Power to the People

The Princeton Economic History of the Western World

JOEL MOKYR, SERIES EDITOR

Power to the People

ENERGY IN EUROPE OVER THE
LAST FIVE CENTURIES

Astrid Kander
Paolo Malanima
Paul Warde

PRINCETON UNIVERSITY PRESS

Princeton and Oxford

Published by Princeton University Press, 41 William Street, Princeton,
New Jersey 08540
In the United Kingdom: Princeton University Press, 6 Oxford Street, Woodstock,
Oxfordshire OX20 1TW

press.princeton.edu

ISBN 978-0-691-14362-0

Library of Congress Control Number: 2013950070

British Library Cataloging-in-Publication Data is available

This book has been composed in Sabon

Printed on acid-free paper ∞

Printed in the United States of America

10 9 8 7 6 5 4 3 2 1

Contents

Preface

THIS BOOK HAS ITS ORIGIN in a network on energy history, the LEG network (Long-term Energy and Growth). This came together in 2003 with the aim of providing standardized and comparable statistics on historical energy use for a range of European countries, as the basis for developing more reliable analyses of energy history. This has been a long and often arduous task, but one enlivened by many convivial and memorable workshops along the way. We thank heartily all of those who have helped us in producing and sharing the datasets and developing our methods: Silvana Bartoletto, Kerstin Enflo, Ben Gales, Sofia Henriques, Magnus Lindmark, Mar Rubio, Lennart Schön, David Stern, Enric Tello, Richard Unger, and Tony Wrigley. This book is in some sense the collective output of them all, although we do not seek to blame them for its flaws. We are especially grateful to Ben Gales, Mar Rubio, Silvana Bartoletto, and Sofia Henriques for devoting substantial amounts of time assembling data series for individual countries and sharing them with us to use in this book. Sofia Henriques deserves an extra heartfelt thanks for checking the consistency of our data and linking it with the International Energy Agency database from 1960.

After some years of hard work collecting data and seeking funding, three of the network set out to write a book together, that could synthesize, analyze, and push forward the research that we had assembled: Paul Warde (England), Paolo Malanima (Italy), and Astrid Kander (Sweden). This book is the result of our efforts. It is a co-authored work in that we have collectively produced the overall shape of the book, written some of the sections together, shared ideas, and subjected each other to an unending stream of criticism and advice (sometimes more welcome than at others). However, we have also divided the writing of parts of the book to reflect the particular expertise and approaches of the authors, and each author takes responsibility for our own part. Paolo Malanima writes about the pre-industrial energy system (chapters 3–4), Paul Warde about the first industrial revolution (chapters 5–7), and Astrid Kander about the second and third industrial revolutions (chapters 8–10). The approaches taken necessarily differ at times because of the scope of the subject and the data available. However, we also take collective responsibility for the whole manuscript that we have discussed for many years, and sought to build into a coherent whole. We hope it reflects our shared perspectives on energy history, but also our distinct contributions and the assistance of the many colleagues who have aided us.

One legacy of the LEG network is the construction of a new database of time-series of energy use in Europe, including both modern, and for the first time, traditional energy carriers. This full database is available at www.energyhistory.org.

Producing a book like this requires—dare we say it—a lot of energy, and we know only too well that consuming energy very often requires money. We would like to express our thanks to those who have provided financial support for our project: the Centre for History and Economics, Magdalene College, Cambridge; the Leverhulme Trust; VINNOVA and CIRCLE in Sweden, the Faculty of Economics and Management at Lund University, the European Science Foundation through GLOBALEURONET for workshops; the Institute of Studies on Mediterranean Societies (National Research Council) in Naples. We have received the enthusiastic support of Princeton University Press, and our editor, Joel Mokyr: we thank them, and the anonymous readers of the manuscript who have assisted us greatly in improving it. We owe thanks to Annelieke Vries-Baaijens and Peter Robertson for preparing some of the maps and illustrations. Piotr Widulinski, Roberta Scotti, and Rūta Gentvilaite have helped us with the reference list. We would also like to thank those who have participated in our many discussions and given us words of wisdom of all kinds, commented on our papers, or read drafts of the manuscript: Francesca Antolin, Bob Ayres, Nina Brandt, Martin Chick, Roger Fouquet, Chris Jones, Fridolin Kraussman, Leos Müller, Alessandro Nuvolari, Peter Pearson, Heinz Schandl, Benjamin Warr, and Chris Wigley. We hope that this volume will not be the end of our conversation, but a further stimulus to work in a field where we still have much to learn.

Astrid Kander
Paolo Malanima
Paul Warde

Power to the People

CHAPTER ONE

INTRODUCTION

WHAT NEEDS TO BE EXPLAINED

THIS BOOK IS AN ECONOMIC history of Europe viewed through the role that energy has played in that history. As such, it also aims to provide an account of the role energy can play in economic history more generally, and how energy consumption and economic development have been, are, and may be, entwined.

All things need energy, and all actions are transformations of energy. Every step, small or large, that a human takes, is part of an energy economy, and every object we treasure, use, or discard is similarly the product of that economy. We have always been "children of the sun,"[1] the final source of nearly all of the energy that those living on the surface of this planet will ever consume. The way this energy, with its origins in the nuclear processes at the heart of our nearest star, is obtained and used has put its stamp on human societies since time immemorial, whether of hunter-gatherers, farmers, industrial cities, or astronauts; and whether that energy is consumed as food from plants or animals, as the driving force of wind or water, as the heat of combustion or flow of electricity. All humans that have ever lived have been equally dependent on energy, but each society's energy economy has taken on distinct forms, and some previous great societal transitions have also been, in their own way, energy revolutions.

But in a very long human history nothing quite like the past couple of hundred years has ever occurred. No previous transformation has been of the scale and intensity of modern times. Indeed, this explosive and ongoing change in scale and speed is what we now evoke with the very word "modern." While the human population had for the first time advanced to a full billion by the early nineteenth century, less than two hundred years later there are seven times more of us. Yet this sevenfold advance pales beside the increase in our production, which has risen more than seventy-fold in the same period (fifty-five times in the case of Western Europe, the focus of this book). By this measure, the "average" inhabitant of planet Earth is today more than eleven times better off than in 1820, and in Western Europe, eighteen times better off.[2] Our technology can achieve feats barely

---

[1] Crosby, 2006.
[2] Maddison, 2003.

imaginable to our great-great-great grandparents, a mere five generations ago, and each generation continues to be astounded and bewildered by the achievements of the next, even in a world where such change is so commonplace as to have become the norm. Alongside such transformations we are also witnessing a "great acceleration" of impact on our environment, and the possibility that our economy is transgressing the "planetary boundaries" that provide a "safe operating space for humanity," threatening the functioning of ecosystems and threatening rapid climate change.[3] However we value the modern world, it is hard to describe the changes that have occurred without reaching for the lexicon of the big.

Unsurprisingly, a short era that has witnessed more economic growth than in the whole of previous history also has required much more energy. There have been many kinds of revolutions during the modern age. There has been an industrial revolution, or rather three industrial revolutions, which we will use as the organizing principle of the book. There has been an energy revolution or several energy revolutions too, as new energy conversions have been enabled or new energy carriers have been exploited.

We could provide an almost endless list of how radically different our lives have become in the modern, industrial period. Take the case of light. In the premodern world, darkness reigned once the sun slipped below the horizon. Only a handful of cities provided street illumination that cast a weak light into nocturnal streets where only a bright moon provided a guide for the eyes.[4] Indoors, most people, if they used artificial light at all, struggled with candles or rush-lights, dried strips of vegetation dipped into animal fat and giving off a foul smell for the short time they burned. How different were the summers and winters then in northern climes, the difference between long, bright nights and short, dim days. Heating was generally provided only when considered an absolute necessity, and then only for one chamber. Even the houses of the well-to-do have well-documented cases of wine freezing in glasses or ink in inkpots. Today manufacturing runs round the clock. Central heating raises temperatures to summer levels in every room irrespective of its use, while for some of us air conditioning seeks to keep the high summer temperatures at bay, out of doors. As centers of population cast their glow into space, we wonder if today's children will ever see the "true" night sky. By one estimate, the average Briton now consumes six and a half thousand times more artificial light than did their ancestor in 1800.[5]

The services we get from energy may be the same: heat of low and high temperature, motive power, and light. But in most of Europe in the twenty-first century, none of those services in a domestic home, aside from the work done by the people themselves, are coming from the same sources as they

---

[3] Costanza et al., 2007; Rockström et al., 2009.
[4] Koslofsky, 2011.
[5] Fouquet and Pearson, 1998.

did in the nineteenth century. Not a single one. Such a turnaround has never happened since humans learned to harness fire. And the heat, motion, and light do not just deliver much more of what we used to have, but entirely new services: pictures that come from screens (and can be seen in the dark), voices and music from speakers, conversations in real time that span the globe. This new technology did not just come from changes in knowledge, from the accumulation of generations of ingenuity, but required the use of "energy carriers" that, globally, had only previously been used on a trivial scale and that were inaccessible to most (such as coal, oil, natural gas), or were entirely new (electricity).

As societies and as individuals, our command over resources, and the degree of choice open to us, has vastly increased as a result of these transformations. In a very everyday sense, we have been empowered by the energy revolution; in the choice of what we can do with our time, in our liberation from heavy labor, and in that while we earn much, much, more, we have also benefited from a reduction in working hours since the nineteenth century. This empowerment has come above all in our material life, but in our political and social lives, too. There have also been costs; for many, there may be a sense of disempowerment: a sense of alienation from the natural world that has come with urbanization and the capacity to consume resources with little direct relationship to them. In this book we will stress material changes, but in the broader senses of the word, this is why we think this is a story of bringing power to the people.

Energy also redistributes political power (the more familiar use of "power" to historians). It has not done so in a standard, linear way. Greater energy availability does not, by any means, simply translate into greater democracy or indeed greater governmental control (which are not, in any case, necessarily contradictory). But new systems of harnessing and consuming energy have certainly greatly influenced the options open to governments, individuals, corporations, and countries, and given rise to new areas of contestation and co-operation. Even in the least liberal of European states, people have generally been greatly empowered as consumers relative to their forebears. Sometimes new energy systems have conferred power more directly, whether to the rulers of countries who held major oil reserves, or the political muscle of coalminers, railwaymen and dockers in periods when they populated key parts of the infrastructure.[6] The spread of information, whether via steam-powered printing, television, or the Internet, has provided significant new ways to hold leaders to account. Resource endowments have shaped geopolitics.

We can also put numbers to the expansion in energy use: indeed, one of the main contributions of this book is to provide, for the first time, reliable numbers on energy consumption for much of Europe and individual

---

[6] Mitchell, 2011.

countries within it, including traditional as well as modern energy carriers. The data we can now provide are path-breaking in two regards. First, they provide much more reliable estimates than previously existed on pre–fossil fuel era energy consumption, making much greater use of contemporary sources than pioneering work.[7] Second, we have established a consistent methodology for quantifying the economic consumption of energy that can be used for cross-country comparison and aggregation of our datasets.[8] These data, focusing on energy as an input into the economy, can then be combined with available long time-series of GDP, capital stocks, and labor to shed new light on what we characterize as "three industrial revolutions" that have occurred over the past two centuries, and their varied impact on energy use in society.

What do these numbers show? We can see in figure 1.1 that the path of the modern economy has not been a straightforward story of a constant rate of increase in the use of energy. Instead, the overall trajectory of energy use within Europe follows a logistic S-shaped curve. It is possible to discern three phases. The first phase, 1500–1800, was marked by little growth in overall energy consumption, and even slightly falling per capita energy consumption in the sixteenth and the eighteenth centuries. The second phase, 1800–1970, is the Industrial Age, which saw explosive expansion in energy use, except for during the World Wars and interwar period. However, industrialization took place at different moments and at different speeds in the countries of Europe, and the curve in figure 1.1, which aggregates the European experience as a whole, makes this change appear smoother than it might seem from a national or regional perspective. The third period, 1970–2008, is exceptional in that it was marked by stabilization in energy consumption per capita. It seems that after around 1970, economic growth has no longer been accompanied by the same level of increase in energy use. Rises in consumption have been modest, and in per capita terms, changed little. At the end of the twentieth century, we seem to have entered a new phase in the relationship between energy and economic growth.

The main thing we set out to explain in this book is why the shape of this curve looks the way it does.

In so doing, we need to investigate the relation between energy and economic growth. This relation is influenced by the kinds of energy carriers involved in the aggregate energy consumption at any point in time. Industrialization has not been just one change in the energy regime, but many: the transition to the first fossil fuel, coal, has been followed by the adoption of oil and natural gas, and the diffusion of electricity. This has affected energy consumption as well as economic growth. For instance, as the main shift

---

[7] Martin, 1988; Schurr and Netschert, 1978, for the United States; Smil, 1994; Fouquet, 2008.

[8] Etemad, 1991; Reddy, and Goldemberg, 1990.

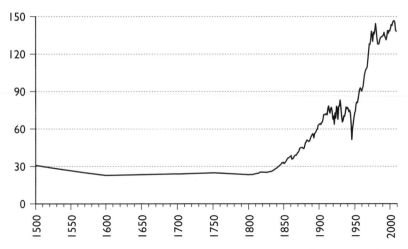

Figure 1.1. Energy consumption per capita in Europe (Gigajoules, 1500–2008)
Sources: Own detailed data, 1800–2008, see www.energyhistory.org. For the period 1500–1800 the trend is nothing more than a rough estimate. See chapter 3.

into the oil economy happened almost simultaneously across Europe after the Second World War, we see most clearly in the postwar decades, that "golden age" of growth, the explosive increase in energy use that swept the whole continent. Consequently, energy transitions are an important part of our story. Last, but not least, energy transitions influence the economic efficiency of energy use, expressed by the ratio GDP/energy, since different energy carriers form part of new growth complexes, which we call development blocks, using energy to different degrees.

Of course, bare numbers on energy consumption can only give a bare sense of how everyday life has been transformed, whether through improved access to information, or the much greater ease and speed with which we can accomplish domestic tasks (which means, in turn, that we also do them much more frequently than before, whether washing clothes or heating food and drink at home). Unsurprisingly, ours is a book that stresses material flows and our dependency on physical things. This is not to underplay either changes in, or the role of "wishes, habits, ideas, goals" in this history,[9] and these, as they relate to energy, are part of our story (although histories of such things very rarely touch on the role of energy in generating and disseminating them). More energy is not just a consequence of other revolutions, as if it could be hauled up from nothing, like the proverbial man lifting himself by his own bootstraps. We also see the energy revolution as

[9] Mumford [1934], 1963, 3.

one of the causes of the modern world, and we want to explain why and how this was achieved.

RESEARCH QUESTIONS AND MAIN ARGUMENTS

At this stage we would like to spell out the main arguments we will make, and the three interrelated research questions we will address, and in doing so position ourselves relative to other approaches:

1. Energy and economic growth;
2. Drivers of energy transitions;
3. Economic efficiency of energy use.

Energy and Economic Growth

The relationship between energy and economic growth is the first and core research question that we deal with throughout the book. Is energy a driver of economic growth, or does economic growth simply bring about sufficient increases in the supply of energy? We think that the energy revolution of modern times was not optional, merely one path that was taken among a number that could have brought about similar changes. Major innovations in the field of energy were a *necessary* condition for the modern world and energy continues to play a large role in the economy, as intuitively grasped by the continuing general preoccupation with the geopolitics of energy, whether oil or natural gas.

Yet although it might seem commonsensical today to say that energy plays a central role within the economy, most economists do not include energy in their models of economic growth. According to some economists, raw materials (including energy) played virtually no determining role in the development of the economy. We can take as an important example Robert Solow, who claimed in 1974 that actually the economy can progress without natural resources.[10] Growth depended and continues to depend on knowledge, technical progress, and capital. The contribution of natural resources to past and present growth has been almost non-existent, in their view: the supply of energy and resources has always simply followed the demand generated by new forms of knowledge and techniques and has never played a constraining role in the economy. The implication is that energy resources have never exercised any significant restraint on growth, or shaped its course. Equally, and quite optimistically, this implies that future energy transitions, whether necessitated by the imperative to mitigate climate change

[10] In fact, as early as the 1860s, opponents of Stanley Jevons were arguing that the future exhaustion of coal reserves would not be a problem for Britain because it would shift to activities more reliant on skill than raw materials; see Jevons, 1866; Solow, 1974.

and pollution, or combat rising relative prices of fossil fuels, are unlikely to impose major costs on the economy. For such thinking, the fact that the energy sector presently makes up only a small part of the income of modern economies, generally less than 10 percent, indicates its insignificance.

We dispute the logic that cheapness means a lack of importance. In fact, it is the cheapness of energy that underpins much of the infrastructure of modernity, and an approach that apportions economic importance solely on the basis of the size of a sector in the national accounts misses out on essential qualitative drivers of economic development and success. In a pure cost sense, energy is certainly less of a limiting factor than it was in the pre-industrial era. Then, as we will show, a majority share of total economic activity in most places was devoted to obtaining energy in the form of food, fodder, and wood fuel. An advantage of modern energy sectors is that the energy return on investment (EROI) is very high, although this is something that might change again in the near future.[11]

The decrease in the cost of energy, at the same time that much greater quantities of it could be supplied, has allowed vast reserves of capital to be employed, delivering other kinds of goods and services rather than covering only basic energetic needs. Nevertheless, the expansion of many sectors of our economy has also depended on particular *development blocks*[12] with energy provision at their heart; and infrastructure whether in the design of suburbs and transportation systems almost wholly dependent on the Internal Combustion Engine (ICE), or the electric or gas-fired heating and cooling systems that make domestic and office life bearable in a variety of climates. The shrinkage of what we might consider as "the energy sector" to a much smaller part of the economy has not, then, allowed economic development to escape from dependence on particular forms of energy carrier. The fact that our economies have been built around development blocks based on certain energy carriers and their associated technologies also means the cost of energy transition may be high, requiring renewal of a significant part of our capital stock.

Drivers of Energy Transitions

The scale and drivers of each historical energy transition is the second of our main research questions in this book. Energy transition is a major preoccupation of twenty-first-century politics, but has already been a defining feature of modern life for at least one and a half centuries. The first of these transitions was between a variety of "traditional," or "organic" energy carriers that primarily were based on the products of the soil, to fossil fuel; at

---

[11] Cleveland, 2008; Murphy and Hall, 2011.
[12] For a technical definition of this term, see chapter 2.

first, coal.[13] These early energy carriers included wood, peat, fodder for draft animals, and food for humans. It may come as a surprise that human food is considered part of the energy sector. But much of what our ancestors consumed was fuel to power their muscles. Of course, there is more to human nutrition than calories; there is more to human work than brute power. Yet without understanding how agriculture was also an essential part of the energy regime, that an essential task of this sector *was* to produce calories that drove work, as well as proteins and vitamins, it is impossible to understand the organization of the pre-industrial world, or the nature of the transition to modern energy regimes. The capacity of the land to grow plants useful to humans and draft animals imposed a fundamental limit on our economy. Without the need to feed these "biological engines," much greater areas could have been used to supply firewood; these sources of energy stood in competition. The ability to transcend both the land constraint through the use of fossil fuel, and the muscle constraint through mechanization which increased power (largely fueled by coal) were founding acts of the modern world.

The transition to fossil fuels was not the end, but only the beginning of modern energy transitions, even if it has been (at least up until now) the most profound shift. Transition has continued, both in fossil fuels such as coal, oil, and natural gas, but also harnessing new forms of carriers—most importantly for generating electricity. This history of transition is in part a history of substitution, with societies shifting demand between, for example, wood and coal, or coal and natural gas according to their price, but some of the uses of certain energy carriers have no or very poor substitutes. Electricity is absolutely necessary to run a wide array of household devices such as vacuum cleaners, and technology with much wider applications: lighting, computers, machines in industry. Cars are best run on liquid or gaseous forms of energy. So historically there has been a strong complementarity between certain energy carriers and associated technology, something we will deal with extensively. Indeed, the most significant changes in the energy regime have required very major infrastructural developments and shifts in technology and the organization of society to accommodate them, and make best use of their capacities.

Transformation in the energy system derived from the progress of technical knowledge and associated innovations. These advances did not just occur in forms of energy generation or the invention of new processes (such as steam power or the internal combustion engine), but had to occur across a wide array of the supporting infrastructure required to put new technology into use. We use the expression *development blocks* to describe the series of systems of technology, infrastructure, energy sources, and institutions by which economic growth proceeded (for a fuller description see chap-

[13] Greenberg, 1992.

ter 2).[14] Shifting transportation networks to automobiles required a new infrastructure of tankers, refineries, gas stations, and metaled roads. Even when the end product is the same, such as electricity, the use of different forms of generation (wind, nuclear, coal) requires capital of different scales and capacities in the increasingly international supply network. Because of their scale, complexity, and level of interconnection or complementarity, development blocks formed discontinuous phases in economic development, and mean that there may be a significant lag between early inventions and the widespread adoption of a technology. Thus, while transition has been a common feature of the modern economy, and the process of growth is fairly continuous, we argue that this has been achieved through fundamentally *discontinuous* processes involving major structural shifts that take time to achieve. We develop a novel historical account of what forces have led to the emergence of the development blocks marking different periods and thus permitted the energy transitions of industrial society. This will be developed more fully in chapter 2.

Economic Efficiency of Energy Use

The third research question we address is the change and impact of the *economic efficiency of energy use*, indicated by the ratio of GDP/energy. We investigate how economic energy efficiency has developed in time and space. This is, among other things, a contribution to the debate about *dematerialization* of production and how far that can take us in reconciling ecological concerns with economic growth.[15] We find not only that increased economic energy efficiency has long been seen as desirable; it has also been the normal experience of some countries and sectors of the economy. Both energy transitions from lower to higher quality energy carriers and increases in the thermal efficiency of machines have stimulated increases in economic energy efficiency, i.e., unsurprisingly, producing more useful light or motion or heat out of the same input of energy has often contributed to the amount of income that can be won from each input of energy.

Nevertheless, the long-term story is more complex. Technological shifts related to development blocks and industrial revolutions have caused structural changes in the economy (changes in the relative importance of different activities) which have also affected economic energy efficiency to a considerable degree. Development blocks can be primarily *energy saving* or *energy expanding*. Yet these processes can interact. Efficiency improvements in a particular technology, like iron-smelting or the steam engine, can reduce the energy costs of production, but in doing so make the technology more

---

[14] Dahmén, 1950, 1988.

[15] Ausubel and Waggoner, 2008; Herman et al., 1990; Ming Sheng et al., 2010; Sun, 2000; Tapio et al., 2007; Vringer and Blok, 2000.

widely affordable, creating a huge expansion in its use. The net effect of a local saving can be an absolute expansion, paradoxical as that might seem. These *rebound* or *take-back* effects are an important part of the story of modern growth (see chapter 2 for a fuller explanation of these concepts). We also perceive a sequence in the historical evolution of development blocks, where they have become relatively more energy-saving over time.

However, this historical evidence of improving economic energy efficiency does not suggest a very strong dematerialization over time. Many economists believe so strongly in general efficiency increases (total factor productivity increases) being the reason behind modern economic growth that they also believe the economy can dematerialize, or get rid of its dependence on energy or other material resources almost entirely. We show that this is a false belief. Over the last two centuries the efficiency in the use of energy has doubled. The size of the economy is fifty times as large as it used to be and energy consumption, twenty-five times higher. This is very far from a dematerialization, and we offer as one of the main contributions of our book a resolution of this paradox of the economy being on a high-energy path, despite all of the advances in productivity. The "capital deepening" path of modern economic growth has been so strong as to outweigh most advances in the thermal efficiency of that capital. Technical change has been indeed *biased*, saving on labor much more than capital and energy in the long run. Indeed, it is this greater advance of capital and energy use compared to labor that has brought "power to the people."

Still, we also have a somewhat more positive message with regard to the prospects for some dematerialization. This pattern has changed since the 1970s; from this decade we show that the rate of improvement in economic energy efficiency has sped up as a consequence of the third industrial revolution, both affecting energy use in the manufacturing sector and contributing to a structural change in the economy, with a relative increase of the service sector. Energy consumption has ceased what seemed an inexorable rise, presenting some hope that future growth may become more energy-saving.

Our book is written at a time when there is large concern for and interest in the role of energy in economic growth.[16] This interest is related to contemporary urgent issues that humankind is facing: global warming, peak oil, and so on. We are neither the first to produce a quantitative energy history, nor to have engaged with our research questions. Looking back over four decades we can highlight the work of (among others!) Netschert and Schurr on the United States; Václav Smil and Arnulf Grübler respectively on global energy economies; Jean Marie Martin on long-term energy intensities for several countries; work undertaken independently of each other by Rolf-Peter Sieferle and Tony Wrigley on the European energy economies of the first industrial revolution; recent quantitative reconstructions by Fridolin

---

[16] Ayres and Warr, 2009; Stern, 2010b.

Krausmann, Heinz Schandl, and Roger Fouquet, and the team of Bob Ayres and Benjamin Warr; and a very wide range of literature that has touched on energy to a greater or lesser degree in examining historical change, whether the first industrial revolution, village-scale agricultural change, shifting "networked" cities, or the economic history of particular sectors of the economy.[17] Nearly all of these works would also argue that energy was important to industrialization and modern economic growth. Our book differs from these, in the provision of new time-series data, but also in our focus on long-term and internationally comparative economic development. We also differ with some of our colleagues on key points of interpretation. We do not, as do Ayres and Warr, argue that energy, or energy services, were the engine of growth in a unified way throughout modern history.[18] We argue that the influence of energy changed and was a discontinuous process during the three industrial revolutions. Equally, we want to draw attention to the varied, but interlinked, regional and national manifestations of these changes. The role of energy relative to shifts in technology that employs it altered especially from the 1970s, with the emergence of a development block founded on Information and Communication Technology (ICT).

The great revolutions of modern times have been phenomena of great breadth and have had an equally great breadth of academic studies and explanations devoted to them. Too often such texts are read and interpreted as if they are seeking to be all-embracing or mono-causal explanations, even when they insist they are not. When we say an energy revolution was part of these processes of modernity, this is not seeking to negate the validity of other approaches. We do not think that energy history is the key that by itself unlocks everything else; the transformation of the pre-industrial energy regime was *not* a sufficient condition for the industrial revolution or modern economic growth. It was however a necessary condition.

Energy resources could only be useful insofar as there was "useful knowledge" and the appropriate "state of mind" to make use of them.[19] The accumulation of knowledge, institutional change, and market expansion played an important role in the birth of the modern economy, as stressed nowadays by most economic historians and economists. But we strongly believe that knowledge and states of mind were only useful insofar as they have the right kind of material to work on, and in fact are only likely to develop if the uses are a realistic and imaginable prospect. In places that lack certain kinds of resources, ingenuity will flow in other directions, and rapid economic

---

[17] Schurr and Netschert, 1978; Martin, 1988; Sieferle, 1982, 2001; Smil, 1994; Grübler, 1998; Wrigley, 1962, 1988a, 2010; Krausmann and Haberl, 2002; Krausmann et al., 2009; Fouquet, 2008; Ayres and Warr, 2009.

[18] In their major book, *The Economic Growth Engine*, it is energy services that drive growth, but in a more recent publication from 2010 they also see information and communication technology as important for growth since the 1970s.

[19] Mokyr, 2002.

growth will not be the result. Consequently we take issue with accounts of economic change that give little place to material considerations and resource availability.

This debate has been most prominent in the vast literature about the industrial revolution, frequently asking why Britain took a clear early lead (especially as opposed to its near neighbor and political rival, France), or more generally, why western Europe and not the economies of south and east Asia industrialized first.[20] An earlier generation of scholars had explained national or regional economic advantage and its character broadly in terms of resource endowments, especially of fossil fuels.[21] In the 1970s, revisionist views argued that there was little to distinguish the economies of Britain and France in the eighteenth century, and that the British lead was thus entirely the result of contingent factors or even inexplicable in theoretical terms.[22] More recently, and following on from the work of Douglass North, who placed greater emphasis on the role of education or institutions in facilitating growth, many scholars have explained differential economic performance by variations in human capital, institutional capacity, or cultural differences.[23] Limitations or advantages did not lie in the availability of material resources, which imposed no essential restriction on supply; rather, conservative habits of mind had to be overcome to stimulate demand and ingenuity, and local success was steered by the disposition of key groups among the population, or the diffusion of Enlightenment values.[24] In these accounts, countries *were* significantly different, but in how they thought, not what they possessed. In contrast, a strong line of argument has persisted that the advantages of Britain and Western Europe more generally lay in the relatively low price of energy found where fossil fuels were easily accessible, stimulating the move into an industrial and capital-intensive economy.[25]

These intense debates among economic historians about the wellsprings of modern growth have had very little influence on modern growth theory, which has rarely perceived energy or natural resources in general as a constraint upon growth at all.[26] This has generally been because they think that other resources can substitute for energy or natural resources. Ecological economists on the other hand see energy as a limiting factor to growth. They think that substitution between capital and resources and technological change can only to some degree mitigate the scarcity of resources.[27]

[20] For a recent summary, see Griffin, 2010.

[21] Landes, 2003; Pollard, 1981; Habakkuk, 1962.

[22] Milward and Saul, 1973; Crafts, 1977.

[23] Rostow, 1960; North, 1973; Clark, 2007.

[24] Clark, 2007; Mokyr, 2009; McCloskey, 2006; Voigtlander and Voth, 2006; de Vries, 2008; Sharp and Weisdorf, 2012.

[25] Wrigley, 1988a, 2004, 2010; Pomeranz, 2000; Allen, 2009.

[26] Aghion and Howitt, 2009.

[27] Stern, 1997, 2010b.

We do not argue for a false choice between "ideas" and "materials" in driving growth, but will examine how they must advance in mutual interaction and co-dependence. In that sense we actually think that some of the debates in economic history today are a little artificial; dare we say it, some of their participants would concede that they generate more heat than light, and different rhetorical and analytical emphases in the literature may not represent genuine disagreement in principle.[28] Nevertheless, we firmly place ourselves among those who think that the availability and relative price of energy was a key determinant of growth patterns and differential economic performance. We will present clear evidence that the resources of the pre–fossil fuel economy were not sufficient to have underpinned modern industrial growth.[29] We agree that the accumulation of physical capital, requiring particular raw materials, and its utilization in ever more productive ways by using the complementary modern energy carriers, has been an essential part of the history of modern growth. Human capital, the set of knowledge and skills we possess, and our institutions for steering economic life, are necessary but not sufficient parts of this story.[30]

THE STRUCTURE OF THE BOOK

In this book we adopt a commonly used division in economic history, of "three industrial revolutions."[31] We use them as the organizing principle of the book, and relate them to four development blocks that have played a particular role in shaping our modern energy economy and society over the last two centuries (figure 1.2).

To understand the transformation of the five centuries we take as our subject, we must first understand the energy economy of the premodern world, and its reliance on "traditional" energy carriers, largely the products of the land, but also water and wind power. The premodern world and the pressures upon its energy economy are set out in the first part of the book,

---

[28] In the Economic History World Congress of 2009, Joel Mokyr and Bob Allen had an intense debate about the roots of the industrial revolution. Mokyr confessed in the beginning of this debate that he actually agreed with Allen about many things and it is clear that he does think that technology, steam, and coal mattered, although he has come to stress the mind-set of people more in his recent writings. Mokyr has also rightly pointed out that the Industrial Revolution is one event with many competing explanations, and since it is only one event it is in fact overdetermined. We can never empirically distinguish between them.

[29] In distinction to authors such as Clark and Jacks, 2007, or Kunnas and Myllyntaus, 2009.

[30] Prados De La Escosura and Rosés, 2010b.

[31] The third industrial revolution does not only affect the manufacturing sector, but also the growth and content of the service sector to a large degree. It describes a general process of enhancing productivity by the use of ICT technology across sectors, and has seen continued advance in industrial production despite the shrinking share of industrial workers in the total workforce.

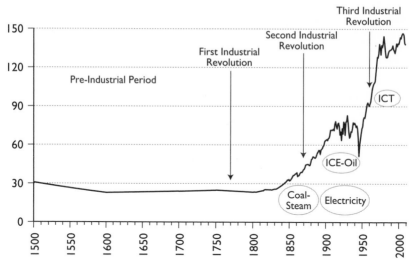

Figure 1.2. Three industrial revolutions and four development blocks
Source: See www.energyhistory.org.

written by Paolo Malanima. It has long been debated whether premodern, or "pre-industrial," society was profoundly trapped by its dependency on the land and thus a fundamental scarcity of resources that in the long run would lead to falling real wages as populations grow. We argue that this scarcity was real: the evidence points to stagnation or real falls in many parts of Europe. Growth, modest by later standards, was an exception, linked to very few regions that often had exceptional energy economies, like the Netherlands, and Britain. This is not to deny significant changes in the organizational and technological basis of this society that was an essential precursor to the revolutions that followed; not least, localized trends toward mechanization and the use of fossil fuels.

The first industrial revolution is the subject of the second part of the book, written by Paul Warde. This great transition emerged in a highly re-gionalized fashion out of the pressures and resource endowments of the premodern economy. This led to rising per capita energy consumption in the nineteenth century, after a long pre-industrial history of stagnation or even decline over much of the continent. This gradual rise at the aggregate level disguises much more rapid transitions in sectors, regions, and countries.[32] The core innovations associated with coal use were steam power and new iron-smelting techniques. We argue that both qualitatively and quantita-tively coal was a necessary condition for the emergence of modern growth from the pre-industrial past. To us the evidence points to the impossibility

[32] Pollard, 1981.

of sustaining high levels of growth or transformation in a world wholly dependent on "organic" or vegetable sources of energy. Wood could not have done the job.

The third part of the book, written by Astrid Kander, covers the much more complex patterns of development to be found in the twentieth century. The second industrial revolution, based on electricity and oil, was already emerging in the late nineteenth century but only brought about a very major impact in Europe in quantitative terms in the Golden Age of growth after World War II. A third industrial revolution grounded in ever-widening use of electricity combined with Information and Communication Technology (ICT) has been a major factor in the stabilization of per capita energy consumption levels since around 1970. The alternative propositions that it is the transition to a service economy that have led the decline, or that it was driven by outsourcing energy-intensive production to less developed countries, are critically investigated.

Energy productivity (or its reciprocal energy intensity) will be affected by the structural changes brought on by the emergence of development blocks, since economic sectors differ with respect to their energy needs. We argue that the development block of the first industrial revolution was energy-expanding, with the importance of metals and steam technology widening the use of fossil fuels enormously. The second industrial revolution presents two different kinds of development blocks: one around oil, which had the same expansive character as the steam-coal-steel block; and another around electricity, which to a large degree increased energy productivity and was energy-saving. The third industrial revolution only had one large development block. It is basically a continuation of the electricity block, but is even more energy-saving than the electricity block. The different properties of the development blocks with respect to energy demand mean that the economy's dependence on energy (in a quantitative sense) will change over time; increasing with the first industrial revolution and also the second, but becoming less dependent on energy since the 1970s.

Across all of the five centuries we examine, we also wish to set out how energy relates to, and has indeed driven, the relative price of factors of production like capital and labor; shaped the structure of the economy; and related to physical constraints such as land or the possibility of "dematerialization." We trace these stories by using "seven propositions" in each part of the book, although as the economies examined changed, so must the emphasis and precise focus of each set of propositions. Some can be followed throughout the book; others must be more particular to the specific historical period. Through these propositions we aim to show both the continuous and the changing character of key relationships that relate energy and the economy.

Before we proceed to explaining the concepts we will use in more detail in chapter 2, we should add a brief discussion about the geographical coverage of this book. The energy data we have collected so far only covers Western Europe, and while we will at times discuss data from countries not covered by our own datasets, predominately in Eastern Europe, the weight of our analysis falls on the west. The three parts of the book also differ in what countries they emphasize. These are to some degree a reflection of the particular expertise of the authors of each section; the reader will find more of Italy at first, Britain in the second part, and Sweden in the third. Nevertheless, there are also solid intellectual grounds for these choices. Italy was a leading economy at the very start of our period that fell behind in early industrialization. Britain, it hardly needs repeating, was the flag bearer of the industrial revolution. Sweden was one of the countries that saw a growth spurt during the second industrial revolution, making major use of new technologies in manufacturing, and electricity. Although this book is mainly about Europe, we also seek to provide some global comparisons, especially as a contribution to the debates comparing Europe and East Asia in the eighteenth and nineteenth centuries, and in the third part of the book, with the inclusion of other rapidly growing economies like the United States and Japan in the twentieth century.

CHAPTER TWO

DEFINITIONS AND CONCEPTS

THIS CHAPTER WILL DEFINE SOME IMPORTANT concepts that we use in this book as we deal with energy in the economic context.

ENERGY CONSUMPTION IN THE ECONOMIC SENSE

In daily life we have direct contact with matter, but not with energy. Matter can be touched, its form described, and it is found underfoot and all around us. With energy, things are different. We only perceive the indirect effects that derive from changes either in the *structure*, that is, the molecular or atomic composition of matter, or in its *location* in space, such as in the case of a stream of water or wind, whose potential energy we can exploit. In both cases, indirect effects such as movement, heat, or light reveal the presence of what has been called "energy" for about two hundred years. Indeed, the fact that energy is not directly observable helps explain why it only emerged as a concept unifying a range of "forces" at a comparatively late date.

The first law of thermodynamics states that energy is always conserved. This means that the level of energy in the universe cannot alter and energy cannot actually be consumed or used up. It can only change form. The second law of thermodynamics states, however, that energy always has a tendency to change into less organized forms, known as entropy or disorder. In practice, this usually means less useful forms for human purposes. In the combustion of an engine, the chemical energy bound up in a fuel, for example, is converted into the movement of a car (which is the high-quality form of energy that we want) plus low-temperature heat and smoke (waste products). An amount of energy has been transformed, but the total remains the same as before. The entropy has, however, increased. There are only very limited possibilities of making further use of the kinetic energy of motion and the waste heat and smoke. What has been consumed is the fuel used for the engine, and in practical terms this is what is referred to when we speak of energy consumption. Some physicists prefer to say that *exergy* has been consumed, that is the potential work the energy can accomplish before reaching an equilibrium with its environment. However, in this book, we will retain the commonplace and familiar usage of the term energy.

Figure 2.1 shows a range of possible energy conversions as they appear to people today. Several forms of energy can provide different energy

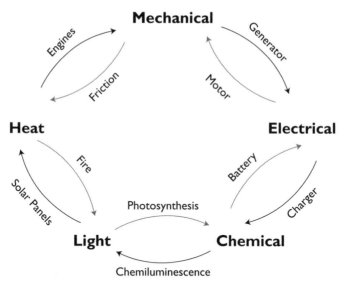

Figure 2.1. Energy conversions

services thanks to devices able to convert one form of energy into another: from thermal to mechanical, from mechanical to electric, from chemical to electrical, and to light and heat. Plants and animals can also, of course, accomplish a limited range of conversions, from chemical energy into heat or mechanical energy. The range above is not exhaustive.

In physics, energy is defined as the capacity of bodies to perform work. Work as defined by physics is restricted to some concrete services: motion, light, heat, and electricity. In economic terms, we could define energy as *the capacity to perform work, useful for human beings, thanks to changes in the structure of matter or its position in space. These changes are not free, but imply some cost or effort.* In other words, the use of energy by humans has an opportunity cost, meaning that the time and resources allocated to using this energy could have been used differently.

The idea of opportunity cost constrains what we include in our analysis of energy. Only when there is an alternative use of human time do we consider the energy to have a cost. Solar heat is of decisive importance for the existence of life, heating the atmosphere and driving the process of photosynthesis in plants. It is, however, a free source of energy from a human's perspective, because we do not need to do anything to make it flow; we do not devote any time to this, and thus it is not included in our economic definition; whereas the capture of solar radiation by means of some technical device in order to heat water or produce electric power is included in our definition, because time was once spent in producing these technical devices and it takes time to maintain their proper functioning. In the first case, solar heat is not an economic resource, while it becomes one in the second case, where an opportunity cost is involved. Similarly, the formation of biomass in a forest is a transformation of the sun's energy by plants through photosynthesis and is not included in an economic definition of energy. On the other hand, firewood is included, which is that part of forest biomass used by human beings for warmth, cooking, or smelting metals, because people need to cut the wood and this takes time, for which there is an alternative usage.

Food is a source of energy in an economic sense, since its consumption enables the performance of work and its production implies some cost, either when provided directly by plants or animals consumed by humans. Another rationale for including food in our energy measure is that food production requires land and hence there is always competition over scarce land involved in the provision of food or other renewable sources of energy.[1]

Food for animals is only exploitable as a source of power by humans when metabolized by those animals utilized for agricultural work. It is not a source of work for men when consumed by wild animals in a forest. Therefore we only include fodder for domesticated animals that are used for productive purposes.

Both fossil fuels used today and nuclear energy exploited to produce electricity are also energy carriers that we obviously include in our definition of energy that can be consumed. All these sources are the basis of the productive activity necessary to satisfy the human demand for commodities and services.[2]

These observations help us to understand a crucial development in the modern history of energy use. In one sense, all energy is "free"; it is delivered to us by natural processes, and has existed since the beginning of the universe. This sounds fortunate and only to our benefit, but it also has the implication that people cannot invent energy carriers. If we run out of high-quality energy carriers like oil, we cannot simply invent a new one. All we can do is transform one form of energy into another. But different forms of energy place very different demands on humans if they are to be made useful (or "extracted") for us. Some forms of energy place large demands on our available energy reserves simply to be extracted; they have a high opportunity cost (or put another way, the net return on investment of energy

---

[1] In certain circumstances including food in energy calculations can create problems; if we want to include the cost of energy in models of economic growth that also include the cost of labor, are we then double-counting? This would be a particular risk in examining past economies where a very high share of the wages of labor were spent on food. But we do not attempt any formal modeling of these societies, so there is no double-counting. In the third part of the book, where we present some modeling of the twentieth-century economy, the cost share of energy embodied in food has become so small that we can safely ignore it.

[2] On concepts and definitions see Grathwohl, 1982, 7–14 and Siddayao, 1986, 4–18.

is relatively low). Most "modern" energy carriers, such as fossil fuels, give very high returns on energy invested for their extraction, even if the initial investment required to access them (such as constructing an oil well) is high. The opportunity cost of the energy embodied in oil or natural gas, which amounts to the cost in terms of resources already at people's disposal required to make it useful, is low.

In the economic sense, energy consumption entails both private and social costs. Social costs are mainly negative effects like environmental and health costs.[3] These social costs are mostly external to the market economy, i.e., they are not captured in the market prices of energy although energy has often been relatively heavily taxed, in part because of the ease of doing so. In a few countries, and only quite late in the twentieth century, energy taxes and CO_2 taxes have aimed to capture external costs to a degree. We will examine some of the social costs of energy consumption, primarily in relation to CO_2 emissions.

PRIMARY AND SECONDARY CARRIERS OF ENERGY

According to this economic definition, the energy carriers we end up counting are: food; fodder for draft animals; firewood; water and wind power; peat; coal; oil and natural gas; and electricity from nuclear or hydropower, or wind, water, or geothermal sources. These are ordinarily defined as *primary sources of energy*: that is, inputs of energy that have been only harnessed rather than transformed by human work, or subject to only limited transformations.[4] By contrast, *secondary energy carriers* are those that have been subject to extensive transformations by us before they reach the point of final consumption, whether in industry, agriculture, or the home. Charcoal for example is a secondary source of energy created by the chemical transformation of wood, where most of the water is removed from the fuel. The same extensive transformation holds true for coke produced from coal and electricity produced by burning coal or oil or gas.

In our series of energy consumption we count only *primary sources of energy*: the calorific content in the firewood used to produce the charcoal, rather than the calorific content that remains in the charcoal actually used to smelt metal; or the energy contained in the coal used to fuel a power station. We do not therefore count the energy content of electricity that is generated

---

[3] Pigou, 1920.

[4] In fact all electricity is a secondary energy carrier, refined from some primary source of energy: wind, nuclear energy, water, fossil fuels, or biofuels. "Primary electricity" is treated differently, because the forms of generation or "extraction" of energy from the environment via water, wind, and nuclear power can then be delivered immediately into the economic system without further transformation, and we treat this as a primary source. We follow the normal procedure of the IEA and national accounts.

by fuels. We only count the electricity that was generated by hydropower, nuclear, or other means except for fossil fuels. This avoids the double counting of energy sources in our balance of energy consumption. If all electricity was added up, including that produced by means of the fossil fuels, it would result in a duplication of some sources in our calculations; we would treat both the coal and the electricity produced from it as an input into the economic system.

This difference between primary and secondary energy sources could be questioned by a physicist. The chain that leads from consumption by humans to a primary source is in fact only defined in our schema by the human relationship with energy. This would not be a matter for a physicist, who could rightly point out that all these sources of energy have already been transformed, and are already a secondary source of some other energy source stretching back millions or billions of years. We return, however, to our concern with the relationship between energy and the economy. For us a primary energy source exists as it is being utilized by people and is not free.

POWER

The amount of energy we have consumed is not the only important point. The speed and manner in which we can do so is also a key attribute of our economy. This is measured by *power*, how much energy is consumed in a second; that is, Power = Energy/Time. Often power is measured in horsepower (hp), but it may equally well be measured in watts or in joules per second. The common unit for electrical energy, kWh, is thus a combination of the power unit kilowatt multiplied by how many hours this energy has been flowing in the system. One kW is the same as one kilojoule per second. In a sense any biological or mechanical engine has a specific power, depending on its capacity to collect energy sources in order to accomplish a specific task or work; such as a magnifying lens that can collect and focus diffuse solar radiation toward a specific work. A draft animal collects diffuse energy inputs, such as the grass of a meadow, and uses the resulting chemical energy for a specific task. Its capacity to utilize the chemical energy of fodder per second for mechanical work is its power.

While the adoption of new energy carriers in the past two centuries has greatly expanded the *quantity* of energy at our disposal, an equally key development has been new technology (machines) able to concentrate large ✓ amounts of work in particular locations in order to carry out specific tasks, or in other words, increase available *power*. This *concentration of power* allows humans to accomplish tasks that were barely imaginable just a few lifetimes ago. In the eighteenth century, the idea of "horsepower" was invented as a means of comparing the power performance of animals and machines. Obviously, a horse could exercise roughly one horsepower; the most advanced mills several horsepowers at most. Today a rocket blasting off from the surface of the Earth develops several tens of millions of horsepowers, without which we would not be able to use satellites as central nodes of the communications infrastructure that carries the Internet and other forms of rapid information exchange around the globe. Of all the quantifiable changes in energy that have occurred over the past two centuries, our ability to concentrate power is perhaps the greatest.

Thermodynamic Efficiency and Energy Productivity

There is a difference between the basic dependence of all economic activity on energy flows, and the way in which we value the economic output generated by those flows. The size of the energy flow is not necessarily closely correlated with the value we give to a particular resulting economic output. Similarly, there is a difference between the thermodynamic efficiency of the physical conversion of energy from one form to another, and the economic efficiency in turning energy into units of value (like dollars or euros). This is illustrated in figure 2.2.

The diagram shows the different kinds of conversions by which economic output is achieved. Energy carriers, whether primary or secondary, are converted into energy services, which are what people actually want: heat, motion, and light. All these conversions of energy from one form into another entail losses, in line with the second law of thermodynamics, and the part of energy that is successfully retained in the next stage is expressed in thermodynamic efficiency rates. If 90 percent of the energy of wood is lost when it is burned in an open stove and only 10 percent actually is required to heat the room to the temperature it is, we say that the thermal efficiency is 10 percent. Thermodynamic efficiency (η) can be expressed through the following ratio (and then multiplied by 100):

$$n = \frac{E_u}{E_i}$$

where E_u is useful energy (or energy services) and E_i is the input of energy in the form of a primary or secondary source.

The last step, converting energy into the value of goods and services, can also be expressed as a ratio. Energy inputs combine with other factors of production (labor and capital) and together produce economic value. There is a change in kind: energy input, which can be measured in physical units (joules for instance), is related to products that are usually given monetary values. Nevertheless, we can still measure the ratio between value and energy inputs: this is economic efficiency, sometimes called *energy productivity*, and is for instance expressed in dollars per joule. Usually this ratio is

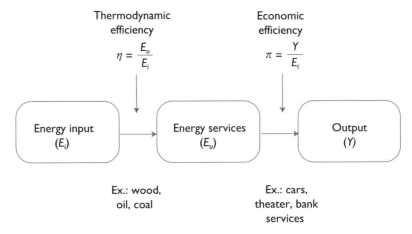

Figure 2.2. Input of energy, energy services, and GDP

measured between the economic output and the energy input, rather than the energy services. This is both because it is the energy input that represents an actual cost, and also because of the difficulty, in many cases, of accurately measuring the service. So our measure of economic efficiency is:

$$\pi = \frac{Y}{E_i}$$

where Y is output in monetary terms and E_i is the raw input of energy (and not energy services) into the economic flow.[5] We would expect the two kinds of efficiency to be linked. For example, over the very long term the transition from biological engines to mechanical engines, which is the main change in the energy system during the industrial revolution, implied both a rise in thermodynamic efficiency and energy productivity measured in economic terms (although the first engines were often more inefficient than biological converters).[6] While the first formula deals with the mere technical structure of an engine or a series of engines, the second is more comprehensive and includes, at the same time, both technical and organizational and institutional changes that determine the final relationship of value generated to energy inputs.

[5] We could wonder why, at this stage, we do not express energy productivity as a ratio of Y to E_u energy services rather than to total energy input. Actually to express the thermodynamic efficiency of the economy as a whole is, in practice, very difficult; while it is much easier at the level of specific technical engines.

[6] We will see, however, that, at the beginning, the substitution of biological engines resulted in a decline of energy productivity, given the low efficiency of the first steam engines.

The Determinants of Energy Productivity

Energy productivity is a partial measure of productivity, like labor productivity. A total productivity measure relates economic output to all the combined inputs of capital, labor, energy, and materials. If some of these inputs can be substituted for each other, it is not necessarily the case that improvements in the productivity of one factor (like energy, or labor, or capital) will increase total productivity if in doing so other factors must be used to a greater extent and become less productive. However, although limited, the measure of energy productivity is simple and easy to interpret and it further serves the purpose of informing us about how productive the economy is in relation to that one scarce and limited input. Energy productivity is an indicator that furthermore has important environmental implications, since most energy use also emits pollutants, fossil fuels in particular.

At the level of the whole economy, changes in energy productivity can occur as a consequence of one or more of the following:

1. Progress of *technical knowledge* and associated innovations, such as the introduction of new machinery or better organization of a factory
2. Changes in the *general level* of knowledge and competence, social relations, or the *institutions* that rule the working of the economy and society as a whole and greatly contribute to the performance of the individual and economic inputs in combination
3. *Structural change*, where we see changes in the composition of goods and services in total production, or put another way, in the relative weight of productive sectors and subsectors. Thus, if parts of the economy that are more energy efficient than others also grow faster, and provide a greater share of national income, then the energy productivity of the economy will increase, although technical knowledge and thermal efficiency have not changed.

Energy productivity is then not only influenced by the technical capacities of the converters we use, or by the balance of factors of production, but also by other variables, such as the specialization of an economy in particular sectors, the level of gross output, and also climate (especially the average level of temperature in a region). In a cold, rich, northern country, specializing in heavy industry, energy productivity can be much lower than in a warm, southern region specializing in light industry; although this difference by no means implies a higher total factor productivity of the latter economy. Today, energy productivity in Sweden is 62 percent of Italian energy productivity on the national level,[7] although total factor productivity is more or less the same.

---

[7] Series of energy intensity in the world from IEA.

Energy Intensity

Discontinuities in energy history are marked by major changes in technical knowledge, as well as institutions and the structure of economies. In an economy that shifts from primarily agricultural into industrial production, one would expect to use an increasing amount of energy in relation to its GDP, although, as we will see, the historical experience of this transition is quite varied. It may also be the case that richer people exhibit a preference for consuming goods that are not so energy efficient, but that they value highly. Nineteenth-century consumers preferred wheat bread if they could afford it, for example, although contemporaries such as R. D. Thomson calculated that this was not an efficient way of obtaining energy; modern preferences for meat and dairy products are less efficient still.[8] But people want more from food than energy. Likewise, if an economy undergoes a transition from the industrial to a post-industrial era, or a service economy, this would be expected to reduce energy consumption in relation to its GDP. Psychotherapy or hairdressing do not consume the same amount of energy as steel-making per unit of income, and any society that has relatively more of the first two will have a higher energy productivity. Again, although the transition to a service economy is thought to be prevalent in the developed world, historical data show that in terms of real production, this discontinuity is not as big as normally believed, as we will discuss in chapter 10. The transition has been more marked in terms of shifts in occupational structure than the real balance of goods and services produced.

Economists and historians dealing with energy prefer to use another efficiency measure, which is the reciprocal of the previous formula of energy productivity. This is called energy intensity (i):

$$i = \frac{E_i}{Y} = \frac{1}{\pi}$$

where E_i is total energy input and Y is GDP. The formula represents the quantity of energy employed for the production of one unit of output. This is thus an inversion of the idea of energy productivity. An economy that is energy intense has low energy productivity. These two measures inform us about different things. While energy productivity says how much value has been created in relation to a certain amount of energy, energy intensity informs us about how much energy was used to produce a certain amount of output. We will use both of these concepts. Energy intensity is particularly useful for calculating pollutants and environmental damage, because this is often a function of the amount of energy consumed, which allows a simple conversion from units of output to environmental "bads."

[8] Porter, 1995, 56.

MACRO-, MESO-, AND MICRO-INNOVATIONS

Economic historians have employed the terms "macro-" and "micro-" inventions to describe the relative significance of inventions. Joel Mokyr has defined a macro-invention as "a radical new idea, without clear precedent [that] emerges more or less ab nihilo." Micro-inventions, alternatively, are "the small, incremental steps that improve, adapt, and streamline existing techniques already in use."[9] In contrast, while Bob Allen defines a micro-invention in similar terms, he sees a macro-invention more formally as something that radically realigns factor costs. This generally makes the employment of capital much cheaper relative to labor, and puts society on a new "capital deepening" track, where capital is used relatively more than labor.[10]

We find these terms useful, but would apply a different set of meanings. Macro-inventions are indeed usefully understood as novelties that open up new applications, or open up the possibility of completely new ways of doing old tasks.[11] However, for our purposes we wish to adopt the increasingly used distinction between an "invention," which is a purely technical step forward (a new device or way of arranging things) and an "innovation." which is a new development in economic markets (for example, diffusing the use of the new device in processes that generate economic value). This is often a difficult step to make. To have economic value, an invention must first also become implemented as an innovation in economic life.[12] Since we are more interested in the market adoption and diffusion of inventions in society, we will henceforth rather speak about macro-, meso-, and micro-*innovations*. When a macro-innovation becomes the driving force behind the evolution of a new development block, we call it a *core innovation*: that step from invention to innovation requires more than the original spark of genius—it requires a whole supporting cast. To become core innovations,

---

[9] Mokyr, 1990, 13.

[10] Allen, 2009.

[11] Whether they emerge *ab nihilo*, out of "nothing," is rather harder to determine empirically, especially because many inventions or ideas involve the transplantation of a principle from one field of endeavor to another very different one, and often these connections are hard to trace. Truly "new" ideas must be counted as extreme rarities. However, it is also true that a realignment of factor costs created by a new invention is often only realized with hindsight, although the *prospect* of such a realignment might be driving the inventor. Again, it is rather hard to measure, but we can reasonably suppose that most attempts at invention fail. This is not always because of the "badness" of the idea, but because the infrastructure or incentives are not in place to develop and use it. In other words, it must be nested or embedded in a particular development block to fully realize that potential.

[12] This reflects our interest in the economic consequences of technology, rather than the precise conditions that give rise to technology, which may be quite varied. The history of technology is of course a very important and interrelated area of study, but cannot be a main focus of our concern in this text.

macro-inventions are dependent on the structure of particular development blocks, and energy sources.

This process takes time. The steam engine was a macro-innovation, but for more than one hundred years it was very expensive to use it in any sites distant from coal supplies. Wide diffusion required further micro-innovations that improved the efficiency and reliability of engines. However, some further changes in the technology were of such profundity that characterizing them as micro-innovations seems to underplay their significance. They might at least be seen as meso-innovations that made a brilliant (although sometimes very simple) idea *applicable* across a much greater range of economic activities. It was often the meso-innovation that could really establish a development block. One might even say that a macro-innovation or a core innovation remains only potentially so until a series of meso-innovations has cemented its status. These are traits that emerge only in a specific historical context; they are not properties of the innovation itself, which might emerge in people's minds or workshops many times throughout history. The paradigmatic example of a meso-innovation was the application of high-pressure steam to a piece of technology that was already quite venerable in the form of the "atmospheric engine." In this case, the innovation was attached to a deliberate desire for innovation: people realized the wider potential of the steam engine and wanted economic gain from it. Out of this came the steam train and the steam ship, and a revolution that could be continental, and indeed global, in scope. They permitted kinetic energy to be employed to move objects horizontally over the surface of the Earth, rather than simply providing turning or lifting on one spot. What the meso-innovation offered was a radically new end application to which the technology could be put, although it also had the benefits of raising its efficiency and lowering costs.

This conceptualization of innovations of different levels of importance also helps clarify what we mean by *biased technical change* and capital deepening. Capital deepening, or an increase in the physical capital to labor ratio, can come about in two ways. First, simply because capital has become relatively cheaper, producers who can choose among different combinations of factors of production will then naturally choose more capital. The fact that capital or labor become relatively cheaper in certain circumstances does not necessarily push society on a different course; circumstances can change, and it can return to previous practices. But in the second case, capital deepening means that the actual possible combinations of capital and labor have changed. This is what is also called biased technical change. This means some kind of innovation has occurred that is more directed to saving labor than saving capital. Macro-innovations have a certain capacity to bring about such biased technical change, which can have very pervasive effects.

Like many authors before us we believe that technical change is biased. Macro-innovations offer the possibility of a radical rebalancing in the use of capital and labor. But the uptake of such macro-inventions for wider usage depends on both the local resource endowment, which determines more immediately relative prices and the affordability of new technology; and the potential people perceive of micro- or meso-innovations.[13]

DEVELOPMENT BLOCKS

We find discontinuities in energy history when a critical macro-innovation comes into existence and transforms economy and society. The implementation, diffusion, and wider impact on society of such macro-innovations are described by the concept of the development block, first coined by E. Dahmén in the 1950s.[14]

A development block is begun by one or more central macro-innovations. Once this initial innovation has occurred, a large set of factors needs to be put in place before there can be a wide economic impact (figure 2.3). Often the potential of the macro-innovation is realized only in a niche market before other changes allow it to be widely diffused, showing at first a very gradual uptake followed by an explosive growth and finally, market saturation.[15] As we have seen, the realization of the potential of a macro-innovation usually requires a series of further micro-innovations, and possibly meso-innovations, to widen its application, and adapt complementary technologies to be used in combination with it. However, the challenges faced are not just purely technical. New firms must be created by entrepreneurs to make and market the innovation, or old firms must adapt. There is a need for capital investment by the financial markets to fund these entrepreneurial activities. Knowledge and competence must rise among the users of the innovation, and specific forms of energy, for instance coal or gasoline, will be needed to make the best use of it. New infrastructure such as grids or roads or refueling stations are often required and institutions need to act, whether to provide investment, planning, and coordination, or to adjust laws in order to facilitate the development of the wider socio-technical system. The overall web of relationships established can be very wide, complex, and mutually dependent. On many occasions innovations may not have a big impact because one or many of the necessary complementary elements is missing. The complexity of the processes that go in to building a development block also help explain the usually slow initial diffusion of the macro-innovation, followed by explosive growth when the full set of complementary goods, infrastructure, and institutions are in place.

[13] Habakkuk, 1962; Hayami-Ruttan, 1985; O'Rourke, Taylor, and Williamson, 1996; Federico, 2005; Antràs, 2004; Acemoglu, 2003; Koetse et al., 2008.

[14] Dahmén, 1950, 1988; Schön, 2000, 2010.

[15] This of course follows a classic logistic S-curve model of growth. See Kuznets, 1930; Wright, 1936; Dean, 1950; Bass, 1969; Young, 2009.

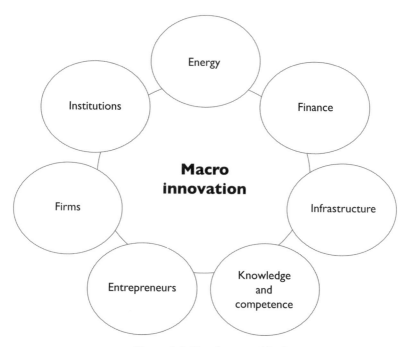

Figure 2.3. Development block

We refer to macro-innovations that become the essential building block of a development block as a core innovation. Sometimes, but not always, this also takes the form of a *general purpose technology* (GPT), that is, a technology that has a very wide range of potential applications and that becomes a key part of the capital stock for many different sectors of the economy.[16]

MARKET WIDENING AND MARKET SUCTION

Complementarities in the development block mean that some parts cannot work without others. On the positive side, this can lead to interactions that reinforce the power of the system, so that the whole becomes more than the sum of the parts. On the negative side it means that, as parts of the development block emerge and demand rises for complementary products, for instance particular energy carriers, bottlenecks and tensions will occur in the system.

---

[16] Bresnahan and Trajtenberg, 1995; Lipsey et al., 2005; Crafts, 2004.

In relation to these complementarities and imbalances, Dahmén coined the concepts "market suction" and "market widening," which we will use in our analyses of energy transitions and the diffusion of new technologies. The distinction between *market suction* and *market widening* relates to the demand side of the adoption of the new technology. Market suction describes the relationship between an innovation and its requirements for complementary resources, such as a machine requiring a particular form of energy to function. The machine exercises "suction" on the market for the complementary resource, meaning there is a large *demand pull*. In contrast, market widening means the widening of demand for the innovation itself, or any of its complementary resources, as an effect from lower prices. This means changes in the availability of the service that the innovation provides come about from a *supply push.*

Market suction and market widening thus have opposite effects: in the case of suction, goods that are complementary to the innovation may rise in price. In the energy sphere steam engines are best run on coal and internal combustion engines on oil, for example. The engine is complementary with that particular energy carrier and substitutes are few, always poorer, and may even be non-existent. Steam engines thus create market suction for coal, and internal combustion engines do the same for oil. The few alternatives mean that market suction is not very sensitive to the price of the fuel. In contrast, market widening is totally dependent on relative prices; the fall in price of using the core innovation provides a stimulus to demand. In energy history, the market widening effect often comes from the transport and communications revolutions inherent in all major development blocks. When transport and communication are cheapened, the new energy carrier can be transported at affordable costs even to remote places and will be used for purposes even where substitutes exist. Both market suction (demand pull) and market widening (supply push) thus make the new energy carrier diffuse more widely in society, but the two forces can differ in strength over time and in different development blocks; and they present the economy with different kinds of challenges.

ENERGY EXPANSION AND ENERGY SAVING

Technical change has a double impact on energy, or works as a two-edged sword. On the one hand, technical change means thermal efficiency increases, which will reduce energy losses and lead to *energy savings.*[17] On the other hand, technical change also leads to the inventions of new end applications of energy (for instance think of the numerous electrical house-

---

[17] Clapp, 1994, stresses the economic incentives to cut down on waste and use energy more efficiently, which have spurred innovation in the area.

hold gadgets that were invented during the twentieth century), so it is *energy expanding*.[18] In addition there are logical relationships between the energy saving and energy expansion, in the form of so-called *rebound* effects, or *take-back effects* (also known as the Jevons Paradox, or Khazzoom-Brookes postulate).[19] In plain words this means that some of the energy savings from thermal efficiency improvements are "eaten up" by increased energy consumption. A classic example is that when a car engine becomes more efficient it needs less fuel to drive a mile, but the lower price paid for driving a mile can stimulate people to take longer car rides.

In short, the rebound effect means "to do more because it is less costly."[20] In the sense of the wider economy, there are three kinds of rebound effects:

1. direct effects: the saving reduces the price of a good or service and leads to people consuming more of the same. This may include stimulating further *biased technical change* in an energy-using direction;
2. indirect effects: the saving increases demand for complementary activities;
3. scale effects: the saving frees up money to invest in all kinds of activities, and this investment affects the scale of the economy: it grows.

Because of rebound effects, every development block stimulates both energy savings and energy expansion, but one force will be more powerful than the other. To indicate this relative strength of the contrasting forces in various development blocks we use the concepts "energy saving" versus "energy expanding." The distinction is mainly applicable for characterizing different development blocks as being generally more prone to stimulate either energy savings or increased energy consumption.

It is common to speak about *economy-wide rebound effects*. This is the impact that the energy efficiency gains have on the aggregate demand for energy in the economy, and this is the most difficult to assess.[21] It encompasses all of the three rebound effects noted previously. In practice, it is possible to estimate rebound effects from particular efficiency savings within particular uses or contexts; in these cases we can say, for example, that a 10 percent rebound effect means that one-tenth of the energy savings are taken back in the form of more energy consumption, while a rebound that exceeds 100 percent means that more energy is consumed as a consequence of the energy efficiency improvement. But achieving this kind of accuracy at the level of the economy from one particular technical change, especially when a range of energy saving and expanding processes are operating simultaneously, is much harder to assess—if at all. We do not attempt this. Indeed,

[18] Grübler, 1998, 341–47.
[19] Jevons, 1866; Khazzoom, 1980; Brookes, 1990; Saunders, 1992; Howarth, 1997.
[20] Hertwich, 2005.
[21] Guerra and Sancho, 2010; Sorrell, 2010.

our understanding of the complexity and range of complementarities embedded in each development block means that effects can only be considered in terms of the functioning of a whole system, rather than individual elements. Instead, we assess the general tendencies toward energy saving or expansion of particular development blocks over time.

DECOMPOSING ENERGY CONSUMPTION

Throughout the book, we use the so-called Commoner-Ehrlich decomposition to show what forces affected changes in total energy consumption.[22] This is, first, a way of demonstrating how much of the change in energy consumption over a certain period was because of increasing population, and how much was because of increasing income. The change in energy use that cannot be explained by these two scale effects (meaning that the economy has become larger) must be a result of changes in energy intensity. As we have seen, energy intensity is the energy required to produce one unit of GDP, and can go up and down. When it goes down, it counteracts the scale effects and means the economy becomes more efficient in creating value out of its energy consumption; the total rise is less than the scale effects of population and income growth would suggest. If, of course, energy intensity rises, it compounds the effects of scale increases.

The Commoner-Ehrlich identity can be written:

$$E = P \cdot \frac{Y}{P} \cdot \frac{E}{Y}$$

where E denotes Energy, P is population, Y/P is income per capita, and E/Y is energy intensity. The Commoner-Ehrlich identity can also be rewritten as annual growth rates:

$$e = p + y + e_y$$

where e denotes the annual change in total primary energy supply, p is the annual change in population, y is the annual change in income per capita, and e_y is the annual change in energy intensity. We use this decomposition in chapters 7, 10, and in our concluding chapter looking to the future.

This kind of decomposition is quite straightforward, but it does not answer the questions we raise about driving factors behind energy intensity and the possibilities for dematerialization in the economy. In this analysis energy intensity is a residual, that is, the result of changes in the ratio between energy consumption and income. It does not tell us precisely what

---

[22] Ehrlich and Holdren, 1971; Commoner, 1972.

caused these changes; it is only an indicator to what might be important, rather than the answer. Such analyses require more data and more advanced calculations.

When we have information about energy consumption in each sector of the economy, at least at certain benchmarks, it is possible to further decompose the energy intensity into effects from structural change ("between sector changes," that is, changes in their relative share of the whole economy) and from technical change ("within sector changes"). It is important to note that technical change is still meant in quite a broad sense. It may pertain to new technology permitting changes in thermal efficiency that has a knock-on effect on the economic efficiency of energy use, but it may also come from changes in organization that gets greater productivity out of the same inputs. However, this further decomposition into structural and technical change can help us answer some questions, such as how important the transition to a service economy was for the decline in energy intensity. The more detailed information required for this kind of analysis means that currently, at least, it can only be applied to the history of the twentieth century. The much greater availability of a range of sectoral-level information gives the third part of the book a different character, as we can engage to a much greater extent in these kinds of decomposition and technical analyses.

DEMATERIALIZATION OF GROWTH

One of the most important things to remember in the context of natural resources and growth is that GDP is a measure of value and *not* a measure of physical throughput per se.[23] GDP is *not* a measure of quantities with a clear correspondence to material and energy needs. Every product sold is measured by its quantity multiplied by its price (price indicating quality, among other things). Some things are big and require lots of energy and material for their production, and others are small and require less energy and material. The small things can still be valued more highly, that is, command a higher price. If we have miniaturization of products, which is typical for the transistors and other products of of the ICT development block, and they increasingly make up a larger share of the GDP, then the growth of the economy becomes based relatively more on increases in the quality of goods than on increases in their quantity measured by weight or volume. Likewise, if we have new materials that are lighter and can be applied more precisely in their use, another dominant feature of development in the later twentieth century, this can also reduce energy and material needs. There is a similar effect from constructing things that can be recycled or used longer before they are worn out.

[23] Daly, 1992, does not quite understand this, while Ekins, 2000, does.

GDP growth that is based on qualitative improvements is better for the environment. Such growth is not so much based on increasing throughput of energy and material, but rather on achieving more *services* for people from that throughput.[24] This is sometimes called dematerialization of the economy. However, this expression can mislead; all services and products produced require at least some materials, so we will never be free of material needs.[25] Nevertheless, output of goods and services based on higher quality in relation to quantity can be regarded as dematerialization and energy intensity can be used as an indicator of such dematerialization.

[24] Boulding, 1966.
[25] Vringer and Blok, 2000; Lawn, 2001.

PART I

Pre-Industrial Economies

Paolo Malanima

CHAPTER THREE

TRADITIONAL SOURCES

1. ENERGY IN PREMODERN SOCIETIES

ENERGY SOURCES AND ENERGY CONSUMPTION IN PREMODERN EUROPE

OVER THE LAST TWO CENTURIES energy has been plentiful, its price relatively low, and the influence of its consumption on the environment profound. In agrarian economies of the past, in contrast, energy was scarce, expensive, and its productivity low; environmental, and particularly climatic, changes heavily influenced its availability. Almost all of the energy exploited by humans was directly obtained from products of the soil, the main converters of solar radiation.

The energy system of these agrarian societies developed between 5000 and 3000 BC, the epoch that also saw the birth of the major agrarian civilizations, and that energy system remained the basis of the economy until the modern energy transition. It was dominant for 5–7 millennia. The energy carriers exploited in this long phase of human history were food, the originary input of energy; firewood, the main source in quantitative terms since the discovery of fire between 1 million and a half million years ago; and fodder for working animals, the main "biological machines." Water- and wind power, although important, added very little in mere quantitative terms to the three aforementioned sources. Since those three main sources were produced through the exploitation of the fields and forests, the energy system was almost identical with the output of agriculture and forestry.

Although direct information on the energy basis of pre-industrial societies is scarce, we can provide some order of magnitude about both the per capita level and structure of energy consumption, and establish the main differences between the past and the present.

At the end of the twentieth century, per capita energy consumption on the world scale was about 50,000 kilocalories per day; that is 76 Gigajoules per year, including traditional sources. In western Europe it was about 100,000 kilocalories per day (153 Gigajoules per year). In the first half of the nineteenth century, it was 13,000 kilocalories per day or 20 Gigajoules per year, excluding coal, and 15,000 and 23 respectively, when coal is included.[1]

---

[1] On the methods followed in order to quantify energy consumption in premodern Western Europe, see Kander, 2002; Malanima, 2006a; Warde, 2007; Henriques, 2009. Our estimates

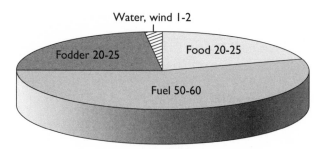

Figure 3.1. Share of any source of energy on total
consumption in early modern Europe (%)
Note: The figure is based on table 3.1 and the
actual consumption per source c.1800
(see www.energyhistory.org).

TABLE 3.1
Energy consumption in early Modern Europe (in GJ per year per capita and kcal
per capita per day)

Sources of energy	Minimum (Gj/year)	Maximum (Gj/year)	Minimum (kcal/day)	Maximum (kcal/day)
Food for human beings	3.1	6.1	2,000	4,000
Fuel	4.6	45.8	3,000	30,000
Fodder for animals	4.4	6.9	2,870	4,500
Water and wind	0.2	1.1	95	690
Total	12.3	59.9	7,965	39,190

Source: Malanima, 2006b.

Although in the middle of the nineteenth century the European energy
transition was already in progress, the shares of total consumption taken
by the different carriers at that time allow us to outline the previous structure of energy consumption. Food for humans and draft animals accounted
for approximately 20–25 percent each and firewood for the remaining 50–
60 percent (figure 3.1). The importance of water and wind was very modest:
1–2 percent of the total. But together they represented a remarkable share
of energy transformed into mechanical power.[2]

---

do not agree with recent data proposed by Morris, 2010a, 2010b, based on diverse procedures
of calculation, and that are too high in our view. For a wide discussion of Morris's data, see
Malanima, 2013, and forthcoming).

[2] The topic is more widely discussed in the following chapter.

Within the European continent, however, differences in energy consumption between regions were relatively wide. In the seventeenth and eighteenth centuries, the average per capita daily consumption of traditional sources varied around 20 Gigajoules per year, or 13,000 kcal per day, although the range between minimum and maximum actual values was much wider given the different climatic conditions found within the continent (table 3.1).

The Photosynthetic Constraint

In past agricultural societies more than 95 percent of the energy input was represented by phytomass, that is, vegetable products. The problem any economy had to face was how to combine different ways of exploiting the soil in order to cover its primary needs of mechanical power and heating.[3] The specific combination of these essential needs distinguished the various premodern agricultural systems.[4] In modern societies, energy is not a resource produced by the exploitation of soil, but it is extracted from fuel reservoirs found in the subsoil, with the exception of food, water and wind, nuclear power and biomass, which represent, in nearly all of Europe, only small shares of total consumption.

We know that the photosynthetic yield of vegetable matter is relatively low. Of the 400,000 kilocalories which annually reach one square meter of soil in the form of solar radiation, only 4,000, that is 1 percent, are transformed into vegetable matter or phytomass. The difference in yield among the diverse ecosystems is, however, remarkable, as the data in table 3.2 suggest. In addition to the share of phytomass used by humans to meet their needs in heating and food, these data include the share that is generally not used for energy purposes (e.g., the leaves of trees; the ears of cereals). Net primary productivity can be defined as the rate at which radiant energy is stored by photosynthetic activity of producer-organisms, chiefly green plants.[5]

Today forests, together with swamps, lakes, and streams, are the most productive ecosystems. Cultivated lands come next, before oceans and deserts.[6] The organic production from cultivation is, however, high indeed by premodern standards. The production of organic matter from pre-industrial

[3] However, agriculture has to provide other basic nutrients for metabolic function—proteins, vitamins, etc.

[4] In any case, it is important to note that the forest was also used for grazing which was, in some cases, the first cause of deforestation. The exploitation as fuels of crop residues and peat does not modify these main features in the use of soil in premodern economies.

[5] The topic has been the object of a wide research. See especially Ajtay, Ketner, and Duvigneaud, 1977. See also Duvigneaud, 1967.

[6] Here "cultivations" refer to agricultural soils.

TABLE 3.2
Extent (km²) and net primary product (grams per square meter per year)
of different ecosystems

	km² (millions)	gr/sqm per year
Swamps, lakes, streams	4	400–3,000
Forests	89	140–2,200
Cultivations	14	650
Oceans	361	155
Deserts	42	3–90
Total	510	336

Source: Whittaker and Likens, 1973b, 1975, 224.

European arable land was 5–10 times lower, including the non-edible part of the harvest.[7]

The problem facing agriculture in the past was always raising the output of consumables, primarily edible goods, per unit of land, or the intensification of productivity per hectare, since food demand was the most inelastic energy need. The push in this direction was always the result of the pressure of population.[8] Intensification in the cultivated fields had to be combined with pasture and forests, the other two energy bases. This combination has been met in endlessly diverse ways. Although in Europe different paths were followed in different regions, some original characteristics existed that distinguished European agriculture from many coeval agricultural systems around the world.[9]

The photosynthetic yield deeply depended, in past agricultural systems, on the changing climate, that is, temperature and precipitation. Historians have stressed the consequences of yearly variations in weather conditions for food availability. Less attention has been paid to long-term climatic change and its influence on energy. A mere drop of 1 degree C for several years could have important effects on the energy balance of the agrarian civilizations.[10] To summarize the main consequences:

1. kilocalories from solar radiation diminished by about 10 percent per cm;²

[7] In table 3.2, data refers to the organic product of any ecosystem. Thus the non-edible by humans part of the output is included.

[8] The analysis of intensification by Boserup, 1965, is still important.

[9] We will come back to the specific character of the European agriculture in the following section of this chapter.

[10] On the subject, see Li, 1998b, and Galloway, 1986.

2. hours of solar light decreased in the temperate zone from a yearly average of more than 2,000 to less than 1,900, causing an approximately three-week decrease in the growing period for crops, pastures, and forests.[11] In cold northern European regions, cereal cultivation became more and more difficult;

3. microbial activity in the soil declined, and with it the decomposition of organic material and the activation of latent fertility;

4. the marginal frontier of cultivated land was lowered by 150–200 meters; the negative effects on cultivation could be serious especially in mountainous regions;

5. it was harder to feed livestock in late winter and early spring: stored grass and hay could be insufficient until pastures grew again in April or May.[12]

Higher temperatures, on the other hand, meant the formation of free capital and a possibility for humans of exploiting a wider range of natural energy resources.

Thus, in premodern agrarian regimes a correlation existed between long-term population movements and climatic variations.[13] Ordinarily warmer temperatures implied more energy from the fields and woods, and then the ✓ possibility of supporting a larger population. This was not true in every case, however.[14]

2. ORGANIC SOURCES AND AGRICULTURES

FOOD DEMAND

Differences among past civilizations regarding the calories consumed daily as food per head were modest, whether calorific requirements were met primarily by rice, maize, wheat, or potatoes.

The intake of food varies in relation with the age, sex, and kind of work undertaken by the population, as well as the climate. On average, however, a human being needs a minimum intake of 1,000 Calories per day in order to stay alive. For light labor, the intake grows to about 2,000 Calories. In case of particularly strenuous work, a man may need up to 4,000–5,000 Calories

[11] Marks, 1998, 217.

[12] Pfister, 1988, 38ff.

[13] See especially the 1800 year reconstruction by Mann and Jones, 2003, and data in IGBP PAGES/World Data Center for Paleoclimatology. Data Contribution Series #2003-051. NOAA-NGDC Paleoclimatology Program, Boulder CO, USA. We return to this topic in the following chapter.

[14] As we will see in the next chapter, where we discuss the influence of climate on land productivity.

TABLE 3.3
Energy requirement as food per sex and per age (kcal per day)

Age	Men	Women
1	757	700
5	1,323	1,226
10	1,984	1,762
15	2,700	2,400
20	2,903	2,285
25	2,683	2,083
30	2,600	2,083
35–65	2,600	2,117
65	2,200	1,883
70	2,200	1,883

Source: Jongman, 2007, 599. See also Fogel, 1993.

(table 3.3 and figure 3.2). Ordinarily, however, food intake rises until 15–20 years of age; and is stable around a daily consumption of 2,600 kcal for men and 2,000 for women until the age of 60, followed by a decline.

Part of the intake of energy is not digested and is expelled as waste. The main part is used for metabolic energy in order to repair the cells, digest food, and maintain the body's heat. As for all mammals, the homeothermic system maintains the same body temperature irrespective of external variation, and it is very expensive in terms of energy, since the metabolism requires energy even when a person is not active, in order to keep the inner temperature stable. What remains can be called the *productive or useful energy*, which is converted into movement and work (or, increasingly in modern times, excess body weight). The ratio between this output of useful work (U) and total input (E) represents the efficiency or yield of energy (η) of any animal:

$$\eta = \frac{U}{E}.$$

For humans this ratio is low, around 0.15–0.20; only about 15–20 percent, that is, of the input of energy becomes useful energy, while 80–85 percent goes into the production of heat.[15] In terms of power, the maximum

[15] Herman, 2007.

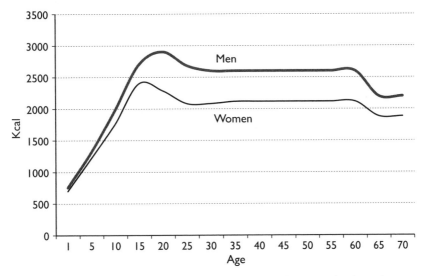

Figure 3.2. Energy requirement as food per sex and per age (kcal per day)
Source: Table 3.3.

effort that the human body can reach, around 5 hp, can be maintained only for a few seconds. One-tenth of this power, that is 0.5–0.6 hp, can last for a few minutes, while in ordinary prolonged work the power averages 0.05 hp.[16] Mowing with a scythe or cutting trees for 10 hours could require, in historic agricultures, more than 7,500 kcal; hoeing and weeding for the same 10 hours, 5,700 kcal, while ploughing requires 6,600 kcal and building labor, 6,300.[17]

THE EUROPEAN AGRICULTURE: A GLOBAL PERSPECTIVE

If the needs for food were similar, the extent of land necessary to meet the annual requirements of a human being were very different in the diverse ecosystems of the past. In order to produce the basic energy requirement consumed as food, the various forms of exploitation of the soil can be classified according to their intensity, or the quantity of output per unit of area.[18] Proceeding from the least to the most intensive agricultural systems of the past, we find, first of all, temporary cultivation (such as slash and burn agriculture, or swidden systems, or shifting agriculture); then crop rotations, when a portion of the soil—half, one-third, or less—is left uncultivated; to agricultural systems where no field remains uncultivated; and finally to

---

[16] Edholm, 1967.
[17] Muldrew, 2010, in particular table 3.8.
[18] The topic has been further developed in Malanima, 2006b.

the continuous cultivation of the same soil with more than one harvest per year.[19]

When population rises, less intensive systems of cultivation are replaced by more intensive ones in order to balance rising demand for energy with a rising supply. In hunting and gathering economies, people need more than 200 hectares per person to provide 2,000–3,000 Calories, and with slash and burn some 10–20 hectares; but in a dry agriculture (such as the cereal cultivation common to much of Europe) with a three-field rotation, only 0.5–2 hectares are required, and much less than half a hectare in the case of continuous multi-cropping. As the density of population rises, land intensification progresses, which means more output per unit of land, more working hours per year, and more workers per family. Not every piece of land, however, can be exploited with the same intensity. Intensification depends on the physical and climatic characteristics of any region and the kinds of crop available. In fact, the main crops—rice, maize, wheat, and potatoes—have very different yields per hectare.

In Europe, wheat and other minor cereals such as rye, barley, and oats were the most important crops, whereas in wet agricultures rice, maize, and potatoes were often the main products. Their yields were much higher than those of the wheat and minor cereals cultivated in Europe.[20] The spread of rice and maize in Europe, starting from the late sixteenth century, and of the potato, from the seventeenth, were only important in some regions and only well into the eighteenth century.[21] Despite the use of these new products, the cereal yield of European dry agriculture was much lower than that of wet agricultures. Energy in the form of food per unit of land was comparatively scarce.

Vegetable products harvested in Europe absorbed virtually all the water necessary for their ripening from rain. Rainwater, however, is poor in the minerals required by the plant during the growing cycle. The land was therefore subject to sharp drops in fertility during brief periods of continuous cultivation. It was of fundamental importance to allow the land to recover by leaving it uncultivated for periods of time, known as fallows, which were usually one year in every two or three. In the medieval and early modern European agrarian system, based on a low yielding cereal such as wheat and on dry methods of cultivation, land was certainly much less productive than in the irrigated agricultures prevailing in the coeval civilizations based on wet agriculture.

Geographers have stressed that, for thousands of years, 60–70 percent of the world population lived in regions where agriculture based on irri-

[19] Boserup, 1965.

[20] On the relative productivity of wheat, rice and maize, see Grigg, 1974, 109.

[21] We will discuss the introduction of maize and potatoes into European agriculture in the next chapter.

TABLE 3.4

Yield per hectare of rice, maize, and wheat in sixteenth-century traditional agricultures (kilograms per hectare)

Cultivation	Place	Kilograms per ha
Rice, irrigated fields	Southern China, Taiwan	2,500
Rice, dry cultivation	Northeast Thailand, Part of India	2,500
Rice, floating cultivation	Deltas of Mekong, Chaqhraya, Ganges	1,500
Rice, slash and burn	Areas of Southeast Asia	1,500
Maize, irrigated areas	Mexico	1,000
Maize, dry cultivation	Central America	1,000–1,300
Wheat, rye, dry cultivation	Europe	400-500

Note: One should, however, allow for husking, which reduces the weight of rice by about 20–25 percent; that of wheat only by 10 percent.

Sources: Data on Asian agricultures: Tsubouchi, 1990, 6–20; on Mexico: Bray, 1968, 119ff.; on Central America: Wilhelmy, 1981, ch. 4; on Europe: De Maddalena, 1972–76.

gation or flooding, known as wet agriculture, prevailed.[22] In 1500, out of a total world population of 450 million,[23] 20 percent was represented by comparatively backward farmers practicing shifting agriculture, and by nomads, shepherds, and other pastoralists. These were the inhabitants of the wide ring of lands at the margins of the agricultural world. The inhabitants of countries supported by wet agriculture, about 60 percent or more of the world's population, were concentrated in fertile narrow valleys in warm regions. The rest—another 20 percent—mostly lived in Europe.

Europe was, then, an exception in the early modern world. In Europe agriculture was in most cases not based on river water, and the dominant crop, wheat, had the lowest yield of the three main cereals.[24] Wheat cultivation was not unknown outside of Europe; it existed also in China and India. In these civilizations, however, most inhabitants depended on cereals different from wheat. As a consequence, when we compare the European cereal yields of the sixteenth–seventeenth centuries, on average about 400–500 kg of edible matter per hectare, with those in the regions of maize and rice, the difference is striking (table 3.4).

[22] Kostrowicki, 1980, 310. This same difference between Europe, on the one hand, and the other agricultural civilizations, on the other, was already pointed out by Max Weber, 1898.

[23] See Biraben, 1979, 15 for data on population density in different ecological areas.

[24] Together with some minor crops, whose yields were lower than those of wheat. On the difference in yields between Europe and Asia and its consequences, see Bray, 1986, 26, and Bray, 1994.

Intensification and Population

In the most productive wet agricultural regions, a family of four or five members could support itself on just one hectare of land, or even less. No fallow land existed there, and pastures were of limited extent since few animals were used in agriculture. In Europe, to regenerate fertility, people had to leave part of the arable land uncultivated (usually a third). In addition, extensive pastures were necessary to make cultivation possible since animal power was essential. Growing seasons were relatively short and did not allow multiple cropping. It has been calculated that in Europe, on reasonably fertile flat land, a peasant family of five members would require 5–10 hectares to survive (forests, providing firewood, excluded, but pastures and fallow land included).[25] In comparison, in China only 0.50–1 hectare was sufficient to meet the requirements of rice for a family of five people.

Intensification, that is, the attempt at increasing the productivity of the land, was much harder in Europe's non-intensive dry agriculture than in Asia's wet, intensive agrarian systems.[26] European agriculture is highly demanding of land, and land per worker was higher in Europe than elsewhere. As a consequence, the density of population attained in traditional Asian agricultural societies was never reached in Europe. Japan and Europe represent two extremes. While in seventeenth-century Japan the highest population density per km[2] of arable land was 850, in Europe it was only 60. The figures for China are much closer to those of Japan than those of Europe, while India is midway between Japan and Europe.[27] In China, as early as the eleventh century, 1 km[2] of rice fields could support 500–600 people.[28]

As the agrarian civilizations won most of their food from cultivated crops rather than pastoralism, it is important to relate population data to arable land. This was relatively abundant in Europe, while it was actually quite scarce in parts of Asia (table 3.5).[29] In parts of east Asia such as Japan, this reflected the very mountainous topography of the country, and hence the limited acreages suitable for wet agriculture. Such a diverse relationship between humans and land constitutes an important difference when considering Europe in a comparative perspective.

Different agricultural systems can be placed along an imaginary line according to their land productivity (Q/R or the quantity of calories per unit of resource, e.g., hectare) and density of working population (L/R or workers per hectare). At one end of the line we find swidden cultivation, whose

---

[25] De Vries, 1976, 35; Abel, 1966, chap. 6; Lis and Soly, 1979.
[26] See, however, Elvin in Sörlin and Warde, 2009.
[27] Grigg, 1992, 93.
[28] Cartier, 1985, 58.
[29] Data on population and demographic trends will be examined in the following chapter.

Arable land, ratio population/arable land, and ratio arable/population in Japan, China, India, and Europe in 1600

	% arable	Population/ arable (km²)	Per capita arable (ha)
Japan	11.0	856	0.12
China	8.6	477	0.21
India	24.2	269	0.37
Europe	28.4	60	1.66

Source: Grigg, 1992, 93.

productivity in terms of the soil was low,[30] and, on the other extreme, we find wet cultivation with rice. The European dry system lay in between, although closer to the swidden system than to wet agriculture. Both density of population and land productivity were relatively low (figure 3.3a). Furthermore, it was not easy, on European soils, to proceed along the line of our graph toward the higher density of population and land productivity of the irrigated agricultures.

The same concept can be expressed by taking the reciprocal of the previous ratios into account: that is R/Q, or resources (e.g., the cultivated area) per unit of output and R/L, or resources per worker (figure 3.3b). As soon as the extent of land per worker diminishes, because population is rising, resources per unit of product must diminish as well. In other words, the productivity of the land must rise. It has been maintained that since in Europe labor was scarce and costly, there was "a historical trend towards the substitution of machinery for labour."[31] Actually the real problem facing the European agrarian system was the relative scarcity of soils capable of supporting high yields of the main converter of energy: growing plants. In any premodern agrarian system the scarce factor was land, while labor was relatively abundant.

As early as the middle of the eighteenth century, Montesquieu, comparing rice and wheat agricultures, pointed out the difference between these two systems of cultivation as to the extent of land required to support a family. "In those regions where rice is cultivated [. . .] one needs less soil to support the living of a family." The difference was even greater because of the need for animals in European wheat agriculture. In Asian rice economies, he

---

[30] Whenever we include in the extent of the soil the temporarily uncultivated share. Otherwise, if we take only the cultivated part, temporary cultivation is highly productive.

[31] F. Bray, 1986, 113. Actually labor rewards were in any case close to the subsistence, as shown by Broadberry and Gupta, 2006.

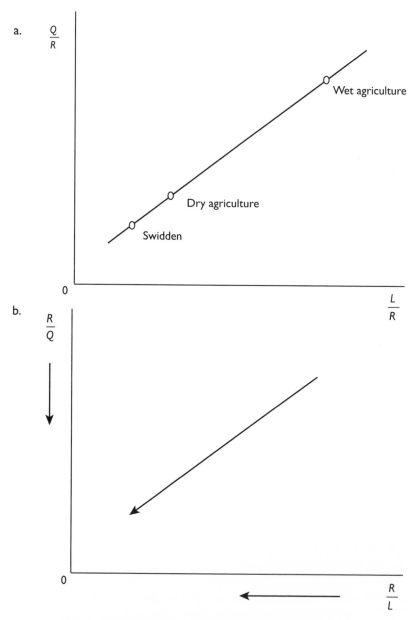

a. $\frac{Q}{R}$

Wet agriculture

Dry agriculture

Swidden

0

$\frac{L}{R}$

b. $\frac{R}{Q}$

0

$\frac{R}{L}$

Figure 3.3. The relationship between land productivity and density of population

wrote, "the work done elsewhere by the animals is done there by humans and agriculture is an immense manufacture."[32] The need to cultivate much more soil to support a peasant family in a dry than in a wet agriculture also implied the exploitation of much more mechanical force. When a hectare is enough to support a family, many agricultural tasks can be accomplished without the help of a working animal.[33] This is not the case when the living of a family depends on the cultivation of 5–10 hectares such as in Europe. The nature of the agricultural ecology as a whole implies a wider use of animal power.

WORKING ANIMALS

Animals were important in Europe as sources of mechanical power. The European peasant needed not only more land, but also more capital in the form of working animals. Working animals were the early machines used by humans and fodder was their fuel.

During the agricultural Neolithic revolution, humans made a decisive step forward with the taming of animals. As far as we know, this new phase occurred from 4000 years BCE or even earlier. G. Childe defined this period as the most fertile in inventions and discoveries of any epoch in human history before the industrial revolution.[34] The central change was represented by the taming of animals—ox, donkey, horse, camel—and their utilization in agriculture and transportation.

It was not so in all agricultural regions of the world. In some areas, animals such as the ox, horse, donkey, and mule were unknown; these animals were only introduced to the Americas after Columbus's arrival. Although originally native to America, the horse and camel spread toward Asia, Africa, and Europe, ultimately disappearing from the continent between 40,000 and 10,000 years ago.[35] Humans and their daily work remained the main source of power in Chinese agriculture, in some areas the only source. In a seventeenth-century treatise on agricultural technology, Sung Ying-Hsing mentioned the use of manpower to draw the plow together with the "water buffalo and the yellow ox,"[36] the working animals utilized in Chinese agriculture. Furthermore, when transport by water was impossible, men's shoulders were the most frequent substitute.

[32] Montesquieu, 1979, II, 114, Livres XXIII, XIV.
[33] All this refers especially to southern China, where rice was the dominant crop cultivated. Where wheat was the main cereal, as in the north, matters were different and more similar to other dry agricultures.
[34] Childe, 1936, 1942.
[35] Crosby, 1972, chap. I.
[36] Sung Ying-Hsing, 1966, 8.

In Europe, animal power began to be employed to a much greater extent from the eighth century onward. It has been calculated that, as a result of this development, 70 percent of the available mechanical power in eleventh-century England was provided by working animals (still mostly oxen in this period) and only the remaining 30 percent by human muscle power or by water mills.[37] Yet, from the late thirteenth century, as a consequence of the rise in population, per capita animal power diminished. In England, by 1300 it was lower than in the eleventh century.[38]

Animal Power

Until the taming of animals during the Neolithic agricultural revolution, √ humans' endowment with energy consisted of food and firewood. Every-day energy consumption could average 4,000–5,000 kcal. How much did it increase with working animals? This question cannot be answered with certainty for Antiquity and the Middle Ages. Reliable estimates of animals and the ratio of working animals to workers only exist from the nineteenth century. If we convert all draft animals (oxen, cows, mules, donkeys) into horse equivalents,[39] on the basis of their relative power, we discover that an agricultural worker in nineteenth-century Europe could exploit the equivalent of 0.3–0.5 horses (table 3.6).[40]

Since we are interested in the availability of energy in per capita terms, we can look at a working animal as a machine and divide its daily input of energy as food among the people who employed it. Since agricultural workers represented about 30–40 percent of the population of Europe, the ratio of animals to humans in the nineteenth century could be obtained by multiplying the previous ratio of horse equivalents to workers by 0.30–0.40. The result we attain is a horse equivalent for every 5–8 people.

Fernand Braudel was probably right when, for the second half of the eighteenth century, he proposed an estimate of 14 million horses and 24 million oxen in the continent: 38 million working animals in total. Since the European population was then about 150 million,[41] the ratio of animals to humans was about 0.25: that is a working animal to every four people, more or less the same as in medieval England.[42] If we convert the oxen into

---

[37] Langdon, 1986, 20. Only mechanical energy is included in this estimate. See also Langdon, 2003. See also Vigneron, 1968; Lefebvre De Noëttes, 1931, I; Haudricourt and Delamarre, 1955.

[38] Campbell, 2003, 187.

[39] "One ox equals two thirds of a horse, one donkey is one-half of an ox, and one cow is one-third of an ox": Kander and Warde, 2011.

[40] Kander and Warde, 2011.

[41] Without Russia.

[42] Langdon, 2003, 216.

TABLE 3.6
Number of horse equivalents working in agriculture in selected European
countries, 1815 and 1870 (in 1000s) and ratio horse equivalent/workers (H/W)

	1815	1870		1815	1870
Sweden			France		
Horse equivalent	466	525	Horse equivalent	3,078	2,857
H/W	0.69	0.50	H/W	0.48	0.40
Germany			Italy		
Horse equivalent	2,945	3,741	Horse equivalent		1,377
H/W	0.31	0.37	H/W		0.14
England (& W.)			Spain		
Horse equivalent	700	802	Horse equivalent		2,055
H/W	0.44	0.54	H/W		0.48
Netherlands			Portugal		
Horse equivalent	142	168	Horse equivalent		293
H/W	0.37	0.30	H/W		0.28

Source: Kander and Warde, 2011.

horse equivalents, the ratio diminishes to one to every five persons, since, in terms of power, three oxen correspond to two horses (thus 24 million oxen are equivalent to 16 million horses). The result tallies with what we find in nineteenth-century agriculture.

The rough estimate of a working animal to every five people hides deep differences between northern and Mediterranean regions. Around the middle of the nineteenth century the range of variation was wide (table 3.7). In Italy and Spain, the number of horses and oxen was lower, as was the ratio of animals to workers.

From what we know about these animals' weight, size, and physical exertion, their daily intake of food must have ranged from 83 to 105 MJ (that is 20,000–25,000 Calories). For oxen, we can assume a figure of 21,000 kcal per day; for horses, mules, and donkeys, 24,000 kcal.[43] A working horse of

[43] The daily consumption is close to that proposed by Kander, 2002, 46.

TABLE 3.7

Number of horses and oxen employed in agriculture and ratio of animals to workers in agriculture in Italy, Spain, France, the Netherlands, and United Kingdom, 1850–1870 (number of horses and oxen in 1000s)

	Horses	Oxen	Horses per worker	Oxen per worker
Italy	401	1,351	0,04	0,14
Spain	435	928	0,09	0,18
France	1,715	1,535	0,23	0,20
Germany	2,193	2,178	0,20	0,20
Netherlands	153	0	0,28	0,00
England & W.	802	0	0,54	0,00
Sweden	299	352	0,29	0,34

Source: Kander and Warde, 2011.

about 350 kg requires 7 kg of hay and oats; that is digestible nutritive substance, with an energy content of 4,000 Calories per kg. If we assume a daily average of 94 MJ for these "biological engines,"[44] this would mean about 12–19 MJ for each inhabitant of Europe (that is 2,800–4,500 Calories).[45] If we add these calories to the food consumed by each person, we reach about 6,000–8,000 Calories per day.

As with humans, the useful energy or mechanical work performed by working animals represents only a fraction of the whole caloric intake. The efficiency of an animal is lower than that of a human as a converter and averages about 10–15 percent (about 10 percent for horses and 15 percent for oxen).

Assuming the rough number of 38 million working animals in the continent around 1750, and thus a total power availability of around 10 million hp, power from animals per European inhabitant was equivalent to 0.07 hp. This means that, with the use of animals in agriculture and transport, the power available to any European was more than twice what could be exerted by his or her body alone.

[44] Smil, 1994, 76ff. I assume that the average draft animal horse or ox, weighing, as was usual in the pre-industrial world, 300–400 kg, and subjected to relatively heavy agrarian labor, consumed about 11 Forage Units, corresponding to 10 kg of dry substance—hay, for instance—per day.

[45] A more precise estimate should distinguish between the different energy intake of the horse and ox: higher for the first—100 MJ per day, than for the second—88. I have assumed here an average of 96.

FORESTS

Demand for food was the most inelastic energy need. While the potential for variation according to the kind of labor task being done at any one time was large, the long-term metabolic and basic working needs of a population fell within a narrow range. Eating is of course *sine qua non* of any economy. However, in pre-industrial Europe the most important energy carrier, in quantitative terms was fuel, and in particular, firewood.

During the later centuries of Roman civilization and in the early Middle Ages, forests had been felled in many densely inhabited areas of the Mediterranean in order to extend arable land.[46] At this time, dense woods still existed in many numerous uninhabited or sparsely populated zones of northern and eastern Europe. Following the fall of the Roman Empire in the west, the population declined in the Mediterranean and consequently in many places forests returned. There were fewer than 30 million people living in Europe in the eighth century, with a population density of less than 3 inhabitants per km². Cultivated lands and inhabited sites were superficial scars in a never-ending green forest.[47]

Before the year 1000, demographic growth began to intensify in Europe, thus bringing renewed inroads into the forests (figure 3.4). As the demand for food gradually increased, farming families, monasteries, and landowners made clearances in the thick forests in order to gain land for agriculture. Since population growth resulted in land clearing, due to the increasing need for arable land, the reduction of forests in Europe mainly occurred in periods of demographic expansion, such as the twelfth to thirteenth and the sixteenth centuries, whereas in intermediate periods, the woods advanced.[48] By the end of the sixteenth century, "around one-third of France, the German speaking lands, Bohemia and Poland was wooded. Most of northeastern Europe and Scandinavia was rather more forested. Denmark had at most a quarter of its surface area under trees, but quite possibly much less. At least 12 per cent of Ireland was probably wooded, of England 6 to 7 per cent and Scotland 4 per cent and of the Netherlands about 4 per cent."[49]

The attack on the forests occurred not only in Europe but also China, where in the high Middle Ages there was a sharp rise in population. Many forests were cut down for heating requirements, building, and industrial use, especially for the smelting of metals. A consequence was an increase in China in the use of coal in metal-working during the high Middle Ages.[50] During the early modern age, however, all major agricultural civilizations

---

[46] Harris, 2011, devoted to the Antiquity, is important for the following epochs as well.

[47] Higounet, 1966.

[48] These estimates can provide, at most, an approximation: Williams, 1990.

[49] Warde 2006, 34. See also the very long-term reconstruction by Kaplan, Krumhardt, and Zimmermann, 2009.

[50] Elvin, 1973, 85; and above all Hartwell, 1967.

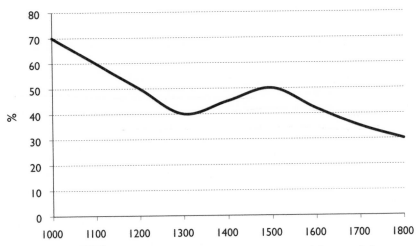

Figure 3.4. Estimate of the extent of forests in Europe (% of the wooded area on total extent) (1000–1800)
Note: The graph shows the changes over a long period and in the percentage of forest over the extent of the whole continent. See also Williams, 1990; Saito, 2009; and Kaplan, Krumhardt, and Zimmermann, 2009 (on the recovery of the forests after the Black Death and the trend).
Source: Malanima, 1996, 57.

with high population densities were situated in relatively warm or temperate areas of the world, such as the belt stretching from Peru to Mexico, northeast Africa, parts of the Middle East, India, and China. In these areas people needed less firewood for survival than in most of Europe; at least if we exclude mountainous regions, where the population density was much lower.[51] On a world scale the forested area covered a little less than 50 percent of the surface in 1700.[52]

More reliable figures on the extent of the forests of Europe only go back as far as the end of the nineteenth century. Woods then covered about 30 percent of the whole surface area. The differences among countries were remarkable (table 3.8).

Excepting sparsely populated regions such as Scandinavia, and much of Russia and Austria-Hungary, the extent of woods was less than 30 percent of the total area of western and central Europe, and often less than 20 percent. The percentage was especially low in some of the most dynamic coun-

---

[51] I have dealt with the subject of fuel consumption in Malanima, 1996, 47ff.
[52] Richards, 1990, 160.

TABLE 3.8
Surface, extent of forests, population, and forests per inhabitant Europe around 1900 (A, B and D, in 1000s)

		A	B	C	D	E
		Surface (000) km²	Woods (000) km²	B/A (%)	Population (000)	Woods per c. (ha)
1	Scandinavia	1,198	479	40.0	12,490	3.84
2	Great Britain & Ireland	317	13	4.1	41,300	0.03
3	Netherlands	33	2	7.5	5,140	0.05
4	Belgium	30	5	17.7	6,710	0.08
5	France	544	99	18.2	40,600	0.24
6	Italy	301	42	14.0	33,800	0.12
7	Spain	505	66	13.0	18,570	0.35
8	Portugal	92	5	5.1	5,420	0.09
9	Switzerland	41	8	19.3	3,300	0.24
10	Austria (Hungary)	626	188	30.0	47,200	0.40
11	Germany	543	140	25.8	56,100	0.25
12	Poland	240	56	23.3	9,000	0.62
13	Balkans	516	129	25.0	33,000	0.39
14	Russia (European)	5,400	1,928	35.7	109,700	1.76
	EUROPE	10,383	3,163	30.5	422,330	0.75
	EUROPE (without Russia)	4,983	1,233	24.8	312,630	0.39

Source: Lunardoni, 1904, 81; Chierici, 1911, 258–59. On the sources of data concerning population see Malanima, 2009, 9.

tries such as Great Britain and the Netherlands. The push toward substitute fuels was much stronger in these countries.[53]

Firewood Consumption

Since firewood was consumed both at home for heating and cooking and in manufactures for metal, glass, and ceramics production, total consumption depended on two main determinants, at least looking from the demand side: air temperatures and the industrial specialization of any region. In southern Europe the daily quantity of wood consumed per capita was low since temperatures were higher and less heating was required. On the plains of Italy, 1 kg of wood per capita per day was sufficient for survival. In the mountainous Piedmont it was not so: in the eighteenth century per capita daily consumption was 2.3 kg for domestic uses and 0.5 kg as fuel in industry: a total of 2.8 kg. For the cities of northern Europe an estimate has been proposed of 1–1.6 tons per capita per year, that is 2.7–4.3 kg per day (8,000–13,000 Calories).[54]

For eighteenth-century France, Fernand Braudel suggested a yearly consumption per head of 1.3–2 tons, not far from the previous estimate for urban centers.[55] In Paris it was 9,600 calories daily per capita at the end of the eighteenth century, and in Dijon, 7,300.[56] In Denmark, urban domestic daily consumption between 1500 and 1800 averaged 7,000–14,000 Calories, while in the countryside it was lower: 6,900 Calories without industrial consumption.[57] In 1811, Danish consumption was 1.75 cubic meters per person, that is about 2 tons per year or 5 kg per day.[58] In eighteenth-century Germany a per capita consumption of 1.5 tons has been suggested, that is 4 kg;[59] whereas up to 7–8 kg per person were necessary in Sweden and Finland. While in southern Sweden about 3 kg were consumed per day per head, in the north 8–9 was the usual level of consumption. Thus, from southern Italy to northern Scandinavia,[60] daily firewood consumption could range from about 1 kg per capita to a little less than 10.[61] Across the whole

---

[53] As we will see in the next chapter.

[54] Hayami, de Vries, and Van der Woude, 1990, 8. According to different estimates the caloric content of firewood is comprised between 3,000 and 4,000. The differences depend, at least in part, on the different qualities of firewood in use in various regions.

[55] Braudel, 1979, I.

[56] Devèze, 1982d, 188 and 192–93.

[57] Lovins, 1991, 14.

[58] Kjaergaard, 1994, 122.

[59] Sieferle, 2001, 141. According to Warde, 2003, 590, firewood consumption in Germany can be estimated at 2.33 kg per day per head.

[60] Estimates for Sweden are from Kander, 2002 and 2003.

[61] On the theme of the industrial uses of firewood, see Sieferle, 2001, 61ff.

continent, the daily average per capita was about 2–3 kg, corresponding to 6,000–9,000 calories per day.[62]

According to our results in western Europe around 1800, firewood was by far the chief source of energy, with the only exception being England and Wales, where coal had already long been the dominant source, becoming more important than firewood around 1620 and second only to draft animals. In northern European countries such as Sweden, Norway, and Finland, firewood accounted for 80 percent of total consumption, while in central and southern Europe it represented about 45–65 percent. On the whole, in this part of the continent, firewood consumption accounted for about 50 percent of the total energy consumed (table 3.9).

Fuelwood consumption at the beginning of the nineteenth century was, in Western Europe, 0.24 Toe per year per head (2.4 million calories per year or 6,500 kcal per day).[63] The average was 0.17 Toe per year or 4,700 kcal per day around 1850. At that time, however, the use of coal in Western Europe was developing and per capita firewood consumption diminishing (see chapter 5). We would suggest an average of 0.25–0.30 (6,800–8,300 kcal per capita per day) for the previous centuries, when the European population relied almost entirely on fuelwood. Thus we can estimate that the annual growth of more than one hectare of forestland was necessary to supply the needs of one single person, although yields varied significantly from place to place.

It is hard to specify precisely the relative share of total consumption used by domestic and industrial demand respectively. Only for iron do we have quantitative estimates of the European output as a whole. If we accept the estimate of a production of 100,000 tons in 1500 and 1 million tons in 1800,[64] and the need of 30 kg of wood per kg of iron, the firewood exploited at the beginning of the sixteenth century was about 5 percent of the total consumption and in 1800, some 20–25 percent.[65] It is only a rough estimate, however. We should add to iron production firewood consumed for other industrial usages such the working of non-ferrous metals, glass, bricks, salt, food. The total may have reached something like 20 percent at the beginning of the early modern period and certainly more, probably approaching 40 percent of total firewood consumption, at the end.[66]

The availability of firewood placed a constraint on urban growth, especially in northern Europe, where the need for firewood per head was higher than in the south. In a northern European region, where the daily demand of wood per inhabitant was 3–4 kg, one needed about a hectare of forest. Then

[62] Previous data are confirmed by Warde, 2006, 38–39.

[63] See our data appendix at www.energyhistory.org.

[64] Braudel, 1979, I. The estimate by Braudel represents probably the higher margin of the range. With reference to western Europe, we found a much lower estimate in Van Zanden, 2001, 83.

[65] See also the lower estimate of 10–20 percent by Warde, 2006.

[66] We revisit the topic in the next chapter.

TABLE 3.9
Firewood consumption as a percentage of total energy consumption
in Western–Central Europe around 1800

	%
Sweden	80.0
Netherlands	38.2
England & Wales	4.3
Germany	49.6
France	65.4
Italy	60.0
Spain	46.3
Portugal	57.4
Western Europe	*50.0*

Note: For Italy the percentage is based on an indirect calculation; for Spain
the estimate refers to 1850, and for Portugal to 1856. Actually we have no
direct data concerning Italy, Spain, and Portugal in 1800. Peat is included in
the percentages; it was important in relative terms only in the Netherlands.
The estimate for western Europe is only a plausible suggestion.
Sources: See www.energyhistory.org.

a city of 10,000 inhabitants needed 10,000 hectares. This firewood had to
be transported to the city. A city of 10,000 inhabitants needed to employ
30–50 carts daily to transport wood from the nearby forests, unless it was
easily accessed by water.[67] Since draft animals have to be fed, the area required to support the city's fuel need is greater still. Although this constraint
worked in southern European cities as well, higher temperatures made the
provision of wood easier, especially when woodland or woody offcuts from
agriculture were available. This is certainly one of the reasons why, until
about 1500, big cities were scarce in northern Europe. They became numerous in this part of the continent where the main source of heating could be
peat or coal. With these alternative fuels, the volume that had to be transported diminished because of the greater energy density of these fuels, and,
with this, transport costs fell. Thanks to the widespread use of peat and coal,
usually transported by water, big cities such as Amsterdam and London
were able to expand rapidly from the sixteenth century on.[68]

[67] We follow here the calculations in the introduction to Hayami, De Vries, and Van der
Woude, 1990.
[68] We return to this topic in the following chapter.

In Chinese agricultural society, fuel needs per capita "were probably significantly lower" than in Europe: "less heating was needed in a warmer climate; Chinese cooking methods were much faster and more fuel efficient than European ones."[69] China, however, and especially northern China, can be bitterly cold in winter months, so it is likely that a lot of wood was consumed there.[70] On the whole, however, the European average temperature, and especially in the north, was "much lower and the surface cover was stripped off by Pleistocene glaciers, inhibiting natural regrowth."[71] In the other civilizations practicing wet agriculture, located in more southerly climes than Europe, fuel consumption was certainly much lower than in France, Germany, and England.

We know that a hectare of European forest could produce 1.5–2 cubic meters of wood,[72] and a well-managed woodland, even 3 or more,[73] whose weight was about 625 kg per cubic meter, and provided 1,875,000 kcal (table 3.10). If we assume a per capita consumption of wood in Europe of 2–4 kg per day, the annual consumption would be 0.7–1.5 tons: from 6,000 to 12,000 kcal per day. We can accept the calculation by Braudel that to meet the annual consumption of 150 million Europeans in the middle of the eighteenth century, the need for forest would have been 160 million hectares, which is about a third of the extent of the continent without Russia.

The efficiency of the use of firewood was very modest. Depending on the different methods of domestic heating—open fireplaces in the center of the room, fireplaces with chimneys set into the walls, or stoves—the yield was about 5–15 percent.[74]

Up to this point, we have examined both energy demand and the need for the products of soil in order to meet this demand. All in all, taking into account fields, pastures, and forests, any European inhabitant needed around 1–2 hectares. We will see that possibilities of intensification existed within the European agricultural system and that these possibilities were exploited in the nineteenth century. However, the dependency of energy consumption on organic or vegetable carriers did not allow the kind of development subsequently experienced by the European economy and that we now call modern growth, by which in the long term a faster growth of output than population leads in turn to an improving standard of living.

[69] Pomeranz, 2000, 231, and also appendix C for a comparison between firewood consumption in Lingnan China and France.

[70] The books by Smil, 1988 and 2004 deal especially with energy consumption in contemporary China. Few elements are provided on pre-modern energy consumption.

[71] Saito, 2009, 403.

[72] Sieferle, 2001, 141.

[73] Warde, 2006, 39.

[74] In the following chapter, we will discuss the topic of the changing yield of heating. See Fouquet, 2008, 95 and 394.

TABLE 3.10
Equivalence of measures concerning wood (volume to kg, to kcal)

cubic meter	625 kg*
firewood (kg)	3,000 kcal
charcoal (kg)	7,300 kcal
charcoal (kg)	5.5 kg firewood**

* This is the coefficient for dry wood from coniferous trees: see *Energy Statistics*, 1987 (Table 14, Coniferous fuelwood). A coefficient of 450 kg is sometimes used, although *Energy Statistics* 1987 suggests an average of coniferous and non-coniferous of 725 kg. Obviously the difference can deeply affect our statistics.

** 5.5 kg are used in order to produce 1 kg of charcoal.

We can now examine the carriers that did not need the soil in order to be produced. Although these sources were of secondary importance before the nineteenth century (with some exceptions), they would become the basis of the energy balance in the following epoch.

Two New Fuels: Coal and Peat

From a geological viewpoint, coal is a sedimentary rock formed by a mixture of components of vegetable origins. Vegetable matter is composed of carbon, hydrogen, oxygen, and also inorganic materials. When vegetable matter decays under water in the absence of oxygen, the carbon content increases. Peat is the initial product of this decomposition and is formed in bogs, marshes, and swamps. The pressure of sedimentary materials that accumulate over the peat deposits causes the transformation of peat into *lignite*. Greater pressures and heat cause the transformation of lignite to *bituminous* and *anthracite* coal. Some coal deposits formed more than 400 million years ago and bituminous and anthracite coal formed during the so-called Carboniferous period between 360 million and 286 million years ago.

Fossil fuels were known and used in Europe long before the industrial revolution. Coal was known in antiquity in England and probably elsewhere in northern Europe.[75] Dated remains from archaeological sites in England show that coal consumption peaked in the late Roman period between the second and fourth centuries CE and then diminished with the decline in population. Its consumption expanded again in the high Middle

[75] Smith, 1997.

Ages following the rise in population.[76] Coal was also widely used in medieval China.[77]

Peat (or turf), another fossil fuel, is formed over centuries in areas of marshland. Its caloric content or energy density (calories per kg) is 60 percent of that of coal (17 MJ per kg). It was already employed for heating when the Romans reached the Dutch lowlands. A traveler from north Africa in the second half of the tenth century mentioned peat being cut in the western Netherlands.[78] It also enjoyed a long history of use up to recent times in Ireland, upland and fenland Britain, and the north European plain stretching east from the Netherlands. By the fifteenth century, coal was widely used around Lièges and near Newcastle. In urbanized areas such as Flanders, the quantities of peat used were sufficient to exhaust the local supplies.[79]

Overall, the use of coal in most of Europe during the seventeenth and the greater part of the eighteenth centuries remained modest and was of no particular importance to the economy. This, however, was not the case in England or in the northern areas of the Netherlands, where much of the economy's success from the seventeenth century onward was a result of these newfound energy resources.[80] Without coal, could a city such as London have grown from 50,000 inhabitants in the sixteenth century to almost 600,000 in the eighteenth and 1 million by the nineteenth? It would have been impossible considering the restrictions that the limited availability of wood imposed on every human settlement. Such growth was possible, nonetheless, thanks to the coalfields in the north-east of the country.[81] In the whole of England the production of coal increased 7–8 times between 1530 and 1630, and coal very probably became more important than wood as a provider of thermal energy by the 1620s. The share of coal in total energy consumed was 12 percent in 1560, 20 percent in 1600, and 50 percent in 1700.[82]

More and more industrial activities turned to these new sources of energy: from weapon and gunpowder production to that of alum, bricks, tiles, and glass, and from salt, beer, and soap production, to sugar refineries.[83] Until the end of the eighteenth century the use of coal in the iron industry was limited.[84] Coal contains a high quantity of sulphur that, when combined with minerals during smelting, produces a poor-quality product. Coal could, however, be used in the blacksmiths' forge when the metal utilized was solid

---

[76] Nef, 1952.

[77] Hartwell, 1967.

[78] Unger, 1984, 223.

[79] De Zeeuw, 1978.

[80] Hayami, De Vries, and Van der Woude, 1990, 12.

[81] On these developments see Nef, 1932.

[82] Warde, 2007.

[83] Nef, 1936, 169–70. See also Mathias, 2003, on the topic and Hatcher, 1993.

[84] Tylecote, 1962, 190–91; Sprandel, 1981, 419.

and compact and did not absorb sulphur. In 1650, 55 percent was used for heating, 33 percent in industry, while the rest was employed for other uses and exported. Until 1800, about half of the coal extracted in Britain was employed in industry and half in domestic hearths, excluding exports.[85]

The Dutch civilization of the seventeenth century also owes much of its splendor to its fuel resources, above all peat. With the rise in population, the forests had almost totally disappeared and the country's salvation was peat, the presence of which had long been known.[86] The total volume of peat dug in the four hundred years between 1550 and 1950 corresponded to the heating provided to 175 million people for one year, or the equivalent of the total annual energy consumption of the European population in the second half of the eighteenth century.[87] Peat exploitation on a large scale started in the late Middle Ages, and reached a peak in the second half of the century, declined during the eighteenth century, and grew again in the nineteenth century especially after 1825. The peak of extraction was reached between 1850 and 1925. Coal imports from England, however, contributed heavily to Dutch energy consumption in the seventeenth and eighteenth centuries.[88] And the importance of coal continued to rise during the eighteenth century.

Until 1900, the trend of peat digging followed the trend of the Dutch economy. In around 1650, 3,000 workers plus their families were employed in peat-bogs, while 2,500 found seasonal work in this industry. Almost 4,000 boatmen were involved in the shipment of peat for at least 100 days per year. Not only was domestic heating largely based on peat, but also several industries such as brick and tile production, brewing, baking, and distilling. About 30–40 percent of total energy consumption in the Netherlands was based on peat during the seventeenth and eighteenth centuries. Turf and wind were the foundations of the Dutch Golden Age.[89]

3. NON-ORGANIC SOURCES

GUNPOWDER

It is often claimed that the first transformation of heat into orderly movement occurred with the steam engine, but it would perhaps be more correct to say that this came about with gunpowder. "The cannon is the first known example of controlled conversion of thermal energy to kinetic energy: it is

[85] Hatcher, 2003, 501.
[86] See the important article by De Zeeuw, 1978.
[87] Gerding, 1995.
[88] Cornelisse, 2008; Unger, 1984, 222.
[89] De Zeeuw, 1978.

Figure 3.5. A fifteenth-century war machine
Source: Valturio, 1462–70.

a one-cylinder internal combustion machine."[90] Naturally, the manner in which the motive power is used—for destruction (by a cannon) or for production (a steam engine in a factory)—makes a difference (figure 3.5).

Gunpowder was a compound of potassium nitrate, sulphur, and charcoal in the proportion of 4-1-1 when used for cannons and 6-1-1 for arquebuses (the precursor to the modern rifle). It is said to have been found in China as

[90] Mokyr, 1990, 85, n.2.

early as the ninth century, but was not used for weapons. The first Chinese cannon was in fact recorded in 1356.[91] In Europe, gunpowder made its first appearance in the early fourteenth century and may well have had no connection with the Chinese invention.[92] After its first recorded appearances, in 1314 or 1319 in Flanders and in 1326 in Florence, it soon reached every corner of Europe. By the middle of the fourteenth century, gunpowder was already well known everywhere. On closer consideration, gunpowder was perhaps the fastest growing source of energy in the early modern age. This explosive mixture of substances, along with the construction of ever more effective means to utilize it, in the shape of artillery and firearms, played an important role in the expansion of Europe into the rest of the world. Explosives also began to be used in mines from the last decades of the sixteenth century.[93]

Saltpeter was the main component of gunpowder. It could be produced artificially from the sixteenth century and probably as early as the fifteenth.[94] As firing a cannonball required 10 kilos of gunpowder, of which more than 6.5 kilos were made up of saltpeter, this component was often in short supply. The European chemical industry took its first steps in supplying armies and obtained saltpeter by mixing nitrogenous organic residues (for the most part sheep excrement) with earth, before adding urine and lime, then filtering the mixture with water, and finally repeatedly distilling the liquid.

WATER

The mechanical contribution of a water mill to energy availability in traditional societies was relatively modest when we compare it to human and animal energy consumption from food and fodder; even more modest if the comparison is made with total energy consumption, including firewood. The mechanical energy produced by a water mill endowed with the power of 2 hp working 12 hours is equal to about 15,000 kcal (65 MJ), and since in a day a man consumes 3,000 kcal, consumption of gravitational energy by a water mill is five times the food energy consumption of a man. A working animal consumed fodder containing about 20,000–25,000 kcal a day, as we have seen. Energy consumption by this animate machine was higher than that by a water mill. We also have to take into account, however, that, while the yield of a mill is high—the transformation into mechanical, useful work is about 70 percent or more of the gravitational water energy falling on a vertical wheel—the yield of an animal body is low, as we have seen:

---

[91] Needham, 1956–2004, V, 34.
[92] As Braudel also suspects; 1979, I, chap. 6.
[93] Vergani, 2003.
[94] Panciera, 1988.

10–15 percent for working animals and a little more for a man. Useful energy is about 2,000–2,500 kcal for an animal and 500–600 for a man. The inanimate machines of today are much more efficient: usually more than 30 percent of the energy of our cars is transformed into useful work (the transportation, that is, of people or commodities).

While small in quantitative terms, water and wind were central components of the European pre-industrial energy system, being the only sources of non-muscular mechanical energy in a world where all other energy was ultimately derived from the transformation of the products of the soil. They appear much more important if we refer only to mechanical power. In mid-nineteenth century Sweden, water and wind accounted for 20 percent of total motive power, while animals represented 79 percent and steam engines, 1 percent. The percentage diminishes greatly if we take human power into account.[95] Since the main constraint of premodern energy systems was the lack of a technical means to convert heat into mechanical work, we can exclude firewood in our calculation of power.

If in terms of energy consumption the contribution by a water mill is modest, in terms of power, or the capacity of doing work in a second, things are a little different. In the eleventh and twelfth centuries the ratio of water mills to the population was approximately one mill to every 250–300 people,[96] which means that more or less every village had at least one mill. The same ratio of population to mills prevailed in early modern Europe until the end of the eighteenth century. From late medieval and early modern documentary sources, we know that an ordinary water mill seldom exceeded the power of 3 hp (figure 3.6). In the nineteenth century, more powerful mills were much more common. Often in the late Middle Ages it was lower: around 2 hp or less. As a comparison, we can remember that the ordinary Watt steam engines in 1800 had 10–15 times this power. The contribution of water power in traditional economies is more apparent if we imagine a fairly typical village of 300 people, each of whom consumes a little more than 2,000 kcal as food and works with some assistance from draft animals. Amidst all of these hungry people the importance of a mill with the power of 3 hp would actually be substantial. Without it there may not be enough muscle power to grind the grain. In table 3.11, we see a hypothetical quantification of the power, or the capacity to do mechanical work, for such a small village. We see that looking at the problem from the side of mechanical power, the existence of a mill represents a remarkable addition (10 percent) to the total power of the village. Vannoccio Biringuccio from Siena wrote in his *De la pirotechnia*, published in 1540, that a water mill could replace the mechanical work of 100 men.[97]

[95] We return to the topic in the section 4 of this chapter.

[96] Makkai, 1981.

[97] Biringuccio, 1914; Reynolds, 1983 derived the title of his book from Biringuccio.

Figure 3.6. A big seventeenth-century water mill
Source: Ramelli, 1588.

According to Marc Bloch, there was a connection between the disappearance of slavery in medieval Europe and the introduction and spread of water power in the early (fifth to tenth centuries) and high Middle Ages (eleventh to thirteenth centuries); in fact, emphasizing that medieval invention implied "a more efficient use of natural inanimate forces," he concluded

TABLE 3.11
Estimate of the endowment with power in a small village of 300 inhabitants, with 60 draft animals and 1 water mill (in HP and %)

	HP each	Total HP	% on total HP
300 people	0.05	15	30
60 animals	0.5	30	60
1 watermill	3	3	10

Source: Makkai, 1981.

that this endeavour to "spare human work" derived from the fact that "the master had fewer slaves."[98] Many new contributions have been published recently on medieval and early modern water technology and, on their basis, we can question the actual rise of waterpower in this period (and, even more, of the ratio of waterpower to men).[99]

In the high Middle Ages, however, many other forms of production benefited from waterpower: fulling cloth,[100] beating hemp, milling paper, pressing olives, spinning silk, beating oak bark for the production of tannin, boring gun and canon shafts, crushing cereals, preparing tobacco, working clay, producing cement and gunpowder, grinding glass, and milling flax. In the sixteenth century, hydraulic energy was used for at least forty different industrial processes.

WIND

The windmill (figure 3.7) is said to have originated in Asia. The first evidence we possess refers to the seventh century CE.[101] Whatever the origins really were, windmills were long known in Europe as Persian mills. Although the first European region where windmills spread was twelfth-century Italy, the regions where wind power played a more important role were the great plains of northern and western Europe, where the winds are more constant and there are no mountains; from northern France, to Holland, Denmark, and across the plains of Poland and Russia. On the Atlantic Coast, windmills were still rare in the fourteenth century, only multiplying in the fifteenth.[102] In England, however, about 4,500 windmills already existed in

[98] Bloch, 1935.
[99] Munro, 2003, 226–27; Brun, 2006.
[100] Malanima, 1986, 1988. See also Ludwig, 1994.
[101] Forbes, 1956.
[102] Forbes, 1956. For the diffusion of the windmill toward Eastern Europe: Davids, 1990.

Figure 3.7. A seventeenth-century windmill
Source: Ramelli, 1588.

1300, when there were 9,000 watermills.[103] In Holland the number rose continually, reaching 3–4,000 in the seventeenth century and 9,000 in the second half of the nineteenth century. Toward the year 1900, 30,000 existed in the area surrounding the North Sea.

The windmill, like the water mill, had many uses apart from grinding cereals. In sixteenth-century Holland, windmills were used to spin cotton,

---

[103] Campbell, 2003, 187.

full cloth, beat leather, manufacture gunpowder and tannin, saw wood, produce oil, paper and tobacco and to drain water. Fulling windmills became relatively common in the sixteenth century in Dutch towns such as Leiden, Rotterdam, and Groningen, and were well known in Flanders at an earlier date.[104]

At the end of the eighteenth century, the power of a windmill was 2–3 times higher than that of a watermill, varying on average between 5 and 10 hp. In seventeenth-century Holland, a windmill supplied 60 kilowatt-hours per day, equal to that of 100 men.[105] On a European scale the number of these installations was much lower than that of the watermills, and it has been calculated that, in the eighteenth century, the overall power was equal to one-third or one-quarter of that of hydraulic wheels: the first varied from 1.5 million horsepower to 3 million and the second from a minimum of 300,000 to a maximum of 1 million. Their number was therefore between approximately 30,000 and 100,000 whilst that of hydraulic wheels (for mills and other devices) could well have reached 1 million. In the first half of the nineteenth century the total number of windmills in France, England, Germany, the Netherlands, Belgium, and Finland numbered between 50,000 and 60,000.[106]

It is much more difficult to quantify the importance of wind power used by shipping. Uninterrupted progress was made in the use of wind: great increases in the number of sails on the seas from the commercial revolution of the Middle Ages implied a growth in the magnitude of energy exploited.[107] We know that, in the second half of the nineteenth century, the ratio of a steamship's tonnage to its power (expressed in hp) was 2.8.[108] Thus, power is the result of tonnage divided by 2.8 (we are speaking here of net rather than gross tonnage). In the same period—the late nineteenth century—we know that, tonnage being equal, a sailing ship was usually estimated to have one-third of the power of a steamship.[109] Thus, to calculate the power of a sailing ship, all we need to do is divide its tonnage by 2.8 × 3, that is, 8.4.[110]

The next step is to estimate how much of this power was actually used. We lack any information whatsoever on this matter. Since ships were not used every day and did not always travel at full speed, less than half a day at full power all year round seems a reasonable assumption in order to

[104] Van Uytven, 1971, 11–12.

[105] See the comments and calculations on windmills' power in Davids, 2003, 275ff.

[106] Davids, 2003. These figures, collected by Davids, suggest a total number of windmills closer to 100,000 than to 30,000, although there is a difference of a century between the previous estimates and the figures presented by Davids.

[107] Unger, 1980 is an important work on the topic.

[108] Malanima, 2006a, 36–37.

[109] Barberis, 1908, II.

[110] Important technical information can be also found in Rossignoli, 1922, 34ff. and Rossi, 1915.

reach a magnitude. If an engine with a power of 1 hp works 10 hours, the energy consumed is 10 hph. The final step is to convert hph into calories or joules. In 1780, when the tonnage of the European merchant fleet has been estimated to be 3,370,000,[111] the power of the European merchant ships can be estimated to have been 400,000 hp[112] We have seen that, at the same time, animal power is estimated to be 10 million hp for all of Europe. Animal power was then twenty-five times higher, although both water and wind machines were more efficient than the biological converters and modern thermal machines. Their yield was 60–85 percent.[113] Using a different method, an estimate of wind power consumption has been made for the seventeenth-century Netherlands, an important maritime region of Europe: the result is surprisingly low. Wind supplied about 8 percent of the thermal energy from peat.[114] Magnus Lindmark has devised an alternative method that makes an assessment of wind energy hitting the rig. Allowing for loss largely because of the interference of sails with each other, Lindmark calculates that the energy input is approximately 0.6 kW per ton. This figure gives an estimate approximately twice that proposed above.[115]

4. SEVEN LONG-RUN PROPOSITIONS

Until now we have followed the composition of the energy balance in Europe before the great changes brought about by the large-scale exploitation of coal. We can now stress some of the distinctive aspects of this organic energy system based on phytomass conversion by biological transformers. As previously stated, since the energy system of premodern societies involved the cultivated fields, pastures, forests, streams of water, and wind, its importance in everyday life was wide-ranging. It directly governed the use of the land in a way unlike the subsequent fossil fuel–based regime.

PREDOMINANCE OF REPRODUCIBLE SOURCES

Vegetable energy carriers are reproducible. They are based on solar radiation, and since the sun has existed for 4.5 billion years and will continue

[111] Romano, 1962.

[112] In any case, such an estimate is a rough approximation. Debeir, Deléage, and Hémery, 1986, estimated the power of the English merchant fleet at the same time at 655,000 hp. Since the English fleet was 25 percent of the European merchant fleet, the power would be 2,620,000. The estimate by Braudel, 1979, III, is much lower than ours: 150,000–233,000.

[113] Smil, 1994, 107ff. This estimate refers, however, to overshot water mills. The efficiency of an undershot water mill was considerably lower.

[114] Unger, 1984, 231.

[115] The method has been followed by Warde, 2007, 46.

to exist for another 5 billion years, plants can be considered as an endless source of energy. Water and wind, the marginal components of the old energy regime, are also endless sources of energy. Organic or vegetable economies were in principle sustainable since the sun's energy allowed a continuous flow of exploitable phytomass and the circulation of water and wind. However, only a negligible part of the sun's radiation reaching the Earth, less than 1 percent, is transformed into phytomass by plants. Of this 1 percent, only an insignificant part could actually be utilized by men and working animals. On the other hand, the exploitation of more vegetable sources implied the expansion of arable land and pasture and the increased gathering of firewood, which was hard to transport over long distances. The different ways of utilizing the phytomass were also in conflict, since more arable land implied less pasture and woodland. While the availability of these carriers was endless, increasing their quantity was hard and time-consuming. A big part of the working time of these past civilizations was devoted to providing energy. Agricultural output was almost completely made up of energy sources exploited by humans and draft animals both as food and fuel; and agricultural output represented more than 50 percent of total output. Investment in fixed capital was also largely aimed at providing the means to make possible the exploitation of energy and then was indirectly aimed at procuring energy. Although the wearing of clothes did not only relate to energy needs, one important function was to diminish the dispersion of heat from the body and thus to improve the thermodynamic yield; and this remained a primary function in cold climates. Buildings originally were also aimed at creating and preserving a microclimate inside that differed from that outside the home. All things considered, at least 60–70 percent of economic output directly or indirectly aimed at providing or conserving energy in premodern agrarian societies.

We will see that, since the beginning of its utilization in England, the demand and supply for coal followed an exponential curve. With organic vegetable sources of energy it could not be so. The development of the curve was periodic, such as the one also represented in figure 3.8. This is the reason why the supply of energy per head oscillated around a basic level, although with cycles, while in the last two centuries it described a continuously growing curve. This is the main difference between past and modern energy exploitation.[116] The passage from the old vegetable sources to the modern ones was expressed by Paul Bairoch as "from the bottleneck of renewable energies to the *infinite* resources of fossil energy."[117]

---

[116] This refers, of course, to past energy systems. Future exploitation of renewable sources can even support a new rise in per head energy consumption.

[117] Bairoch, 1983, 403; emphasis in original.

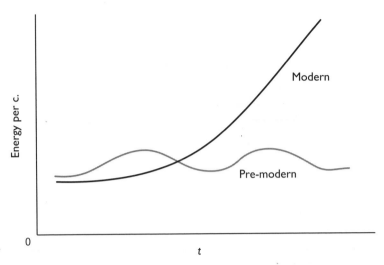

Figure 3.8. Past and present trends of energy consumption

ENERGY SUPPLY AND DEMAND ARE CLOSELY RELATED TO CLIMATE

Since in premodern organic energy systems the transformation of solar radiation by plants into phytomass by photosynthesis was central, and since the sun's heat is not constant across the surface of the Earth or over time, the "fuel" of any human activity was subject to changes occurring in the environment. Climatic phases marked the past history of humankind. Glaciations, which ended before the Neolithic agricultural revolution, diminished the available energy from hunting and gathering and influenced the number of humans and the evolution of their settlements. Agricultural civilizations were also deeply influenced by climatic variations. While warm periods were favorable to the spread of cultivation and the multiplication of humankind, cold epochs coincided with periods of demographic decline. Roman civilization flourished in a period of warm climate and was accompanied by population increase, while the early Middle Ages was an age of demographic decline and cold climate. The warm so-called Medieval Climatic Optimum coincided again with population increases across the whole world, while the period 1270–1840, referred to as a Little Ice Age, was, at least in the first part, until about 1700, a period of economic hardship and population stability.[118] While it is relatively easy to increase the extraction of fossil fuels, it is not so with phytomass. The supply of energy carriers in

---

[118] We must except the fifteenth century, when demographic decline prompted rising living standards.

a fossil-based economy is relatively elastic and can easily follow the trend of production and demand. Past agricultural systems were instead relatively rigid and static in their supply of energy.

In Europe especially, the influence of climate on population and economy was remarkable. Periods of warm climate favored the spread of cultivation and settlements toward the center and the north. In the Mediterranean regions too, milder temperatures allowed the extension of cultivation on the hills and mountains and the multiplication of population since the volume of available energy was consequently rising. In the long term, one degree more in average temperature resulted in a longer period of ripening for crops, a rise in the frontier of cultivation on the hills, and the possibility of farming more marginal environments. The size of the population that could be fed increased remarkably.

Today energy systems heavily influence the environment and climate, as we know. Until a few centuries ago the opposite was true. Of course CO_2 emissions from burning firewood are not so different from those from other fuels: however, it is equally true that, when a plant dies, it releases into the atmosphere the carbon that had been absorbed during the period of growth through the process of photosynthesis (although sometimes with a considerable lag). The balance of CO_2 in the atmosphere is not modified when firewood is burned; the release is only faster. If the forest is allowed to regrow in the same form, the net effect is zero; net contribution to emissions occurs only if large forest stocks are removed and not replaced. In contrast, as the accumulation of carbon in a forest, absorbed in millions of years and then mineralized, is released in a relatively short period of time, as has occurred in the past two centuries, the content of CO_2 in the air has been suddenly and heavily modified by this human intervention with the consequence of global warming that climatologists have identified today.[119]

Transport Costs Are a Major Barrier to Growth

Scholars interested in the topic of market formation in premodern economies have paid a lot of attention to transaction costs, that is, to costs "of externalities, of information, and of risk,"[120] as an impediment to growth. According to some historians, we may consider economic progress as a gradual reduction of exchange costs, increase in the volume of the exchanged goods, progress in the division of labor and, subsequently, productivity. Economic progress would be equivalent to the sum of the rise in welfare as a consequence of the elimination of inefficiencies in market mechanisms and

---

[119] As we will see in the final chapter.
[120] North and Thomas, 1970, 5–6; North and Thomas, 1973; more recently Persson, 2010.

TABLE 3.12

Transport costs in premodern economies and at the start of modernization (in kgs of grain per ton-kilometer transported)

	Kg of grain per Ton/km
Porterage	8.6
Pack animals	4.1
Wagon	3.4
Boat	1.0
Steam boat	0.5
Railways	0.45

Source: Clark and Haswell, 1967, 189 (median figures).

increasing incentives to innovation. This Smithian approach to economic history had, and continues to have, considerable explanatory strength.

Much less attention has been paid to transport costs, at least in recent times, though these are much easier to quantify, determined as they are by the state of the roads, the means of transportation, and locomotive energy. These did not really improve in the agricultural societies prior to the combination of the steam engine and coal to power locomotives and railways as far as overland trade is concerned. It is equally unclear that there were significant advances in trade in the Mediterranean since maritime trade was already well developed during the Roman period. A huge increase occurred in oceanic trade in early modern times.

It has been calculated that the average transport cost over land equaled 4–5 kg of cereals per ton of a commodity transported per kilometer; by river, 0.9, and by sea, 0.3–0.4 (table 3.12).[121]

The transport costs of internal overland traffic, which related to the vast majority of all exchanges, were no different in the eighteenth century from what they had been two millennia earlier.[122] The system of energy consumption based on vegetable energy carriers thus remained at the core of the premodern economy, and was little affected by progress in long-distance transactions because self-sufficiency was dominant due to the high cost of transport. Market formation meant first of all reduction in transport costs, and these large reductions became possible only with railways and steamships.

[121] See the interesting table 47 in Clark and Haswell, 1967, 184ff.; and Bairoch, 1990, 141.

[122] See the recent modernizing views on ancient Roman economy presented in Lo Cascio, 2000.

TABLE 3.13
Animal power (in HP)

	HP
Horse	*1*
Bullock-Ox	0.75
Mule	0.7
Cow	0.4
Donkey	0.4

Sources: Kander and Warde, 2009.

THE ECONOMY IS LIMITED BY LOW POWER

Power is defined as the maximum of energy liberated in a second by a biological or technical engine. The low level of power attainable was another consequence of the usage of biomass converted into work by these past economies. We saw that the power of a man using a tool is about 0.05 horsepower (hp). That of a horse or donkey can be 10–20 times higher (table 3.13 and figure 3.9).

Water mills generally provided 3–5 hp (although this power could be increased remarkably in particular cases), while a windmill can reach 8–10 hp. In comparison, the very largest steam engines could attain 8,000–12,000 hp around 1900.[123] The conquest of power meant an incredible advance in the possibility of processing or manipulating the forces and materials of the environment (table 3.14).[124]

Thus, together with the low availability of energy sources, another main constraint of all premodern energy systems was the low power of the converters, which resulted in a low working capacity per unit of time. The high standard of living of modern societies is the result of the higher output per unit of time, or higher labor productivity. The power of a man in everyday work is the same as a 40-watt lamp. The power of a horse is 15–20 times higher. In premodern civilizations, the most powerful engines were water mills, producing on average about 3 hp, and sailing ships, which could even reach 50 hp.[125] To clarify this central point about the differences between past and modern energy systems, we must remember that the power of an average car (80 kilowatts) is today equal to the power of 2,000 people and that the power of a large power station generating electricity (800 megawatts)

[123] See chapter 6.
[124] The values in the table refer to averages and only suggest orders of magnitude.
[125] We neglect here the employment of power for military purposes. A catapult was an ingenious concentration of power, but with limited economic uses.

Figure 3.9. Water pumping before steam power
Source: Ramelli, 1588.

is the same as that of 20 million people. The electric power of a medium-sized nation of 40–60 million inhabitants, some 80,000 megawatts, equals the power of 2 billion people. Today, a nuclear plant or a nuclear bomb can concentrate millions of hp, or the work of many generations of humans and draft animals, into a small space and a fraction of time. This *concentration of work* allows humans to accomplish tasks that were barely imaginable just a few lifetimes ago.

TABLE 3.14

Chronological advances in power from traditional societies to the steam engine (in hp)

Man pulling a lever	
Ox pulling a load	0.5
Donkey mill	0.5
Vertical water mill	3
Post windmill	8
Newcomen's steam engine	5
Watt's steam engine	40

Source: Cook, 1976, 29.

HIGH ENERGY INTENSITY AND LOW ENERGY PRODUCTIVITY

We have seen the low efficiency of converters in traditional economies. We can now summarize the main results (table 3.15). On the whole, taking a weighted average, the efficiency of the energy system was between 15 percent and 20 percent. Today it is around 35 percent in advanced economies. We have seen that, in the first half of the nineteenth century, energy consumption per capita was around 13,000 kilocalories per day or 20 Gigajoules per year, excluding coal, and respectively 15,000 and 23, if coal is included. Useful energy was then about 2,000–2,500 Calories per day without coal, which means around 3–4 hph (such as a simple water mill) working for an hour or a man working 60–80 hours or a Watt's steam engine working 6–7 minutes.

When the yield of energy converters is low, energy intensity is low as well.[126] Energy intensity represents the energy needed to produce one unit of GDP. Premodern agrarian systems were high-intensity systems. The production of one dollar of GDP (in constant prices) in 1800 required about 20 Megajoules in Western Europe, in contrast with only 9 today. As we have seen, energy productivity is the reciprocal of energy intensity.[127] One unit of energy (Gigajoule) produced about 50 dollars in 1800, while today it produces 115 dollars.[128] Energy transition meant remarkable progress not only

---

[126] The problem is, however, more complex, as we have shown in the introduction. The composition of output is also an important determinant of energy intensity. We will come back to the problem in part III of the book.

[127] In the introduction.

[128] We refer to International Geary-Khamis 1990 dollars.

TABLE 3.15
Efficiency of energy converters in 1700–1800 (%)

	%
Humans	20
Animals	15
Fireplaces	15
Water- and windmills	70

Sources: See text.

in the volume of energy exploited by humans, but also in the capacity to produce. The passage to an economy predominantly using machinery meant a considerable rise in the productivity of the economic system as a whole.

A DIFFUSE GEOGRAPHY OF ENERGY

Energy transition implied a major change in the geography of energy, whether we look from the supply side or the side of consumption. When plants were the only sources of energy, the production of this main input of economic activity was spatially diffuse or areal, as stated by E. A. Wrigley.[129] More or less any inhabited region of the world could avail itself of this energy basis, but the capacity to concentrate it was everywhere limited. The productivity of arable lands, as we have seen, was different in diverse agricultural civilizations. Yet populations could only harvest their food in close proximity to where they lived. Some wider circulation of agricultural products took place, but it was relatively modest in comparison to demand. Wheat traded in the early modern Mediterranean represented no more than 1 percent of the total need of the inhabitants.[130] The commercialization of firewood was even more limited—constrained, as it was, by the high costs of distribution of such a heavy and relatively cheap commodity.

The geography of energy was equally profoundly different from that of the last two centuries when we examine the problem of consumption. Today 25 percent of the world population consumes 75 percent of energy, and the other 75 percent of population consumes the remaining 25 percent. Between Niger and Mali on one hand and the United States on the other, the current difference in per capita consumption of energy is 1 to 40. In the past so great a difference did not, and could not, exist. This is not to say that there were no meaningful differences. In order to survive, an inhabitant of

[129] Wrigley, 1988a, 1988b.
[130] Braudel, 1966, sections III, II.

northern Europe had to consume much more firewood than the inhabitant of northern Africa, and had to employ much more animal power than did a Chinese peasant, since, as we know, a dry agriculture can not subsist without working animals. Food consumption was also higher in cold climates than in warm regions. This difference, however, did not result in a very different standard of living. The organization of agriculture and economy as a whole required more or less energy in relation to diverse geographical conditions rather than differences in wealth. We know that today is different and that the variety of energy consumption corresponds to the variety of levels of income. The rich consume much more than the poor. The diversity of climatic conditions contributes relatively little to the diversity of levels of energy consumption.

HIGHER EUROPEAN THAN NON-EUROPEAN CONSUMPTION

It would be interesting to compare pre-industrial Europe to other coeval civilizations. Unfortunately we lack direct information about energy consumption in other densely populated regions of the world. Indirect information suggests that:

a. fuel consumption was lower than in Europe, because of the warmer climates of these non-European civilizations, usually located farther to the south (in Europe, the average temperature in January ranged from −10 to 10°C, while in the other early modern agrarian civilizations it was between 0 and 20°C);

b. the surface area required to feed one person had to be less than in the European continent, because of irrigation and the cultivation of higher-yield cereals and tubers in advanced non-European agrarian societies;[131]

c. pastures were, on the whole, certainly scarcer than in Europe, because of the lower utilization of animals for agriculture and transportation—if we disregard, obviously, non-agrarian societies, such as nomadic peoples.

While, as already suggested above, an average energy consumption of about 63–84 MJ per day may seem reasonable for a European, in non-European agricultural societies this average was probably less than 42 MJ, or 10,000 kcal, and, for those situated in the warmest regions, close to 21 MJ, or 5,000 kcal. On the whole, the European energy system, because of its lower land productivity and the higher levels of per capita consumption, appears much more vulnerable to pressure from the increasing needs of a growing population. Resources per worker—in terms of fields, pastures, and forests—had a greater significance in Europe than in other regions.

---

[131] We refer to the centuries before the eighteenth, when in Europe as well the cultivation of maize and potatoes spread, as we will see in the next chapter.

5. CONCLUSION

There were undoubtedly margins for improving the productivity of the old biological energy system, notably by increasing the productivity of land and peasant labor. We will see in the following chapter that agricultural intensification progressed in the continent along the seventeenth, eighteenth, and nineteenth centuries and that coal consumption replaced an enormous share of the biomass production in the English advanced organic economy. We will see also that in the Netherlands, remarkable progress was achieved in the use of power. Yet England and Wales together with the Netherlands contained only 6 percent of the European population in 1750. A major advance in agricultural productivity across the continent as a whole only occurred in the age of chemical fertilizers and tractors, which are both technologies made possible by changes brought about by the transformation of the energy system.

As argued by C. M. Cipolla[132] some decades ago, and more recently by E. A. Wrigley,[133] the agricultural energy basis of past civilizations was the main obstacle to their economic progress. Since the metabolism of their system depended on the availability of soil, which is limited, labor productivity declined as human beings grew in number and the ratio of population to natural resources and animals increased as a consequence. This resulted in decreasing energy for converters to translate into motion and work. Improvements in the division of labor, and the invention of more effective implements, could stretch these limits, but not remove them, within the boundaries imposed by the dominant energy system. Only the passage to the new, modern system, starting in the nineteenth century, opened up new potentialities for growth to the agricultural civilizations. Examining the dynamics of the early modern European economy will highlight both the possibilities for development and the constraints of the old European world.

[132] Cipolla, 1962.
[133] Wrigley, 1988a; and the essays collected in Wrigley, 2004 and 2010.

CHAPTER FOUR

CONSTRAINTS AND DYNAMICS

1. POPULATION AND CLIMATE

OUR PERSPECTIVE

OUR VIEW OF THE EARLY MODERN European economy is more pessimistic than that proposed by many historians. We think that, while in aggregate terms agricultural output was growing in the continent from the late Middle Ages, in per capita terms the reverse was true. Since energy consumption almost coincided with agricultural output, energy per capita declined as well.

The start of the energy transition in Britain from the second half of the sixteenth century was a reaction to this constraint in a period when population pressure on resources, as well as prices, were rising. This reaction or "escape from the constraints of an organic economy,"[1] as Wrigley wrote, consisted of two main changes:

1. *saving land*: the increasing resort to coal, since the end of the sixteenth century, and the agricultural innovations from the seventeenth, were aimed primarily at *saving land*. Thanks to the success of these changes, labor, better endowed with resources than before, became more productive, and as ordinarily happens in such circumstances, wages began to rise;
2. *saving labor*: the second main change, aimed at *saving labor*, or put another way, endowing laborers with more *mechanical power*, was favored or caused by the level of English wages, which were higher than in other European regions. This change occurred from the eighteenth century with the increasing mechanization of the economy, especially with the rapid expansion in the use of the steam engine in factories from the later eighteenth century.

The first change implied a *transition in the kind of energy carriers*; the second, a *transition in the kind of converters* used to engender mechanical work. Energy transition was the result of the positive interaction of both changes, which made for a discontinuity in the performance of the economy. In this chapter we will examine some main determinants of the availability

---

[1] Wrigley, 2010, 239.

of energy such as population and climate, then the consequences of the changes in these variables on the actual energy consumption, and, finally, the reactions represented by saving resources, and saving labor.

THE DEMOGRAPHIC TRANSITION: THE FIRST WAVE

A first push toward change came from population growth. World population doubled in the 1,600 years after the birth of Christ: from 250 to 500 million.[2] The rate of increase in this long period was, on average, 0.04 percent per year: barely perceptible. In the 200 years from 1650 to 1850, world population doubled again: from about 600 to 1,200 million. The rate of increase was then 0.4 percent, or 10 times higher than in the previous 1,600 years.

The first wave of the *demographic transition*,[3] starting from about 1670–1700, meant the acceleration of an already slowly upward-moving trend from the late fifteenth century on. It was not only a European event. The same demographic trend was shared by other Eurasian regions such as India and China (figure 4.1). These figures are, however, far from conclusive: their

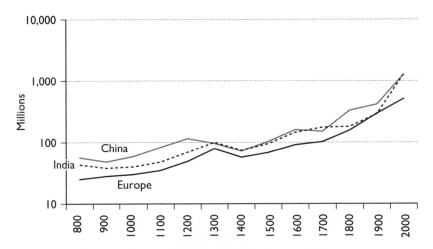

Figure 4.1. The population of Europe, India, and China from 900 to 2000 (millions) (log scale).
Source: For Europe and India: Biraben, 1969; for China, Biraben, 1969; Madison, 2006c; and Caboara, 1998.

---

[2] Biraben, 1969. The figures reported by Biraben for the beginning of our era refer to orders of magnitude. See a summary of the demographic series relating to very far epochs in Cohen, 1995, appendix.

[3] On the transition see the general overview in Chesnais, 1986.

TABLE 4.1

European population (000), yearly rates of growth (%), and densities (inhabitants per km²) 1400–1900

	Population	Rates of Growth	Density	
	(000)	%	With Russia	Without Russia
1400	67,850		6.5	11.4
1500	84,850	0.22	8.2	14.0
1600	107,050	0.23	10.3	18.3
1650	105,310	−0.03	10.1	17.5
1700	121,850	0.29	11.7	20.4
1750	143,230	0.32	13.8	24.3
1800	188,630	0.55	18.2	30.8
1870	310,320	0.71	29.9	49.6
1900	422,330	1.03	40.7	62.7

Note: Data in the table refer to the European population within the present borders of the continent.

Source: Malanima, 2009 (with the addition of data on 1650 and 1900, from the same sources quoted in the book).

margins of uncertainty are still wide, especially for more distant periods and for non-European countries. There is no doubt, however, on the rising trend in population since the end of the seventeenth century.

As far as the European countries are concerned, we discover everywhere an upward trend (table 4.1). After a relatively long period of decline and then stability due to the Black Death and subsequent epidemics, the European population growth rose about 120–130 percent in the 300 years between 1500 and 1800 and 80 percent in the 150 years from 1650 to 1800. The annual rise was still weak when compared to nineteenth-century rates of growth; taking the two centuries 1600–1800 as a whole, it was 0.28 percent per year.

In traditional agricultural economies, the densities of population represent the ratio between the two main factors of production: labor and land. During the eighteenth century this ratio increased by 50 percent and, between 1700 and 1870, it doubled. Land was becoming a scarce factor of production in comparison with the other factor: labor.

Although the rates of growth in diverse parts of Europe are similar, they reveal the slower rise of the southern, Mediterranean regions and the faster

TABLE 4.2
Population in Europe (in 1000s) and annual rates of growth (%), 1600–1800

	1600 (thousands)	1800 (thousands)	1600–1800 (% per year)
North	2,400	5,250	0.39
North-West	9,250	21,080	0.41
West	18,500	29,000	0.22
South	21,400	31,500	0.19
Center	32,500	54,800	0.26
South-East	7,000	12,000	0.27
East	16,000	35,000	0.39
EUROPE	107,050	188,630	0.28

Note: North: Denmark, Norway, Finland, Sweden;
North-West: England, Scotland, Ireland, the Netherlands, Belgium;
West: France;
South: Portugal, Spain, Italy;
Centre: Germany, Switzerland, Austria, Poland, Bohemia, Slovakia, Hungary;
South-East: Balkans;
East: European Russia.
Source: Malanima, 2009 (ch. 1).

increase of the centre and north (table 4.2). This slow change was the continuation of a process already under way from the early Middle Ages. The balance of the European world was moving toward the north in the early modern age. Europe was less and less Mediterranean and more and more continental. As we will see, this change influenced the modern path of the energy system. The European demographic balance was in fact moving toward regions where the productive capacity of soil in producing cereals, the main foodstuff and an important carrier of energy, was higher,[4] and where fossil sources of energy were much more abundant.

Rising industrial production brought additional pressures on energy resources.[5]

THE LITTLE ICE AGE: THE LAST PHASE

Energy availability in pre-industrial agrarian societies depended not only on the technological ability to tap known sources, but also on variations in the

---

[4] See, with data relating to 1800, Van Zanden, 1999a, 359.
[5] As already stated in chapter 3.

sun's energy reaching the Earth. A long-term small variation in temperature could determine, year by year, many more changes than important technical discoveries.[6]

The effects of sudden climatic changes on harvests, agricultural prices, and mortality have been stressed repeatedly in agrarian history. Assessments by historians of long-term climatic variations and their influence have been much more cautious, because until recently our knowledge of the subject remained limited and speculative, with few available series relating to climate over the very long term.[7] But recent reconstructions of temperatures over the last two millennia by paleoclimatologists have shed light on the influence of variations in solar radiation on energy sources.

We know that in the 2,000 years before 1900, annual temperatures varied within a narrow range and that long-term changes depended especially on the variability of solar radiation and volcanic eruptions.[8] Research on the topic has not yet reached definitive conclusions; indeed, some historians even think that the Little Ice Age might be a statistical artifact without any support in the existing series of temperature.[9] The first long-term annual series of temperatures[10] showed the shape of the so-called hockey-stick: a long stability before the sudden contemporary increase due to CO_2 emissions. Temperature curves "behave as almost independent draws from a distribution with a constant mean but time-varying volatility,"[11] without any clear trend. But this view has already been revised by paleoclimatologists, on the basis of new reconstructions less dependent on dendrochronological data.[12] A constant long-term mean over the past millennium disappears from these new series. Uncertainties on the precise timing and trend of temperatures in 1500–1800 are still wide, such as figures 4.2 and 4.3 reveal, and some remarkable criticism of the concept of the Little Ice Age has been raised. The majority of paleoclimatologists believe, however, that the "existence and extent of a Little Ice Age . . . is supported by a wide variety of evidence including ice cores, tree rings, borehole temperatures, glacier length records, and historical documents." According to the same paleoclimatologists, during the Little Ice Age "there was a widespread contraction of rural settlements in upland regions of Europe to lower-lying terrain."[13]

The decline in temperatures ordinarily defined as the Little Ice Age occurred from the end of the thirteenth century, after the so-called Medieval

---

[6] As already recalled in chapter 1.

[7] Still useful for the historian, however, is Le Roy Ladurie, 1967.

[8] On these two main causes, see Crowley, 2000.

[9] Kelly and O'Grada, 2010.

[10] Published from about 2000.

[11] Kelly and O'Grada, 2010 although in this paper the authors do not only refer to the "hockey-stick" series.

[12] Lohele, 2007; Lohele and McCulloch, 2008.

[13] National Research Council of the National Academies, 2006.

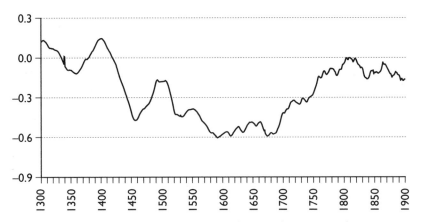

Figure 4.2. Mean temperature trend in Northern Hemisphere, 1300–1900 (running average)
Source: Lohele, 2007; Lohele and McCulloch, 2008.

Climatic Optimum (figure 4.2). In the following centuries, low temperatures were a constraint to raising the land's productive capacity.

It seems highly probable that the negative effects of colder temperatures on energy from vegetable sources were especially remarkable in the seventeenth century, when the lowest levels of the entire millennium were reached: 1–2 degrees lower than the average for that whole period. Some correlation between the changes in population and that of temperatures is apparent. In particular, the decline or stability in population during the seventeenth century coincided with low temperatures. "During the cooling period from around 1590 to 1670, grain yield, measures of fertility, and life expectancy were low, and the population growth rate declined."[14]

Recent research has shown that temperatures rose somewhat at the end of the seventeenth century or first years of the eighteenth.[15] The recovery in population from the late seventeenth century coincided with the new, more favorable climatic period. Fernand Braudel stressed that the simultaneous start on a world scale of a population rise from the late seventeenth century would be hard to explain without the influence of some common determinant.[16] This common determinant cannot but be climatic change. We can note, however, a decoupling of temperature trend and population since the

[14] Galloway, 1986, 12. See also Eddy, 1977a and 1977b; and Eddy, Gilman, and Trotter, 1976.

[15] However, the modern rise in temperatures actually took place only in the second half of the nineteenth century.

[16] Braudel, 1979, I chap. 1.

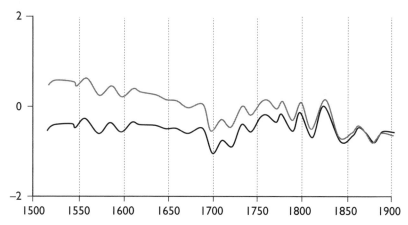

Figure 4.3. The range of European spring temperatures, 1500–1900
Source: Based on National Research Council of the
National Academies, 2006, 41.

late eighteenth century.[17] From 1760 and until about the 1820s many bad
harvests occurred in Europe. According to paleoclimatologists, in fact, the
Little Ice Age continued well into the nineteenth century, while the population was rising more and more. The available curves of temperatures in
Europe show that, after a period of increase from the end of the seventeenth
century, a fall occurred from the 1780s until the low level of the 1810–20
period (figure 4.3).

In northern Italy and the Alps bad harvests became more frequent from
1764 until 1773, and again from 1815 to 1818.[18] There is a correlation between data on temperatures and the advancement of glaciers in the Alps.[19]
In Tyrol, glaciers progressed from 1760 on, reaching their maximum extent
in 1816–18.[20] In Switzerland, temperatures diminished after 1750, dropping
by 1.5 degree C between 1760 and 1780, then increased from 1780 to about
1795, to decline again and reach its minimum between 1810 and 1820.[21]
Both for England and France the period from the end of the seventeenth century until about 1740 was characterized by a significant warming, followed

[17] Although there remain differences and contradictions among the curves constructed by
the paleoclimatologists, as a simple comparison of figures 4.2 and 4.3 shows.
[18] Serre-Bachet, Martinelli, Pignatelli, Guiot, and Tessier, 1991. More recent research on
temperature in Italy, such as Brunetti, Maugeri, Monti, and Nanni, 2006, deals with the years
after 1800 or after 1750.
[19] Mangini, Spötl, and Verdes, 2005.
[20] Corona, 1992.
[21] Pfister, 1988 and 1992.

TABLE 4.3

Indices of gross agricultural product, per capita product, and population between 1300 and 1800 (1500=1)

	Gross Product	Per Capita Product	Population
1500	1.00	1.00	1.00
1600	0.94	0.74	1.26
1700	1.06	0.78	1.44
1750	1.37	0.81	1.68
1800	1.72	0.76	2.26

Note: Countries on which the estimation of agricultural production is based: England, central-northern Italy, Germany, Spain, France, Poland, Belgium, the Netherlands, and Austria (including Hungary and Czech lands).

Sources: The table is based on the estimations proposed by Allen, 2000. For Italy, Allen's data has been replaced by those of Federico-Malanima, 2004 and Malanima, 2009.

by a subsequent cooling.[22] Between 1740 and 1820, winter temperatures dropped about 1.5–2°C.[23]

Sunspots, usually associated with periods of higher solar activity and high temperatures on the Earth, almost disappeared between 1790 and 1820–30.[24] The eruption of the volcano Tambora in Indonesia in 1815, throwing vast amounts of dust into the atmosphere, was followed by two "years without a summer," as contemporary observers noted, in several parts of the world.[25]

THE OUTPUT OF THE SOIL IN EUROPE

From 1500 to 1800, while the European population rose by 120–130 percent, agricultural output increased by 70–80 percent.[26] Per capita agricultural output diminished especially from 1750–60 until 1820 (table 4.3). If we take the centuries 1500–1800 as a whole, per capita agricultural output fell by about 25 percent. The decline was especially notable in the sixteenth century. A partial recovery occurred in the seventeenth century and first half of the eighteenth, followed by a new fall in the second half. This trend

[22] Michaelowa, 2001, 201ff.

[23] Both in the older series by Lamb, 1984, and in the recent Hulme-Barrow, 1997.

[24] Mann, Gille, Bradley, Hughes, Overpeck, Keimig, and Gross, 2000, present a graph of solar irradiation from 1600 on.

[25] For a narrative account of the Little Ice Age, see Fagan, 2000, 167ff.

[26] From Allen, 2000.

TABLE 4.4
Agricultural product per capita in England, Germany, Spain, Italy, France, Poland, Belgium, the Netherlands, Austria
from 1500 until 1800 (1500=1)

	England	Germany	Spain	Italy	France	Poland	Belgium	Netherlands	Austria
1500	1.00	1.00	1.00	1.00	1.00	1.00	1.00	1.00	1.00
1600	0.70	0.76	0.81	1.00	0.78	0.78	0.78	0.84	0.60
1700	0.85	0.67	0.94	0.96	0.76	0.87	0.87	0.84	0.71
1750	0.92	0.67	0.81	0.81	0.78	0.82	0.82	1.02	0.82
1800	0.68	0.76	0.75	0.66	0.78	0.90	0.90	0.96	0.68

Source: As in table 4.3.

has been identified both in Italy[27] and Spain.[28] In Belgium, "agriculture developed rather gradually when seen from a long-term perspective."[29] In the eighteenth century, however, "the increase in cereal crop productivity was lower than the average national population growth."[30] Despite the rise in labor productivity in the seventeenth century,[31] in England too, "the total available food energy per capita dropped after 1780 as population grew."[32] Calories per capita from food may have diminished by 25 percent between 1770 and 1800, while they had increased between 1600 and the first half of the eighteenth century.[33]

In table 4.4, we report data on agricultural output per capita, from 1500 to 1800, in some European countries, representative of the north, center, and south. Here the beginning of the series is 1500, equalized to 1. If we start from 1600, that is, from an already low level, in most cases we find stability rather than a fall.

2. ENERGY SCARCITY

ENERGY PRICES

The trend of energy prices can further strengthen our argument about the constraints of the premodern agrarian economy. If food was becoming scarcer we would expect its relative price to increase.[34] This is what we find. Since for England and Italy we can avail ourselves of longer series of prices and wages, we will refer mainly to these countries.

A first piece of evidence on the rise in prices is provided by wheat, a basic source of energy (figure 4.4).[35] Its price began to rise rapidly in the second half of the sixteenth century and, after a period of stability or decline, again from about 1730–50. The rate of increase in the second half of the eighteenth century and the first two decades of the nineteenth was more or less the same as that during the "Price Revolution" two centuries earlier. From about 1820, wheat prices fell or stabilized. The growth in agricultural pro-

---

[27] Malanima, 2011.

[28] Prados De La Escosura and Alvarez Nogal, 2013.

[29] Dejongh, 1999, 9.

[30] Dejongh, 1999, 26.

[31] Wrigley, 2006.

[32] Muldrew, 2010, 322.

[33] Muldrew, 2010, 143.

[34] According to the quantitative theory of money, a population rise cannot determine an increase in prices. It can, however, if the demographic rise is accompanied by a rise in the velocity of money circulation and in the stock of money. This is precisely what happened in Europe in periods of price inflation such as the sixteenth and the eighteenth centuries.

[35] The correlation between the series is 0.75, higher than we could expect.

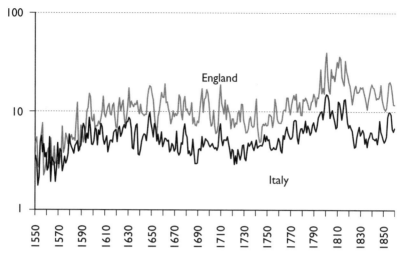

Figure 4.4. Wheat prices in Italy and England 1550–1860
(Florentine soldi per kg, –Italy; pence per kg, England)
Source: For England, Allen in www.iisg.nl; for Italy,
Malanima in www.paolomalanima.it.

ductivity allowed a larger population to be supported without any rise in prices, contrary to what had previously occurred.

The price of wheat is an important indicator of the price of energy, since bread was a main source of energy for the population of past agrarian regimes: ordinarily, it accounted for 40–60 percent of the total expenses of the lower and middle classes. The cost of food as a whole took up 70–80 percent of total income in premodern Europe. Together with bread and other cereals, the main sources of energy in the form of food were a little meat, some fats, and drinks.[36]

Since food represents such an important share of total expenses, the price of energy sources in the form of food heavily influenced the general consumer price trend. If we again look at England and Italy, as representative of the north and south, we notice in both cases a remarkable eighteenth-century rise: stronger and longer in Italy than in England. Changes in the quantity of money, on one hand, and the performance of these two economies, on the other, certainly played a role and explain the differences in the price trends. The intensity of the changes was, however, similar in the final decades of the eighteenth century (figure 4.5).

Despite considerable differences among the various regions, price trends in the south, north, and east of the continent show similar long-term trends: the sixteenth-century rise; the seventeenth-century decline or stability, and the renewed eighteenth-entury increase (figure 4.6).

[36] Consumption in premodern Europe is analysed in Malanima, 2009, chap. 7.

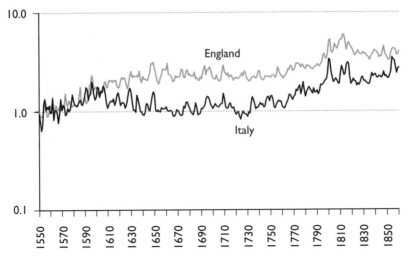

Figure 4.5. Consumer price indices in Italy and England, 1550–1860 (1550–60=1)
Source: For England, Allen at www.iisg.nl; for Italy, Malanima, 2011.

Figure 4.6. Consumer price index in Europe 1500–1850 (1500–50=1)
Source: Malanima, 2009, ch. 6.

However, while prices of food and firewood rose remarkably, prices of non-energy goods rose much less and in real terms (divided, that is, by the consumer price index) they diminished: as happened in the case of textiles.[37]

[37] See section 4, "Saving Labor." Textile fibers come from the soil as well; but in this case the value added from the industrial transformation of the raw material represents the main share of the total price (with the exception of silk).

The trend of European prices was thus greatly influenced by the price of energy, which represented 70–80 percent of the whole basket of goods consumed. Whenever the technology of energy is based on the exploitation of the products of the soil as the main converters of energy, since the availability of soil is given, diminishing returns to labor imply a rise in prices of the aggregate supply of energy carriers. We are not far from the model the English classical economists provided in their works between the second half of the eighteenth century and the first half of the nineteenth.

REAL WAGES AND LIVING CONDITIONS

Rising population and declining resources per worker within a relatively stationary technical framework imply a drop in labor productivity and consequently in wage rates.[38] Series of real wages bear witness to a declining trend from the fifteenth century. Data referring to wages in different European cities reveal a sixteenth-century slump that continued into the first half of the seventeenth century. Losses could reach as high as 50 percent. Stability followed for about a century, but subsequently, during the second half of the eighteenth century, a uniform decline, although of different intensity, brought real wages to a level 20–60 percent lower than that at the beginning of the sixteenth century (table 4.5). This trend confirms previous conclusions about the decline in agricultural output and rise in agricultural prices.[39]

Converted into wheat, the wage in Western Europe in the building industry "fell from about 12 to 15 litres of grain in 1500–20, to 6 to 10 litres in 1780–1800."[40] This trend is not very different from that of agricultural real wages.[41]

An average European trend more clearly summarizes the phases of decline and growth in urban real wages (table 4.6 and figure 4.7).

In the first half of the seventeenth century, European real wage rates were 23 percent lower than in 1500–50. They recovered between 1650 and 1750. Subsequently they fell again between 1700–50 and 1800, reaching their nadir since the late Middle Ages in 1780–1818. After 1818, prices began to diminish and wages to rise.

---

[38] Here we use "wage" and "wage rate" as synonyms. Actually, while wage rate is the wage paid in the unit of time, e.g., day, wage is the product of wage rate by the number of worked days. Series of data on wages in premodern Europe always refer to wage rates.

[39] For a family, it is possible to face a decline in real wage rates either working more or changing the basket of purchased goods. In any case, both working more or purchasing cheaper consumption goods, the conditions of the family worsen. This worsening is represented by the wage rates as a decline in the level.

[40] Van Zanden, 1999b, 188.

[41] On agricultural wages see Malanima, 2009, chap. 6.

TABLE 4.5
Real wage rates in the building sector in some European cities 1500–1900 (1500–50 = 100)

	1500–50	1550–1600	1600–50	1650–1700	1700–50	1750–1800	1800–50	1850–1900
Antwerp	100	94	94	88	93	88	83	94
Amsterdam	100	80	96	99	100	91	74	82
London	100	85	83	95	101	101	105	153
Paris	100	103	97	99	91	85	122	152
Strassbourg	100	68	54	64	49	52	64	57
Augsburg	100	66	52	85	77	61	52	—
Munich	100	67	56	58	45	41	—	—
Vienna	100	70	60	72	72	61	46	—
Valencia	100	66	59	63	65	50	—	—
Florence	100	96	105	122	106	78	59	56
Danzig	100	105	109	124	123	82	66	—
Krakow	100	99	60	71	65	60	68	100
Lwow	100	95	84	52	50	42	—	—
Istanbul	100	83	77	83	80	69	77	110

Source: Based on Allen, 2001. For Florence the wages are those in Malanima, 2002, app. IV; for Istanbul data are from Pamuk, 2000.

TABLE 4.6
The European trend of real wage rates 1500–1850
(1500–50 = 100)

1500–50	100
1550–1600	83
1600–50	77
1650–1700	83
1700–50	80
1750–1800	69
1800–50	77

Source: Average of the series in table 4.5.

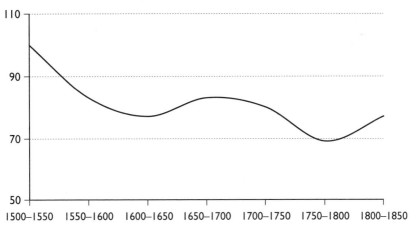

Figure 4.7. Trend of the European real wage rates,
1500–1850 (1500–50 = 100)
Source: Table 4.5.

Recent anthropometric research has shown the effects of the worsening living conditions on the height of Europeans born between 1770 and 1820: several centimeters lower than the preceding and succeeding periods.[42] The trend appears to be more or less the same all over the continent, although the average decrease varies from one region to the next. Stature is particularly sensitive to nutritional deficiency in childhood (but it is also influenced by other variables, such as the disease environment of a specific society).

[42] There is a wide array of literature on the topic. See the summary articles by Komlos, 1998, and Fogel, et al., 1983.

Researchers in historical anthropometrics tend, however, to correlate the decrease in stature between the eighteenth and nineteenth century with the worsening diet and, then, diminishing availability of energy in the form of food.[43] Later, with the start of modern growth, stature recovered the centimeters lost. Since food is the most income-inelastic need, we can suppose that the supply of working animals and of firewood suffered even more as a consequence of declining per capita availability of energy.

FUELS

If we take fuel prices (that is firewood in most European regions, coal in England, and peat in Holland from the seventeenth century on), we find the same trend as already seen in the primary energy input, food. All of the carbon compounds (food and fuels) exploited by the Europeans as sources of energy were growing in price from the sixteenth century on. Firewood prices rose about two to three times from 1500 until 1700. There was only a modest increase in the first half of the eighteenth century, and it became much stronger again in the second half (table 4.7).

Robert C. Allen noted that, if we look at real fuel prices, that is, at fuel prices divided by the consumer price indices of any country, the rise disappears completely and "what impresses is the narrowness of the range of the real price of energy across Europe"[44] during the early modern age. His conclusion is that "the theory that all of Europe faced an energy crisis by the eighteenth century is an attractive theory since it makes the industrial revolution the solution to a contradiction in the pre-industrial economy." This theory is, however, false, in his view, since an "energy crisis" simply "did not occur. There was no general crisis, only local adjustments."[45]

This conclusion is correct only when we look at premodern energy sources in a partial way; in other words, only when we consider firewood and other fuels as the only sources of energy and we exclude the other sources, primarily food. Since in this book we adopt a wider perspective and look at energy sources as a whole, including food for humans and for other animals, we cannot but disagree with Allen's view. In this case, since both food and fodder were, in the eighteenth century, rising in price just as the fuels, in real terms fuel prices were stagnant. In fact, food represents the main share of the consumption basket used to compute price indices. If its price increases, the price index increases as well. Dividing the price of fuels by the price index and then calculating real price of fuel results in an apparent, but only apparent, stability. Actually fuels rose in price just like the other sources

[43] Consumption in Europe is more widely analyzed in Malanima, 2009, chap. 7.
[44] Allen, 2003, 474.
[45] Allen, 2003, 477.

TABLE 4.7

Indices of fuel prices in some European cities 1500–1800 (1700 = 1)

	1500	1550	1600	1650	1700	1750	1800
Antwerp	0.39	0.80	0.79	0.90	1.00	0.91	0.93
Amsterdam	0.37	0.54	0.92	0.92	1.00	1.31	2.38
London	0.35	0.51	0.62	0.95	1.00	1.23	1.55
Paris	—	—	0.98	0.96	1.00	1.09	—
Strasbourg	0.36	0.70	0.87	0.88	1.00	1.60	3.31
Florence	—	0.56	0.83	1.13	1.00	0.99	1.82
Naples	—	1.42	1.68	—	1.00	1.14	1.63
Valencia	0.78	1.32	1.55	1.50	1.00	1.32	—
Madrid	—	1.43	1.89	1.57	1.00	1.34	1.88
Leipzig	—	0.83	1.16	0.72	1.00	0.88	—
Vienna	0.43	0.69	0.88	0.89	1.00	1.20	1.27
Danzig	0.56	0.97	1.00	1.06	1.00	1.68	2.73
Warsaw	—	0.59	1.25	1.05	1.00	1.71	—
Lwow	0.90	1.08	1.14	1.07	1.00	1.49	—

Source: Allen, 2003, 479 (fuel prices on which the Table is based are expressed in grams of silver per BTU). See, however, figure 4.10 on the prices of firewood and coal in England in pence.

of energy.[46] "In the absence of coal," Joel Mokyr writes, "the price of timber would have risen more steeply [. . .], and British land use would have shifted to a higher proportion of trees."[47] As already stated, the rise in price did not concern only firewood, but energy sources as a whole. Firewood is not the only source of energy in the premodern world. The problem was to safeguard the level of energy consumption, and since nearly all sources of energy were rising in price because they had produced through the use of the main converter—land—the problem was saving the scarce factor—soil. As we will see, the resort to coal was a way, indeed the main way, of facing up to the increasing relative scarcity. Thus we do think that "had Britain

[46] Further on, in the beginning of section 4 of this chapter, we will come back to the problem of prices, showing that the non-agricultural component of the CPI rose much less than the agricultural component.

[47] Mokyr, 2009, 105.

not been fortunate enough to find itself located on top of a mountain of coal [. . .], its economic history would have looked quite different."[48]

THE FALL IN ENERGY CONSUMPTION PER HEAD

Since energy consumption in vegetable or organic economies almost coincided with the agricultural output,[49] we can hypothesize that energy per capita was diminishing at roughly the same rate as output per capita. It is important to note, however, that the data on which the estimate of per capita agricultural output is based are in money values and not calories or other unit of energy.[50] Certainly the spread of potatoes and maize during the eighteenth century, whose prices were lower than that of wheat, but whose calories produced per hectare were far higher, countered this declining trend, but not sufficiently to reverse it, as we will see.[51]

Rise of population, low temperatures, decline in agricultural output per head, and increasing prices of energy sources resulted both in a diminishing availability of energy per capita and in reactions aimed at compensating for this decline.

The fall in energy availability from the soil per head, by about 25 percent in the period 1500–1800, and 15 percent in the period 1750–1820, is observable in all of the European regions (table 4.8 and figure 4.8).[52] One could still entertain doubts, until a few years ago, about agricultural output in England. Today we see that, in England too, where a remarkable growth in labor and land productivity had occurred in the seventeenth century, the second half of the eighteenth was not a prosperous period, at least looking at the agricultural output in per capita terms. In this half century, "food consumption per person fell, reaching its nadir during the Napoleonic wars. In terms of food consumption, the idea of absolute immiseration during the early industrial revolution was no myth."[53] It appears that, in England, per

---

[48] Mokyr, 2009, 104.

[49] With the exception of the raw material, that ordinarily did not represent more than 5–10 percent of the total—water and wind power and coal and peat.

[50] We will try, however, further on to present data in calories.

[51] Later in this chapter.

[52] We lack direct estimates of energy production and consumption, with the exception of England and Wales, for the period before the nineteenth century. Table 4.8 is based on table 4.4. We assume that, since energy consumption as defined in this book almost coincides with real agricultural product, the trend of agricultural output represents quite well the trend of energy consumption. On the basis of the relationship between energy and agricultural output in the first half of the nineteenth century, we went back in time and reconstructed the series presented in table 4.8.

[53] Allen, 1999, 217.

TABLE 4.8

Per capita energy consumption in Europe
(Gj per year) 1500–1800

1500	22,4
1600	16,6
1700	17,4
1750	18,1
1800	17,0

Source: Allen, 2000; and, for Italy (included
in the European average), Federico-Malanima
2004.

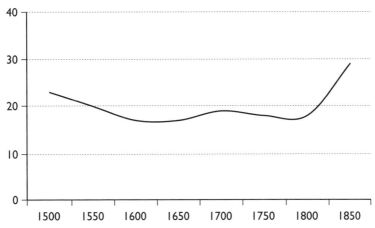

Figure 4.8. Per capita energy consumption in Europe,
1500–1850 (Gj per year)
Source: Table 4.8.

capita agricultural product dropped as elsewhere in Europe—as in Italy,
Belgium, and the Netherlands.[54]

EFFICIENCY

Was the decline in average energy consumption in Europe compensated by
an improvement in the yield of the converters?

[54] For Italy, see Federico and Malanima, 2004; see table 4.4 for the other countries.

In the case of the human body, the thermodynamic yield is around 20 percent.[55] Thermal efficiency of the body cannot change. The same holds true for working animals, whose efficiency is 10–15 percent. Yet in big animals the "body surface is relatively smaller and so heat losses are relatively smaller too. So over time as the draught animals grew bigger they needed less feed per body weight unit in rest and their technical energy efficiency increased"[56] (although this increase in animals' size occurred especially in the last two centuries and not the period we are dealing with in this chapter). Changes in the relative number of draft animals, using more horses, could increase the economic efficiency as well, since horses worked faster.

In the case of firearms, efficiency probably rose much more than in other fields; although in the seventeenth and eighteenth centuries, that is, before the industrialization of war occurring from 1850 onward, the improvements were relatively modest.[57]

In the exploitation of wind power, several remarkable improvements were achieved in the early modern age. The efficiency of windmills certainly rose both in grinding cereals and other industrial activities. Wind-powered sawmills "sporting multiple blades spread rapidly after an explosion in their use in the Netherlands in the 1590s. They could be found in Brittany by 1621, Sweden in 1635, Manhattan in 1623, and soon after Cochin, Batavia and Mauritius."[58] It has been suggested that a windmill in 1800 was able to produce 70 percent more flour than four centuries before.[59]

As the capacity of sails rose, gears became better and better, friction in the mechanisms was reduced, and so industrial tools put into action by the force of the wind became more efficient. An expert of maritime history wrote that "wind energy use also rose dramatically from 1500 to 1800. That increase did not pace with the growth in coal use but it did outstrip the rise in use of other sources. The English were in 1800 not only the greatest users of energy from coal but also the greatest users of energy from wind. The rapid growth of the merchant marine indicated that, alongside the new technology of exploiting coal, the English were effective in using the old technology of exploiting wind by deploying more ships and much more shipping tonnage."[60] The labor productivity increase for ocean shipping was apparently superior to gains in almost all other sectors of the economy. "From 1500 to 1800 the number of tons per man doubled and then almost doubled again. Tons served per man in 1800 was 3.6 times that in 1450." Unger is certainly right in his statement about the rising importance of maritime trades and then the

---

[55] As seen in table 3.15.
[56] Kander, 2003, 809.
[57] McNeill, 1982.
[58] Warde, 2009.
[59] In Davids, 2003, 180, the author quotes a calculation done by Ch. Vandenbroeke in 1986.
[60] Unger, 2004. See also the important article by Lucassen and Unger, 2000.

use of wind. Looking at the subject from the side of energy in mere quantitative terms, this rising importance translates into a very marginal rise in the efficiency of total energy exploitation.

Much more scope for improvement lay in firewood consumption. In domestic heating, coal burning became more and more efficient. In the seventeenth and eighteenth centuries, "the rate of growth in the consumption of coal for domestic heating and cooking was linked to far-reaching developments in domestic architecture."[61] Recent research on heating technology before the nineteenth century is, however, rather pessimistic on the progress in combustion yield in the period we are dealing with.[62] Open hearths, that is, a heating source without a chimney, rose in efficiency during the late Middle Ages, although the rise was very modest. The disadvantage of this form of heating was that the smoke remained in the room. The advantage was that more heat also remained inside.

The fireplace was probably introduced for the first time in twelfth- or thirteenth-century Venice.[63] Its efficiency could reach 15 percent, while that of the open hearth was less than 10 percent.[64] The spread of the brick or tile stove in central Europe (Switzerland, Austria, Germany, Hungary, Poland, and Russia) improved the use of fire for domestic heating; while in southern and eastern Europe the stove was almost totally unknown. Iron or cast iron stoves developed during the eighteenth century and progressed in the Netherlands and northern Europe (in the form of the so-called Franklin stove),[65] and even more with the invention of the Cronstedt and Wrede stove in the 1760s (figure 4.9), with several vertical smoke channels. In domestic heating, coal burning became more and more efficient only during the nineteenth century. "Slowly but surely they discovered the means of rendering houses tolerably free of smoke, through the development of narrower hearths and flues, raised coal-baskets, tall chimneys, and improved internal ventilation."[66]

The spread of the stoves in northern Europe and more efficient fireplaces ushered in an improvement in heating technology from the nineteenth century on. In Sweden, the "efficiency of stoves increased substantially during the nineteenth century,"[67] although the technical devices that allowed this rise in efficiency already existed in the previous century. With these innovations, thermal efficiencies could even attain 50 percent. These stoves spread all over Sweden, Norway, and Finland. Mary Wollstonecraft, when traveling through Sweden in 1795, noticed the stoves "made of earthenware, and

[61] Hatcher, 1993, 409.
[62] Crowley, 2001, 14 and 29.
[63] Sarti, 1999, 105.
[64] Fouquet, 2008, 393–95; see also fig. 4.17, 95 in the same text.
[65] Sarti, 1999, 106.
[66] Hatcher, 2003, 495.
[67] Kander, 2002, 28.

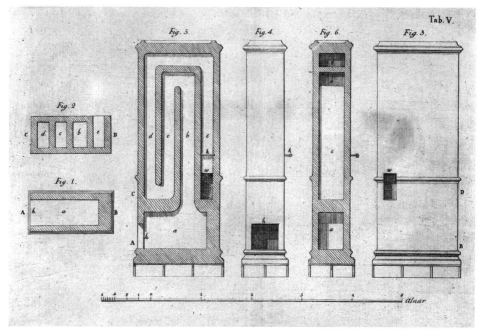

Figure 4.9. The Cronstedt stove

often in a form that ornaments an apartment, which is never the case with the heavy iron ones I have seen elsewhere."[68] When a stove needed to be rebuilt, every forty years or so, the new technology could be exploited. The climate was cold and collecting firewood time-consuming. The novelties in domestic heating did not imply, before 1800, a dramatic increase in the efficiency of heating, but only a slow advance.

On the whole, the rise in efficiency was found especially with sources, such as wind and gunpowder, that represented a small percentage of total consumption. The rising efficiency in the use of firewood in some northern regions of Europe was unable to countervail the trend toward a per capita decline in the exploitation of energy in early modern Europe.

3. SAVING LAND

Under the pressure of population and in the face of a declining per capita availability of energy and rising prices, any traditional agricultural society reacts by trying to intensify the use of land, and especially the arable land, in order to provide the most inelastic need: food. Intensification means a

---

[68] Wollstonecraft, 1796, p. 86.

higher ratio between harvest (in quantity or value) and the cultivated soil, in other words, a rise in yields per hectare.[69]

The developments that allowed intensification of land use in Europe were:

a. the colonization of new lands;
b. the introduction into European agriculture of new, more productive, crops;
c. new forms of rotation;
d. the resort to coal.

These reactions to the decline in per capita energy could only partially compensate the fall. The productivity of the land only rose faster than the population after around 1820. Agricultural prices, as we have seen, clearly bear witness to this change.

COLONIZATION: WITHIN EUROPE AND OUTSIDE

Colonization of new lands accompanied the rise in population and often meant deforestation. On one hand new arable lands supported the growing demand for food, but, on the other hand, they implied a reduction in the availability of the main fuel: firewood. On the basis of contemporary literature on forest degradation and the frequent attempts to control and limit wood destruction, Pomeranz wrote of a European ecological crisis in the eighteenth and nineteenth centuries.[70] The same rate of ecological decay is observable in China, although there it was "slower than that seen in eighteenth-century Western Europe."[71]

It has been estimated that, between 1750 and 1850, 146,000–186,000 km² were cleared in Europe (excluding Russia)[72]—30–35 percent of the whole surface—only a little less than the land cleared from the late Middle Ages to 1650.[73] This process of conquering new space for agriculture continued throughout the nineteenth century, and also spread beyond Europe, opening up new lands on other continents, especially the Americas. These vast areas of natural resources were for the most part only exploited at a very low intensity by the indigenous inhabitants. The importation of textile fibers (cotton) and foodstuffs (sugar) in England meant the exploitation of "ghost acres," that is, the substitution of domestic soils by those in far distant lands. Since neither cotton nor sugar "could be cultivated in temperate latitudes, their purchase by English customers must have involved 'annexing' land

[69] Boserup, 1965.
[70] Pomeranz, 2000.
[71] Pomeranz, 2000, 236.
[72] Williams, 1990, 180.
[73] Büntgen et al., 2011.

elsewhere."[74] Before 1800, however, most "ghost acres" came either from sugar produced in the Caribbean or wood products from North America. In ecological terms the New World really made little difference to European resource availability in this pre-industrial period.

NEW PRODUCTS

Although present in some areas during the sixteenth century, it was not until the end of the seventeenth century that maize spread more widely through southern Europe, extending from the north of Spain and Provence, through the whole of the north of Italy (especially the Po Plain) to Slovenia and Hungary and subsequently to the Balkans. For the farmers of this vast region, maize represented a considerable contribution to the availability of energy in the form of carbohydrates, being 50–100 percent more productive per hectare than other cereals.[75]

The potato was another plant that originated in America. One hectare cultivated with potatoes could supply a calorific value two- to threefold that of a hectare cultivated with grain; sometimes even higher.[76] In eighteenth-century France it was calculated that the yield of grain per hectare was equal to 600–900 kilos, whereas that of potatoes was 5,000.[77] Already well known in Europe at the end of the sixteenth century, potatoes spread into the countryside of Germany, Austria, and then Switzerland, northern France, Flanders, and Ireland in the second half of the seventeenth century. Major progress was made during the first decades of the eighteenth century, although in England it was slow and hard-won, whereas in Flanders, Ireland, and parts of northern Germany it was considerably faster and po-tato cultivation almost totally replaced that of grain. Diffusion was greatly boosted due to a general shortage of cereals. However, the potato was not particularly popular in France and Spain until the end of the eighteenth century. In northern Europe (Sweden and Norway), southern Europe (Italy), and eastern Europe (Poland, Russia) it was introduced later and was little cultivated until the beginning of the nineteenth century.[78]

How significant was the contribution of the new converters in terms of energy? A cautious calculation of their production in kcal per hectare would suggest a 100 percent increase compared to traditional crops. As regards their diffusion, we know that, in the first decades of the nineteenth century,

---

[74] Wrigley, 2006, 471 and the comments in n.137 to Pomeranz's calculation of "ghost acres."

[75] Levi, 1991, 156 and 164. See also Gasparini, 2002. The diffusion of rice was more limited, only interesting the North of Italy and some areas of Spain. Rice was of Asian origin and was already well-known in Italy in the high Middle Ages.

[76] Grigg, 1982, p. 84.

[77] Toutain, 1961, 94.

[78] Masefield, 1967, 346.

the potato—in England, the Netherlands, Belgium, Germany, and Northern France—and maize—in Southern France and Northern Italy—occupied more or less the same area: more than 2 million hectares each. Including also the expanding cultivation of rice, we obtain something like 5 million hectares out of the 42 million hectares of arable land in this core area of the European continent.[79] The need of carbohydrates per head was covered through a smaller extent of arable land. With the spread of potato and maize, the possibility of accumulating carbon, the main "fuel" for biological engines, rose considerably.

ROTATIONS

Another means to intensify production was changing rotations to eliminate fallow. The amount of calories available rose in particular as a result of the introduction of *mixed farming* or *convertible husbandry*. This system of cultivation, already known in several parts of the continent and even recorded by Latin agronomists,[80] progressed especially in England during the seventeenth and eighteenth centuries. It was based on the cultivation of fodder crops on land that previously lay fallow.[81] Fodder crops impoverished the land less than cereals, while at the same time they could be used for the raising of farm animals. A system of continuous rotation thereby replaced the traditional three-field rotation system with no field ever remaining fallow. As a result, the pastures no longer in use could be turned into arable land or could produce fodder. Greater quantities of fertilizer rendered the land much more fertile and helped raise the yields.[82]

Although mixed farming developed primarily in England, intensification to achieve a higher amount of calories from the same extent of arable land also developed in continental Europe. Intensification was often associated with the introduction of new crops. The spread of convertible husbandry in England represented an important change, as it was able not only to increase land productivity, but labor productivity as well. This progress in agricultural productivity was an aspect of the first stage of the energy transition in England.

[79] From data in Mitchell, 1975.

[80] Ambrosoli, 1992.

[81] On agricultural rotations, see also chapter 3. While in chapter 3 we dealt with the importance of rotations in the European agriculture, here we deal with changes.

[82] Overton and Campbell, 1999, 200; Chorley, 1981.

SAVING LAND IN THE EAST: THE POVERTY TRAP

We know that in China the agrarian energy system was able to bear a far greater density of population than in Europe. This is a feature of irrigated agricultures, where peasants are able to raise land productivity much more than in dry agricultures such as those of Europe and North America. While the first economies are "skill oriented," the second are "mechanical."[83] In the first case it is possible to meet decreasing returns by simply employing more labor. In the second, investment in fixed capital is the main reaction in order to counteract declining returns, rising prices, and increasing wages and labor costs.

During the eighteenth century, the Chinese population doubled, while that of Europe rose about 50 percent. From 1700 to 1800, Qing China, in the words of J. A. Goldstone, "added to its numbers a population equivalent to twice the total population of Europe c. 1700." The result is much more remarkable because it was attained without a notable deterioration in nutritional levels. "It is hard to exaggerate this achievement, probably unequaled in preindustrial history."[84] As Bozhong has shown for the Jiangnan region, improvements in hydraulic installations, variations of spatial cropping patterns, a lavish use of fertilizers, progress in techniques of cultivation, and diffusion of the best cropping systems, brought a major rise in wet-rice productivity.[85] Chinese peasants were able, according to Dwight H. Perkins, "to reverse the usual Malthusian direction of causality, which has the pace of agricultural development determining the level of population."[86] We could add to this that in Europe too the Malthusian direction of causality was reversed, but with other means, as we will see.

There is evidence, in some Chinese regions, of a growing use of manure to fertilize the soil, the progress of new crops such as potato and maize, the diffusion of multiple harvests, and the expansion of the cultivated area.[87] For instance, as Robert Marks has shown, in the Guandong province, in the eighteenth century, every year, on the same land, the "cropping pattern consisted of two crops of rice followed by wheat or vegetables.[. . .] With just two or three weeks between the harvesting of one crop and the planting of the next, there was hardly an agricultural slack season in the rice-rice-wheat cycle."[88] Why substitute labor with a machine, when labor is so cheap? The path toward the intensification of labor may turn out to be a

---

[83] This was the conceptualization put forward by F. Bray, 1986, 1994.

[84] Goldstone, 2002.

[85] Li, 1998a.

[86] Perkins, 1969, 23.

[87] Already at the beginning of the eighteenth century, foreign observers maintained that, in some Southern Chinese regions, not an inch of soil was free from cultivation. See the comments by the French agronomist Pierre Poivre in the 1720s in Marks, 1998, 285.

[88] Marks, 1998, 203–4.

"trap," a "poverty trap." More workers mean more production, allowing more demographic growth which, in its turn, stimulates the use of still more labor and less capital.[89] This development was quite clear to Malthus, when he wrote about China that "the country is rather over-peopled in proportion to what its stock can employ, and labour is, therefore, so abundant, that no pains are taken to abridge it."[90] Once this trend is under way, it may become hard to disentangle oneself from it. The paradoxical conclusion is that the standard of living tends to decline precisely in those agricultures where production per unit of land is the highest.[91]

After 1800, Europe and China traveled on two deeply divergent paths. In China the intensification of labor continued, while its economic performance was declining. The low yield of wheat in Europe led "to increase yield per unit of labour by labour saving and introduction of external means of energy other than man."[92]

Even in a rice-producing economy, the possibilities for intensification could not be endless. Chinese economy "was finally hit by both the absolute shortage of land" due to a limit to the new lands in which to expand, and the relative scarcity of land due to the lack of any new land-saving technology.[93] "In the second half of the nineteenth century China was poor compared to the West and much less industrialised."[94]

The Transition to Coal

Coal resources are distributed in the world among 2,000 different fields.[95] Within Europe, coalfields are virtually non-existent in the Mediterranean countries. They are almost entirely found in the central, northern, and eastern regions, and especially Britain and the Ruhr region of Germany, where the main deposits were located. The gradual displacement of the demographic and economic balance of the continent from south to north, starting in the early Middle Ages and continuing in the following centuries, also meant a shift in the population toward the areas of continental Europe where coal was available.

England was the first country in Europe to resort to coal on a wide scale. Looking at the dynamics of fuelwood and coal prices in England, we notice

---

[89] The problem was stressed by Tawney, 1979, 21ff.

[90] Malthus, 1798, ch. XVI.

[91] On this "Asian paradox," see Lattimore's remarks, 1962.

[92] Hayami, 1990, 1.

[93] Deng, 1999, 179.

[94] Vries, 2003, 43.

[95] The geography of coal will be more widely examined in part II.

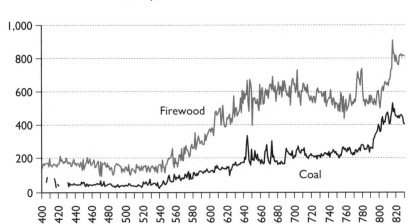

Figure 4.10. Prices of firewood and coal in the south of England,
1440–1830 (pence per Toe)
Source: Clark, 2004 and agricultural prices collected by Clark in
www.iisg.nl. The price of coal (excluding the North, where it was
far lower) was primarily the price in London.

that, in the long period between 1400 and 1830, the price of coal for the
same quantity of calories was far lower than that of wood (figure 4.10).[96]

If we look at figure 4.11, however, we see that the price of wood was,
until the end of the eighteenth century, between two and four times higher
than that of coal (always for the same calorific content): closer to four times
at the beginning of our curve and two at the end. It is quite apparent that,
if in the long run prices of inelastic goods are increasing and real incomes
are stable or diminishing, people will resort more and more to the less expensive substitute. When income is not far from subsistence for the majority of the population, if there is a less expensive possibility for meeting
the same needs, people will replace the expensive good with the cheaper
substitute. In a Mediterranean country such as Italy, totally lacking in coal,
real prices of firewood followed a gently rising trend in the eighteenth century and a remarkable increase in the nineteenth century (figure 4.12). The
only possibility to deal with the rising price of fuel was to resort to imports
of coal, primarily from Britain. The first documented imports of English
coal in Genoa—300 tons—occurred in 1820. Imports grew in the following
decades.[97]

In England, the resort to coal as a form of land saving was contemporaneous with the changes in agriculture described earlier. Until the widespread introduction of steam power, the increasing utilization of coal in

[96] Fouquet, 2008, 2011.
[97] Lupo, forthcoming.

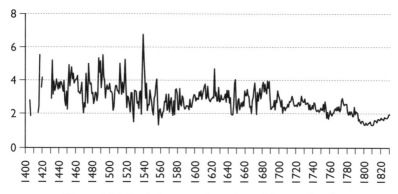

Figure 4.11. Ratio between the prices of firewood and coal in south England, 1500–1830
Source: Based on Clark, 2004.

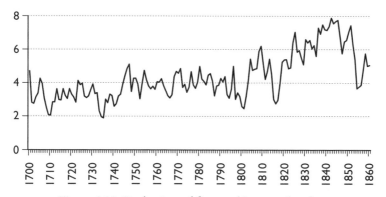

Figure 4.12. Real prices of firewood in central and northern Italy, 1700–1850
Note: Here wood prices per ton have been divided by the consumer price index.
Source: Based on data from De Maddalena, 1974a.

England still occurred within the framework of an advanced traditional economy, or as Wrigley calls it, an "advanced organic economy."[98]

Peat also contributed to saving land in several European regions. The case of Holland in its Golden Age is the best known. Although its role has been overestimated in the past, its importance in domestic and industrial consumption was remarkable. "Per capita energy available to Dutchmen from peat was greater than energy available from all sources in many less

---

[98] Wrigley, 2006.

developed countries in the 20th century. The Dutch enjoyed a comparative advantage in industries which relied on thermal processes."[99]

COAL IN BRITAIN

We saw that in England coal began to be exploited more and more in early modern times as a consequence of the increasing relative price of firewood as the density of population rose. Fears of a general "timber famine" by the early seventeenth century were alleviated by the very early and rapid expansion of coal use.[100] From the middle of the sixteenth century, coal consumption in England and Wales described an exponential curve whose slope appears almost stable—2 percent per year—if the curve is represented through a log scale (figure 4.13).

At the beginning of the seventeenth century, coal already represented a significant share of total energy consumption. Around 1700, half of inland consumption was covered by coal; in 1800, that had risen to more than three quarters, and in 1900 it had reached hardly less than total consumption of energy (table 4.9). In other central and northern European countries

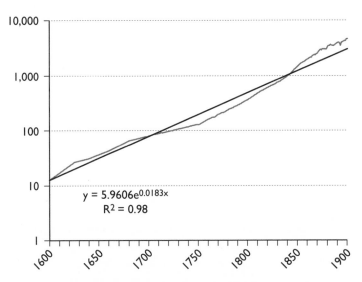

Figure 4.13. Coal consumption in England and Wales, 1600–1900 (Petajoules) (log scale)
Source: Warde, 2007.

[99] Unger, 1984, 222.
[100] Warde, 2007, 38.

TABLE 4.9
Composition of energy consumption in England and Wales 1600–2000 (%)

	1600	1700	1800	1900
Food	27.5	19.9	7.4	2.5
Firewood	28.7	13.4	4.4	0
Fodder (draught)	25.6	16.4	8.8	1.7
Wind	0.5	0.8	2.3	0.3
Water	1	0.6	0.2	0.03
Fossil fuels	16.7	48.6	77	95.5

Source: Warde, 2007, 69.

TABLE 4.10
The consumption of coal by use 1650–1830 (%)

	1650	1700	1750	1775	1800	1830
Domestic	55	48	43	43	36	38
Industrial	33	39	40	42	50	46
Exports	8	5	8	5	3	4
Other	4	8	9	10	11	12

Source: Hatcher, 2003, 501.

coal consumption was fed by imports from England. "For all English coal exports even in the second half of the seventeenth century the main destinations were Amsterdam and Hamburg."[101]

Until the end of the eighteenth century, coal was nearly all used either as a domestic fuel or as an industrial fuel, but, in this case as well, only for its heat content and not in order to produce work. The resort to coal in Britain was a way of saving land and not fixed capital or labor (table 4.10).

As Adam Smith stated, as long as firewood was widely available, people preferred to use it rather than bear the bad smell of coal smoke in their houses.[102] As land became scarcer and increasingly expensive, people were forced to turn to the less expensive past solar radiation. It is hard to say whether this transformation ultimately derived only from the fortuitous circumstance that Britain had easily accessible abundant coal deposits close

[101] Unger, 1984, 239.
[102] Smith, 1776, 72ff.

to the surface. This circumstance, at any rate, played an important role in a context where per capita availability of land was diminishing as a consequence of an unprecedented demographic rise and hard climatic conditions. A combination of factors existed for the transformation of a chance into a necessity. The phase of resource shortage had come to an end thanks to the use of coal as a land-saving development. First in England, and then elsewhere in the continent, per capita energy consumption was rising, although a fast rise occurred especially after 1850. The point can be illustrated by an example taken from Fred Cottrell.[103] 3,500 kcal consumed by a coal miner in the form of food were exploited by the same worker to extract in a day a weight of coal equal to 500 times his sustenance in terms of calories.

COAL AND PEAT IN EUROPE

The extensive exploitation of peat in the Netherlands was a major underpinning of the economic growth occurring from the sixteenth century.[104]

While firewood prices were rising, peat exploitation in Holland ran along similar lines to the exploitation of coal in England: a way of saving land, and permitting the expansion of arable land, since the soil under the peat layer could be cultivated once peat had been removed. Peat exploitation rose in the sixteenth century and the first half of the seventeenth. Then, after 1670, the trend of peat extraction fell until 1740. Its extraction grew again from then on together with its increasing price. The volume extracted did not compete, however, with the level of the 1650s, which was only exceeded in the middle of the nineteenth century.[105]

We have seen that European annual consumption per head varied, if we except coal and peat, between 15 and 25 Gigajoules. The limits of this range were exceeded by the Netherlands and England in the seventeenth century, thanks to the introduction of peat and coal (figure 4.14). Yet, while the English consumption per head continued to rise, it stabilized in the Netherlands and then declined during the second half of the eighteenth century.[106]

This change offered parts of Europe a new way of saving land: not by intensifying the exploitation of present insolation, as the Chinese were doing, but by exploiting remote insolation now hidden underground. Without the resort to coal, England's agricultural advancements would have "never sufficed on their own to engender an industrial revolution."[107] Wherever possible, the British were rapidly followed by other Europeans. A country such

[103] Cottrell, 1955, 85 and recalled by Wrigley in the forthcoming article.
[104] Unger, 1984, summarizes the main achievements in the field of energy during the seventeenth century.
[105] Gerding, 1995.
[106] Gales, Kander, Malanima, and Rubio, 2007.
[107] Wrigley, 2004, 64.

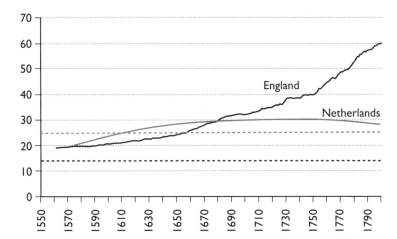

Figure 4.14. Estimate of per c. energy consumption in England
and the Netherlands, 1550–1800 (Gj/year)
Note: The graph illustrates the range (between the straight lines)
into which average European consumption was presumably
comprised together with Dutch and English energy consumption.
Sources: English data are taken from Warde, 2007 and are based
on direct information; data concerning Holland are based on
assumptions on peat and wind exploitation and on their
increasing diffusion in the seventeenth century.

as Russia, even though well endowed with coal, but also rich in forests,
utilized wood extensively during the nineteenth century. At the end of the
nineteenth century, woodland per inhabitant amounted to 1.77 hectares,
while the European average was 0.75. In Germany, coal was available and
forest per inhabitant relatively scarce; thus we see from the close of the
eighteenth century a rapid rise in coal production and then the substitution
of coal for wood.[108] Other countries, lacking coal almost completely, still
continued to rely heavily on firewood and charcoal. Italy, however, began to
import coal from the beginning of the nineteenth century, especially through
the port of Genoa.[109]

It is true that the European agriculture remained within the boundaries of
the traditional energy regime for a long time. In agriculture some intensification was still possible through the generalization of the already known techniques and products, especially for example potato and maize. It is not easy
to determine how much this intensification also depended on opportunities
indirectly offered by the rising "fossil environment," such as the circulation

[108] Sieferle, 2001, 139, and data on production, 174.
[109] As the research in progress by Maurizio Lupo already reveals.

of agricultural goods, the possibilities of importation of fertilizers through railways and steamships, the widening of the internal and external demand deriving from the rise of the industrial sector and services. In the second half of the nineteenth century, fossil energy carriers began to contribute directly to saving the soil. A remarkable growth in land productivity took place during the so-called first green revolution,[110] from 1870 on, partly as a consequence of the introduction of new fertilizers, and these new fertilizers were either by-products of fossil fuels or made using the energy provided by fossil fuels and later, electricity.[111] The fossil system of energy was embracing agriculture as well, indirectly, through the changes in economic life outside of agriculture and the wider possibilities of communication and specialization, and later directly, through the introduction of new fertilizers and machines.

LAND SAVING: INDUSTRIAL HEAT PROCESSES

"The fact—Wrigley writes—that in 1800 British coal output was providing as much energy as would otherwise have required the devotion of perhaps 15 million acres to the production of wood for fuel on a sustained basis is a telling instance of the scale of the changes which had been taking place."[112] Wrigley calculated that 1 ton of coal could replace the calories of 1 acre of forest (or 0.4 hectares).[113] If we follow this calculation, coal extraction in Britain in 1700 was replacing 12,000 square kilometers, which we could call "ghost square kilometres," that is, 5 percent of the extent of Great Britain, and in 1800, with 15 million tons of coal annually extracted, 60,000 square kilometres, that is a quarter of the extent of the island. Thanks to these innovations, natural resources were no longer fixed. According to another calculation, the area needed to replace with firewood the coal consumed in Great Britain was about 2,000 km^2 in 1560; a negligible surface on the total of 228,000 km^2. In 1850–60 an extent twice as large as the whole island would have been required.[114]

Iron was to become the largest single industrial consumer of coal, but a myriad of other processes used intensive heat and could potentially benefit from a switch away from firewood and charcoal to coal. Governments concerned about wood shortages promoted coal as an alternative fuel, but generally with little success until the middle of the nineteenth century. In most parts of Europe, coal remained too expensive to obtain until a late

[110] Van Zanden, 1991.
[111] Smil, 1994, chap. 5.
[112] Wrigley, 2004, 65.
[113] Wrigley, 1988a, 54–5.
[114] See the calculations in Sieferle, 2001, 104.

date. The Prussian government resorted to subsidies and compulsion, with limited results.[115]

Where there appeared to be commercial potential in making the switch, many industries experimented with coal, and it is clear that those who attempted innovations saw the cost of firewood as a major incentive to do so. By the end of the seventeenth century, key British industries such as soap (largely used in textile manufacture), sugar refining, copper-smelting, and the production of saltpeter, paper, alum, copperas, and glass all relied on coal. From around 1700, coke-smelting using a reverberatory furnace was successfully employed in the production of lead, tin, and copper, a little before Darby's innovation in making pig iron.[116] At the beginning of the nineteenth century, coal was already employed in many industrial processes, such as smith's work, nailmaking, limeburning, brewing, dyeing, salt making, brickmaking, glassmaking, maltmaking, steel manufacture, chemicals' production, brassmaking, and earthenware production.[117]

Thanks to its combination of vast stocks of coal and expensive alternative fuels that made the switch worthwhile, England came to assume an internationally dominant position in nearly all of these industries, many of which (such as soap and alum) contributed to holding down costs in the largest industrial sector, textiles. By the nineteenth century, British dominance in non-ferrous metals was as great as it became in iron, supplying three-quarters of the world's copper, half of the world's lead, and three-fifths of its tin by 1850.[118]

Coal was also applied to further "land-saving" processes, economizing not just on fuel, but substituting timber and raising yields. By the seventeenth century, coal was extensively used in brick-making, although it was many years before techniques were developed to reduce the high rate of wastage in the "clamps" of bricks being fired. Brewers and maltsters were largely using coal in England by the late seventeenth century. So too were lime-burners, providing an important material for construction, but also one that was very widely used on the land to reduce the acidity of the soil and raise crop yields.[119] Coal use did not necessarily kill off industrial processes that used charcoal and firewood, because by easing pressure on the land, the use of coal kept wood fuel cheaper than it would otherwise have been. Some firewood users were thus permitted a longer lease on life and remained competitive due to low fuel prices. It was reported as early as the 1630s from the Weald of Kent, one of the most heavily wooded areas

[115] Dietz, 1997, 9; Piasecki, 1987, 212; Schäfer, 1992, 156; Sieferle, 2001, 162–66.

[116] Hatcher, 1993, 54, 451–57; Nef 1932, 206–20; Zahedieh, 2013.

[117] Harris, 1992, 9, introduction.

[118] Musson, 1978, 102; Flinn, 1984, 232–33; Burt, 1995, 39–40. The high quality of English ores was also an added advantage.

[119] Hatcher, 1993, 442; Nef, 1932, 205; Evelyn, 1661; Flinn, 1984, 238–39; Clow and Clow, 1952, 476–78.

of England, that the heavy local demand for wood from iron-smelters and brass-founders had led others to import coal.[120]

4. SAVING LABOR

NOMINAL WAGE AND LABOR COST

Our view is that the start of the energy transition was brought about by the need to replace natural resources that were becoming scarce in the face of rising demand from more consumers and more industries. England shared, with the rest of Europe, the rising trend in prices and the decline of real wages. We have seen that the saving of resources was successful in England from the end of the sixteenth century. This meant a rise of resource per worker in relation to the rest of Europe. The consequence was a relatively higher labor productivity and higher wages, although real wages were declining at the end of the eighteenth century in England as well as elsewhere (see table 4.4). The need developed in England to replace labor by means of mechanical engines, as we will see.

It has recently been argued that the British industrial revolution was the consequence of the high level of British wages, higher than those of the continental workers.[121] "England found it profitable to use technology that saved expensive labour by increasing the use of cheap energy and capital. With more capital and energy at their disposal, British workers became more productive—the secret of economic growth."[122] Since wages, however, represent marginal labor productivity and since productivity was higher in the eighteenth and nineteenth centuries in England than in other European countries, the obvious conclusion is that growth had already taken place in the country. We can also hypothesize that the British growth, although slow, derived from the ongoing energy transformation, both in food production, that is agriculture, and industry. Certainly the possibility of widening the coal economy was limited without the steam engine, which represented a great discontinuity in Britain and then in Europe as a whole.

On the other hand, however, when we deal with the level of wages and with their fallout on the economy, it is important to look at nominal and not real figures. Real wages represent the standard of living of workers.[123] Nominal wages represent the cost paid by entrepreneurs in order to carry out their activity. Prices of the commodities produced, on one hand, and

---

[120] Hatcher, 1993, 420; see discussion in Yarranton, 1681, 59.

[121] Allen, 2009. The same topic is discussed by Allen, 2011a.

[122] Allen, 2011b, 32.

[123] We already examined real wages and living conditions in section 2 of this chapter.

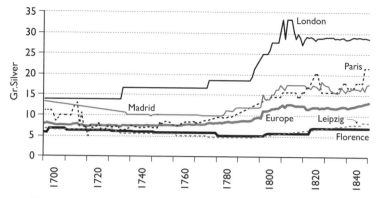

Figure 4.15. Nominal wage rates in Europe and in some
European cities, 1700–1850 (grams of silver)
Source: Based on data in Allen, www.nuff.ox.ac.uk/users/allen.

wages in money paid by employers, on the other, are the basic elements of his economic calculation.

Nominal wages, that is, wages expressed in the silver content of the money of any country, show that British wages were already higher during the second half of the eighteenth century (figure 4.15). Whenever the value of something expressed in precious metal rises, it means that the commodity or service purchased is more expensive, or that precious metals are cheaper, in that country; and probably, in the case of England during the so-called commercial revolution,[124] both things were true at the same time. On the other hand, we also know that the purchasing power of English wages was higher than those of other European workers. We note also that everywhere in the continent, nominal wages were increasing during the second half of the eighteenth century. Since any input of energy was rising in price, entrepreneurs, both in the cities and the countryside, had no choice but to grant their workers an increase in their nominal wages, although in real terms it was not enough to keep their standard of living stable.

In different branches of economic activity, the gap between prices and costs, and thus the profit margins, also varied. It seems reasonable to suppose that agricultural entrepreneurs were favored by the upward trend of agricultural prices, followed, but only with some delay, by nominal wages. In the case of industrial entrepreneurs it was different. Prices of manufacturing goods were growing much less than agricultural prices. In the case of industry, margins of profit could be endangered by the rising trend of nominal wages, primarily determined by the rising prices of food from about 1730 on.

[124] See especially Davis, 1967, 1979.

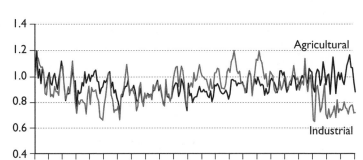

Figure 4.16. Real prices of agricultural and industrial goods
in England, 1600–1830 (1600–10 = 1).
Source: Based on data in Allen, www.nuff.ox.ac.uk/users/allen.

If we look at industrial real prices in England and agricultural real
prices,[125] we discover, in fact, that, although the eighteenth-century trends
were fairly similar, at the end of the century industrial prices fell relatively
(figure 4.16). In other European countries, the trend of divergence was similar to the English one.[126]

If we take the longer period from 1300 until 1830, we see that industrial prices were increasing much less than agricultural prices from the late
Middle Ages (figure 4.17). As David Ricardo already convincingly showed
at the beginning of the nineteenth century, this differential behavior of agricultural and industrial prices can be explained partly as the consequence
of the influx of innovations in industry and trade. "The natural price of all
commodities . . . ," Ricardo wrote, "has a tendency to fall, in the progress
of wealth and population," thanks to "improvements in machinery," "better
division and distribution of labour," and "increasing skill both in science
and art of the producers." On the other hand, the diminishing returns in
agriculture also tend to increase "the natural price of the raw material of
which they are made."[127] Although the development of agriculture in the
nineteenth century contradicts the opinion expressed by Ricardo, when we
deal with premodern economies we cannot but share his opinion.

Was the replacement of expensive labor possible through a more efficient
and widespread use of the "old machines" that delivered mechanical work?

[125] Agricultural and industrial price indexes are real, since they are deflated by means of the
consumer price index.
[126] Malanima, 2009, chap. 6.
[127] Ricardo, 1821, chap. 5.

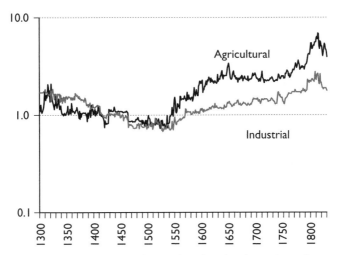

Figure 4.17. Real prices of agricultural and industrial goods
in England, 1300–1830 (1420–40=1; log vertical axis)
Source: Based on data in Allen, www.nuff.ox.ac.uk/users/allen.

OLD MACHINES

As regards water mills, both Braudel and Makkai independently suggested
that they grew in number from the late Middle Ages to the nineteenth century at more or less the same rate as population. There was, however, an increase in the wheel's power over the centuries, and hence a rise in per capita
hp in the long term, from 2, to 3 (table 4.11). We can speak of stability
rather than true growth in the use of this form of energy. It seems that only
later, during the first wave of industrialization in the nineteenth century,
growth was accompanied by a rise in the utilization of water power. Per
capita power from water rose markedly at that time (figure 4.18).

The exploitation of wind by mills progressed more rapidly.[128] In Holland
and northern Europe wind began to be exploited more and more in several industrial processes, such as fulling, iron production, hemp processing,
paper manufacturing. Between the end of the fifteenth and the end of the
eighteenth century, while the population only doubled, tonnage of European ships rose 10–15-fold, generating the most substantial increase in the
exploitation of energy sources (table 4.12).[129] In 1780, the power of the
European merchant ships is estimated to have been around 400,000 hp. If

[128] Davids, 2003, 286–91.
[129] Lucassen and Unger, 2000; Unger, 2004, 2011.

TABLE 4.11
Per capita power from water wheels in 1200 and 1800 (hp)

	Average power for wheel (hp)	Inhabitants per water wheel	Per capita hp
1200	2	250	0.008
1800	3	250	0.012

Source: Braudel, 1979, I, ch. V; Makkai, 1981.

Figure 4.18. Pumping water by means of the water power in the seventeenth century
Source: Ramelli, 1588.

the navy and the numerous small vessels and boats were to be added, these figures would increase much more.

The exploitation of wind power by sails grew at an astonishing rate. The use of European sails on the seas of Europe and the rest of the world increased throughout in the early modern age; even though per capita avail-

TABLE 4.12

Estimates of the carrying capacity of the European merchant fleets from 1470 to 1780 (thousands of tons and indices) compared with demographic movement (index)

	A		B		Population
1470–1500	350	*100*	200–250	*100*	*100*
1570–1600	800	*229*	600–700	*289*	*127*
1670	1,350	*386*	1,000–1,100	*467*	*139*
1780	3,856	*1,102*	3,372	*1,498*	*210*

Sources: Maddison, 2001, 79; Van Zanden, 2001, 82.

able energy from the exploitation of wind by sails remained very small compared to energy derived from the soil. Richard Unger is, however, correct when he writes about the "increasingly effective use of ships, use which opened the possibility of 'Smithian growth' through specialization because of falling costs of shipping goods and people."[130]

Unfortunately we lack estimates of energy consumption for military purposes. Considering, however, the growth of armies in early modern Europe, it is certain that, together with wind power, the use of gunpowder was rising both in absolute terms and as a ratio to the population.

Although we should not underrate the rise in the exploitation of these sources in absolute figures and even in per capita terms, they represented a negligible share of total energy consumption. Even allowing for a 100 percent increase in sources representing less than 2 percent of the whole consumption in the first half of the nineteenth century, the result we reach is, after all, modest indeed. Although in many regions of Europe the first industrial revolution was accompanied by rising exploitation of water power, water power could not be the support of modern growth (see chapter 6). The path toward the replacement of expensive labor by capital was in the end the result of the exploitation of thermal energy through nonbiological ✓ engines.

Population growth, per capita decline in the availability of land, unfavorable climatic conditions, price increases, diminishing real wages, but rising nominal wages, all pushed entrepreneurs and workers toward the replacement of traditional biological converters of energy with machines. We could also say that a "latent demand" existed for the replacement of labor with capital (figure 4.18). The solution of the economic problems Europe was dealing with depended on the availability of a different and plentiful energy

---

[130] Unger, 2004.

source and the development of techniques able to exploit this different energy source. We saw how the introduction of coal was spurred by the need for land saving. The replacement of workers through machines able to exploit the new fossil carrier in order to engender mechanical work are the topics of chapters 5–7.

NEW MACHINES

Without doubt the pace of invention and economic innovation accelerated across the eighteenth and early nineteenth centuries. Many changes were labor-saving and few of them required any major breakthrough in scientific or theoretical understanding. They continued processes of tinkering and adaptation that had been under way during the early modern period.[131] Often it was a combination of previously known mechanical devices that allowed significant progress and economies on labor. In some cases, however, notably the chemical industry, new theoretical and experimental knowledge was essential to developments.[132]

The most famous of these changes is the employment of new machinery in the textile industry, but perhaps more novel, and of greater lasting significance, was the expansion of precise engineering skills that allowed both a vast array of machinery to be made, and the engines to drive those machines. The development of precise cutting and boring skills was thus essential for technological advance. Skills developed in clock-making were central to this progress, especially in the manufacture of metal gear wheels. This happened, again, to be a particular strength of Britain that had emerged because of the importance of its merchant and military fleets for national welfare and security, and the need for precise navigational instruments. Lancashire became a repository of these skills, which greatly aided the early development of mechanization in the textile industry in this region.[133]

Although some individual machines had wide influence, it could only be the progress of mechanization across a broad front that allowed substantial advances in productivity and avoided the problem of bottlenecks in the production process. In the case of cotton production, this included processes such as carding, batting, scutching, and others, as well as the more familiar spinning and weaving. The physical embodiment of the new mechanized work was the factory, gathering the processes together under one roof. Factories had existed for centuries in relatively isolated cases as a way of imposing labor discipline, or for processes that simply required a lot of space, such as winding ropes in naval dockyards. With the advent of mechanization,

---

[131] Musson, 1978, 80; MacLeod, 1988, 2004.
[132] Clow and Clow, 1952; Landes, 2003, 269–76.
[133] Allen, 2009, 204–5; Mokyr, 2009, 107–15.

however, concentration of activity could permit single sources of power—water wheels, or steam engines—to drive many machines through systems of gears and belts.

For many, the paradigmatic case of the industrial revolution is the explosion of cotton production in England from the 1770s, "the wonder industry of the industrial revolution," Initially this was based on a quite traditional power source: water. This is not to say that the cotton industry could have expanded at such a dramatic rate solely with traditional sources. The capital of cotton, Manchester, was by the 1860s consuming as much coal as the whole of the world had done less than two centuries earlier.[134]

The innovations that transformed cotton production, and that later would be applied across the textile industry, took place in the eighteenth century. Just as with the contemporaneous development of steam engines, there was a long process of trial-and-error, perfecting combinations of machinery and the organization of labor. Just as with steam engines, some of the key early machines were not very widely applicable; they provided forms of motion suited only to very limited processes and thus could not promote an industry-wide leap in productivity. In the background of the technical changes we are speaking of was the idea that "material progress could be achieved through increasing human knowledge of natural phenomena and making this knowledge accessible to those who could make use of it in production."[135] The fact that the center of world cotton production was India, where wages were markedly lower than in north-west Europe, may well have been a spur to labor-saving devices in this sector.[136]

Three key inventions underpinned the dramatic history of cotton. These were the "spinning jenny," the first model of which was made by James Hargreaves in 1764; the water frame of Richard Arkwright, introduced in the 1770s; and Compton's mule, essentially a combination of the virtues of the two previous inventions, also introduced in the 1770s.[137] All of these innovations were the end result of numerous attempts to mechanize that stretched back to the start of the century. They also borrowed from techniques widely employed elsewhere.[138]

Mechanization was massively labor-saving. These machines greatly accelerated the spinning of cotton yarn, and meant that instead of one person working with one spindle, one person could supervise the operation of many

---

[134] Allen, 2009, 182; Mosley, 2001, 16; Balderston, 2010.

[135] Mokyr, 2009, 40.

[136] According to Parthasarati, "cotton textiles, were the most important manufactured good in world trade and were consumed from the Americas to Japan. British efforts to imitate Indian cloth propelled a search for new techniques in production, which culminated in the great breakthroughs in spinning of the eighteenth century"; Allen, 2009, 182; Broadberry and Gupta, 2006; Riello and Parthasarathi, 2009; Parthasarathi, 2011, 2.

[137] Musson, 1978, 81.

[138] Allen, 2009, 195–201.

spindles at once. In the case of coarse cotton, the ratio of labor to capital costs per pound of spun thread was 18:1 in 1760 but had fallen to roughly 1:1 by 1836! Overall costs halved during this period, and by the 1830s were almost entirely taken up by the cost of the raw cotton itself. As Robert Allen has shown these productivity gains were even more pronounced in the case of high-quality yarn, which required much more labor than coarse thread to produce.[139]

Mechanization did not change the power source itself, but the manner by which that power was transmitted and made to work. The first spinning jenny, for example, improved the spindle by which the spinner imparted a twist to the cotton "roving," which made it more robust for use in weaving. The jenny allowed this twisting to be done by several spindles at once, moved by a single hand-driven wheel.[140] This could be used in cottage industry, although its introduction was immediately perceived as labor saving and provoked rioting by workers. As spinning was only a small proportion of the total cost of cotton, and the jenny itself was very expensive compared to the old-fashioned wheel, the impact of this innovation was quite small. It was not taken up at all where labor was cheap, even though the technology was known.[141] The mechanization process was self-reinforcing. Any breakthrough at one stage of the production process could speed up the supply of "intermediate" products in the production chain and create potential bottlenecks, which provided an incentive to mechanize other activities.

Continental inventors also made significant contributions to the new technology, such as the Jacquard loom in the 1800s and Heilmann's wool-combing machine of 1845.[142] But although jennies and other machines were widely available by 1800, uptake was quite small where labor remained very cheap, and in such places there was no incentive to engage in long years of tedious experimentation with new gadgets. Indeed, even where machines were introduced, they were often run well below capacity where the cost of power was high, resulting in lower labor productivity. By and large continental Europe lagged behind in expertise and because of its cheaper labor.[143]

Mechanization by itself did not massively enhance the power at people's disposal, and could not have brought about the huge expansion of productivity that occurred during the nineteenth century. But precisely because the new machinery was not attached to a particular source of power, it could be harnessed to the core of the newly emerging development block of the first industrial revolution, built around coal and iron. The machinery

[139] Allen, 2009, 184–88.
[140] Mokyr, 1990, 96.
[141] Allen, 2009, 193–95.
[142] Mokyr, 1990, 100–2.
[143] Allen, 2009, 206–13; Crouzet, 1996, 42; Fohlen, 1973, 64–66; Landes, 2003, 172; von Tunzelmann, 1995, 152, 160–61; see also on the 1840s and labor saving, von Tunzelmann, 1978, 217; Herrigel, 1996, 43; Kleinschmidt, 2007, 3; Milward and Saul, 1977, 190–94.

was "modular," in that it could be driven by many alternative sources of power, and put to many diverse uses once the principles of operation were understood.[144]

Although the initial spectacular expansion of mechanized cotton production in regions such as Lancashire and Alsace rested on water, it was eventually sustained by the steam engine, and coal. By the 1870s, the dominant Lancashire cotton industry was consuming 5.5 million tons of coal a year directly, aside from the great domestic demand of a highly concentrated population. This was more than the entire coal output of southern and eastern Europe, and 5 percent of the British total. Without this source of heat and power, the search for suitable streams to provide power would have both raised costs and caused the dispersal of the industry as it did in other parts of the world, removing a major efficiency benefit from concentrating production and many firms in one place.[145]

The final part of cloth production, weaving, was not widely mechanized until a later date, even though Cartwright invented the power loom in 1787.[146] Given the bottleneck created by the mechanization of cotton spinning, it was unsurprisingly taken up in cotton weaving first, but the invention of the self-actor was crucial for its wider employment. The self-actor produced a more uniform fiber, which could be more reliably spun by power looms.[147] An experienced hand-weaver could expect to produce 48 yards of cotton shirting each week. By 1825, a steam-powered loom supervised by a teenager could produce 168 yards, and by 1833, up to 432 yards! Britain led the way, steadily increasing its number of power looms from 2,400 in 1813 to a quarter of a million by the end of the 1840s. Diffusion only became rapid in the 1850s.[148]

In other textile industries, progress was much slower—at least by the accelerated standards the revolutionary age was now setting. Around 1800, much of Europe's textile output was still in woollens, worsteds, and linens. The nature of the fibers meant that these industries were much harder to mechanize. When Britain had a quarter of a million power looms churning out cotton in 1850, there were still only 9,500 producing woollens. The first steam spinning flax mill for linen production opened in the great center of Belfast only in 1829. British and Irish producers were again far ahead of rivals, operating 40 percent of the world's spindles working linen and jute by mid-century, and 60 percent of the power looms. These industries

---

[144] Baldwin and Clark, 2000, 6, 11, 63.
[145] Balderston, 2010; Mitchell, 1988, 464–65; Milward and Saul, 1977, 318–20.
[146] Landes, 2003, 86; Musson, 1978, 89; Greenberg, 1982, 1246.
[147] Mokyr, 1990, 100; von Tunzelmann, 1978, 196–99.
[148] Musson, 1978, 88.

destroyed old established hand-weaving industries in Belgium and Silesia in a traumatic 1830s and 1840s.[149]

5. CONCLUSION

If there is stagnation in technical progress in the primary sector, rising population implies growing pressure on the main resource: land, the primary energy converter in the pre-modern world. The price and the rent of land rises. Agricultural returns to labor (and then rural wages) diminish, while agricultural prices grow. Landowners' income increases since they own the scarce production factor, land. Coal and land intensification could actually engender the saving of the scarce input, since both saved land.

The same concepts can be clarified by a neoclassical production function:

$$Y = AF(L, K)$$

where Y represents the output, L and K respectively labor and capital, and A represents technical knowledge able to increase the efficiency of the system. The so-called intensive form of the production function can be obtained by dividing both the dependent variable (Y) and the independent variables (L, K) by labor. The result is:

$$\frac{Y}{L} = AF\left(\frac{K}{L}\right)$$

where the average labor productivity (Y/L) is a function of capital per worker (K/L) times A. Since in a premodern, agrarian, traditional economy, natural resources (R) cannot be excluded from the production function, we obtain:

$$\frac{Y}{L} = AF\left(\frac{K}{L}, \frac{R}{L}\right).$$

In the last equation, labor productivity does not depend only on produced resources (that is capital), but also on non-produced (that is natural) resources. Labor, according to classical economists, is more productive the more factors are employed along with it. Since workers were rising in number from the late Middle Ages and especially from the beginning of the demographic transition at the end of the seventeenth century, and since wage rates, and then labor productivity, diminished, the conclusion is that the

---

[149] Musson, 1978, 88, 91; Solar, 2003, 818–19; Milward and Saul, 1977, 325, 447–48; Pierenkemper, 1992, 18.

endowment of any worker with resources and capital was decreasing and that technical progress was unable to arrest the downward trend.

Land saving, supported in England by the introduction of coal and by the successful intensification of land, together with progress in technical knowledge, was beginning to reverse the trend. Capital incorporating technical knowledge was rising as well.

Since labor was endowed with more capital (incorporating more advanced techniques) than before, labor became more productive. All of this meant an increase in wages and then labor costs and a tendency to replace labor with capital.[150] Technical progress in the production of capital goods implies a decreasing price of capital relative to labor. The replacement of laborers by machines became a strong tendency of the economy and became the basis of the continuous replacement of biological converters (workers) with mechanical converters (machines) fed by means of new energy sources (see also chapter 7). The energy transition has been and still is a process of substitution of capital, fixed and circulating, for labor.

The level of nominal wages was higher in England than elsewhere, and labor costs for entrepreneurs were rising as a consequence. Since, at the same time, industrial prices were diminishing, due to relatively more efficient techniques and less scarce resources in the secondary sector, industrial entrepreneurs were particularly hit by the negative conjuncture and decline in profits. In a classical perspective, technical progress could not, or only temporarily, reestablish previous margins of profit. While the British classical economists were right about the working of a traditional, agrarian economy, they underrated, or were not able to single out, the technical perspectives opened up by the changes in progress before their eyes. It is to these perspectives that we now must turn our attention.

---

[150] This perspective is suggested particularly by the important book by Salter, 1966.

The First Industrial Revolution

Paul Warde

A MODERN ENERGY REGIME

1. THE TAKE-OFF OF COAL

THE RISE IN ENERGY CONSUMPTION

BY THE EARLY NINETEENTH CENTURY, Europe had become a far more populous continent than three centuries previously, at the beginning of the early modern period. A mixture of opportunism, an "improving" ethic, and response to price pressures had led to efforts at saving land and labor, so that the soil supported that much larger population and the maritime powers of Europe had acquired vast and growing empires overseas. There were increasingly widespread efforts to develop engineering, convert scientific knowledge into innovation, and we can see the rapid growth in some parts of the textile industry using mechanization powered by water. Yet for the average European, energy remained scarce and expensive and its productivity low. Only two countries had clearly succeeded in heaving their real income upward: Britain and the Netherlands. Both of these had energy regimes heavily dependent on "new" fuels, coal and peat.

We know now that Europe stood on the cusp of an industrial revolution. It was the British achievement that pointed the way to the future, because coal would permit a vast expansion in the quantity of energy that could be productively consumed by human society. This marked the end of the constraints of the "organic economy," barriers already being surpassed, as we have seen in part I, during the seventeenth and eighteenth centuries in parts of north-west Europe.

Between 1820 and 1910, the "British model" of energy consumption rolled out over Europe. Consumption grew sevenfold in per capita terms and 21–22-fold as a whole (figure 5.1). This was spectacularly more than its population, which rose from 192 million in 1800 to 401 million in 1900. The rapidity of the rise in energy consumption over a single century was unprecedented in human history.

As we shall see, not all, or even most, countries became like Britain. But in every case the major changes in the energy regime were almost entirely wrought by the greater consumption of coal, and the aggregate development of the whole continent was also largely driven by coal consumption. Already in 1820 nearly a third of energy consumption in western and central Europe

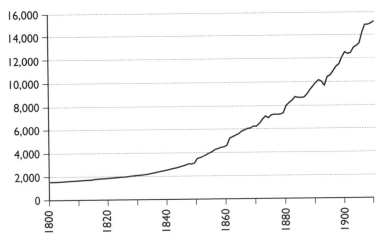

Figure 5.1. Total energy consumption in western Europe, 1800–1910 (PJ)
Note: Data from eight countries: England & Wales, France, Germany, Italy, Netherlands, Portugal, Spain, and Sweden. Prior to 1850 for Spain, 1856 for Portugal, and 1861 for Italy, it is assumed that per capita consumption remained static and then total energy consumption increased with population.
Sources: See http://www.energyhistory.org.

was of coal. Britain accounted for most of this. By the First World War more than four-fifths of Western Europe's aggregate energy supply came from coal, which accounted for more than 90 percent of the total increase in energy consumption between 1820 and 1910.[1] By the later date, "traditional carriers" accounted for only 16 percent of total energy consumption, as we see in table 5.1.

Energy was now plentiful, relatively cheap, and had begun to have major effects on the health of city-dwellers. Buildings disintegrated under the assault of sulphur dioxide emissions, slum-dwellers suffered vitamin deficiencies from lack of sunlight, and deaths from lung diseases soared. Over time, recognition of the damage became more dispersed: the acidification of lakes and habitat destruction. As early as 1896, it was hypothesized that coal-burning and the emission of carbon dioxide would warm the Earth's atmosphere.[2]

If Britain was already emerging from the "photosynthetic constraint" in the seventeenth century, why did an industrial revolution, and a "take-off"

[1] These figures are calculated on the basis of data from England and Wales, France, Germany, Italy, Netherlands, Portugal, Spain, and Sweden.
[2] Arrhenius, 1896.

TABLE 5.1
Shares of energy carriers in total consumption in Europe, 1820–1910 (%)

	Food	Fodder	Firewood	Water and Wind	Coal	Oil
1820	17.4	14	38	1.7	28.9	
1840	15.6	12.5	31.7	1.4	38.8	
1880	8	6.3	11.9	0.8	72.6	0.3
1910	5.6	4.2	5.5	0.3	83.5	0.8

Note: Data from eight countries: England and Wales, France, Germany, Italy, Netherlands, Portugal, Spain, and Sweden. Prior to 1850 for Spain and 1861 for Italy it is assumed that per capita consumption remained static.
Sources: See www.energyhistory.org.

of energy consumption, not occur earlier and more widely? This was because the increase in the quantity of available energy was only one of the shifts required to build a modern energy economy. The second, and perhaps more profound, was a qualitative change: the capacity to convert thermal energy into kinetic energy, or stated simply, to turn heat into motion. This was achieved by the use of steam engines. Combustion could drive machines, and the use of machines vastly raised the amount of work any single individual could do. But without being able to use coal for transportation, the new fossil fuel coal economy remained hemmed in by the limitations to power of the traditional and organic economy. The quantitative and qualitative developments in the energy economy had to be closely linked to bring about general progress, because the use of engines powered by coal would be essential to two processes that undid constraints still operative even in eighteenth-century Britain. The first was to dig deeper mines and access seams that were not exploitable in an earlier age. The second was to drive a transport revolution that meant, through the use of locomotives and steam ships, that bulky coal, raw materials and machinery could be affordably brought to sites across the continent and beyond. This brought a revolution in the use of energy and power beyond anything that could be achieved by the most ingenious millwright with water and wind.

By tracing per capita consumption at the aggregate level of Europe, we can see how developments that were at first highly regionalized and concentrated on accessible coalfields became a more general phenomenon as the century progressed (see figure 5.2). Between 1800 and 1850, total consumption more than doubled, but per capita consumption changed relatively little until the 1840s (although this was still a dramatic reversal of the eighteenth-century trends: see figure 4.8). Advances in total energy consumption were eaten up (a certain proportion quite literally!) by population growth. Most

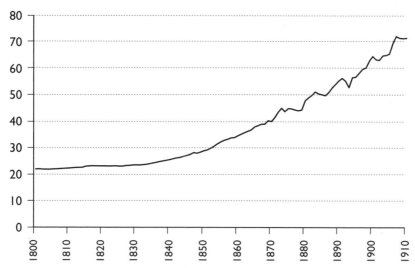

Figure 5.2. Per capita energy consumption in Europe, 1800–1910 (Gj)
Note: This is an average weighted by population of England & Wales,
Sweden, the Netherlands, Germany, France, Spain, Italy, and Portugal. Per capita
consumption levels for Spain, Italy, and Portugal are assumed to be the same
as those found in 1850, 1861, and 1856 respectively for all prior dates. This is
likely to bias the trend for the first half of the century very slightly downward.
Sources: See www.energyhistory.org.

countries could not exceed an annual consumption of 20–30 GJ, or 15,000–
20,000 kcal per person per day, that had characterized the pre-industrial
economy. It was from mid-century that energy consumed per person began
to advance more rapidly. By the early twentieth century on average each
person had almost three times more energy at their disposal than a century
before, most of this advance achieved since 1850. A great juncture in human
history was reached: people began to have ever greater energy supplies per
person at their disposal.

It was the combination of coal, engine, and the raw material out of
which much of the new technology was made, iron, that coalesced to form
the "development block" that characterized and drove the first industrial
revolution.

Decomposing the Energy Growth

We have seen that the scale of energy consumption is a function of the
amount of economic activity, and the efficiency of energy use in undertaking
that activity. This can be expressed by the identity discussed in chapter 1:

TABLE 5.2
Energy, Population, and Income in Western Europe, 1820–1910

Year	Energy (PJ)	Population (000)	Income per capita ($1990)	Energy Intensity (MJ/$)
1820	2,510	108,687	1,212	19.2
1910	15,189	212,723	3,192	22.8
% (per year)	2.04	0.76	1.08	0.19

Note: Sample includes France, Germany, Great Britain, Sweden, Netherlands, Spain and Italy. Prior to 1850 for Spain and 1861 for Italy it is assumed that per capita consumption remained static.
Source: See www.energyhistory.org.

Energy = Population · Income per capita · Energy Intensity.

More precisely the formula can be written:

$$E = P \cdot \frac{Y}{P} \cdot \frac{E}{Y}$$

where E is energy, Y is aggregate output, and P is population.

As we see in table 5.2, per capita GDP rose by around 150 percent in Western Europe in 1820–1910, while the population doubled.[3] Energy intensity only rose around 25 percent, meaning the efficiency with which energy was turned into income fell over the century, but not dramatically. The entire increase in energy intensity occurred after 1850.

The relationship between income and energy consumption was a two-way street. We might think today that it is hardly a surprise that wealthy economies have greater energy consumption, as people with higher income have access to more consumer goods, travel more, and expect a higher degree of comfort. Seen in this way, energy consumption in much of modern Europe is the consequence of economic growth. In the nineteenth century, however, the greatest use of the new fossil fuels came not on the consumption side, but on the production side of the economy. The largest share of fossil fuel energy was not involved in the final consumption of a good or service, but was used in the process of manufacturing those goods, often in making intermediary products like steel. In other words, high levels of energy consumption were not the consequence, but part of the cause of wealth. The easy availability of cheap energy was itself a spur to more economic

---

[3] Maddison, 2003.

activity, and hence greater consumption. But as energy supplies themselves were not evenly distributed, this created a new economic geography for the continent.

COAL AND THE NEW GEOGRAPHY OF ENERGY SUPPLY

The supply of coal was highly localized. As Tony Wrigley has noted, it is available in a "punctiform" manner, in small, concentrated seams.[4] Famous and economically important concentrations of coal supplies are found in many parts of northern and Midland England, south Wales, the central belt of Scotland, the Sambre-Meuse coalfield of Belgium and north-eastern France, the Saarland and in the Ruhr district of western Germany, Upper Silesia in what is now south-western Poland, and the Donets basin of Ukraine. However, beyond these centers and a few smaller coalfields, access to fossil fuel depended on good transport links, greatly facilitated in England by the proximity of coal seams to coastal ports. Until the middle of the nineteenth century some of these coal seams were also relatively inaccessible because they lay deep underground and were expensive to mine.[5]

Coal is not a homogeneous good, however. There are many different types of coal, and they have different uses. Hard, anthracite coals were difficult to ignite in the nineteenth century and burned with little flame. When they did burn, their heat was intense, although smoke pollution was low. For many users, this made them unattractive, although they were much desired for use in steam ships. Bituminous coals were easier to light but gave off strong odors and waste gases. These were easy to handle but could create problems if used as a fuel in some chemical processes. These differences mostly related to the carbon content of the coal, which was highest in the anthracites. Different coals could also have substantially different energy content, from the poorest lignite (brown coal) containing as little as 8.3 MJ/kg, to the best hard coals with up to 32 MJ/kg, with most coals falling into the 20s of MJ/kg.[6] The best coals with the highest energy content could allow a significantly lower amount of fuel to be carried as freight, an important factor when it came to powering vehicles and ships. As the coal found in many fields tended toward being one or the other type, this to some degree determined the geography and diffusion of coal usage. It also meant that certain coalfields became heavily orientated toward supplying particular consumers.[7]

[4] Wrigley, 1988a.
[5] Pounds, 1979.
[6] Smil, 2008a, 204–6.
[7] Jones, 2010; Thorsheim, 2006, 5.

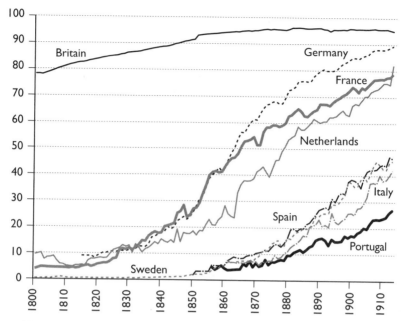

Figure 5.3. Share of coal in total energy consumption, 1820–1900
Note: The values on the vertical axis refer to the percentage of coal in total energy consumption. On the horizontal axis you find the total energy consumption in Petajoules (PJ).
Sources: See www.energyhistory.org.

This geography of coal use is in stark contrast to the widespread but limited accessibility of energy derived from organic matter. The shift from an "organic economy" that is "areal" to a fossil fuel economy that is "punctiform" thus permitted much greater concentration of economic activity in urban centers and around industries that developed on the coalfields. But where transport remained relatively expensive, those coalfields could also remain isolated, as little islands of transition among a sea of tradition. Equally, there was little incentive to develop coalfields if they remained distant from sources of demand.

Unsurprisingly then, the advance of coal across Europe was thus very uneven (figure 5.3). We can distinguish three groups of countries, or more accurately, Britain and two other groups of "latecomers." Britain was already a coal economy by 1800; its transition was long and drawn-out, as we have seen in chapter 4. A cluster of western European nations comprising France, Germany, and a little later the Netherlands saw a slowly rising trend in coal use turn into a dramatic transition in the middle of the century. In both France and Germany, coal became a greater provider of thermal energy than firewood in 1854, while in the Netherlands it supplanted peat and firewood by 1865. The experience of Belgium almost certainly lies somewhere between British precocity and these mid-century revolutionaries.

Much less dramatic and later increases in coal use are to be found in the Mediterranean lands, Portugal, and Sweden. These countries had to wait until the final phase of transition when the steamship and railway brought coal at cheap rates to the quaysides of their port cities. Limited infrastructural development meant that coal use remained quite restricted, to the vicinity of those ports and particular industrial uses. Coal did not attain a half share in energy consumption in any of these nations by the First World War, and energy from coal only outstripped that from firewood in 1894 in Spain, 1904 in Italy, and 1907 in Sweden.

GLOBAL PERSPECTIVES

The advantages that the new fossil fuel economy delivered to those European regions with rich coalfields were replicated on a global scale. Coal is also very unevenly distributed across the globe, and aside from Australia and parts of South Africa, is almost entirely found in a few parts of the Northern Hemisphere: in North America, north-west and eastern Europe, Russia, and China. Of course, the simple presence of coal reserves (even if they were known to the inhabitants) was no guarantee of rapid economic development. Industry still needed access to capital, skilled labor, and consumer markets. Yet those regions that possessed these assets, but no coal, fell behind those regions that possessed these assets and cheap fuel. On a global scale, continents with only limited coal reserves, such as South America and Africa, became increasingly dependent on supplying raw materials to the burgeoning industrial capacity of "the north."

The growth of the economies of Europe and the United States opened up a yawning gap in average incomes between global regions. By 1913, income was hugely skewed toward the industrial world, with the United States, Russia, Japan, and Western Europe accounting for two-thirds of global GDP. These countries now dominated global manufacturing, a reversal of the situation pertaining in 1800. In the pre-industrial economy, income may have varied to the degree that the tiny number of inhabitants of the very richest regions of the planet were perhaps twice or three times better off than most of the global population. In the modern economy, this would expand by almost an order of magnitude.[8]

The north-eastern corner of the United States enjoyed similar advantages to Europe, with the large Pennsylvanian coalfields within easy reach of commercial centers such as Philadelphia and New York. By 1860, these cities

[8] Barbier, 2011, 373, 391.

were coal-fired, and a significant iron industry had arisen using coal.[9] By the early twentieth century the new metropolis of the mid-west, Chicago, was also a vast consumer of fossil fuel.[10] It has sometimes been treated as a puzzle why the great coal reserves of China, which became a very major part of global consumption early in the twenty-first century, were not exploited earlier. But by and large they were far from the commercial and agricultural heartlands of the country, which were clustered toward the southern and eastern coasts. In the cities of China, fuel remained very expensive relative to the centers of European growth. Charcoal in Canton was five times the price of coal in London.[11] By the end of the nineteenth century all of Europe had relatively easy access to the products of the industrializing regions. Most of the world had no such good fortune, and when coal-using technology was employed, the fuel had to be shipped across the ocean. India had coalfields in Bengal, allowing some "modern" industrial growth in the imperial metropolis of Calcutta, but most of the subcontinent remained dependent on traditional fuels, and its railways ran, rather inefficiently, on wood.[12]

DIVERGENCE IN ENERGY REGIMES

Energy consumption per capita was much higher in coal-using countries, in coal-using regions, and above all in the vicinity of coalfields themselves. This was a radical departure from the pre-industrial age, when energy use fell within a more narrow range determined by the photosynthetic yield, and where this yield was highest, in forested regions, the use to which that energy could be put was limited. Consumption of "traditional" energy carriers around the globe is very unlikely to have exceeded northern European levels anywhere. In warmer climates consumption may have been substantially less; while the wet agricultures of Asia permitted intensification and high yields per hectare of food, they suffered from a lack of fuel.

Yet differences in coal consumption were enormous. Europe as a whole had a lead in coal production per capita until 1880, when it was overtaken by the Americas. By 1910, the rapidly expanding Australian coalmining industry had overhauled Europe in per capita terms too. In contrast, production in the rest of the world was negligible. Coal production was in reality concentrated in small pockets. British per capita production remained ahead of the United States until the 1970s, and the only other significant producers globally, South Africa and Australia, were both well under a third of the British per capita level in 1910 (see table 5.3). The scale of imports to

[9] Jones, 2010.
[10] Mosley, 2001, 19.
[11] Pomeranz, 2002.
[12] Anderson, 1995.

TABLE 5.3
Per capita coal production, 1800–1910 (TJ per 1000 inhabitants)

	1800	1850	1880	1910
Africa	—	—	—	1,374
Americas	109	3,717	20,870	76,145
Asia	0	0	55	975
Europe	1,493	7,139	20,414	35,582
Oceania	0	0	9,822	41,082
World	321	1,758	6,475	17,887

Source: Etemad and Luciani, 1991, 202.

TABLE 5.4
Per capita coal consumption 1815–1913 (GJ per year)

	England	Germany	France	Netherlands	Sweden	Portugal	Italy	Spain
1815	48.5	1.5	0.9	1.2	0.2			
1840	62.2	3	3.5	3.8	0.3			
1870	112.4	20.4	14.8	14.8	3.2	1.2	1.2	2
1890	136.5	45.6	27.6	24	10.2	3.3	4.5	5.2
1913	135	86.8	46.8	51.8	29.3	6.1	9.6	11.6

Source: See www.energyhistory.org.

regions without major coal production was not remotely large enough to affect such imbalances.[13] Fossil fuel consumption was completely dominated by coal before the First World War, at 99–100 percent through most of the nineteenth century, and still 93 percent of the total in 1910.[14]

Britain's per capita coal consumption was vastly ahead of any continental country in 1800, consuming more than fifty times as much as France (see table 5.4). This had reduced to only twelve times by 1850, but even in 1913 each Briton consumed almost twice as much as a German, and nearly three times as much as a resident of France or the Netherlands. Britain continued to have an exceptionally energy-intense economy. The per capita consump-

[13] Etemad and Luciani, 1991, 199–202. For recent estimates of *consumption* in Latin America, see Rubio et al., 2010.

[14] Etemad and Luciani, 1991, 185.

TABLE 5.5
National share of energy consumption in total consumption of six-country sample, 1820–1910

	Great Britain	Sweden	Netherlands	Germany	Italy	Spain	France
1820	29	5	2	17	14	10	22
1850	41	3	2	16	11	8	19
1900	39	2	2	33	5	3	15

Source: See www.energyhistory.org.

tion of coal shows groupings very like those for the share coal took as a proportion of total energy consumption: Britain far ahead; a "chasing pack" of Germany, France, and the Netherlands; and a significant gap back to the nations of the south and far north. Out of the laggards, only Sweden began to close the gap as the twentieth century dawned.

England had a population less than half that of Germany and a third that of France in 1820, but consumed far more energy than either (see table 5.5). By 1850, Germany and England combined consumed 60 percent of the energy in our six-country sample, despite having only 38 percent of the population. By 1900, these two nations alone consumed 73 percent of the total energy in a seven-country sample, while containing 46 percent of the population.[15] As income is related to both energy consumption and population, this represented a huge shift in economic power. In medieval and early modern times, the countries of south and central Europe had the largest populations. This lead was eroded during the nineteenth century. Combined with their much higher energy intensity and growing incomes, the bigger populations of the "coal countries" became the driving force on aggregate total energy consumption.

URBANIZATION AND POLLUTION

Thus, the new geography of energy contributed to a new geography of population. Fossil fuel use developed in a closely bound system of feedbacks with urbanization. Previously, great urban centers had largely arisen either on the basis of dominance in interregional trade or as "central places" for regional markets, or perhaps even more so, as great political centers that drew in the income of their polities through rents and taxes. With the rise of coal use, industrial growth became the major force driving population change, drawing it toward sources of heat and power. In turn, the expansion

[15] The additional country is Portugal.

TABLE 5.6

Urbanization rate in Europe, 1800–1870 (percent living in settlements of 10,000+)

	1800	1870
Scandinavia	5.1	9.1
England and Wales	29.9	49.6
Scotland	36.6	40.1
Ireland	8.5	15.6
Netherlands	37.7	37.2
Belgium	24.2	32.2
France	12.5	21.6
Italy (central-north)	14.2	13.4
Italy (south)	21.0	26.4
Spain	19.3	24.7
Portugal	14.3	14.4
Switzerland	6.2	15.3
Austria (incl. Czech lands, Hungary)	3.9	10.7
Germany	9.7	23.4
Poland	7.7	9.6
Balkans	15.3	14.2
Russia (European)	4.6	9.2
Europe	*12.4*	*19.7*
Europe (without Russia)	*11.5*	*17.3*

Source: Malanima, 2010a, 260.

of urban markets well beyond anything that could have been sustained in the "organic economy" stimulated demand for coal.

Urbanization grew rapidly across Europe and North America, especially after 1850. As one might expect, the coal-producing regions led the way, taking in large numbers of migrants.[16] However, previous urban centers that had good transport links could also benefit from the expanded levels of

---

[16] For example, see Griffin, 2010, 55–57; Wrigley, 2007; Wrigley, 2010, 113–39.

population and economic activity. After all, the relative decline of the organic economy meant that some industries were *less* dependent on having access to energy supplies—whether water, firewood, or favorable winds—in their immediate vicinity. Coal could be delivered from afar. As ever, the ideal combination for growth was where a generous resource endowment was matched by good access to overseas and domestic markets.

As the rate of urbanization rose, so did the absolute size of cities. The most famous, paradigmatic case of such development was Manchester in England, which grew from a population of 93,000 in 1801 to over half a million by 1881, each person consuming more than six tons of coal a year by the latter date.[17] The combination of concentrated industrial activity, great masses of population, and a smoky, stinking fuel brought new challenges regarding the pollution of air and water. Pulmonary diseases became the major killers in large, coal-fired cities, and people came to fear that the pall of smoke obscuring the sun was causing vitamin deficiency and stunted growth. By 1902, the Manchester Guardian newspaper could argue that, "Our pride in an Empire on which the sun never sets should be tempered by the reflection that there are courts and slums at home on which the sun never rises." The term "acid rain" was coined by meteorologist R. A. Smith in 1872, as people began to notice and measure the corroding effects of coal smoke on buildings and plants. The pH of Manchester's rain in 1900 was 3.5, and already in the nineteenth century "black snow" in Scandinavia was blamed on British smokestacks.[18]

In turn, such problems called forth campaigning movements to reduce the hazards of smoke pollution, and new debates emerged about whether the environmental challenge of "smoke abatement" should be met by encouraging improved, less-polluting technology, or outright bans on smoky fuels. People began to sense that the greatest "environmental" hazards were not a capricious climate or the risks of rotting matter causing "miasmic" airs, but the waste products of human activity. Coal fires had been used in early modern London as a remedy against airborne plagues and could even be recommended as a treatment against tuberculosis as late as the 1840s. But by the closing decades of the nineteenth century, a long-established sense that coalsmoke was an unpleasant nuisance was transformed by the medical profession's recognition of the its catastrophic impact on the lungs.[19] Industrial cities became characterized by forests of tall chimneys which helped disperse the dangerous pall, although these were originally built to improve the draught of air in steam engine boilers, not for their benefits to

---

[17] Mosley, 2001.

[18] The neutral pH value is 7, so 3.5 is highly acidic. Mosley, 2001, 4, 18–19, 26, 34, 49, 96–99, 103; Brimblecombe, 1987; Brüggemeier, 1996.

[19] Thorsheim, 2006, 17. Such fears about pulmonary damage from coalsmoke were already expressed in the seventeenth century.

health.[20] In many cases the domestic consumer, whose smoke was delivered near ground level, was collectively the greatest polluter. Ironically in Manchester the worst day for smoke was Monday, because of the large number of women starting fires to launder clothes on the traditional wash-day.[21] Densely packed housing also presented new challenges in the development of sanitation systems.[22]

A lesser but still great toll was inflicted on those who supplied the energy. Mining was still backbreaking manual work and highly dangerous, subject to frequent tunnel collapses, gas explosions, and flooding. More insidious was the lung damage caused by breathing in coal dust, a condition first noted by medical men in 1813 but known long before as "black spit."[23]

2. TRADITIONAL SOURCES: RISE BUT RELATIVE DECLINE

The age of coal did not mean the banishing of traditional energy carriers. They may have declined in relative importance, yet consumption of energy in the form of food, fodder, water, and wind for the most part rose to unprecedented heights. In this sense the "organic economy" did not end with the industrial revolution, and indeed has no prospect of ending: humans still need to eat. Draft animals were essential for farm work and short-distance haulage until the appearance of the oil-fueled tractor, while in some uses water and wind power remained competitive with steam throughout the century. Keeping pace with population growth was no mean feat and requires some explanation. But it is a mistake to use these facts to argue "the inference 'no coal, no Industrial Revolution' is untenable." In fact, as we will see, the opposite is the case (we will discuss counterfactuals of what might have happened in the absence of coal in the final section of the book).[24] Per capita supplies of energy from traditional sources did not increase. This was despite major successes in raising output. There was never any prospect of them rising to a degree sufficient to underwrite a new pattern of economic growth. The economies that could not take advantage of fossil fuels fell behind until new opportunities arose with the second industrial revolution. The new dynamic of growth, the developments that clearly differentiate the modern economy from the pre-industrial, belonged to those regions and sectors that used fossil fuels, or that depended on supplying those regions.

[20] Mosley, 2001, 128, passim.
[21] Mosley, 2001, 8.
[22] Schott, Luckin, and Massard-Guilbard, 2005; Melosi, 2008.
[23] Flinn, 1984, 412–23; Nye, 1998, 88–89.
[24] Mokyr, 2009, 102–4; Clark and Jacks, 2007.

CALORIES FROM THE SOIL

Food production increased. So much can be read from the simple expansion of population, and the continued ability to feed them. Although agricultural statistics become widely available by the second half of the nineteenth century, they are generally aggregated in terms of value rather than calorific content. The various regional agricultures of Europe grew different crops and raised different animals, partly in response to local environmental conditions, but also consumer preferences and the possibilities offered by trade. Aggregate figures of agricultural output are not, therefore, a sure indicator of energetic content and give only a rough indicator of trend.[25]

In the high-yielding agricultures of England and the Netherlands, annual growth rates in output were rather slow, on average less than 1 percent in the century after 1815. France managed around 1 percent for most of this century, while Germany's agricultural output is estimated to have grown at around 2 percent up until the 1840s, slowing somewhat thereafter. The decades after 1870 are considered to be a period of agricultural depression for producers, as relative prices fell and European markets faced competition from imports from Russia, the Americas, and Australia. But output across western Europe continued to rise, at around 1 percent p.a.[26]

This growth at least matched the growth of population, which averaged 0.93 percent p.a. between 1800 and 1914.[27] The population more than doubled, but agricultural output, at least in terms of value, may well have trebled over this period.[28] Agriculture was able to reverse the declines in per capita output that had been suffered after 1770, restoring and surpassing the slow growth that had prevailed in the century before 1750. Nevertheless, "pauperism" and the traditional crisis of subsistence still haunted the first half of the century. This was notably the case in the "year without a summer" of 1816–17 triggered by the eruption of the volcano Tambora in Indonesia and with the catastrophic impact of the potato blight across northern Europe in

---

[25] Turner discusses aspects of this problem, but there has not been any proper study of the calorific content of output using the large set of agricultural statistics now available. One exception is the 1939 study of Beilby, driven by the exigencies of needing to feed a blockaded population, which suggested that agricultural output fell in calorific terms between 1870 and 1910. However, the shift toward pastoral agriculture was particularly marked in England during this period. In Denmark, where there was also a shift toward livestock farming, total calorific output certainly grew fast after 1870, but exports were also large. Beilby, 1939, 64–65; Turner, 2004, 146–49; Jörberg, 1973, 396; Van Zanden, 1991, 218; O'Brien and Prados de la Escosura, 1992, 519–26; Kander and Warde, 2011, 17.

[26] Van Zanden, 1991, 229; 1985, 136–37; Federico, 2005, 18.

[27] Livi-Bacci, 2000.

[28] Growth was most rapid in countries with large populations, such as Germany, France and Italy, meaning the western European average must have been in the higher end of the range cited. Kander and Warde, 2011.

the late 1840s, when the tragedy was greatest in Ireland.[29] Yet after this date there were no widespread serious shortages. On the contrary, the quality of the diet improved. Consumption of dairy products and fresh fruit and vegetables rose. Meat production increased by 25 percent in Europe and far more was imported as well.[30]

In the context of the difficulties discussed in part I of this book of raising output in the pre-industrial economy, 1–2 percent annual growth was a great achievement. Part of this growth in value certainly came from the production of higher value foodstuffs, and hence energy supplies may not have risen to the same degree. But more of production was going into animal fodder as an intermediary good, to produce higher-value end products such as milk, cheese, and meat, as well as fueling on-farm draft power. The relative price of grain crops fell significantly after 1870, disguising continuing gains in real output. This growth begs the question of how such advances could be achieved, given that agriculture was touched relatively little by the great technological shifts that powered industry. The achievement was all the greater given that the workforce in the primary sector shrank as a share of the total, from 55 percent in 1870 (and surely a higher proportion before this date) to 46 percent by 1910.[31]

For some regions, this success was a continuation of "land-saving" innovations already introduced in the early modern period: continuing colonization of new land, within the continent and overseas, introduction of new crops, more effective rotations. Imports came to play a much more significant role, the "ghost acres" becoming really significant after 1870. Britain could exchange its industrial products and commercial services for foodstuffs from east and west, as well as raw materials such as the large amounts of cotton required to keep the mills running. By the end of the nineteenth century, meat and grain imports were major contributors to the British diet, much of its wool came from the Southern Hemisphere, and almost all its timber was imported.[32] Britain was able to develop an agriculture that economized particularly on labor and that had a high proportion of pastoral products.

But such a strategy was not open to most of Europe, where farmers had to pursue land- and labor-saving strategies without the benefits of a maritime empire, or where agriculture remained a significant proportion of national income, prompting tariff protection for farmers. As we have seen,

[29] Post, 1977; Ó Grada, 1995.

[30] An exception was the Finnish famine of 1867. In Russia per capita grain supply rose 50 percent between the late 1880s and the First World War. Jörberg, 1973, 399; Van Zanden, 1991, 227; see also O'Brien and Prados de los Escosura, 1992; Munting, 1996, 340–1. On German output, Bittermann, 1956.

[31] Van Zanden, 1991, 219. This figure refers to the male and female workforce in fifteen countries.

[32] Pomeranz, 2000; Koning, 1994; O'Rourke, 1997; Tello and Jover, forthcoming; Floud et al., 2011, 159.

New World crops became increasingly important in agricultural production and the diet. Potatoes, maize, and sugar beet were notable successes. Fodder crops altered rotations and, combined with stall-feeding for livestock, eliminated large areas of fallow from European agriculture. The gradual diffusion of improved agricultural techniques, better drainage, and new breeds of crops and animals made an almost imperceptible but significant difference.[33]

Innovation in nineteenth-century agriculture continued the trend toward increasing the use of animal manure on land as a fertilizer, by increasing the fodder throughput. In 1800, more than 50 percent of German agricultural output had gone to food or raw material for industry and 31 percent to fodder. By 1900, the respective figures had reversed, to 32 percent and 55 percent, and the output of stall-manure had risen sevenfold.[34] This process could not continue indefinitely. The answer would come in the form of new concentrated feeds, and above all artificial fertilizers that began to become important from the 1870s after several decades of experimentation (and the use of limited alternatives such as guano): nitrates, phosphates, and mineral potash. Artificial fertilizers were hugely both land- and labor-saving, and pointed the way to the huge productivity increases of the twentieth century.[35]

The widespread adoption of motorized traction did not come until the internal combustion engine was adopted in the farm after the First World War, or in some countries even later. The "depression" period after 1870 was marked by new technologies that were cheap enough to be widely used by small family farms, which increasingly became the backbone of production on much of the continent. Equipment such as the centrifugal cream separator, invented in Sweden by Gustav de Laval in 1878, led to the industrialization of small-scale farming. Such capital investments became increasingly shared within farming co-operatives, with rapidly increasing numbers of sowing, mowing, and threshing machines.[36] Both artificial fertilizers, mechanization, and later motorization were products of the new fossil fuel economy; indeed, the production of fertilizers was highly energy-intensive.[37]

FOOD DEMAND

By the 1900s Europe was better fed than it had been for many centuries. However, as the quality of the diet improved, it may not have been so important to increase its quantity. Industrialization saw a shift from an economy where a large proportion of the working population performed heavy

[33] O'Rourke and Williamson, 1999, 93–117; Chorley, 1981.
[34] Schremmer, 1988, 40, 52.
[35] Van Zanden, 1991, 231–32.
[36] Van Zanden, 1991, 216, 233; Schremmer, 1988, 41–45; Jörberg, 1973, 397.
[37] Milward and Saul, 1977.

manual labor, often in agriculture, to an occupational structure that had shifted toward more sedentary, indoor tasks. This may have reduced per capita demand, in that the population found it easier to acquire the food necessary to perform the desired amount of labor. Satisfaction and nutrition could improve even without markedly increasing the historically low levels of consumption found in 1800. Specialization increased the availability of higher-value foods and proteins, especially in northern Europe, advancing the consumption of eggs, dairy products, meat, and green vegetables. Here urbanization promoted a virtuous feedback effect with agriculture, as the growth of reliable urban markets and higher industrial wages encouraged farmers to invest in higher value products, specialize, and raise output.[38]

Diets in Mediterranean Europe remained almost static, average intake remaining at around 2,300 kcal per day in Portugal and rising from around 2,500 kcal per day in Italy in 1861 to nearly 3,000 kcal by World War I. In Italy there was widespread malnutrition, such as the incidence of pellagra caused by dependence on a maize-based diet, inducing protein and Vitamin B3 deficiencies. However, at these margins, significant numbers could be pulled out of malnutrition by small shifts in the average, and by the early twentieth century Italian under-nutrition was in decline.[39]

The effects of industrialization in England are much debated. Did the reduced demand for physical labor counteract the rise one might expect from improving incomes? As it stands, estimates of calorific consumption diverge widely, especially at the beginning of the period. This partly depends on the method adopted. The difficulty of extrapolating from limited survey data to the whole population has led historians to use data on production, but considerably different estimates as to losses in the production process leave us with widely differing estimates of per capita consumption, shown in table 5.7.

As we noted in chapter 3, differences in food availability may have had important implications for the amount of work individual laborers could perform. However, the evidence may as easily point to the reverse—food consumption measured by calories tended to adapt to the work people had to perform, and differences in income were reflected in quality, both in terms of nutritional balance and taste, rather than a hierarchy of calorific intake.[40]

---

[38] Wrigley, 1985; Kopsidis, 1996.

[39] Malanima, 2002; 2006a, 26–7,105–6; Vecchi and Coppola, 2006; Henriques, 2009, 28–32; 2011, 28; Italian estimates rest on food production, and do not account for wastage. Henriques has estimated Portuguese consumption per capita to be stable at around 2 300 Kcal per person per day, based on assuming a calorific intake that varies according to the physical activity demanded by the occupational structure, and taking into account age structure. For other attempts, see Segers, 2004 and Grigg, 1995, also collected in Floud et al., 2011, 267. For a discussion of the complexity of interpreting averages, see Humphries, 2011.

[40] It seems likely that the picture across Europe is quite mixed. In some places there does appear to have been a calorific hierarchy, e.g., Beck, 1993, 201, 520.

TABLE 5.7
Estimates of daily per capita caloric consumption in England

	Muldrew	Floud et al.	Broadberry et al.	Warde	Oddy
1750	5,047	2,237	2,112	—	—
1800	3,977	2,439	1,996	2,900	—
1850		2,544	2,036	2,400	2,000–2,300
1900		2,977	—	2,000	2,100

Note: Estimates of Muldrew, Floud et al., and Broadberry et al. are of available calories, while Warde and Oddy are of actual consumption.

Sources: Muldrew, 2011, 156; Floud et al., 2011, 160; Broadberry et al., 2011, 59; Warde, 2007, 25–32; Oddy, 2003, 4, 63–69.

Certainly by the end of the nineteenth century the greater proportion of the European population had sufficient food to fuel their necessary labor. Health and longevity improved too, although these were related to exposure to disease and periods of rapid urbanization could even see local reverses in generally positive trends.[41]

WORKING ANIMALS

Increased food production and mechanization in agriculture increased the demand for draft power. Across most of Europe the amount of draft animals available expanded across the century, especially favoring horses that could work at greater speed than oxen (see table 5.8).

In many countries, however, the rise in (literally) horse-power was also subject to a countervailing long-term decline or stagnation in the use of oxen and cows for draft power. By the First World War, horses provided the majority of draft power in Britain, the Netherlands, Scandinavia, Germany, and Spain. But Italy and much of Eastern Europe still relied heavily on oxen and cattle.[42]

The animals were also getting bigger, so the availability of on-farm power increased at a greater rate than sheer numbers of animals would suggest, almost doubling in Germany, the Netherlands, and England. As industrialization advanced in these countries, and the agricultural workforce shrank as a proportion of the total, this tended to raise the amount of power

[41] Postel-Vinay and Sahn, 2010; Cinnirella, 2008.
[42] Kander and Warde, 2011; Collins, 2010.

TABLE 5.8
Draft livestock in selected countries (000s)

	England and Wales		Germany		Sweden		Italy		
	Horses	Oxen	Horses	Cattle	Horses	Cattle	Horses	Oxen	Other
1815	950	<200	1,790	1,920	311	278			
1850	1,350	40	2,040	2,095	329	333			
1880	1,835	—	2,655	2,080	356	348	510	1,452	935
1910	2,175	—	3,370	2,135	449	275	725	2,038	1,180

Note: In Germany and Sweden, an estimate of cows used for draft purposes is included in the cattle figure. "Other" in Italy includes working donkeys and mules.
Sources: Kander and Warde, 2011; Collins, 2010, 193, 213.

available per worker. The increased use of fast-moving horses was also labor-saving. However, much of the scope for "efficient" use depended on the output mix. The kind of agriculture practiced determines whether animals are needed continuously or only episodically. Although the fodder consumed by animals is closely related to their usage, large amounts of time and fodder still had to be used to keep animals alive when not in use. Overall, the nineteenth century undoubtedly saw a great improvement in the return to capital that on-farm draft power represented. The expansion of draft power in the north tended to reflect the greater capital intensity of agriculture, but there is no straightforward correlation between the availability of on-farm power and labor productivity.[43]

General economic growth drove higher demand for food, transport, and raw materials, all of which expanded traffic and draft animal use. Canals and railways, for example, could supplant horse-drawn traffic on some routes, but their overall effect was to greatly increase the volume of medium- and long-distance traffic. This stimulated demand for short haulage still performed by animals. Canals often required horse traction to move boats along and simply made its use far more efficient by reducing the problem of friction from pulling a load along a solid as opposed to a liquid surface. Thus, the new canal networks that were constructed from the eighteenth century tended to encourage higher demand for transport services and horse traction. Railways created demand for haulage to and from the rail heads.

Industrialization and urbanization initially brought the increased presence of horses on roads and in city streets: hauling carts and wagons, omnibuses, or laden with packs, as well as riding for pleasure and transport. By 1900, only a third of English horses worked in agriculture, around half of French,

---

[43] Kander and Warde, 2011.

TABLE 5.9

Draft livestock fodder consumption per person, 1815–1913 (GJ per year)

	England	Germany	France	Netherlands	Sweden	Portugal	Italy	Spain
1815	3.2	3.6	2.3	3.3	5.7			
1840	2.9	2.4	2.7	2.9	5			
1870	2.6	2.3	3.4	3.1	4.4	3.2	3	5.1
1890	2.6	2.5	3.4	2.8	4.5	3	3.4	3.8
1913	2	2.6	3.9	2.7	4	2.7	3.8	3.3

Note: Total annual energy consumption by draught livestock is calculated and divided by the human population.

Source: See www.energyhistory.org.

and two-thirds in Sweden.[44] Well over a million horses were set to work in the transport sector in Britain at this point in time, nearly the same number that had existed in the whole country a century earlier. Numbers of urban horses fell very rapidly after World War I as they were supplanted by electric tramways and motor vehicles, but horses still provided a considerable amount of motive power to the armies of the Second World War and were not supplanted on the farm across much of the continent until the 1950s.[45]

Nevertheless, we should not imagine that increasing animal numbers signaled the potential of an "organic" or "vegetable" economy to sustain modern rates of growth. Even in these circumstances, the per capita supply of energy from draft livestock declined or was static nearly everywhere. The general trend in fodder consumption by draft animals per person (as a proxy for their power) was downward across most of the continent. The situation was more favorable in agriculture, where draft livestock remained essential; here numbers relative to the workforce remained more stable or showed slight increases. Yet overall, even as herds grew greatly in size, the amount of energy consumed by draft animals per inhabitant of Europe fell (see table 5.9).

FIREWOOD

In countries with no indigenous supplies of coal, and more remote from coalfields, firewood remained the dominant source of thermal energy.[46] As we have seen in chapter 3, in the Scandinavian north 80 percent of total

[44] Kander and Warde, 2009.

[45] Collins, 2009; Thompson, 1983, 80.

[46] It remains an important share of household fuel consumption in some countries, even in the twenty-first century: Henriques, 2011, 41.

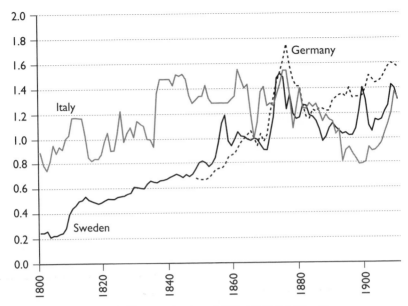

Figure 5.4. Firewood prices, 1800–1910 (1866 = 1)
Sources: Hoffmann, 1965; ISTAT, 1958; Kander, 2002.

energy consumption came from wood at the beginning of the nineteenth century, and in western Europe as a whole the share was around 50 percent.

As population grew, firewood prices rose across the century (see figure 5.4). The opening up of European markets to overseas products of the land, along with competition from coal, depressed prices in the 1870s, but even with alternative sources of energy the general trend was upward, continuing the experience of the eighteenth century.

This is despite some great achievements in increasing the productivity of European woodland in this period. The general trend in woodland area continued to be downward across the nineteenth century, and 1900 represents a nadir in the forest cover of Europe (see table 3.8). The widespread fears of "wood shortage" expressed in the eighteenth century were succeeded in some regions by even greater rates of depletion. But these trends were also counter-acted by localized improvement in yields and increased utilization of the by-products of other crops such as vines in Mediterranean Europe. Germany was the homeland of the "scientific forestry" that spread around the world from the eighteenth century. This was based on the professionalized management of forests, favoring fast-growing species of trees and excluding competing graziers from the woodland, although the implementation of new techniques was slow and not general even in Germany before the

TABLE 5.10
Annual Per Capita Firewood Consumption in selected countries,
1815–1910 (Gj)

	Sweden	Germany	Portugal	Italy
1815	37.8	7.4		
1840	28.4	6.9		
1870	25.0	6.0	10.4	8.3
1890	22.6	4.0	10.3	7.2
1910	23.9	2.7	10.2	5.2

Sources: Italy from Malanima, 2006; Germany estimated from data in Endres, 1905; Henriques, 2009; Kander, 2002.

1860s.[47] Germany managed to double its wood production between 1800 and 1888, driven by improved yields rather than afforestation, although a declining share of this was used for fuel as coal use expanded.[48] Sweden's firewood consumption rose by around half between 1800 and 1914, at the cost of some reduction in the stock of timber. In the south, Italian firewood consumption fell gradually after 1860, but in contrast the Portuguese raised consumption by around a third between 1856 and 1914.[49] The Dutch consumption of peat was a different case, being a clearly exhaustible resource although one that required large areas of moors for its supply. Consumption did not peak until the 1870s.[50]

The widespread achievements of European forestry and wood management showed that the continent was not at the limits of its ecology at 1800, but that it was at the limits of an "organic economy." It proved impossible to raise per capita consumption levels. It is a gross illusion to think that modern growth in Europe could have been supported with the heat content of firewood.[51] In every country for which we have data the trend in per capita consumption was downward (see table 5.10). Contrary to expectations, southern Europeans did not consume less firewood than those living in somewhat more northerly climes, such as Germany and France. This evidence again shows clearly the strong incentives to switch to coal.

Some of this wood was more efficiently used thanks to less wasteful cutting practices, and the improved efficiency of stoves.[52] But Europe probably had less forest cover by 1900 than at any time in its previous inhabited

[47] Rubner, 1967; Grewe, 2007; Hasel and Schwartz, 2006.
[48] Warde, 2006; results calculated from Endres, 1905.
[49] Kander, 2002; Malanima, 2006a, 108; Henriques, 2009, 147–48.
[50] Ben Gales, personal communication.
[51] See chapter 7.
[52] Kander, 2002, 28–29.

history, as the demands of agriculture and grazing expanded to feed the population, as well as to cook the food and provide warmth and industrial fuel. Only the transition to the modern fossil fuel economy relieved this pressure and triggered a recovery of the woodland that was unprecedented in many centuries.[53]

WATER

Falling water was the primary source of industrial power in the pre-industrial age, and it was slow to give up its hegemony. We have seen that while water and wind energy made a small contribution in aggregate terms, its importance lay in the possibility of concentrating power in an era when opportunities to do so were very limited. In those countries where coal was little used, mills and industrial processing clung to waterways until quite late in the nineteenth century. In Midland and northern England, and Lowell's cotton mills across the Atlantic in New England, fast-flowing streams and strong gradients provided ideal sites for industrial development. In fact one of the first major commercial applications of steam power was to provide a smooth flow of water over wheels, especially during drought periods, by pumping water that had flowed past the wheel back up to a reservoir above it. The absolute supply of water power continued to expand for many decades, in Portugal peaking as late as 1958,[54] and in Britain, industrial use of water power probably peaked in the 1870s, although capacity continued to rise until at least 1907, when the largest single user of water power was the railways! Steam engines had surpassed waterwheels as a source of power in Britain by the 1830s.[55] In Italy, water power (excluding hydroelectricity) peaked in the 1880s, four-fifths of which was utilized in industry.[56]

The persistence of water power was aided by great advances in technology, especially in the most industrialized regions. Great vertical iron wheels allowed the concentration of power with a few installations reaching up to 300 hp, although the great majority of European mills remained small horizontal constructions of 2–3 hp, as in medieval times. The use of iron, along with better engineering fittings, also allowed wheels to reach very high rates of efficiency by the mid-nineteenth century, of 85 percent or more. Traditional "undershot" wheels that were driven by the current acting on

[53] Agnoletti, 2007.

[54] Henriques, 2011, 55.

[55] Warde, 2007, 49–57; Kanefsky, 1978; Allen, 2009, 173. Kanefksy and Warde had provided rather different figures on the relative availability of steam and water power; in part because of their different geographical coverage, United Kingdom as against England and Wales, but also because Warde includes estimates for capacity utilization, reckoning that steam engines were used more consistently than waterwheels, especially waterwheels used in cereal milling.

[56] Malanima, 2006a, 37–42.

the bottom of the wheel, with low efficiencies of only 25 percent, were supplanted by overshot or breast-shot wheels where the water fell on the top of the wheel or on to its upper front. Water power could remain competitive for some applications, and the milling gear became increasingly durable as metal replaced oak and elm. From their invention in France in 1827, water turbines advanced steadily. It was the turbine that was widely adopted in the development of hydropower from the 1880s.[57]

WIND

Tens of thousands of windmills also remained in use in Europe during the nineteenth century, mostly used for grinding grain or for drainage.[58] Although windmill design became more sophisticated and better adapted to utilizing the available wind from whichever direction it was blowing, their overall contribution to power output remained small. Individual mills could rarely provide more than 20 hp when the wind was blowing, and most were much smaller.[59]

As we have seen in chapters 3 and 4, the role of sailing ships was much larger. Although steam vessels were being run on coal and wood from the beginning of the century, their conquest of the waters was only gradual. Sailing ships remained competitive for decades, especially on short-haul trips or for small-scale work such as fishing, or on very long-haul routes where the weight of coal needed to fuel the entire voyage imposed, literally, a heavy burden.[60] Fleets continued to expand, with the sailing fleet's apogee in England in 1868. By the First World War it had ceased to have any significance. Italian sail tonnage peaked in 1876, German in 1880, Portuguese in 1899. The decline in the use of sail was less marked in the Mediterranean and Iberian lands, where numbers of small vessels for fishing and coastal journeys continued to expand into the twentieth century.[61] In aggregate terms the importance of wind was, like water, small, but its essential role in propelling coastal and international trade continued into the late nineteenth century.

Yet the trend in per capita consumption of wind and water power was the same as for other traditional carriers: downward (see figure 5.5). Even in an area where the traditional economy did not face the constraints of the area-based photosynthetic regime, energy supply could not keep up with population growth.

[57] Reynolds, 1983, 178, 306, 319; Smil, 2008a, 182–83; 1994, 108; Crouzet, 1996, 41; Gordon, 1983, 244; Milward and Saul, 1977, 207; Kanefsky, 1979, 35–49.

[58] Davids, 2003.

[59] Kanefsky, 1979, 77–79, 227.

[60] Harley, 1972.

[61] Warde, 2007, 45–49; Malanima, 2006a, 114–15; Borchardt, 1973, 144; Henriques, 2009, 150–51.

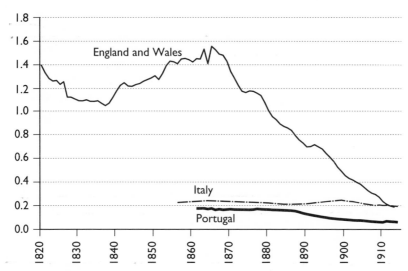

Figure 5.5. Per capita consumption of water and wind power, 1820–1914 (GJ)

Note: The basis for calculating the wind energy captured by sailing ships is slightly different and will tend to exaggerate Britain's advantage over Italy and Portugal.

Sources: See www.energyhistory.org.

3. CONCLUSION

The capacity for growth indicates that Europe had not yet reached an absolute "ecological frontier" in the early nineteenth century, in the sense that it had exhausted its renewable resources, or had overcrowded the sites that could be used for water mills. Long before the application of chemical fertilizers became an essential aspect of European agriculture in the twentieth century, there was scope to significantly increase the output of wood, fodder, food and water, and wind power to supply much larger populations. Nevertheless, the amount of renewable energy available to each inhabitant was falling in the case of every single carrier except food, as population growth outstripped supply. From the 1870s, important supplements to the diet were being imported into western and central Europe, while the supply of fossil fuels had become crucial for the transportation of all goods.

These trends are clearly illustrated in the behavior of prices. We have seen in figure 5.4 how firewood prices rose. Yet the cost of coal to consumers plummeted, as illustrated in figure 5.6. Only Germany shows some upward pressure in prices after 1890. Thus, while total energy consumption became dominated by coal, and expanded to a hitherto unimagined degree, prices of

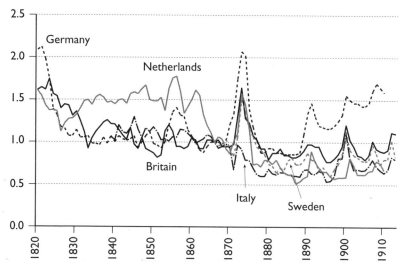

Figure 5.6. Coal prices, 1805–1913 (1866 = 1)
Note: There are no such things as "national" price series at this time.
Italian prices are for coal arriving at the port of Genoa. Britain is
represented by London; Germany by a series of "wholesale prices"
which probably rely on import data for the first half of the century.
Dutch prices are from a large weighted sample from the western
Netherlands. Prices on the coalfields themselves would have risen slightly
over this period, but the price series presented here indicates costs for
consumers removed from coalfields. The Swedish prices show a
weighted series of unit coal costs for consumers.
Sources: Italy: ISTAT, 1958; Britain: Mitchell, 1988; Netherlands:
van Riel at www.iisg.nl/hpw/brannex.php; Sweden 1866–1890, BiSOS;
1890–1910, average from series in Ljungberg, 1990, 345.

fossil fuels fell. At the same time, absolute consumption of "traditional"
carriers rose to a much lesser degree, but prices continued to rise despite
the fact that the energy regime was switching to coal. The different trends
evident in these figures tell us much about what was happening to the energy
regime in the nineteenth century, and the very different constraints under
which each energy regime labored.

Indeed, it can be argued that the modest gains in the supply of traditional
energy were only achieved thanks to the development of new tools and
transport infrastructure that were fueled by coal. The fossil fuel economy
and the "organic" economy were inevitably integrated. Populations had to
be fed, and goods, passengers, and fuels moved. Much of the stimulus for
agricultural improvement came from the concentration of population en- ✓
abled by industrialization and coal-burning.

Even in this age of unprecedented *biological* expansion of the resources that the Europeans could draw on, there is little evidence of increases in per capita terms. It is likely that cost pressures from scarcer resources, which would have been much greater without the presence of coal, would have pulled incomes down.

The transformation of the energy regime also had major implications for the structure of the entire economy. Above all, the new regime was *capital-intensive*. Individual laborers had relatively little scope for increasing their energy consumption. They could not eat that much more food, and with limited technology available, energy consumption could not be a major part of a changed lifestyle once houses were comfortably heated and lit. Humans had tried to augment their *power* through the use of tools and animals for many thousands of years. The wide availability of steam engines and fossil fuels allowed them to do so, on a much greater scale. In other words, it allowed the augmentation of capital per worker.

This was the essence of the industrial revolution: equipping each worker with more energy and capital, thus raising production and raising the average income of the entire population, as we will demonstrate in the following chapters. As people began to expect to be paid better and enjoy the benefits of leisure and consumption allowed by the new energy regime, the gap between wages and capital costs became wider. The incentive to continue on the capital-intensive track would continue, so long as the supply of energy was elastic enough to prevent upward pressure on fuel costs. This trend has continued for most of the nineteenth and twentieth centuries.

CHAPTER SIX

THE COAL DEVELOPMENT BLOCK

1. THE CORE INNOVATIONS

OUR PERSPECTIVE

FROM AN ENERGY POINT OF VIEW, the key aspects of the first industrial revolution were coal, steam, and iron.[1] No doubt individually many of the numerous technological improvements of the age, such as mechanization in the textile industry, would have raised productivity even in the absence of fossil fuel, steam power, and cheap metals. But we argue that they would not have fundamentally changed the trajectory of economic development, launching us on a sustained and historically rapid path of growth in per capita incomes. The most successful of the early modern "advanced organic economies" already made extensive use of fossil fuels. But soon, bottlenecks within the organic economy such as limited supply of transportation or domestic fuel would have provided a brake on growth. Yet it is also true that coal, steam, or iron would not each by themselves have generated a revolution. This is partly because they were basically complementary: there would be no cheap metal without the great stocks of cheap fossil fuel to smelt it. Steam engines would have provided only limited possibilities for extending the use of inanimate power without that fossil fuel, and given the extreme inefficiency of early models, it is highly questionable whether anyone would have bothered developing one without the prospect of cheap and abundant coal to fuel it. In turn, metals and engines provided a major part of the demand for coal itself. As Stanley Jevons wrote in 1866, "None of our inventions can stand alone—all are bound together in mutual dependence. The iron manufacture depends on the use of the steam-engine, and the steam-engine on the iron manufacture."[2] The dynamic interrelationships of these factors, and how they became intertwined in a new *development block*, are the subject of this chapter.

The development block was built around two core innovations, the steam engine and new techniques in metallurgy, saving on both labor and land. Both of them became economic innovations in the context of the new fossil fuel energy regime whose emergence has been described in chapter 4 as

[1] Pollard, 1981, 121.
[2] Jevons, 1866, 107.

The Newcomen Engine

Newcomen's steam engine produced a vacuum by condensing steam into water in a metal cylinder. The pressure of the atmosphere then pushed the piston down into the vacuum, producing motion. Thus the engine required knowledge of both atmospheric pressure and vacuums, ideas that were only clearly demonstrated in the middle of the seventeenth century. If the top end of the piston was attached to a beam, a weight at the other end of the beam then lifted the piston back up once the downward motion had stopped, and steam could be let into the cylinder, to begin the process again. Lifting gear could be attached to the beam to move things up and down with the motion of the piston. Hence these were called "atmospheric engines," although they were also frequently called "fire engines" at the time. Key problems to resolve to make the idea workable were refining the valves to allow the passage of water and steam in and out of the cylinder automatically at the right moments; and finding a way of cooling the steam to create the vacuum, without wasting time and energy in heating and cooling the whole cylinder for each stroke of the piston. It took Newcomen several years to resolve these issues.

a response to pressures encouraging land and labor saving. Cheap coal was their essential precondition. There is a certain irony in the process we will describe. Relatively scarce wood and easily available coal encouraged a switch to fossil fuels in the British economy, and as Robert Allen has argued, the continually low price of energy in turn encouraged capital-intensive and even more labor-saving development.[3] But the technological innovation that was able to link the processes of land and labor-saving, by using coal to fuel mechanization, did not initially aim to save labor. Instead, as the demand for coal and metals increased in the "advanced organic economy," the steam engine was seen as a means to overcome the limits of *power* in a specific sector—the mining industry.

THE EARLY STEAM ENGINE

The steam engine founded a revolution, but it was a long time coming. The sense that society might be transformed by it only gained ground a

---

[3] This is in some ways an updating of the Habakkuk thesis that explained the differential development of the United States and the United Kingdom by the greater resource endowment and relative labor scarcity in the former, an idea further developed theoretically by David. See also Habakkuk, 1962; David, 1975; Allen, 2009.

full century after the first prototype. It was the very first example of an engine that could effectively transform heat into motion, which previously had only been achieved through the use of gunpowder. Eventually these engines would come to drive machines that substituted for human labor. The transformation of thermal into kinetic energy remains the essential underpinning of the very high levels of labor productivity and income that we can achieve today. Yet the first engines did not aim to reduce the relative employment of people. They were applied to mining, and substituted horses and waterwheels, or were used in combination with them (figure 6.1). They were capital-saving, but it might be more accurate to say that the engines were intended to overcome the basic constraints of geography and geology. With coal as a fuel, the new technology allowed power to annihilate space.

Experimentation in the age of the "Scientific Revolution" of the seventeenth century had already led to the Frenchman Papin moving a piston by condensing steam to cause a vacuum as early as 1675. Thus the basic model of early steam engines was established. It was in the experimental milieu of largely well-to-do gentlemen enthusiasts that Thomas Savery produced the first engine in 1697, which he was able to demonstrate before no less a personage than the British monarch, William III. This was a period of significant advances in theoretical knowledge of physics, and the development of an expanding coterie of men with engineering skills who could coax ideas into physical form—and, vitally, fix their machines when they went wrong. This was an essential context to the technological developments of the industrial revolution, and one that would become more important as time went on. But Savery's engine, unsurprisingly for a pioneer, was a rather limited kind of pump that had few applications.[4]

The real breakthrough in steam power came with Thomas Newcomen's first working engine, erected in 1712 (figure 6.2). Newcomen was a tool supplier to the ore mining industry in the south-west of England, who appreciated the potential for such an engine to perform the valuable function of drawing water out of mines by suction. This remained the dominant use of steam engines throughout the eighteenth century.[5]

There was rapid and widespread recognition of the potential of steam, with the spread of engines around England and efforts to export the technology abroad. By the end of the 1720s, engines had been erected in Austria, Belgium, France, Germany, and Sweden. By the middle of the eighteenth century, Belgian engineers had worked out how to construct the engine and begun to export them.[6] In fact, these early efforts to disseminate the technology illustrate well its limitations. Because steam engines could only manage

[4] Hills, 1989, 15–20; Rolt and Allen, 1977, 20–26.
[5] Hills, 1989, 22; Rolt and Allen, 1977, 31–43.
[6] Pollard, 1981; Hills, 1989, 33–35; Rolt and Allen, 1977, 70–81; Dhondt and Bruwier, 1973, 333.

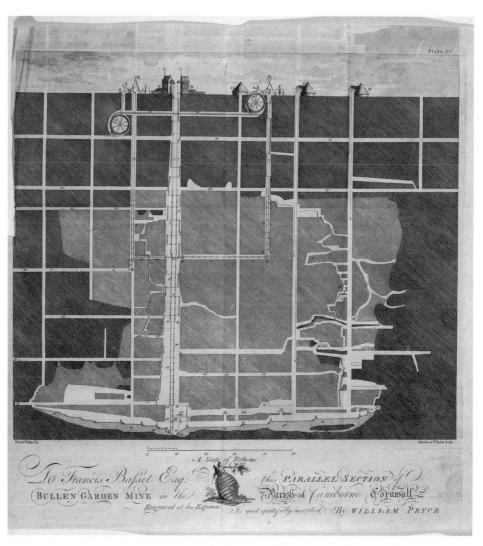

Figure 6.1. Cross-section of Bullen Garden Mine, Cornwall, 1778. Waterwheels (Q) are used to drain the upper sections of the mine, but steam engines (N) to drain the deeper parts.
Source: Pryce, 1778, 172.

an up-and-down reciprocal motion, and a rather uneven one at that, their uses were very restricted. Smoothness of motion remained difficult to achieve long into the nineteenth century, excluding them from mechanical processes that required an even amount of power to be applied, especially more delicate uses in textile manufacture. Early Newcomen engines were often used

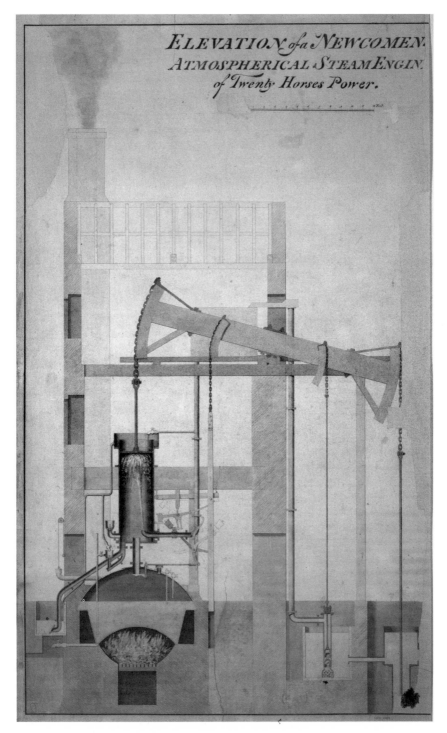

Figure 6.2. Newcomen steam engine

to support traditional sources of power that gave a smoother motion, such as "water returning" engines employed from the 1730s in ironworks and elsewhere to assist waterwheels by pumping water back up above the wheel and assuring a constant flow.[7]

Thus the first engines produced only very limited kinds of motion at very great expense. This changed drastically over the next 150 years. We should imagine a steam engine of the 1880s as being as far removed from the first model built in the late seventeenth century as modern personal computers are from the enormous, room-filling prototypes of the 1940s. There is no mystery about the "slow" uptake of the steam engines any more than there is a mystery as to why most homes did not have personal computers by 1950. Only after a long and complex history of further invention could the steam engine at last emerge in the nineteenth century as the "general purpose technology" of the industrial age, performing tasks as diverse as driving spinning machines, pumping water out of deep mines, or delivering fresh bananas thousands of miles from plantation to city market stalls. We argue that while the steam engine may with hindsight be considered a "macro-innovation," a technological and economic game-changer, it required further "meso-innovations" before it could become the core innovation of a revolutionary development block.

THE COMPLEMENTARITY OF COAL AND STEAM POWER

Could steam engines have run without coal? In places far from coal, many steam engines could be and were run on wood during the nineteenth century, although there was always a strong preference for coal if it could be obtained. But it seems very unlikely that steam power would have been developed without the availability of coal, even though the principle of the engine was at first investigated independently of the fuel. Early Newcomen engines managed efficiencies of only around 0.5 percent, and Savery's engine even less. They consumed a huge amount of fuel relative to the power provided.[8] Nearly 2,300 engines are known to have been erected in Britain during the eighteenth century, more than 80 percent after 1770. A major driver of diffusion was the availability of cheap coal, although their value for industrial purposes permitted a wider use by 1800. None used wood. Only later and rather more efficient engines, with greatly altered boiler designs, would employ wood as fuel.[9]

---

[7] This was a common use as late as the 1840s. Nuvolari et al., 2006; Hills, 1989, 29–30; Rolt and Allen, 1977, 118; Kanefsky, 1979, 176; Nuvolari et al., 2011.
[8] Hill, 1989, 36.
[9] Nuvolari et al., 2006, 189; 2011, 296.

Complementarity cuts both ways. Although the development of steam power as a technology with economic applications needed coal, could coal supply have expanded without steam? If so, an elastic supply of coal might still have been crucial to the industrial revolution, but the coal industry in 1700 would have been just as capable as the coal industry of 1850 in supplying demand.[10] The dynamic for change would have come from outside of the mining industry.

Steam engines contributed little to the direct demand for coal during the eighteenth century, as we have seen in chapter 4. The benefits of the new energy regime were merely quantitative, augmenting the expansion of industries in already established processes. The question is whether coal could have been *extracted* without big increases in cost in the absence of steam engines. A primary use was mine drainage. As coalmining became more ambitious, and mines reached further and further underground, colliers were increasingly presented with the difficulties of keeping shafts and tunnels free of water. In parts of Europe, such as the Harz Mountains of central Germany or quicksilver mines in Idria, sophisticated water management and the use of wheels, and muscle power, had allowed metal mines to reach several hundred feet underground. But in most places in England such techniques were not feasible, although one shaft near Newcastle reached a depth of 300 feet (90 meters). Drainage using muscle power was expensive, and at greater depths, impracticable in the case of many seams.[11]

Steam engines could substitute for both hydraulics and horses, and at first were favored simply because they were cheaper. It was probably not essential for the continued expansion of mining in the early eighteenth century. But the Newcomen engine was able to drain much deeper mines than its rivals, and by the 1770s, these combined advantages had made its use near universal in English collieries for plumbing depths of more than 30 meters. Horses were retained for haulage within the mines and working winding gear, but were gradually supplanted by the use of wire rope and steam power.[12] There was indeed a strong complementarity between coalmining and the development of the atmospheric engine, which was gradually improved and expanded by engineers.[13]

[10] As argued by Clark and Jacks, 2007.

[11] Valentinitsch, 1983, 61; Flinn, 1984, 114.

[12] Church, 1986, 365–67. In 1913, some 73,000 horses and ponies were still used in mines, a figure eclipsed by the 2.4 million hp used in the mining sector as a whole from steam in 1907. Kanefsky, 1979, 339.

[13] Flinn, 1984, 114, 116, 123. Clark and Jacks's alternative argument, that muscle power could have been used with no real influence on cost as drainage costs were only a small part of total retail cost, assume that there would be no bottlenecks where at greater depths costs increased steeply. This contradicts the literature on the mining industry, which argues that the use of muscle power was not technically feasible for many seams; it makes an error common with counterfactual literature in that it ignores the basic material constraints of the real world. Clark and Jacks, 2007; Church, 1986, 318–19.

Steam-powered drainage was the essential innovation that permitted the continual expansion of mines. At the coalface, there was a "continuing primacy of manual labour and physical exertion," with mechanization of cutting only introduced around 1850, often at first using compressed air and later electricity as a source of power. They reduced the widespread and more dangerous use of blasting to assist coal-cutting. However, they were of little importance in overall production before the twentieth century, their advance retarded by the machinery only being effective in particular kinds of seams.[14] Advances in boring and shaft-drilling that speeded up access to seams also increasingly were linked to steam power, as well as the emergence of specialized consultants in boring and mine engineering. Working at greater depths and in difficult geological conditions also required improved ventilation, where steam-powered fans, especially the Guibal fan developed in Belgium around 1860, were a crucial innovation.[15] In 1870 and 1907, around a quarter of British steam power capacity was still in mining.[16]

In mining districts where drainage was not a problem, these early and limited atmospheric engines were not widely employed. In Liège, despite the development of a local capacity to build steam engines, and the presence of coalfields, they at first were little used. By the end of the eighteenth century there were still only a tiny number of engines spread thinly across the continent, mostly in mining districts. After this date, however, the geological complexity and depth of unexploited seams in eastern Belgium was driving up costs; the steam engine became necessary here too, but did not prevent their mining industry from eventually going into decline.[17]

WATT'S ENGINE AND ROTARY MOTION

The great innovation that allowed the application of steam power to manufacturing occurred in the 1770s. This was literally a revolution: the up-and-down motion of a piston was harnessed to produce *rotative power*. Gearing attached to the engine could be used to turn wheels that were linked to industrial machinery that had been designed primarily with the waterwheels or horses in mind. Now, steam engines could become labor-saving: this is one of the great meso-inventions by which steam power was made into a general-purpose technology. Developments in steam power in the late eighteenth century are forever associated with James Watt, a Scottish university–educated engineer who had already won fame for resolving one of the great causes of inefficiency in atmospheric engines: the fact that the

---

[14] Church, 1986, 310, 344–48, 356–57; Greasley, 1982; Mitchell, 1984, 75–77, 81–91.
[15] Church, 1986, 312–13, 324–25; Mitchell, 1984, 79–81.
[16] Kanefsky, 1979, 332–34, 339.
[17] Adits were widely used around Europe. Pollard, 1981, 87; Dhondt and Bruwier, 1973, 333; Pounds and Parker, 1957, 81, 88.

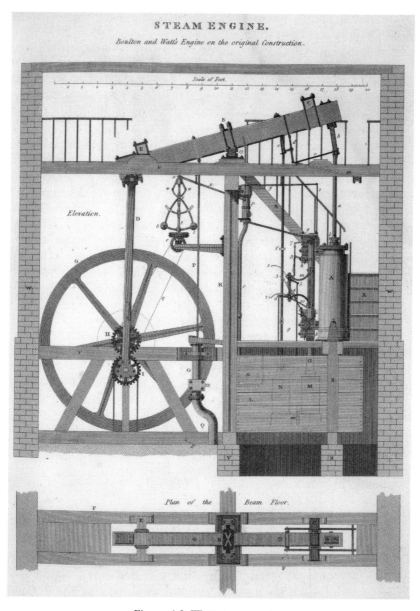

Figure 6.3. Watt steam engine

cylinder containing the piston had to be heated up and cooled with each stroke.[18] Watt realized that the use of a condenser separated from the piston to do the cooling would allow the cylinder to remain permanently hot, making the engine much more efficient.

Watt's work on his engine with a separate condenser began in 1764 and was initially funded by a Birmingham industrialist who needed more efficient engines to drain his Scottish mines.[19] Technical difficulties took time to overcome and the Watt engine was not operable until 1774, by which time he was in business with his famous collaborator, Matthew Boulton (figure 6.3). This period coincided with the rapid expansion of machinery in the textile industry, and it was soon recognized that steam power had enormous potential in this area. Watt was not the first person to think of trying to get rotative motion from a steam engine. It had already been attempted earlier in the century, especially to run the winding gears in mines that brought coal to the surface, but with little success.[20] By 1782, Watt had solved the problem, constructing a gear system to provide rotative power, which meant that his new engines could drive machinery. Credit must also go to Matthew Wasborough, who had already developed a simpler and more effective gearing by 1779. But because Watt was able to create rotative motion in combination with his far more efficient new engines, this was the model that became most widely disseminated and influential.[21]

By the end of the eighteenth century the core design of stationary steam engines had been established, and they were being applied to a wide range of uses, from pumping water to running machinery. Yet there were still only a few hundred in the whole of Europe, and the motion that produced was still too unreliable to be used in processes that required precision or smooth motion. Especially in textiles, uneven motion could easily lead to the breaking of yarn or thread. A continual series of micro-innovations would be required to overcome these difficulties.

Innovation in Iron

Increasingly, the world was bound together by metal. Brass tacks, iron nails, iron beams, copper hulls, and most prominently of all, iron rails. For centuries much of Europe's metal smelting had been concentrated in relatively remote areas, as much for the availability of the cheap wood for fuel as the distribution of ores: the Harz and "Ore Mountains" of Germany, in the Ardennes of Belgium and France, the Weald of England, and the vast

---

[18] Tann, 2004.
[19] Hills, 1989, 54.
[20] Flinn, 1984, 101.
[21] Hills, 1989, 52–69; Rolt and Allen, 1977, 118–23.

forestlands of Sweden.[22] The size of individual operations was curtailed by the availability of wood, and in some areas, shortage and expense of wood led directly to the curtailment or even abandonment of smelting. The introduction of coal into metallurgy would radically alter this picture. This was not because there was no scope at all for expanding charcoal-based metallurgy. Charcoal-smelting iron continued to expand its production in France right up until the 1850s and even longer in Sweden for high-quality iron and steel.[23] But coal use permitted a rapid expansion of production at low prices and in previously unimagined quantities. The changing geography of production also allowed new sources of ore to be exploited, producing new synergies in the economy promoting growth. South Wales emerged as one of the world's major iron and steel producing regions in a landscape largely bereft of trees.

From the fifteenth century, northern European iron production comprised two main stages. First, the ore was smelted in a furnace that produced "pig" iron from the mined ore. This was increasingly done in "blast furnaces" which introduced a blast of air to assist the chemical processes that separated iron from the undesirable slag. But pig iron was brittle and could only be cast rather than worked into different shapes, limiting the uses to which it could be put. The second stage was to make "bar iron," so called because the end product was generally supplied as long, thin bars. This was far more ductile and workable and was used for the great bulk of iron objects. Bar or wrought iron was produced by forging, often with the heated metal being battered by great water-driven hammers, to reduce the carbon content and eliminate dross.[24]

Coal was already used to heat metal in hammer works in the sixteenth century, but it could not be used in any process where the fuel was in close proximity to the metal, because waste gases from the coal altered the chemical composition of the end product. It was recognised at an early date that "coking" the coal, combusting it slowly with limited access to oxygen, would create a more refined fuel that was less at risk of introducing impurities into the metal. The first patent for coking was granted in England in 1620, but it was not until 1709 that Abraham Darby successfully applied coke to the production of cast iron at Coalbrookdale. Clearly the context was the potential saving on fuel costs by using coal. However, this coke iron had a high silicon content, which was helpful in casting molten metal, but made it less suitable for malleable bar iron. More important, according to the recent studies of Peter King, coke iron at first also required greater

---

[22] Kellenbenz, 1974.

[23] Landes, 2003, 217; Arpi, 1951.

[24] For general histories of ironworking, see Hyde, 1977; Kellenbenz, 1974; and Evans and Rydén, 2005.

refining than charcoal-iron, and thus did not provide a cost advantage for several decades.[25]

The key series of innovations that permitted coke to be employed throughout the iron production process occurred in the three decades after the early 1750s. At that time there were only three blast furnaces using coke in Britain, or indeed anywhere. But refinements in the air-blast, rising charcoal and iron import prices, and an elastic supply of cheap coal made coke more competitive. By 1776, coke-pig iron had outstripped charcoal-pig iron production in Britain. From 1753, the Wood brothers introduced the "potting" process as a means of reducing the silicon content in bar iron. The pig was heated with coal to reduce the silicon, but this introduced sulphur into the iron, making it almost unworkable: the problem that had always been the barrier to using coal. The Woods heated this sulphurous iron in pots with a flux such as lime, which eradicated the sulphur. They were able to use coal as fuel for this latter process without direct contact between fuel and metal. Thus the fundamental barrier to using fossil fuels in metallurgy had been overcome.[26] To the modern eye this innovation seems extremely simple but in fact had required a long learning process and experimentation with direct experience of smelting metals.

However, potting could not produce bar iron of the quality of the best charcoal-iron. This was only achieved with the introduction of Cort's "puddling" and "rolling" process developed by 1783–84. The molten iron was stirred in a reverberatory furnace so there was no direct contact between coal and iron. Puddling utilized the fact that wrought or bar iron melted at a higher temperature than the undesirable impurities, and thus the two can be separated out by deft work by the puddler stirring the molten mass and lifting out the lumps of metal left when the impurities melted (see figure 6.4). Introducing oxygen by stirring made the process far faster than potting.[27] Rolling then squeezed out the remaining dross, the function performed previously by hammers. Being a puddler was a horrendous ordeal where men had to stir the molten metal for long hours, making them "an aristocracy of the proletariat, proud, clannish and set apart by sweat and blood." Their lives were commensurately short.[28]

Chris Evans and Göran Rydén see puddling as being driven by an effort to break the labor power of the old forgemen and produce a more refined product that could match the best quality imports; it was a labor-saving

[25] Evans and Rydén, 2007, 251–2; Hyde, 1977, 32–41; King, 2005, 3, 24, 26; King, 2011. Indeed, where good coking coal was expensive, as in France, charcoal ironmaking survived much longer. Fohlen, 1973, 52.

[26] Evans and Rydén, 2007, 253–54, 259; Hyde, 1977, 53–61, 80–83; King, 2011; see also Pounds and Parker, 1957, 55–56.

[27] Hyde, 1977, 89; the advantages were such that it was cost-effective even though up to a fifth of the iron was lost to oxidation; Pounds and Parker, 1957, 74.

[28] Landes, 2003, 218; Paulinyi, 2005, 107–9.

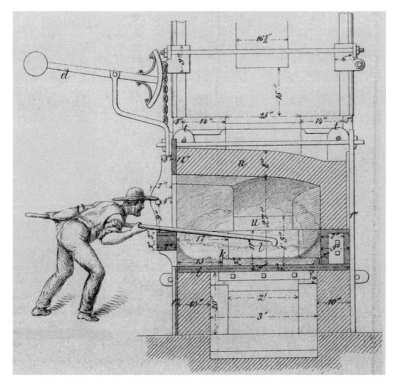

Figure 6.4. A puddling furnace. The puddler stirs the molten metal in the furnace, which is heated by a coal fire in an adjacent oven
Source: Kerpely, 1873.

innovation from the perspective of the firm, although it did not need a machine to achieve. But because this opened up the possibility of a great expansion of iron supply without pressing upon wood resources, it was equally land-saving.[29]

Because of its role in permitting the use of coke to produce quality iron, puddling has received the greatest attention in the literature. The replacement of hammer-works by rolling was a major contribution to the growth of the industry, and often like puddling was disseminated separately from the other components of the "British method" of iron production; it could be applied equally well to charcoal iron. Rolling allowed the rapid production of quality iron plate; the acceleration in production was as much as twentyfold over hammer-works. This opened up new possibilities for production, but only if blast furnaces and puddlers could keep up a high rate of

---

[29] Evans and Rydén, 2007, 260–5, 270.

Figure 6.5. Philip Jacques de Loutherbourg's *Coalbrookdale at Night* of 1801

supply.[30] In the long run these new techniques permitted a huge expansion of production fueled by coal. But as we have seen, this was not what was driving entrepreneurs. A more pressing concern was to economize on labor, and to improve the quality of the product to compete with imports from the Baltic.[31] The long success of Swedish iron-making was not just based on cheap firewood and water power, but on the high quality of the ore, which could only be mimicked in England by more extensive processing of the metal. The pressures of international competition, based on the relative success of the British "advanced organic economy," were also an important part of the story.

The core innovations that would underpin the first industrial revolution followed a remarkably similar chronology. Recognition of the theoretical virtues of steam power and coking coal were understood in the seventeenth century, when coal had already become the primary fuel of the nation, and triggered experimentation. However, economic application was not achieved until the years 1709–12, but in circumstances that allowed only

[30] Evans and Rydén, 2007, 260–5; Evans, 2005, 24.
[31] Before the development of coke-smelting, British iron production had stagnated, but a major part of the reason for the competitiveness of Baltic and Russian iron was its high quality rather than absolute limits to production in Britain. Evans et al., 2002.

limited diffusion of the new techniques. The second half of the eighteenth century would see the key further meso-innovations that allowed the wider dissemination of coked iron and rotative steam power. But even then, it took decades of subsequent tinkering, and declines in the real price of fossil fuels, before the inventions became generalized in the economy: not until the mid-nineteenth century for most of northern Europe. Nevertheless, in limited locales the stimulus to production was impressive. With the possibilities opened up by cheap, high-quality bar iron, demand for pig iron soared. A new age was dawning, lit from the glow and flare of the fires of iron furnaces and foundries portrayed so vividly in Philip Jacques de Loutherbourg's *Coalbrookdale at Night* of 1801 (figure 6.5).

2. THE GROWTH DYNAMICS OF THE COAL DEVELOPMENT BLOCK

IRON AND COAL: MARKET WIDENING AND MARKET SUCTION

The engineer and railway pioneer George Stephenson had no doubt about what constituted the core of Britain's industrial success. "The strength of Britain lies in her iron and coal beds," he proclaimed. "The Lord Chancellor now sits upon a bag of wool; but wool has long since ceased to be emblematical of the staple commodity of England. He ought rather to sit upon a bag of coal."[32] Between the 1780s and the 1840s coal and iron became increasingly intertwined in establishing the key development block of the first industrial revolution. This section will examine how the initial macro-inventions that opened the possibility of a wide application of coal as a source of heat and power were gradually built into an economically dominant block through a continual series of further developments.

Innovations in metal-smelting made iron radically cheaper in the long run, but this change only made sense with two conditions: buoyant demand for metals, and the elastic supply of coal. Cheap metals made all sorts of capital equipment, including steam engines, an affordable prospect. Cheap coal allowed one to run them. We call this expansion of demand driven by the lower costs of iron *market widening*. There was a widening of markets for steam engines as they became cheaper, which in turn had to do with cheap metals, as illustrated in figure 6.6. But both innovation in iron, and the steam engine, increased the demand for coal. Here we also see a process of *market suction*, where the core innovations in steam engines and in iron smelting generated a demand for the complementary resource. If the supply of the complementary goods or materials is not elastic enough, market

[32] Jevons, 1866, 66.

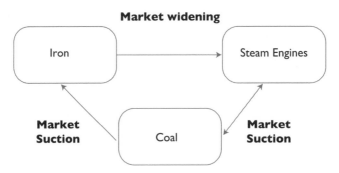

Figure 6.6. The early coal development block

suction will generate price increases, eventually raising the price of the new good and dampening down market widening. The use of a steam engine was still only profitable where coal was extremely cheap. Hence, for many decades, almost the only application of steam power was in coal mines themselves, to provide drainage to reach deeper seams of minerals.[33]

The transportation of coal away from coalfields was still dependent on the "organic economy" of horses and humans, and in fact was only a realistic proposition over any distance when water or wind could be employed along canals, rivers, and relatively short distances over the sea. The price trend in coal was still upward, although to a lesser extent than "organic" fuels.

It was the combination of cheap metal, coal, and steam power in the form of the railway and steamship that made the industrial revolution a general phenomenon, linking centers of raw material supply, production, and consumption. Cheap transport offered the possibility of employing engines for power at sites more distant than the pithead itself. Modern transport technology represented a dramatic market widening, as this innovation cheapened the supply of all three essential elements of the block to a wider market: iron, coal, and engines. This obviated the cost pressures that might have been generated by market suction within the development block (see figure 6.7). In a sense, it was the block that made its own success possible.

The innovation of coke iron led to an explosion in iron production. In the middle of the eighteenth century, total pig iron production in Britain was around 35,000 tons per year. A century later it was 2.25 million tons, around sixty-five times higher. Bar iron production had leapt from about 18,000 tons per annum to two hundred thousand tons.[34] What was just as astonishing was that this great leap forward was accomplished with no pressures on price. Indeed, quite the opposite. Pig iron had cost around

[33] Nuvolari et al., 2006; Jevons, 1866, 61; Rolt and Allen, 1977, 27.
[34] Landes, 2003, 194.

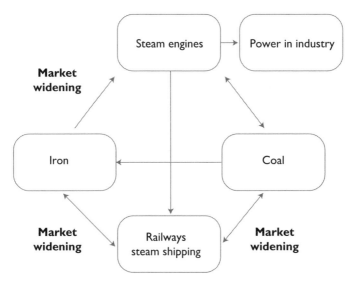

Figure 6.7. The mature coal development block

£6.40 per ton in the 1750s. By the late 1780s charcoal iron generally cost £7–8/ton, but potted pig iron was £5 or less, pushing the former into tiny niche markets. Prices were approaching £3/ton by 1830 and were below this level into the late nineteenth century. Bar iron showed equivalent falls.[35] As coke iron working took off in Germany, the price of pig fell to a similar degree from an average of over 90 marks per tonne in the 1850s to around 48 marks per tonne in the 1880s and 1890s.[36] Per capita consumption of iron in Germany rose tenfold in 1833–74.[37] The cheapening of metals had dramatic impacts across the whole spectrum of life. In the kitchen, it could be observed in England by 1830 that iron stoves and ranges were "within the means of the poorest persons. To find a dwelling, however small, without an oven beside the fire, would be an exceedingly novel occurrence now-a-days." Iron stoves absorbed much heat and were quite inefficient: but both they, and coal, were cheap.[38]

Despite the fact that continental emulators could simply take up techniques already established in Britain, a range of factors delayed this process. The advance of coke-smelting, puddling, and rolling also required the movement of workers who were practiced in the techniques, initially from

[35] Hyde, 1977, 88, 102–6, 138–39. On price relative to other sectors see Crafts, 1985, 25.

[36] German prices are from Feldenkirchen for the Ruhr until 1870, and thereafter use Krengel's national series. Feldenkirchen, 1982, tables 6, 8, 49a; Krengel, 1983, 75; see also Flegel and Turnow, 1915, 468.

[37] Milward and Saul, 1977, 407.

[38] Fouquet, 2008, 82.

Britain, but later from Belgium, France, and Germany once the skills had been mastered. New techniques required not just a new fuel, but new furnace designs, something initially not appreciated on the continent. War and unrest proved a barrier, whether the revolutionary and Napoleonic wars at the start of the century or in Spain the Carlist wars of the 1830s and 1870s. Tariffs also determined market development. The German iron industry only began to invest heavily in coke-smelting once the preferential treatment Belgians received in Prussia was abolished in 1854, coincidentally the same year that the deep seams of coking coal in the Ruhr were first opened up.[39] British products had become so cheap that it created a disincentive to compete. In the 1830s and 1840s it remained cheaper in the Ruhr to obtain pig iron from Britain than from the Siegerland, a mere 50km distant.[40] Britain enjoyed an extraordinary advantage in the proximity of its iron ores and coal seams. In Britain, iron production consumed 12 percent of coal output in 1800, rising to peak at nearly 30 percent in the 1870s.[41] In other regions charcoal iron persisted where distance effectively protected its local markets.

Market suction on supplies of coal thus meant that iron-smelting techniques and engine efficiency had to be raised to become more generally affordable, while competitive pressures within the expanding industry encouraged cost-cutting. Simple "learning by doing" with the new processes brought great economies in fuel. In South Wales a ton of pig had consumed 8 tons of coal in 1791, but this was down to 3.5 by 1830. Scale grew in terms of both size of enterprise and the furnaces employed. Hearths grew from no more than 20 m^3 for the most part in the 1770s, to 3–400 m^3 by 1900.[42] Such advances in scale would not have been possible without the use of steam engines. Much larger furnaces and the vertical integration of furnaces, puddling, rolling, and slitting mills on single sites required new sources of power, not only to drive the mills but to provide hoists for the great weight of fuel and ore being moved around.[43] This rise in capacity was matched by new techniques, notably the "hot blast" invented by the Scotsman Neilson in 1828. The hot blast yielded major fuel savings, of up to a third with coke and as much as two-thirds with coal. It was adopted with

[39] Banken, 2005, 62; Milward and Saul, 1977, 408–9; Kleinschmidt, 2007, 8; Paulinyi, 2005, 102–3; Fernández de Pinedo and Ayo, 2005, 156, 166; Belhoste and Woronoff, 2005, 76–86; Fremdling, 2002, 365, 370–71; Pounds and Parker, 1957, 42–44, 73, 108–9. Tariff barriers presented a barrier to capital as well as products. For example, the lifting of Russia's tariffs on capital investment in Poland led to a rush of German investment that was key for domestic industry when the state-owned industries were restricted by fiscal weakness after the Crimean war. Pustufa, 1992, 263–65.

[40] Henning, 1996, 187.

[41] Church, 1986; nearly half of steam power in France was concentrated in the metallurgical and mining sectors in 1852. Fohlen, 1973, 49.

[42] Fouquet, 2008, 66; Pounds and Parker, 1957, 123.

[43] Hyde, 1977, 109, 119–23.

alacrity where fuel cost pressures were greatest, allowing Scottish pig production to rise by a factor of nearly thirty in the next three decades. The hot
blast technique came to dominate French production too, where particular
expertise also developed in reusing waste gases in furnaces to economize
on fuel—a technique that also allowed charcoal-smelting to survive a little
longer.[44]

By mid-century constraints were being overcome. Belgium was dominated
by coke iron by the late 1830s, which also had won a majority share of production in France and Germany by the mid-1850s. Coal furnaces reached
Silesia in the 1830s, the Saar in 1840, the Rhineland in 1845, and Ruhr in
1849. In these cases the switch was dramatic, with coke pig iron establishing dominance of a rapidly expanding market within a couple of decades.
Coke-smelting reached Spain in 1847, but the local market was small, and
largely agricultural, demanding very pure iron to be worked in smithies of a
quality that even the best coke-smelters could not produce.[45] Isolated pockets of charcoal iron–making persisted until the 1890s, but in essence on a
continental scale the transition was over by the 1860s. Exceptions were the
Austro-Hungarian lands, where after a first coke-blast furnace in Czechia
in the 1830s, dissemination of new technology remained slow with limited
markets, the need to import foreign experts, and expensive fuel. Here the
charcoal iron industry proved dynamic, producing several hundred thousands tons of pig iron by the middle of the century and not being overtaken
until the 1880s. Nevertheless, the Austrian monarchy had to import pig iron
to keep up with demand. Sweden's high-quality industry grew too. Both
Sweden and the Austrian monarchy relied on the introduction of puddling
and rolling in the context of traditional fuels, but output was dwarfed by
growth in the coal users. But charcoal-smelters did not remotely have the
capacity for expansion that would have allowed a leap in per capita consumption of iron.[46] In a century when the population of Western Europe
doubled, iron production had risen twentyfold.

Cheaper metal meant cheaper capital equipment: as we call it, market
widening. "Without it the engine, the spinning-jenny, the power-loom, the
gas and water-pipe, the iron vessel, the bridge, the railway . . . would be
impracticable from the want and cost of material."[47] Although Crompton's
mule had begun life constructed from wood, by the 1790s it was being made
from increasingly cheap cast iron.[48] Even as steam engines became better
engineered and more sophisticated, the cost per unit of power decreased,

---

[44] Fremdling, 2005, 40; 2004, 166; Hyde, 1977, 146–54.

[45] Mitchell, 1988; Dhondt and Bruwier, 1973, 343, 346; Landes, 2003, 177–9; Fremdling,
2005, 159–62; Banken, 2005; Crouzet, 1996, 49; Fohlen, 1973, 56; Broadberry et al., 2010,
185; Fernández de Pinedo and Ayo, 2005, 163, 170.

[46] Paulinyi, 2005, 96, 101; Rýden, 2005; Brose, 1983, 154; Gross, 1973, 267–71.

[47] Jevons, 1866, 135.

[48] Milward and Saul, 1977, 189.

TABLE 6.1

Average Annual Cast Iron production, 1830–1905 (1,000 tons)

	Great Britain	France	Germany	Belgium	Western Europe (F + G + B)	W. Europe as percent of GB	USA
1830	688	266	110	90	466	68	168
1855–59	4,980	900	1,099	312	1,696	57	727
1880–84	8,395	1,918	2,892	699	5,509	66	4,327
1900–04	8,778	2,664	7,925	1,388	11,659	133	16,662
1910–14	9,647	4,278	14,360	2,028	20,666	214	25,429

Source: Mitchell, 1988.

by more than two-thirds between 1760 and 1800, and then halved again by 1870 (although this did depend on the efficiency with which machines were utilized, which might be well below the standards of best practice).[49]

Industrialization in these "modern" sectors tended to come in spurts when the overcoming of cost barriers allowed supply across the whole development block to surge forward. Growth was then explosive, but usually still highly localized. After the deep seams of coal intermixed with iron ore could be accessed in the Ruhr, coal extraction rose at vertiginous pace from under 2 million tons in 1850 to nearly 12 million tons by 1869.[50] Iron production surged from 5,000 tons in 1852 to 227,000 tons by 1860.[51] By 1906, around a third of coal production in the Ruhr, which itself accounted for half of German production, was used as fuel in the iron and steel industry.[52] German industry had begun to erode Britain's market share, and was the continental leader in iron and steel by the end of the century. The United States had become the world's largest pig (cast) iron producer by the first half of the 1890s. In all cases coke iron was essential to this dramatic expansion.[53]

STEEL

The most desirable refinement of iron was steel, whose great strength and tensile properties were a result of its carbon content, falling midway between the high levels in pig iron (which made it hard but very brittle), and the very

[49] Crafts, 2003, table 4.
[50] Holtfrerich, 1973, table 1.
[51] Feldenkirchen, 1982, 27–32.
[52] Feldenkirchen, 1982, table 33; Holtfrerich, 1973, table 29.
[53] Broadberry, 1997, 166.

low levels in bar or wrought iron (which made it workable and ductile but prone to wear and tear). Steel was thus tough but relatively malleable. It had been made for many centuries by traditional techniques, and such was the difficulty of getting the refined product's qualities right—it could only be done with close attention of a master craftsman—it was virtually impossible to produce a standard product. Production was cheapened by the introduction of puddling, but steel remained very expensive compared to wrought iron.[54] A series of innovations between the 1850s and 1870s changed this situation.

The first major change was the introduction of the "Bessemer" process in 1856, which blew air through the molten pig iron instead of using laborious puddling to induce oxidization. It reduced the amount of time required to separate out steel at least seventyfold, and was hence massively labor-saving, but required very high quality ore with a low phosphorous content to work. The Siemens-Martin process, which was developed in its final form by 1864, used a super-heated furnace to greatly reduce the fuel consumption and added scrap iron to the mix to assist carbonization. From 1879, "basic steel" made using the Thomas-Gilchrist process, an adaptation of the Bessemer process that allowed commoner ores with a higher phosphorous content to be used, spread throughout the continent and changed the geography of iron production. Steelmaking costs dropped 90 percent between the 1860s and 1900, while supplying a better-quality, more consistent product. Production exploded, rising at a staggering rate of 10.8 percent per year in Western Europe between 1861 and 1913, or from 125,000 tons to 32 million tons. In the late 1880s and early 1890s, steel replaced wrought iron in many uses, providing cheaper and more durable machines, ships, and buildings.[55]

EFFICIENCY

We have seen in the case of metals how improvements in the energy efficiency of key processes massively increased production. Put another way, there was a high elasticity of supply and demand of metals in relation to the cost of the production processes and the price of the final product. Small decreases in costs could provide bigger benefits in consumption; but in fact, the cost decreases were also big. This is an example of what we call "rebound," where efficiency improvements have startling effects in increasing demand, and the biggest effects of all in areas where the cost of energy is a high proportion of total costs. This particular characteristic was striking to

[54] Landes, 2003, 251–53.
[55] Landes, 2003, 255–68; Milward and Saul, 1977, 199–203; Borchardt, 1973, 135; see also the essays in Evans and Rydén, 2005; Pounds and Parker, 1957, 116–23.

an author like Stanley Jevons in the 1860s and led to the conception of his "paradox."[56] After the initial macro-innovations that permitted the use of fossil fuel to produce motion and smelt metals, the key meso-inventions that followed usually involved large improvements in efficiency.

A crucial breakthrough was the high pressure engine. The initial advantage of using high pressure was that engines produced power with much smaller boilers and cylinders. This opened up new applications to steam power, most importantly in the transport sector, where steam-power vehicles and ships obviously required light, compact engines. But it also soon became apparent that high pressure engines could be run with greater fuel economy, and a reduction of fuel costs encouraged further dissemination of their use. Indeed, fuel economies and a wider fall in the retail price of coal went hand-in-hand, as the successful use of high pressure facilitated those key advances in transportation.

Effective high pressure steam engines were developed independently in the years around 1800 by the American Oliver Evans, who used one to power a dredger, and the Englishman Richard Trevithick, who swiftly moved to apply the technique to vehicles. The most important center of innovation was the tin and copper mines of Cornwall in south-west England, where the desire for drainage of deeper shafts and tunnels was combined with high fuel costs in an area relatively remote from coalfields. This created the kind of bottleneck well-suited to innovative efforts and a willingness of mine owners to invest and experiment.

This has led to the argument that increased use of the steam engine was not because of the relatively low costs of the new technology relative to more labor-intensive processes, but came from efficiency gains that were actually a response to *expensive* fuel. This is to mistake the cost dynamics of a particular industry for the general process. The more important and greater context was cheap coal, and in European terms, the mines of Cornwall still lay very close to the coalfields of South Wales. But once in harness, the engines became a significant aspect of mining costs; steam engine efficiency could be improved, while little could change the productivity of the miners themselves. This explains the context in which the high pressure "Cornish engine" was developed. By 1812 the first classic "Cornish engine," the model high pressure engine for many years, was in operation at the Wheal Prosper mine.[57] The smaller coal reserves and large distances French industry and railways encountered led to drives for fuel economy. As early as 1830, 63 percent of French engines were high pressure.[58]

The development of high pressure steam was part of a drawn-out advance in steam engine efficiency. As process refinement and micro-invention

---

[56] Jevons, 1866.
[57] Hills, 1989, 101–4; Mokyr, 1990, 88.
[58] Crouzet, 1996, 41; Milward and Saul, 1977, 173, 207.

continued over the nineteenth century, engines worked at higher speeds and with better fuel economy. Innovations such as the Corliss "compound" engine in the 1860s and wrought iron boilers in the 1880s, and the Swiss *ventilmaschine* of the 1850s allowed even higher pressures.[59] Quite simple measures such as lagging engines properly gave fuel savings of up to a tenth. New lubricants, including petroleum, allowed superheating of steam and higher pressures without unwanted chemical reactions that damaged the engines. By the end of the century, boilers of steel plate produced by the Bessemer process were needed to withstand the incredible workloads.[60]

Table 6.2 indicates the general progress in the efficiency of steam engines in Britain, which along with the United States remained the center of innovation in power technology. The Watt engine used less than half the coal of the (improved) Newcomen, while high pressure engines came to use only about a third of the Watt engine. The greatest advances came in the middle and latter parts of the nineteenth century. By the 1850s, the best high pressure engines used one-fifteenth of the coal of the early eighteenth-century models, and had very considerably greater power. However, we must remember that technical data often relate to best practice. There was enormous variation in engine efficiency, partly related to the amount of time they were run, and the uses to which they were put. Thus the incentives to adopt steam power could vary from industry to industry and even within factories, depending on the task. What is clear, however, is the move toward very much greater *possible* efficiencies over time.[61]

It was only in the late nineteenth century that steam engines reached the efficiency levels of biological converters such as draft animals (10–15 percent).[62] They lagged far behind the achievements in waterwheels or domestic stoves. We see again how the qualitative and quantitative changes brought about by the new development block were intimately linked. The efficiency with which power could be utilized was no better in the new economy than the old; indeed, it was significantly lower than the best, but geographically restricted possibility of waterwheels. But the sheer amount of coal that could be affordably used at the same level of efficiency allowed total energy consumption to be much greater. At the same time, steam engines concentrated power in a way other converters could not achieve; and this, after all, was the reason they were invented in the first place.

---

[59] Hills, 1989, 182–5, 220–1; Milward and Saul, 1977, 208.

[60] Hills, 1989, 225, 236–40, 253–54.

[61] Hills reckons that the most common high pressure engines still used 18 lb coal per horsepower per hour in the 1840s. The average consumption of coal by engines recorded in a major British parliamentary survey in 1870 was 11.8 lb per hour, indicated and 16.8 lb, nominal, the difference depending on where on the engine one takes the measure of power. Crafts, 2003; Hills, 1989, 119; British Parliamentary Papers, 1871, appendix E, 160–201.

[62] See part I.

TABLE 6.2
Estimates of steam engine efficiency in Britain, 1700–1900

	Engine	lb coal per hour per hp	Efficiency (percent)
1700	Savery	31	0.7
1760s	Newcomen	30	0.7
1768	Watt	8.8	2.3
1780s	Watt	12.5	1.6
1804	Evans	6.7	3.0
1804	Woolf	4.5	4.5
1839	Estimate by Wicksted, cotton industry	12	1.7
1840	Estimate by Armstrong, Lancashire	13.5–14	1.5
1845	Estimate Kane, Irish factories	10–12	1.7–2.0
c. 1850	High pressure	5	4.0
1850s	Elder compound	2.25	9.0
1871	Royal commission report (indicated power)	11.8	1.7
1890s	Best compound engines	1.5	13.5
c. 1900	Very high pressure	2	10.1

Sources: Hills, 1989; Crafts, 2003, BPP, 1871, 160–201; von Tunzelmann, 1978, 68–70; Kanefsky, 1979, 172–73.

POWER

The effect of these innovations was to bring the cost of power tumbling down, and make a power economy based on fossil fuels the primary underpinning of industrial growth. Gains in energy efficiency from Newcomen to the engines of the 1850s offered a 75 percent cut in fuel costs, other things being equal. But other things were not equal. Over the long run, the capital costs of engines fell, possibly by as much as 75 percent in *current* prices between 1830 and 1910, and much more in real terms.[63]

---

[63] There were generally economies of scale in engine-building, although not necessarily in the accompanying housing and boiler costs. The information we have remains scattered, and we have no clear picture on the kind of engines being used across economies. It is equally clear that engine performance was extremely variable, so these results can only be indicative. The information, largely drawn from von Tunzelmann and Kanefsky, is of far too limited value to

There remained many disincentives to the employment of steam engines. Engines took time to construct, with no guarantee of success: many early engines did not function well and disappointed their new owners. The erection of an engine could take 7–12 months, tying up capital and putting the brakes on the process of production. The first steam engine was imported to Portugal to assist with mine drainage in 1804; but it proved too expensive to hire an engineer to erect it![64] Engines frequently broke down. Where there were few manufacturers available, and when expertise in the necessary engineering skills was hard to come by, this represented a major barrier to use. Even late in the nineteenth century much of the demand for industrial and engineering skills and inputs came from the *maintenance*, not the *erection*, of steam engines. Before the infrastructure was in place to provide this, it made little sense to invest in capital that could be rendered useless within a short time, and that was considered unreliable.[65]

The revolution in steam power in industry did not really begin until the middle decades of the nineteenth century. Around 1800, the capacity of stationary engines in Britain was probably no more than 30,000 hp, and concentrations of power were still far greater in mining than in the industrializing cities. The utilized capacity of water power was probably twice as great at this point in time, and from horses much greater still, possibly as much as half a million horsepower. By 1840, stationary steam engines in the United Kingdom supplied around 200,000 hp, nearly twice as much as water. Combined with the power of the rapidly expanding numbers of locomotives, total steam power probably rivaled draft animal power by this point, and easily surpassed water and animal power combined during this decade. By 1870, stationary steam engines supplied over 2 million hp, and this total exceeded 9 million hp by 1900.[66]

Britain's industrial power was far ahead of any of its rivals in the 1870s. It was not just the "workshop of the world." It was the powerhouse of the world too. Although steam engines were widely distributed across northwest Europe from the late eighteenth century, especially in draining mines as in England, their total capacity remained low until after 1850. The rise of the coal-iron-steam development block and decreases in coal prices from this point rapidly expanded the industrial use of steam power (see table 6.3).[67] In Scandinavia and Mediterranean Europe, stationary steam engines remained of very little importance until the end of nineteenth century.[68]

---

make detailed calculations of general productivity or to be applied to national accounts. Cf. Crafts, 2003, 19–20; 2004; von Tunzelmann, 1978, 50, 54–55, 74. Cf. Allen, 2009, 174–75.

[64] Henriques, 2011, 146.

[65] Von Tunzelmann, 1978, 62.

[66] Warde, 2007, 74–75; Musson, 1976; 1978, 166–70. Kanefsky, 1979, 333, 341.

[67] Kleinschmidt, 2007, 6; Milward and Saul, 1977, 186, 401.

[68] On the negligible amount of steam power in the Balkans, see Berov, 1996.

TABLE 6.3

Stationary steam power availability in Europe and United States
in 1840 and 1870 (hp per 1000 people)

	c. 1840	c. 1870
Britain	10.5	81.7
France	1.6	15.5
Prussia	0.4	15.9
Belgium	6.1	34.5
Sweden	0.3	1.8
Czechia	0.1	7.5
USA	2.3	37.1

Sources: Allen, 2009, 179; Warde, 2007, 75; Landes, 1969, 221;
Kander, 2002; Myška, 1996, 255. The population of Czechia is assumed
to be 70 percent of that supplied by Maddison for Czechoslovakia.

Traditional sources could not compensate for lack of coal-fired engines
(see table 6.4). By 1911, steam supplied 51 percent and water, only 28 percent of power capacity in Italian industry, even though Italy had very little
steam power compared to north-west Europe. In Portugal, three-quarters of
stationary power still came from water and wind in 1890, but this put it at
a per capita level far behind any major coal consumer.[69] Seasonal variation
in water flow was a widespread problem.[70] An exception in contribution
water power could make was Sweden. In the last decade of the nineteenth
century, 39 hp of water power per 1,000 people compared favorably with
the use of steam in some of the more industrial nations around 1870.[71]
Across the Atlantic, New England retained a predominance of water power
until around 1890.

But there can be little doubt that, taking Europe as a whole in aggregate
terms, steam engines were far more important for stationary power by the
closing decade of the century. If we include power sources used for transport, this view does not change. The total power exerted by draft animals
was generally much higher than that provided by water and windmills (see
table 6.5). But in many countries, the power provided by locomotives was
very much greater than that employed by stationary engines. "Modern,"
that is coal-fired sources of power overtook "traditional" sources of power

[69] The Italian figure excludes hydroelectricity: Malanima, 2006a, 61; Henriques, 2009, 62.
[70] Henriques, 2011; Pounds and Parker, 1957, 21.
[71] Kander, 2002, 49–50, 202.

High Pressure and Increased Power from Steam

New high-pressure steam engines used steam expansively, that is, power was generated not just by the process of condensing steam to produce a vacuum and move a piston, but through the force of expanding steam that had been heated to a very high degree in a confined space, acting on the other end of the piston. They could provide high levels of power quickly once set in motion, and predominated where machinery needed a great degree of power and traction (or "torque") as soon as it began to operate, as with locomotives or mine winding gear. This is an important consideration in assessing the impact of steam power because animal or water power could not have provided this level of concentration and torque to run the heavy shafting that transmitted power to the machinery. Higher levels of power could not immediately be utilized in industry, however. Poor shafting was a major problem gradually overcome through use of new wrought iron equipment. The idea of a "compound" engine, although decades old, first took off after the model invented by the Scot John McNaught, placing pistons at each end of a beam, thus greatly reducing the inertia present when a piston worked a heavy beam up and down at just one end. Compound engines worked by re-using the expansive power of steam in two or more cylinders, thoroughly exhausting its potential, rather than the single cylinder of traditional engines. By the mid-nineteenth century, above all thanks to the work of Nicolas Carnot in the 1820s (who was directly concerned with issues of steam engine efficiency), the theory of heat was much better understood. This made it apparent that engines still wasted most of the fuel they employed. Motion was generated by the heat gradient within the engine, but the gradient that most engines employed was simply between the temperature of steam under pressure (160 degrees Celsius at six atmospheres pressure) and the temperature of condensation into water (which was generally complete when the temperature reached 40 degrees Celsius). But in order to combust the coal required to produce the steam, temperatures well over 1000° C were used, and most of this heat was wasted. This loss could be reduced by redesigning boilers, and by "compounding," which increasingly employed the expansive power of the high-pressure steam itself to produce motion. Doing so required a complex and tightly engineered series of regulated valves and governors to open and close the valves, a key issue for micro-invention that preoccupied engineers at this time.

TABLE 6.4
Water power availability in selected countries (hp per 1,000 people)

England and Wales c. 1800	6
England and Wales c. 1840	7.1
England and Wales 1907	3.4
France 1845	4.2
Sweden 1890	c.40
Italy 1881	15.2
Italy 1911	7.2
Portugal 1890	5.2

Note: Italian figures exclude hydropower.
Sources: For England and Wales, Warde, 2007; France calculated from Fohlen, 1973, 48, with data originally from Clapham, 1948; for Sweden, Kander, 2002, 49–50; for Italy in 1881, calculated from Poni and Mori, 1996, 168; for 1911, Malanima, 2006a, 61; for Portugal, Henriques, 2009, 62.

(the sum of wind, water, and draft animals) during the 1840s in Britain, in the 1860s in Germany, and 1890s in Italy and Sweden.[72]

In addition to the brute quantities of power, we must also consider the capacity to concentrate it. Despite considerable advances in the size of draft animals, the power they could apply remained largely unchanged; less than 1 hp for any but the briefest moments. Waterwheel technology made impressive advances making use of iron construction; the largest wheels could develop as much as 2–300 hp by the mid-nineteenth century, but the sites where they could be used were restricted. No more than 5–7 hp was the norm. By the 1830s, average mill steam engines in England delivered 48 hp, and by the end of the century engines of several 100 hp had become common. The huge demands for drainage in mines could cause exceptional concentrations of power, with exceptional engines of up to 5,000 hp.[73]

Demand for coal was considerably increased by steam engines. Kanefsky has estimated that by 1870, 30 percent of British coal fed steam engines.[74] This share was relatively low, because of the huge size of the metallurgical sector, and the heavy household use of coal. In Sweden the share of steam

[72] See note to table 6.5 on draft animal power, Collins, 1999.

[73] Reynolds, 1983, 174–77, 280–86, 290–93, 319; Hills, 1989, 116, 217; Church, 1986, 316, 318.

[74] Church, 1986, 28. Tunzelmann estimated that stationary engines consumed 10 percent of British coal output in 1800 and possibly 17 percent by 1856. Von Tunzelmann, 1978, 111–15.

TABLE 6.5
Power availability in selected countries, c. 1880 (hp) (in 1000s)

	Steam	Waterwheels and windmills	Draft Animals
Britain	7,600	240	1,250
Germany	5,120	420	2,425
Italy	500	440	1,260
Sweden	220	c. 200	324

Note: These estimates are based on horse and oxen numbers, with horses providing an effective average horsepower of 0.6 and oxen 0.4; and data on watermills which often was only accurately recorded a little after these dates (1882 in Germany and 1911 in Sweden) but where capacity cannot have been very much different, and almost certainly not larger, in the previous decade. British water power estimates relate to 1870. All estimates must be considered indicative rather than exact.

Sources: Landes, 2003, 221; Kanefsky, 1979, 338; SDR; Kander, 2002, 48–50; Kander and Warde, 2011; Kander and Warde, 2009.

engine consumption was around 55 percent, the greater part by railways, and 8–10 percent each in industrial and agricultural machinery.[75] Given the capacity of German steam power, if the efficiency and use of their engines was roughly equivalent to those in Britain at the time, possibly nearly as much as 70 percent of German coal output was consumed by steam engines (including railways).[76] This share would later decline with the rise to dominance of the German metals and other heat-intensive industries. Nevertheless the wider use of coal was very clearly linked to demand for steam power.

PEOPLE POWER

The most dramatic advances in technology of the industrial revolution related to production and transportation. These delivered more and better quality consumer goods to people, and for a minority of the workforce, saw them shift into new factory environments. Even in Britain, wages did not start to rise until the 1820s, and in the industrial cities, living conditions

[75] Kander, 2002, 196–203.

[76] British engines appear to have consumed around 7.4 tons per hp per year by Kanefsky's estimate. On this basis Germany's 2.48 million hp at this date would have consumed approximately 18.4 million tonnes of coal, from a total supply of 26.4 million tonnes. Assuming the efficiency of engines subsequently improved, this would have dropped. Had it not, the proportion would be very similar in 1896.

were often grim, with life expectancy initially falling and only slowly rising thereafter.[77] As we have seen, while by the end of the nineteenth century dietary conditions had improved for much of the population, calories were by no means plentiful. Unprecedented in human history as it may have been, the onset of industrialization may not have led to many feeling greatly empowered; however, it did not yet radically alter the daily round of activity for most people.

Yet there were also changes in working conditions and possibilities of consumption. Many such changes were not directly connected to the new energy regime, such as the sewing machine or the tin can, although in the great majority of cases, they were made out of metal.[78] In some cases what could be produced was not new, but could be done more cheaply, and with increased demand, on a far greater scale. Steam printing was brought to England by the German entrepreneur Friedrich Koenig and from 1814 was producing *The Times* of London. But it was the emergence of cylinder-based printing that would lead to massive increases in the speed of production. The consequent expansion in the output of information was not driven by a fall in price, so much as the basic physical limits of the previous regime. Hand presses could deliver 250–300 impressions per hour. The earliest steam printers increased output tenfold, but by 1904, Hoe web-rotary printers could deliver 1,760,000 impressions per hour! Previously, a large daily press was impossible because publishers simply could not physically deliver in time to a mass market. Delivering a greater output of information via this huge expansion in productive possibilities was assisted by machinery that did not yet require any more than human power, the typewriter, and the linotype machine.[79] In one very important case, the enhanced spread of information at this time looked to an energy regime of the future: the development of the telegraph working by electricity, used for local and eventually international communication (see chapter 9).[80] The possibility of maintaining family contacts from afar, and gathering up-to-date information on events, was expanding rapidly.

The emergence of a development block also handed power to those able to exercise influence in key sectors of the economy; most obviously the class of capitalists who owned the productive capacity of the new society, but also the workforces of key sections of the infrastructure, such as railwaymen, miners, or engineers.[81] However, the overall development of a

[77] See Griffin, 2010, 144–61; Szreter and Mooney, 1998.

[78] Mokyr, 1990, 140, 142.

[79] In Britain, the main decline in price was initially caused by the repeal of the stamp act on paper. Later, as circulation rapidly expanded, the declining price of paper due to the use of wood pulp became more significant in keeping the press affordable. Lee, 1976, 54–63; Coleman, 1958, 212–22; Griffin, 2010, 94.

[80] Mokyr, 1990, 122–23, 144–45.

[81] Mitchell, 2011, 21.

modern society, concentrating the workforce and increasing urbanization, had a rather greater influence on the emerging labor movement than any particular sector. Miners were famously militant, and engaged in at times protracted, bitter, and violent disputes with employers. Metalworkers and miners emerged as leading groups in obtaining concessions from employers and governments at certain moments, such as the great German strike wave of 1889.[82] Nevertheless, most disputes ended in failure for the workers, and what is equally notable is the continuing, or even increasing militancy and organization in artisanal trades. As Shorter and Tilly have written, "every new stratum of workers which economic modernization tosses to the surface will sooner or later demand participation in the nation's political life," and the new occupational groups of the industrial revolution, and new concentrations of old trades, were no exception to this rule.[83]

Heat: Comforts and Cooking

For all the expansion of production, domestic use remained a highly important consumer of coal. Predictably it was high where coal was cheap close to source, as in much of Britain, or in the vicinity of port cities where other fuels were more expensive, as was the case in Holland, and northern cities like Copenhagen, Stockholm, and Gothenburg. In 1830, domestic consumption still accounted for 38 percent of all coal burned in Britain. By 1870, the share in Britain had fallen to 20 percent at most, and only a little over 10 percent by 1900. In Sweden and the Netherlands, domestic households and businesses used around half of coal burned in the middle of the century, a proportion that only slowly declined.[84]

Part of the relative decline came from efficiency improvements in the home, both in coal and wood-burning. These continued efforts to economize on fuel that we have seen during the eighteenth century, but as new stoves could be comparatively expensive, it was more important either to obtain a cheaper fuel, or enjoy the benefits of a higher income from growth. Changes in cooking and heating equipment also created demand for different types ✔ of coal. Despite containing many other gases and thus giving out an unpleasant smell, bituminous coal was easy to light and popular as a household fuel, reducing handling costs and giving a more cheerful flame. Higher quality anthracite coals that were in demand for steamships and locomotives found it difficult to penetrate the domestic market. In the Netherlands, for example, domestic consumers long preferred the coals of Newcastle to

[82] On metalworkers, see in particular the essays in Haimson and Tilly, 1989; Shorter and Tilly, 1974, 201; on coalminers, Koch, 1954; Reichard, 1991; Church and Outram, 1998; Andrews, 2008.
[83] Shorter and Tilly, 1974, 347–50.
[84] Gales, 2004, 29; Kander, 2002, 202; Church, 1986.

the hard coals of the Limburg coal fields for this reason, which led one politician to speculate that lack of demand for locally mined coal was a consequence of the laziness of maidservants. Alternative fuels like small coals and grit that were formed into balls (as forerunners of briquettes) were also considered time-consuming to handle. But with better stoves, anthracite became the gold standard for domestic fuel in the twentieth century.[85]

From the 1820s, the iron stove and range began to diffuse more rapidly throughout north-west Europe. Again, linkages in the development block were essential because the process was enabled by cheap iron. By the 1890s the stove was almost universal in the Netherlands; the cooking range spread more slowly, and after 1860 faced competition from oil and gas cookers.[86] In Sweden the Cronstedt stove, in fact an invention of the 1760s, reached a thermal efficiency of 50 percent in contrast to more usual stove efficiencies of 10 percent. Its slow diffusion in the country across the nineteenth century reduced demand for heating, which in that case was largely based on firewood.[87] Domestic heating and cooking were assisted greatly by the invention of the friction match in the 1820s, doubtless to the delight of maidservants.

It has long been a source of debate as to why some nations were disinclined to adopt the tile stove and use its more efficient convective heat. In part it seems some places were simply not cold enough to consider the investment worthwhile: the tile stove belongs to the regions of "continental climate" with long, chilly winters. In much of Western Europe there was a clear preference for the cheeriness of the open fire, which also gave light, and provided a draft. Medical opinion insisted on the desirability of ventilation long into the twentieth century, bolstered by the opinion of some that lasted decades as to the dangers of inhaling "re-breathed air," and later based on a more vague sense that fresh air was a good thing.[88] A more simple reason was doubtless that where fuel was cheap, a stove was not considered a worthwhile investment, despite the preoccupation of governments and great minds with the issue.[89] There were also improvements in the efficiency of the traditional open hearth, yet again assisted by cheap iron in redesigning the grate and firewall to radiate heat back into the room.

Efficiency improvements also had "rebound effects," however. Stoves that were easier to light and stoke, and that burned less fuel, created the incentive to heat more rooms, extend the heating period, and to cook more frequently (as did the increasing preference for hot drinks like tea and coffee). For the well-to-do a great shift in lifestyle was now possible, as noted by Benjamin Franklin: "I suppose our Ancestors never thought of warming Rooms to sit

[85] Gales, 2004, 30–1; Jones, 2010, 454.
[86] Gales, 2004, 30.
[87] Kander, 2002, 29. Over time, efficiencies rose to 85 percent.
[88] Mosley, 2001, 133 2003; Thorsheim, 2006, 33.
[89] Sieferle, 2001, 66–67; Crowley, 2001, 171–90.

in; all they purpos'd was to have a Place to Make a Fire in, by which they might warm themselves while cold."[90] By the end of the nineteenth century the fortunate could contemplate regularly heating more than one room in the house, although this only became commonplace long into the twentieth century. Household consumption of fuel rose steadily in the coal-consuming countries, and by World War I had reached well over 20 GJ per person, at least as high as total levels of per capita energy consumption in pre-industrial economies.[91]

LIGHT: COAL GAS

Chemists had sought an effective way of isolating gas while refining coal from the late seventeenth century, but the idea that it had potential as a commercially viable source of light was only taken seriously from the 1790s. The breakthrough to gas lighting was then rapidly made by the Scottish engineer William Murdoch, an employee of the Boulton & Watt's steam engine business, and it was first employed commercially in factories. Gaslight was employed to light the smoggy public thoroughfares of London from 1814, replacing the oil lamps that had previously lit the great cities of Europe since the late seventeenth century. London had the widest price gap of any major city between coal and the lighting substitutes of tallow and oil whose importation was disrupted by the Napoleonic wars. It is thus not surprising that the innovation was realized there.[92] The iron pipelines that bore gas to London's lamps were the first centralized energy network in history. Gaslight spread to most of Europe's major cities over the following decades, and across the middle and second half of the century extended to small towns.[93]

The networked provision of artificial light was a giant step forward from dependence on labor-intensive lighting such as rush-lights, tallow or wax candles, and oil lamps, and by the 1860s was a common feature of cities on both sides of the Atlantic.[94] It was also the founding moment in the history of light pollution, that has banished complete darkness from most of

[90] Crowley, 2001, 172.

[91] Gales, 2004, 34.

[92] Murdoch's work was paralleled by simultaneous experiments, although without commercial success, by Philippe Lebron in Paris. Falkus, 1982, 220–21, 228, 234.

[93] Kaijser, 1986; Flinn, 1984, 245–46; de Vries, 2008, 129; Jevons, 1866, 67; Falkus, 1967, 496–9; Millward, 2005, 36. The production of gas from coal was a by-product of the coking process, as was coal tar which came to provide an essential input into the chemical industry and the production of dyestuffs. However as bituminous coal was preferred for gasworks, which made only low quality coke unsuitable for metallurgy, these industries were not generally complementary before the twentieth century, when major metal-works in Germany began to supply waste gases to neighbouring municipalities. Kleinschmidt, 2007, 11–12, 21–22; Clapp, 1994, 221.

[94] Nye, 1998, 95.

the inhabited areas of the world as the price of being able to work and play for twenty-four hours each day. Gaslight began to be widely used in private homes from the 1850s, and was followed by gas heating and cooking in the 1880s. The uptake of heating was slow, but gas cookers were popular, owned by one in three British households by 1900. While this lighting and cooking technology remained expensive, the services it provided were novel and extremely useful. Diffusion was wide where coal was affordable and where there was access to a gas supply in cities. With the fall in iron prices, the capital equipment became dramatically cheaper during the 1820s and '30s. As a source of heat, coal-gas was expensive and not widely popular; only the use of natural gas from the 1960s would change this preference.[95] By the 1870s, gas production amounted to 7 percent of British coal consumption; a share that was small, but that still accounted for some 7 million tons, more than the entire world's coal production in 1700.[96]

3. THE TRANSPORT REVOLUTION

MARKET WIDENING, ABUNDANCE, AND SCARCITY

When in 1870 British Parliamentary Commissioners looked back over what they viewed as an astonishing rise in the use of coal in the previous few decades, even in that coal-rich country, there was one main reason that they pinpointed for this phenomenon: the rise of the railways.[97] Strictly speaking, we mean the steam-powered locomotive, because the railway was a centuries-old means of conveying wagons for short distances over the land, either relying on horse-power or gravity. The steam locomotive was only part of a transport revolution in the nineteenth century, embracing steam shipping and major efficiency improvements in the quality of "traditional" forms of transport: the metaled road, the canal, faster and more capacious sailing ships, better sprung carriages, and more effective breeds of horses. But among these, the application of steam power to transport was the most important, for it permitted market widening for all of the products of the industrial development block by dramatically slashing costs (see figure 6.8). The use of coal as fuel could become a continent-wide phenomenon, not one largely confined to the immediate vicinity of coalfields, or ports with direct links to coalfields. Of course, every kind of freight and passenger transport benefited from this change, but it was crucial above all for those extremely heavy products of the Earth—coal and ores.

---

[95] Fouquet, 2008, 83–4; Falkus, 1967, 501.
[96] Church, 1986, 23.
[97] British Parliamentary Papers, 1871, appendix E, ii.

This greatly expanded the possibilities for market integration, and the potential benefits from that of "Smithian growth": specialization and a vent for otherwise unused resources, and monopoly positions and rents were eroded, benefiting consumers and undermining inefficient producers. The transport revolution of the nineteenth century compounded trends that were already present to a limited extent in north-west Europe with previous improvements in roads, carriages, and other vehicles, but above all the availability of shipping. But allied with much greater reserves of energy, the nineteenth century was a revolution nonetheless.

ROADS AND SAIL

The importance of transport services in the economy had been steadily rising throughout the early modern period. The volume of European trade was expanding much more rapidly than the economy as a whole. During the eighteenth century nearly all of these advances came from the improved quality of road travel and sailing ships. Parts of eighteenth-century Europe had seen major improvements in journey times, squeezing costs downward. Although improved carriage-building made some contribution, the real barrier to swift road transport was the poor quality of the roads themselves. Hence investment in road surfaces, whether through private companies being granted concessions (as with the turnpike system in England and Belgium), or state investment as in France, Spain, and Germany could make for dramatic changes. In the 1650s, the 290-kilometer journey from London to Chester could be made in six days. By 1704, it could be completed in four days, but by 1837, a it took a mere twenty-two hours, eliminating the need for a costly overnight stay for the determined traveler. Horse-teams were able to pull much heavier loads. This improvement would continue throughout the nineteenth century, not least to haul goods to and from railheads.[98] Nevertheless, away from major arterial routes, most of Europe's road network remained in a poorer state than had existed in Roman times.

A similar story can be told about sail. Per capita shipping tonnage in Europe rose tenfold between 1500 and 1780, an increase ahead of very modest rises in income.[99] Although there were no major technological breakthroughs in shipping after the sixteenth century, incremental improvements in the vessels themselves, and the organization of shipping, squeezed costs over time and made sea transport more attractive. Although the very largest ships were no bigger than in Roman times, average size expanded on routes

[98] Fouquet, 2008, 168; Blanning, 2002, 127–32; Gerhold, 1996, 446, 499–500; Bogart et al., 2010, 88–89; Bogart, 2005; Grafe et al., 2010, 197; Boch, 2004, 22; Kleinschmidt, 2007, 28; Milward and Saul, 1977, 441; Henning, 1996, 200–3; Borchardt, 1973, 109.
[99] Van Zanden, 2001, 80.

where bulky cargoes predominated, especially in the North Sea and Baltic, or to carry sufficient stores for transoceanic voyages. This meant that the ratio of crew to tonnage fell and cut costs.[100] Improved rigging and design meant greater speeds were attained. Factors such as new insurance services, improved navigational tools, and better-wearing parts from tropical hardwoods all made small, incremental improvements that allowed shipping services to expand without raising prices.[101]

Canals

Land freight remained slow and limited in power. Even on tarred roads a horse could at best haul two tons of goods. Land haulage remained ten or twenty times more expensive than going by navigable waterways. In 1800, it could cost as much to ship goods 30 miles from the eastern seaboard of America as it did to take them across the Atlantic.[102] Removing the friction of the road on the wheels, and transferring the load to water, could take advantage of the energy of gravity that simply drew the water downhill in rivers, as well as from the lower friction of the water.[103] But this required trade to follow the natural gradients of watersheds and river systems, orientating it toward the coast and leaving inland regions isolated. The way to overcome this was the canal, which while by no means entirely free of the constraints of geography, permitted bulk transport in new directions and could link up sources of raw materials and sites of production and consumption. Canals benefited above all the transport of bulky goods like coal or grain. Lowering transport costs opened up markets and broke open local monopolies, although until the coming of the railways the canal owners themselves could charge monopoly rents, as being able to command the only source of cheap navigation by which bulk commodities could be shifted. The advance of the network was often slow. It took fifty years to connect the new industrial powerhouse of Lancashire with London. Some major canal-building on the continent was driven by concerns of military strategy or prestige and made relatively little impact on trade.[104] The real florescence of canals did

---

[100] This was also true in coastal shipping. See Willan, [1938], 1967, 13.

[101] Smil, 2008a, 202; Unger, 1978, 2011.

[102] Willan, [1938], 1967, xiv; Nye, 1998, 60.

[103] Downstream transport remained considerably cheaper than upstream, however. It remained cheaper to take goods along the lower Danube to the Black Sea, ship them to northern European ports, and carry them by rail to central Germany, rather than move them upriver. Sieferle, 2001, 23; Milward and Saul, 1977, 211.

[104] As Turnbull puts it, "It is . . . difficult to speak of a country-wide network of canals [in Britain] in any meaningful sense before about 1810." Matthias, 1984, 97–102; Turnbull, 1987, 541; Pollard, 1981, 127–28.

not come until the nineteenth century, and some major routes did not open until the twentieth.

Falling costs due to cheaper canal transport remained a narrowly spread boon. Most journeys on the English system were short, within regions. Even so, literal "market widening" from canals could provide a considerable incentive to local industrialization, especially as coal had become such a major commodity since the seventeenth century. In the great textile center of Leeds in northern England, a third was added to the retail price of coal from carrying it by land a mere two miles to the suburbs of Headingly and Armley. Every mile of water thus made a difference. The effect of canals was to promote more intense regional industrial development in localities relatively near to key resources. Canals were essential for opening markets for early coalfields, as with supplies from the Upper Loire to Paris, later superseded when new canals connected the metropolis to the north-eastern coalfields; or linking Berlin to Upper Silesia.[105] Canal-building was also accompanied by river canalization and straightening, partly as a means of reclaiming land, but also to deepen channels and cut journey times on rivers such as on the Oder or upper Rhine.[106] In countries with much larger river systems, canals could play an important role in linking them for commerce, such as the famed Canal du Midi in southern France, or in America, where most long-distance freight still went by water as late as 1852. Here canals played a key role in breaking open urban markets in Philadelphia or New York, and hastening a general transition to coal.[107] Germany only developed a major canal network for freight after unification, by which time the rail system had already been rapidly expanding for decades.[108]

RAILWAYS

The steam-powered locomotive was not something that arrived before its time. It arrived because of a great expenditure of will and effort to conjure it into existence: "The locomotive is not the invention of one man, but of a nation of mechanical engineers," as Robert Stephenson put it.[109] The innovation of high pressure steam power was crucial, reducing engines to a manageable size. Now transport could benefit from the concentration of power. The first steam-powered vehicle on the road emerged in 1801. Richard Trevithick is credited with the first viable rail engine that was operating

[105] Turnbull, 1987, 543–44; Jevons, 1866, 64; von Tunzelmann, 1978, 64; Milward and Saul, 1977, 333–36; Langton, 1979; Fremdling, 2002, 373; Fohlen, 1973, 51; Pounds and Parker, 1957, 115, 144.

[106] See also Jones, 2010 on the United States; Blackbourn, 2006.

[107] Nye, 1998, 61, 76; Mukerji, 2009.

[108] Bogart et al., 2010, 90–92 ; Boch, 2004, 42.

[109] Jevons, 1866, 69; Mokyr, 2009, 112–13.

by 1808.[110] The railways on which locomotives could run were an already long-established method of reducing friction on heavy loads and easing transport in the mining industry, simply using gravity or horses for haulage. But the steam train's big breakthrough did not come until "the Rocket" of George Stephenson that had its inaugural run in 1829, after many attempts to develop a commercial engine. Railway lines also had to be constructed between towns before the new technology could prove itself. But even an extra ordinary accident, when on the day Britain's second-ever line was opened between Liverpool and Manchester the engine ran over and killed William Huskisson, a leading member of Parliament and government minister, was not a deterrent to the dramatic florescence of the railway network once the first steps had been taken.

Developing a rail network was an undertaking unlike any other that had been previously attempted. There were huge problems in acquiring access to land, the construction of embankments and bridges, the production of rails, and the coordination of people, trains, and multiple companies. After a long catalog of predictable accidents it was railways that provided the impetus for the standardization and synchronization of time, and effectively the creation of time zones, in Britain in 1846 and in the United States in 1883.[111] Railway construction generated huge flows of capital and stretched the capacity of economies to provide finance, providing a major stimulus to the development of financial institutions and share markets, but also equally predictable cycles of boom-and-bust.[112]

Comparing the diffusion of railways is not a simple task. Given that countries are of very different size, the extent of the track may not tell us very much about the benefits derived from it. By 1913, Germany and Russia both had twice the length of track of Britain, while the United States had more than ten times as much. Railway construction in America was particularly rapid, easily outstripping the whole of Europe by 1840.[113] This was of course a key influence on the integration of large land masses, but cannot tell us much about relative economic significance. Certainly great savings could come for landlocked regions with no alternative forms of rapid transport. But the savings could also be large in a smaller region with a dense network of railways. Other countries with easy access to the sea will need to make relatively less use of rail freight. Equally, showing a measure that takes size into account, such as track per square kilometer, is not very meaningful if the population is not equally distributed over the landmass; the important task is to link centers of production, consumer demand, and resources. Thus, what table 6.6 shows is not the length of the railways, but the pace

---

[110] Mokyr, 1990, 127.
[111] Cronon, 1991, 79.
[112] Fritzsche, 1996, 144; Caron, 1983, 29, 34.
[113] Mitchell, 1988; Nye, 1998, 73.

TABLE 6.6
Proportion of railway network completed by date, 1840–1913 (1913 = 1)

	Britain	France	Belgium	Germany	Italy	Habsburg Empire	Russia	USA
1840	0.07	0.01	0.07	0.01	0.00	0.00	0.00	0.01
1850	0.30	0.07	0.18	0.09	0.03	0.03	0.01	0.04
1860	0.45	0.22	0.36	0.17	0.13	0.07	0.02	0.12
1870	0.62	0.38	0.61	0.30	0.34	0.14	0.15	0.21
1880	0.78	0.57	0.86	0.53	0.49	0.26	0.33	0.37
1890	0.86	0.82	0.95	0.68	0.72	0.35	0.44	0.62
1900	0.93	0.93	0.96	0.82	0.87	0.43	0.76	0.73
1910	1.00	0.99	0.98	0.97	0.96	0.51	0.95	0.90
1913	1.00	1.00	1.00	1.00	1.00	1.00	1.00	1.00

Sources: Mitchell, 1988, 737–41.

of diffusion *within* each country. We can assume that the railway networks were all largely complete by the First World War (indeed there were already many lines that required government subsidy to stay in business).[114] The indexes therefore show the proportion of that final network that was completed by particular dates.

Britain and Belgium stand out as the leaders in developing a rail network. They had the advantage of cheap indigenous coal supplies, but also being small. France, Italy, and Germany all expanded their networks with approximately the same chronology, Italy catching up with her northern neighbors after a slower start (the first line in Italy was only laid down in 1839). The much larger nations, of the Russian Empire, the United States, and the Habsburg Empire, expanded their coverage much more slowly, although the absolute mileage could be very large; it is the Habsburg Empire that stands out as particularly "backward" before the twentieth century.[115] Of course, even more than with canals, many railways were built for military reasons and did not necessarily stimulate economic activity where routes were ill-chosen or demand was very weak.[116]

Railways brought dramatic falls in the price of transport in their wake. German freight rates fell 75 percent between 1845 and 1900. In Belgium

[114] Millward, 2005, 67–72.
[115] Nye, 1998, 73; Fenoaltea, 1983, 52.
[116] Pollard, 1981, 208–9.

they dropped by two-thirds, 1845–1913, and in France, passenger rates fell by about 50 percent, and freight rates 85 percent or more over the same period.[117] These are simply nominal prices; they do not reflect transport costs relative to other price movements, or the fact that vastly more freight and people were on the move at the later date. The real fall in price was even greater. This represented the final triumph of the market-widening properties of the new development block over the propensity to diminishing returns in the traditional energy economy.

Railways also benefited from great economies of scale. The greater the reach of the network, the more traffic that could be brought onto it, so the higher the turnover and the lower the unit cost, as the great share of fixed capital in costs encouraged the maximal possible use of the investment. This in turn stimulated further demand and expansion. Travel became much less subject to seasonality, and to the problems of ice or water-logging that afflicted transport by water or un-metaled roads. Even the most ponderous freight train was at least five times faster than a wagon. Railways thus made a significant difference to the cost of coal itself. As we will see, this cheapening can create the illusion that as a small share of costs, transport mattered less. In reality, it was cheap energy that released the possibility of adding other kinds of value in the economy. In London in 1830, a location distant (in British terms) from coalfields, transport made up two-thirds of the retail cost of the fuel in 1830, but only between a third and a half in 1870.[118]

These price decreases reflected not only the expansion of railway networks, but yet again a constant process of improvement in the technology itself. Rails became made of better quality iron and then steel, and thus more durable. Engine efficiencies rose. "Continuous brakes" allowed locomotives to slow more rapidly and consequently utilize higher speeds more frequently between stations. Trains became much larger and able to bear much greater loads.[119] Landscape remained a barrier, because the trains could be used with much greater efficiency in lowland Europe. Mountainous countries like Italy, where trains constantly had to haul up long, steep gradients, inevitably slowed travel and increased fuel consumption. The main Italian rail companies consequently spent around three and a half times more for fuel per unit of traffic than the company that covered northern France. Lower utilization of the lines also meant lower productivity generally, underlining again the geographical advantages where there was proximity of producers and consumers. Thus rail modified but did not overcome the constraints of geography. Italian railways were relatively costly not, for the most part, because coal itself was expensive to the train companies, or even because they had to use more of it per kilometer traveled. Rather, higher general fuel

[117] Caron, 1983, 45; O'Brien, 1983, 11.
[118] Church, 1986, 63.
[119] Caron, 1983, 34; Fontana, 2006, 211.

costs in Italy discouraged heavy industry and the transport of bulk goods and lowered the utilization of the network. The high fixed costs of railways in turn reduced the return they brought.[120]

One of the most important growth-promoting linkages was between railways and mining. In Britain, the railways' share of coal consumption was small, at 3 percent in 1869, and 5 percent in 1913.[121] The effect on coalmining *in toto* was greater, however, because a larger share of exports were consumed by railways than domestically. In Sweden, for example, 30 percent of the almost entirely imported coal went to the railways in 1850, and 37 percent in 1870. Cheaper transportation inevitably meant cheaper coal for the consumer. In turn, a very large amount of traffic on the railways was generated by shifting coal, so mining and rail developed in a symbiotic relationship.[122]

In the wake of the railways came a major advance in transport services, especially of bulky goods, illustrated in table 6.7. In pre-industrial times the amount of freight annually shipped per person must have been very much less than one metric ton.[123] Thus, even the very modest gains to freight achieved by the middle of the nineteenth century, or by the end in the case of the Mediterranean lands, represented significant shifts. In much of northern and central Europe the advance in freight services was very great. As a high proportion of these heavy goods were in fact ores or coal, the figures to a large extent reflect the location of the heartlands of the new development block, but they are equally an indicator of the importance of the railways in expanding the consumption of fuel and metals. Cheaper transport also facilitated the flow of people and information. Migratory movements within Germany were closely linked to the expansion of the railway network.[124]

Britain shifted goods one billion tonne-km in 1850, but by the turn of the nineteenth century, the figure was a staggering thirty times higher. Canals and railways were of equivalent importance in 1845, but canal freight was only a fifteenth of rail freight by 1898. In France, the use of coastal shipping, canals, and roads was stable between 1830 and 1914. But railways had gone from making zero contribution to transport services in 1830 to

[120] Fenoaltea, 1983, 82–6.

[121] Church, 1986, 30.

[122] Kander, 2002, 199–202; Hawke, 1970, 73, 159, 173–74; Fremdling, 1983, 137; the development of coalmining in the Austro-Hungarian Empire was also closely linked with the expansion of railways. Gross, 1973, 265.

[123] Adults consumed around 250 kg of the one bulk foodstuff, grain. A cubic meter of firewood weighs 500–600 kg, and consumption levels were only 1–2 m³ per head. Much of both these goods would have been obtained in the near locality of the consumer, often by themselves. Other foodstuffs and consumer goods would have only come to a few kilograms per year. Even allowing for transport of the bulkier raw materials that went into processing final consumer goods, the per capita amounts must have been small. Malanima, 2001, 61.

[124] Tipton, 1976, 104, 110–11.

TABLE 6.7
Annual per capita freight on railways (metric tons), 1850–1900

	1850	1860	1870	1880	1890	1900
Britain		4.4	7.5	9.3	9.3	11.3
Germany	0.1	0.5	1.7	3.3	4.6	6.6
France	0.1	0.6	1.0	2.2	2.3	3.0
Austria	0.1	0.4	1.2	2.4	3.8	5.0
Belgium	0.3	0.8	1.6	6.4	7.2	8.1
Russia				0.5	0.7	1.3
Italy			0.2	0.3	0.6	0.5
Spain			0.2	0.4	0.6	0.9
Sweden			0.5	1.4	2.2	3.8
Netherlands				1.2	1.5	1.9
Sample excl. Russia				3.4	4.3	5.9

Note: Ton-kilometers is usually the preferred measure of actual railways usage. More data are available on simple tonnage. In the case of Germany, data are mostly in the form of ton-kilometers. However, there is a rough ratio 1 metric ton to 100 ton-kilometers when both data series sets are available, and the assumption of stability has been employed here before 1880.

Source: Calculated from Mitchell, 1988, 748–52. Population data from Maddison, 2003, and Mitchell, 1988, table 6.8.

70 percent by 1914.[125] Of course, this expansion of transport and trade was far larger than the expansion of actual economic activity. But it certainly did promote the employment of more people and more resources, some under the ground, some of them in far-flung parts of the globe that became more integrated with European markets. "Traditional" sectors of the economy such as agriculture enjoyed considerable growth in demand as supply conditions improved, opening up new commercial exporting economies in the midwest of America, the Ukrainian steppes, and Hungary.[126]

Steam Shipping

The desirability of using concentrated steam power in ships to put them beyond the mercy of the winds, currents, and river flows was recognized

[125] Fouquet, 2008, 167, 170; O'Brien, 1983, 7.
[126] Pollard, 1981, 228.

early. Efforts to drive boats with a steam engine began in the 1780s. As with railways, early beginnings were modest and highly localized. Steamships made an early appearance in river transport, first in America, and then in Europe with the *Comet* that worked the Clyde at Glasgow from 1812. The first regular steam-powered route crossed the Irish Sea from 1818.[127] By the end of the 1820s, steamships were active in all European waters, initially in niche markets where speed was of the essence: mail and passenger transport. Unlike railways, steam shipping faced a fundamental problem of fuel supply. Trains could easily be refueled at repeated stops. A ship traveling any distance had to carry all its fuel on board. As early steam engines were both large and inefficient, this put a great constraint on the size of the cargo. Steam navigation also faced an innovative and attractive competitor in sail, especially over long distances. Most early steamships, which had engines propelling paddle wheels, also still used "mixed" methods with sails and rigging in case of engine problems.[128]

Steam power's rise to domination of maritime transport thus required further innovations in engines and metals. More compact and more efficient engines freed space on board for other uses. Improved boiler design cut fuel consumption by half between the 1840s and 1870s, and the introduction of triple expansion engines during the 1880s cut coal consumption by half again by 1913. After 1843, the introduction of the propeller instead of the paddle wheel increased efficiency, especially as higher engine speeds allowed higher speeds to be attained by the vessels. A particularly problematic good to transport by steamship was coal itself, as unless the ship carried an equally heavy cargo back to its home port, it was very considerably lighter and this lifted paddles out of the water. Along with the other technical advances, this needed the development of both propellers, and water ballast tanks that could be filled for return voyages.[129]

Iron hulls, pioneered in a Coalbrookedale barge as early as 1787, became more frequent from the 1840s as the making of iron plates improved, reducing maintenance costs, creating more cargo space, and allowing much larger vessels to be constructed: shipbuilding costs increased by the square of the ship's dimensions, but capacity by the cube. This allowed freighters and liners to expand in dimensions, precursors to the diesel super-tankers of the twentieth century on which the international oil trade rests. Iron was soon supplanted by steel, which came to predominate in ships' hulls in the 1890s.[130] Overall British ocean freight rates fell by around 60 percent

[127] Fenton, 2008, 182; Nye, 1998, 29.

[128] Harley, 1972; 1988, 865.

[129] Fenton, 2008, 181, 184–85.

[130] Fenton, 2008,180–83; Milward and Saul, 1977, 220–21; Harley, 1988, 865; Barbier, 2011, 385.

Figure 6.8. Index of maritime freight costs, 1741 = 100
Sources: Stopford, 2009, 754–57 [from Isserlis, 1938].

between 1855 and 1910. The period after 1870 saw very dramatic declines in sea transport costs around the globe (see figure 6.8).[131]

The supplanting of sail by steam was a drawn-out process. The building of steamships only overtook sail ships around 1870 in Britain.[132] By the early 1870s, steamships were competitive on the Atlantic crossing and by the end of the decade carried cotton to Europe from New Orleans. The opening of the Suez Canal greatly shortened the route to Asia and allowed steam to expand in this market too. But on the longest hauls, to Australia or the Pacific coast of America, sail remained paramount into the twentieth century.[133] Even at this late date, sail still predominated in the fleet of Norway, the third largest merchant marine in the world.[134]

As in so many other matters during the first industrial revolution, Britain enjoyed a dominant position. The role of iron and steel technology, especially the use of the Siemens-Martin process (see the section "Steel" above) in steamship building simply created a new kind of advantage. The high pressure engines in ships also needed anthracite, which was in ample sup-

---

[131] Barbier, 2011, 376. There has been controversy over the extent of the fall of freight rates in British waters, but we follow the method of Ville and Armstrong, which suggests they were significant. Ville, 1987; Hausman, 1987; Armstrong, 1993.

[132] See Mitchell, 1988.

[133] Harley, 1972; Thomas, 2004, 107.

[134] Broadberry, 2006, 152; although the energy consumption from steam shipping was larger than the wind power used for sailing ships. Lindmark, 2006. Steam tonnage only surpassed sail in Germany in the 1890s. Borchardt, 1973, 145.

ply from the "steam coal" of the valleys of South Wales. By the 1860s, the British commanded more than a third of the world's fleet, and this proportion did not shift until after the First World War. The growth in the use of large steamships was labor-saving, just as in all the other key innovations of the new energy economy. British shipping services grew at 3.7 percent per annum between 1871 and 1911, with capital inputs growing at around 3 percent and labor, only 0.8 percent each year.[135] In the "first wave of globalisation" steam shipping made a major contribution to the overall fall in the costs of trade. Although direct shipping costs made up only a proportion of the total cost, the use of coal was "permissive" in allowing a rapid expansion of fast shipping services, and also permitted economies of scale in trade more generally. Falling transport costs on land and sea were a major driver of a growing global food market, international migration, and real wage convergence in the Atlantic world.[136]

ENERGY PRICES

The transport revolution was a revolution in the accessibility of coal. Only when coal-using technology could be put to use in the transport sector, reducing both the capital cost of vehicles, locomotives, and ships, and in turn their own running costs because this new technology itself freighted the coal, could energy prices more widely fall. The trend in prices is clear enough (see figure 5.6), but providing reliable series on the "price" of energy is a complicated business. There are different qualities of most fuels, whether firewood, coal or petrol. Most historical prices we have are "spot prices" from one particular location: a pithead, port city, or paid by a particular company; they are not national prices, which in any case would not be very meaningful unless the national market itself was highly integrated. One only has to drive around a few local petrol stations to see that prices even of identical products can vary over short distances. International coal prices in coal-producing countries are generally quoted at the pithead, which tells us very little about the price actually paid by most consumers. There were, it is true, significant differences. Pithead prices in the mid-1880s were lowest in Britain and Germany, although soon to be surpassed by the United States, while Canada was around 40 percent more expensive, and Spain and France, 85 percent higher.[137] This undoubtedly made industry sited on

---

[135] Broadberry, 2006, 154; Jevons, 1866, 89; Harley, 1988, 861–65.

[136] Harley, 1988; O'Rourke and Williamson, 1999, 29, 43–54; although transport might make up less than half of total trade costs, the combination of rail and steam shipping permitted much greater exchange and access to resources. Again, it was the *cheapness* of supply and low cost share that could allow an expansion in effective demand. For another view, see Meissner, Jacks and Novy, 2010, 127–37.

[137] Henriques, 2011, 142.

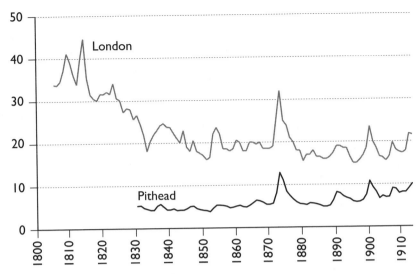

Figure 6.9. Real price of coal in England, 1800–1913
(shillings per ton, 1913 prices)
Note: The coal price series are deflated by a retail price index. We should
remember that this means both numerator and denominator contain coal
prices, as coal is part of the RPI, and is also a component of the cost of most
items in the RPI, which are manufactured or supplied using coal-based
technology. As this fact will have lowered the price of goods over the century,
in line with the price trend in coal itself, the real price of coal appears to fall
less than would otherwise be the case.
Source: Coal prices: Church, 1986; Mitchell, 1984; RPI from Officer, 2008.

the coalfield more competitive in Germany, Britain, and North America.
Yet what mattered when it came to international competition was retail
prices of energy and goods. And comparing a pithead price in one country
with a retail price in another is comparing apples and pears. There are not
"national" prices as such, but prices at a greater or lesser distance from the
source of coal, firewood, or peat.

The different levels of prices at pithead and point of consumption can
be seen if we compare English pithead prices with those from London (figure 6.9), which was in fact a city with relatively good access to coal supplies
by water, even before the railways were built. Pithead prices obviously could
not benefit from changes in transportation, and rose very slowly while retail
prices in London fell: a gradual convergence. In the late 1820s the pithead
price of English coal was around 5s per ton, just as it would be four decades
later. At this time consumers in Manchester paid just over 10s per ton, in
Birmingham 13–14s, but Londoners, 27–30s. The markup on pithead prices
in the capital was as much as 600 percent. By the late 1870s, this markup

would fall to 200–300 percent. The use by the end of the century of steam-powered colliers down the east coast of England would squeeze price differential further, down to as little as 150 percent at times during the 1890s and 1900s. There was still a distinct advantage for fuel-intensive industries to locate on the coalfields, but generally cheap coal had come within the reach of all.[138]

The drop in transport costs brought about by railways and steamships obviously caused a proportionately greater fall in price the further one was from the source of coal, as transport costs made up a greater share of total costs. Nevertheless, this did not make for a convergence of economic activity, as we will see in the next chapter. One consequence of the widened market for coal was greater demand for the energy-intense products of the core industrialized regions.

Transport links thus determined participation in the first industrial revolution. Every government and firm of the day knew it, and said it often.[139] At the pitheads of most European coal mines, good-quality coal generally sold for about 5s (British shillings) in the mid-1860s, just as in England. Yet we can see in table 6.8 how most regions remained quite remote from coalfields, even in "countries" that were well stocked with coal. In this period, the country, we are reminded again, is a somewhat arbitrary economic unit, certainly with little meaning in terms of resource endowment. This situation would change with integrated markets and networked energy systems in the twentieth century, making nations and supra-national bodies more important. The northern coast of Germany still received its coal from Newcastle and South Wales at this point, even though German mining was developing rapidly. Occasionally distance could be transcended by other factors, such as patterns of international trade; in those places where the British ships sought valuable return cargoes they used coal as ballast and sold it at a discount, accounting for the surprisingly cheap rates in some Baltic ports and in distant Bombay.

From the late 1860s the widespread use of the steamship cheapened coal where sea routes were the main artery of supply. After the peak prices in the international crisis of 1873–74, coal prices fell considerably in Scandinavia and Italy, just as steam freight rates saw their most dramatic drop. In the large import trade of British coal to Hamburg, steamships overtook sail in 1866.[140] By this stage, steam engines in transportation had led to market widening for coal in remote areas of Europe, far from the coalfields. But even this revolution in supply still left more "remote" regions facing relatively high bills for coal compared to alternatives, and in many parts

---

[138] Calculated from von Tunzelmann, 1978, 96–97; Church, 1986, 53–4; Beveridge, 1965.
[139] See for example British Parliamentary Papers, 1866.
[140] Fremdling, 2002, 369.

TABLE 6.8
International Coal Prices as Multiple of English Pithead Prices, c. 1865–1882

	England, Pithead	England, Industrial Cities	England, London	Baltic Ports	Germany Landlocked	Russia Landlocked	Mediterranean Western Ports	Mediterranean Eastern ports	South America	USA Industrial Cities	Canada	Bombay
Mid-1860s Shilling	5	10	20	17	40	40	29	40	120	—	—	—
Mid-1860s multiple pithead	1	2	4	3.4	8	8	5.8	8	24	—	—	—
c. 1882 Shillings	5.5	6.2	17.0	22.2	12.3	35.1	26.7	—	—	16.4	20.5	25
c. 1882 multiple pithead	1	1.1	3.1	4.0	2.2	6.4	4.9	—	—	3.0	3.7	4.5

Note: 'Baltic ports' refers to Gothenburg and St. Petersburg in the 1860s and St. Petersburg in the 1880s. Germany Landlocked is the Frankfurt price in the 1880s, although similar to prices quoted elsewhere; and from a range of citations in the 1880s. Russia landlocked is from Moscow. Mediterranean ports cover a range of consular reports from Spain, Italy, Greece and Turkey. These figures are approximations to the level reported. Canadian prices are from Ontario and American prices from east coast cities.

Sources: von Tunzelmann, 1978, 96–97; Church, 1986, 53–55; BPP 1866, passim; Balderston, 2010, 589–90.

of Europe households stuck with firewood or peat.[141] Only more specialized users, such as the railways, switched, and in some areas of Poland and Russia locomotives ran on wood. Coal prices remained markedly different between regions and nations, and these different levels explain much of the course of the industrial revolution, even in its later stages.

A British Revolution in Its Global Context

No one thing made for the industrial revolution. What we need to explain is the *combination* of different processes, not simply the origin of each one. Given that the combination of many things was necessary for a revolutionary effect, it is not surprising that only one place seems to have offered the possibility for the first industrial revolution, at least in the world of the eighteenth and early nineteenth centuries: Britain. The story we tell is thus at first "British." While some important developments, such as in the scientific theory, were European in nature, the very local context of Britain was crucial in providing the combination of opportunities that could allow the new block to emerge. Indeed, even though Joel Mokyr is probably correct to see most macro-inventions of the eighteenth and nineteenth centuries emerging on the continent of Europe, the ones that really mattered: steam engines, locomotives, and innovatory smelting techniques, were all unambiguously British. These factors were local enough that even an apparently similar economy, such as in the neighboring Netherlands, could not replicate them. Indeed, it is important to remember that economic choices are made on the basis of opportunity costs, and even small margins of difference can have a major cumulative impact on the paths taken by different economies.

Much of the development in "followers" occurred where conditions were also relatively favorable for the exploitation of coal, and the vending of the goods produced by new industries: in the north-east coast of the United States near to the great seaboard cities, and in pockets of Western Europe. In all these places the transfer of technology, and perhaps most significantly recruiting personnel to build, operate, and maintain it, was a relatively easy matter. Most of the rest of the world, however, lacked the mineral reserves, the capital for investment, and the commercial networks likely to lure in the necessary expert migrants. Only the *market widening* that accompanied the nineteenth-century transport revolution, and the development of the steamship and railway, could spread this transformation out from small core regions. Even then, the areas where costs worked favorably toward the large-scale introduction of new technology and the people to use it were very limited.

---

[141] Endres, 1905,110–11.

Perhaps more important, however, the industrial revolution evolved in England—if such a statement is not oxymoronic. The combination of its key elements took time, and different factors had different influences on each stage of this evolution. Our explanation is *historical*, and its systematic character cannot be explained by one single driving force.

CHAPTER SEVEN

ENERGY AND INDUSTRIAL GROWTH

1. COAL AND GROWTH

THE COAL DEVELOPMENT BLOCK AND GROWTH

THE ECONOMIES OF EUROPE GREW more rapidly during the nineteenth century than at any previous period in history. This was not simply a consequence of the doubling of the population; per capita income rose too. Given these facts it is hardly surprising that energy consumption also increased dramatically. Some might argue that higher energy consumption is simply a natural function of growth, and requires no further explanation. The economy might grow for any number of reasons, but as people consumed more final goods and services, they also consumed more energy. But we argue that energy consumption, and the availability of coal, helped *propel* economic growth (as did other things). Consumption of coal seems to have been a key part of economic success, as measured by per capita income,[1] and cheap energy was a necessary condition of the industrial revolution.

Nevertheless, this story is complex. It was not simply the case that the richer a country was, the more energy its inhabitants consumed. This *was* certainly true of the single richest country, Britain. However, Britain's high energy consumption was not just a function of its high income, leading to more economic activity, and hence demand for energy. Rather, this high income was underpinned by a capital-intensive economy that required large amounts of cheap energy as inputs. Most of the coal consumption was in the production of *intermediate* products or their distribution, such as metal smelting, manufacturing industry, or transport. This meant that consuming coal was not a consumer preference based on incomes already earned, but a crucial part of the productive processes for a large number of goods. It was not optional for growth, one choice among roughly equivalent alternatives that could also have delivered modern economies.

However, not all countries followed the British path. This is because few countries had the kind of resource endowment of minerals that led to especially energy intense growth: this was only the case in Britain, Germany, and

---

[1] Income is taken here to mean GDP. Of course the limitations of GDP as a measure of welfare and economic activity are well known, although other welfare indicators tend to be relatively well correlated with GDP, especially at early stages of development. See Tilly, 1983.

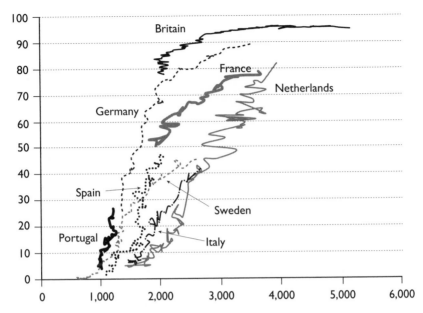

Figure 7.1. Percent of coal in total energy consumption
(on the vertical axis)and per capita income, 1800–1913
Note: Per capita incomes are displayed in 1990 international $.
The countries are England & Wales (1856–1913), Netherlands
(1800–1913), Germany (1820–1913), France (1820–1913), Sweden
(1800–1913), Spain (1850–1913), Italy (1861–1913) and Portugal
(1856–1913). In the case of Germany and France there are no data from
1821 to 1849, and 1821 to 1855. What is clear is the strong relationship
between per capita income and the share of coal in total energy consumption.

Belgium. There was an international division of labor, with other countries
developing different kinds of industrial sectors, specializations in commerce
or food processing, and hence different levels of demand for coal. Consequently there is not a close correlation between per capita consumption of
energy and income in a cross-country comparison in this period, and neither
would we expect to find one. Indeed, to some degree we see economies taking divergent economic paths within the context of international exchange.

What is more striking is a different relationship—between the level of per
capita income and the *share* of coal in total energy consumption, illustrated
in figure 7.1. This shows more clearly the links between the use of modern
energy carriers and economic success. An economy did not have to be particularly energy intense by international standards to be wealthy in the decades before and after 1900, although this certainly did no harm. But it did
need a high share of total energy consumption to be from coal. One did not
need the great metallurgical industries of the Ruhr, South Wales, or Teesside;

TABLE 7.1
Per capita GDP, 1855–1914 (1990 US $)

	Great Britain	Netherlands	France	Germany	Italy	Spain	Sweden	Portugal
1855	2926	2380	1726	1466	-	1163	944	936
1870	3474	2648	1980	1748	1576	1311	1168	975
1890	4161	3111	2477	2347	1848	1621	1404	1120
1913	5150	3937 .	3633	3543	2670	2048	2626	1207

Sources: Great Britain from Feinstein, 1972; Netherlands (Maddison, 2003); France, Spain, and Germany (Maddison, 2008); Italy (Malanima, 2006); Sweden (Schön and Kranz, 2007); Portugal (Henriques, 2009).

but one did need a modern transport sector burning coal and the significant presence of steam power. As time went on, countries migrated more to the upper right of the graph, as coal use and income rose.

Income in Britain remained far ahead of any of its neighbors throughout the century (table 7.1). The Dutch economy had been pre-eminent during the early modern period, but lost this to the British in the early nineteenth century.[2] Dutch incomes remained at about 70 percent of the level of Great Britain from 1850 to 1914, as Holland also became an economy dominated by coal use. This was a weaker performance than both France and Germany, the two other countries in our sample who shifted rapidly to a coal economy in mid-century, as shown in figure 5.3. Germany's per capita income rose most of all, from a little over a third of the British level mid-century to 65 percent in 1911. Sweden and the southern countries lagged far behind. Convergence in these cases was late, and in the case of Iberia, non-existent. Thus, growth after 1850 was a tide that raised all boats, but not to the same degree. Overall the experience of the nineteenth century was of "growth without convergence," with some catch-up from the southern countries toward the end of the era but a marked falling behind of Eastern Europe.[3]

The transition to fossil fuels was marked by new patterns of regional development and specialization, and new forms of interdependence. Centers of coal mining and manufacturing industry were heavily reliant on marketing their products elsewhere, whether within national economies or abroad. Even those countries that made relatively little direct use of the new

[2] It is important to distinguish between income in Great Britain and that of the entire United Kingdom, including Ireland, as average income in Ireland was much lower.

[3] Pamuk and van Zanden, 2010, 220–21; Carreras and Josephson, 2010, 42–43. International convergence in real wages tended to be greater than with per capita GDP after 1870, largely driven by international migration and the development of an international market in basic foodstuffs. O'Rourke and Williamson, 1999, 15–24.

development block relied heavily on the energy-intense economies abroad for the supply of new technology, expertise, and energy-intense goods, especially capital goods. In turn these goods became important inputs into sectors of the economy that superficially appeared more "traditional," such as the use of fertilizers in agriculture. The story of these new interdependencies and patterns of growth will be a central aspect of this chapter.

CONSUMPTION AND WELFARE

If we trace the linkages between the various branches of the economy, we can see how new technology and energy carriers changed prices and promoted growth. Yet on the aggregate level of the economy, the impact of the new development block is not always so clear-cut. Many countries do not appear to have experienced a radical "take-off" in growth rates during the nineteenth century, at least by later standards. The "modern" sectors of the economy still made up a minority of total economic activity. Inevitably starting from a very low base, the growth of these sectors would take a long time to make a big impact on the aggregate size of the economy. The persistence of "traditional sectors" in aggregate national income has led some economic historians to call into question the epochal nature of the industrial revolution. The careful tracing of forward and backward linkages would suggest that modern sectors of the economy did in fact have a big influence on traditional sectors by accessing new resources, lowering transport costs, and increasing effective demand, as well as providing new capital equipment and fuel. But such linkages and all of their effects are almost impossible to trace on the scale of a whole economy, and are easy to overlook. More profoundly, differing opinions also arise because of the way in which we attempt to measure economic growth itself.

In the 1980s, the British economic historian Nick Crafts revised downward previous estimates of the rapid growth rates for the British economy that had seemed to give a quantitative basis to the idea of a "take-off" in the classic period of the industrial revolution from around 1770 to 1830.[4] The reason for this was not that a huge amount of new information had appeared, but because Crafts pointed out problems with the previously accepted index of industrial output, produced by Deane and Cole. They calculated indices of changes in "real output" for all of the sectors of the economy: that is, tons of pig iron, tons of wheat, gallons of beer, and so forth. The problem is, then, what unit of value is used to aggregate these to produce a value for real national income that can be standardized over time? This is done using monetary values per unit of output of a particular

[4] Crafts, 1985; Deane and Cole, 1962; for further revisions, Crafts and Harley, 1992; and see the discussion in Temin, 1997, 66–67.

year (i.e., current prices). However, the relative prices of these goods are not stable over time. In different years it takes different amounts of wheat to buy a set amount of iron. If these changing relative prices are used to "weight" the real output figures, the information on the real output of the economy is lost. Instead we create a series of how much money people are prepared to pay for that output, which is not the same thing.[5]

One way to get around this is to use a single year for the price weights to aggregate the series. Deane and Cole weighted the importance of each branch of the economy using the values of output at the start of the period in 1770, and growth thus appeared to be very rapid. But one of the features of this period growth was very significant changes in relative prices. British consumers no longer valued the goods in 1830 in the way that they had in 1770. If one weighted the importance of each sector of the economy according to the prices of 1830, you got rather different results, and rather slower rates of growth. From the perspective of the consumer of 1770, there has been a Revolution. Seen from the values of 1830, growth appeared much more gradual.[6] What may seem to many as an obscure methodological discussion is in fact crucial for the interpretation of the industrial revolution, and our understanding of the role of resources within it.

Crafts rightly pointed out that "the choice of which index number to use depends on what question it is intended to answer."[7] Thus, when we are measuring the success of the economy according to the welfare levels achieved by final consumers, we must take into account the changing relative valuations of goods over time. However, the point of view of the producer or the environmentalist is likely to be different from the consumer. Unlike consumers who in most cases can switch their expenditure to another product if one becomes more expensive, or preferences change, many producers have no such flexibility. Equally, particular resources may be available in finite amounts. Iron becoming much cheaper does not make it any less important for the production of steel, just as a collapse in the price of apples does not make them any less valued by the producers of apple juice.

It is essential then to always remember Craft's comment, so often ignored, that each measure is only useful relative to the question being asked. He chose to measure economic growth through adjusting the weighting given to each sector according to changing trends in consumer valuations.

---

[5] For the eighteenth century, Crafts used weights based upon occupational structure; Crafts, 1985, 15–17. See also Broadberry and van Leeuwen, 2010, 13. Recent work by Shaw-Taylor and Wrigley suggests that the size of industrial employment was underestimated by both Deane and Cole and Crafts, casting into doubt their weighting. As industry shows the greatest growth over the century, this implies that overall growth was higher in the eighteenth century. Shaw-Taylor and Wrigley, Personal communication.

[6] Crafts actually used a Divisia Index changing weightings at various benchmarks between these years. Crafts, 1985, 25–28.

[7] Crafts, 1985, 25; See also Tilly, 1983 for a general discussion of "index-number problems."

The Apples and Pears Problem

The difficulties in providing aggregate measures of growth can be demonstrated with a simple illustration. If people value apples and pears differently, we cannot judge the benefit of producing particular numbers of apples and pears by simply adding up the numbers of each fruit to get a grand total. We would have to weight each fruit differently, reflecting how much people liked it. If people tend to like apples more than pears, we might count, for example, each pear as 0.8 of an apple. This is what a price does. We value things not "in themselves" but through their cost in money as a means of comparing the value of unlike things. But what if we then imagine that the price of a fruit suddenly falls—for example, a new technology allows it to be delivered from far away, where the fruit can be grown more cheaply (this is what happened to the banana, thanks to the invention of railways and steamships). If this happened to apples, they could then be bought much more cheaply than pears. But the amount people spend on fruit might not change that much. They would eat many more apples, but possibly even spend less in total on them, because they have become so cheap. The change in the benefits people gain from eating fruit would not be captured by the change in the amount of money they spent on it. Yet there are additional problems. The new cheapness of apples might also mean that they fell in people's esteem, and pears became a more highly regarded fruit. People would pay a premium to get pears instead of apples. It may be that people value fruit less when it becomes more plentiful, so they do not think they are much better off. After apples became cheaper, people would not be so impressed by the fact that they had a very plentiful supply, and the increase in apple consumption would not be considered to have made people much better off. So we are left with a paradox. A consumer who was transported from the age before cheap apples would think they had arrived in a fruit heaven. Given that at the later date they are eating a lot more fruit, any commonsensical judgment would be that their welfare has improved. But standard price-based ways of measuring welfare could suggest that they were no better off, or even that welfare had declined.

We could equally argue that the "revolutionary" nature of the change is best established by using the valuations of goods as they appear to a young consumer at the earliest date, to gain a sense of how their world would be transformed by the time they reached old age. Humans do not after all react to new inventions which we imagine will transform our well-being by saying that they will soon become commonplace, fall in relative value,

TABLE 7.2
Increases in key economic indicators in Europe,
1870–1913 (percent)

Population	40
GDP	147
Coal production	254
Pig iron output	326
Sulfuric acid output	572
Raw cotton consumption	250
Beer production	303

Note: Population and GDP are drawn from Maddison, 2003. Whether one uses a more limited 12-country, or larger 29-country sample of European nations, the change in GDP and population is almost identical. Other data are drawn from the major producers, and are likely to be slight under-statements of the real increase. Broadberry et al., 2010, 75–76.

seem less important to future generations, and thus not be worth the fuss. Indeed, Alexander Gerschenkron argued that it is precisely those rapid shifts in relative prices that create index-number problems of measurement that are useful indicators themselves of major structural change in the economy. The problem of measuring the change is itself a sign that something important has happened.[8]

Across the board, as we have already seen in the case of energy, raw material consumption rose faster than both population and total income. Thus, the "material" advance of Europe, or what today we might call its ecological footprint, which also became more dependent on imports from outside its borders, ran ahead of the usual measures of improvement in welfare. Indeed, this fact may be said to be a condition of improvement in welfare at this time that was dependent on steeply falling prices of some key materials and great leaps in their per capita availability. The period shown in table 7.2 already post-dates an era of substantial advance in the north-west of the continent.

[8] This relates to a well-known discussion among economists as to the relative merits of Paasche or Laspeyres indices for measuring change. Gerschenkron, 1962; see also the discussion in Ljungberg, 1990, 67.

SOCIAL SAVING VERSUS THE DEVELOPMENT BLOCK

The most frequently used method to try and assess the importance of an innovation in the economy has been "social savings," pioneered by Robert Fogel in his study of nineteenth-century American railroads.[9] This seeks to quantify the difference a particular innovation made. How important was an innovation really to overall income? Fogel attempted to quantify the difference the railroad had made by calculating what the additional cost would be if all those railroads disappeared overnight and the goods moved by them had to be shifted by the next best alternative, which was canals. The figure arrived at is called the "social saving" and is usually cited as a share of GDP.

Most studies employing social savings have not attempted to analyze anything as general as energy carrier transitions; even Fogel's work focused on the transport of bulk agricultural goods and made only rough calculations of other forms of freight. Perhaps more wisely and more modestly, they have attempted to calculate the benefits that came with very specific pieces of technology, such as the Watt steam engine.[10] The results of social savings calculations in different economies have been very diverse, which one might expect given that economies themselves are diverse. In some countries, particularly landlocked ones, we see social saving rates of the railways at particular dates approaching 40 percent! In other words, GDP would have had to be 40 percent higher to be able to afford the transport of all that real freight by the best alternative means. The implication here is that rail was essential for economic development. But in many cases the figure is far smaller, at 5 percent or less; no more than a hard single year's recession (see table 7.3).

The social savings approach has asked important questions in a relatively clear and straightforward manner. However, it has been subject to fierce criticism, and problems with the method are now well known. For example, in trying to model the impact of change over time, from which year should one take the prices to develop a counterfactual scenario? If we imagine railways disappearing in any given year, we can hardly imagine that in the counterfactual universe the price for canal boats or carts would be exactly the same as it was historically when the railways existed. Indeed, if these still appeared as viable alternatives to railways in some places during the nineteenth century, this was because they operated in regions where the train could not out-compete them. It does not make sense to price all transport services in the counterfactual scenario using historical prices from where those services happened to be cheap. But in areas where rail dominated, alternative freight had gone out of business, so there is no price to use. In a world with no rail, unless the supply of transport services and energy was

---

[9] Fogel, 1964; see discussions and applications of the method in Hawke, 1970, 7–20, 44, 47, 90; Thomas, 2004, 109–12; Herranz-Loncán, 2006.

[10] von Tunzelmann, 1978.

TABLE 7.3
Social savings on freight transport by rail, 1846–1910

		percent GNP
Belgium	1846	1
England & Wales	1865	4.1
England & Wales	1890	11
France	1872	5.8
Spain	1878	3.9–6.4
Spain	1912	18.9
Germany	1890s	5
Russia	1907	4.5
USA	1859	3.7
USA	1890	6.9
Mexico	1910	24.9–38.5

Source: Broadbery et al., 2010, 81.

just as elastic as in the case with coal-based technology, the alternatives would have been very much more expensive.

One solution is to take the relative price of the more expensive alternatives at that moment just before the new technology arrived. Advocates of the method have argued that this in fact makes the new technology seem more advantageous than it really was, because one can assume that without it, there actually would have been pressure for innovation and efficiency savings in the "traditional sector." This rather flies in the face of evidence. Clearly we can actually find efficiency gains, such as in the quality of sail ships, or the size and power of horses. But nowhere were they remotely of the magnitude to permit any great fall in prices while simultaneously massively boosting supply, and there is no reason to think that advances would have been any faster without railroads. By 1900, canal freight traffic in Britain was only a fifteenth of that on rail. In Germany. the ratio held at a steady one to four after the 1870s, where both canals and the great arterial rivers provided greater competition.[11]

The social savings approach is an exercise in "comparative statics," where everything else is held equal aside from the cost of the technology being analyzed, and its alternatives. But in reality, economies are dynamic entities where changing prices stimulate a new distribution of investment, and as

[11] Fouquet, 2008, 145; Fremdling, 1983, 137.

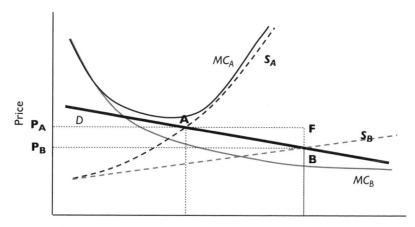

Figure 7.2. Long-term costs and savings
Note: Two curves (*MC*) show the long-term marginal costs over time
for two products, one based on organic products (A) and one that replaces
it and that uses fossil fuel–based technology (B). They have associated
supply curves, S_A and S_B. Because long-term costs fall with the fossil fuel–based
product as technology advances, and as we know empirically that the
long-run tendency was for a relative fall in the cost of fossil fuels, supply is
far more elastic (and hence presented as a straight line here). In association
with the demand curve *D*, the equilibrium for product B is at a much higher
level of output. A social savings approach, which compared the "saving" of
the fossil fuel technology *B* with the earlier technology at the equilibrium
price of *A* that existed before *B* was employed would reckon the saving to
be shown by the rectangle $P_A FBP_B$. But this greatly underestimates the effect
of the expansion of demand that was created by product *B*, shifting supply
outward from the previous equilibrium indicated by the shaded area. At the
higher level of demand at point *B*, in this scenario the cost of good *A* would
in fact be off the scale and the savings incalculable.

we have seen the relative expansion of particular branches and sectors. The
development block is made up of interlinked processes of market suction
and market widening, which would respond in a dynamic fashion to major
changes in any of its core innovations. In fact, it might not function effectively at all. We also know that bulky goods such as coal, metals, and fertilizer saw declining marginal costs in the long run as they enjoyed benefits of
increased scale of production, and the introduction of new, more efficient
techniques as market opportunities and the reach of the transport network
expanded. This market widening was an irreversible change lowering costs
and expanding demand, a process illustrated in figure 7.2.

Without the opportunities presented by the effects of technological
change (in this case steam-driven transport) we can imagine that the economy would have maintained a more traditional structure and supply curve,

and thus operated at a higher level of costs, and lower levels of demand and supply. The savings impact of the changes was thus much larger than the basic cost savings estimated from the switch in transport technology. A similar effect was achieved by lowered transport costs making large amounts of "idle" resources profitable to exploit, thus expanding the real resource base of the economy.[12] A clear example of this is the expansion of railways into previously isolated parts of the American midwest.[13] This is of course precisely what pumping engines did in making far more coal accessible to miners. One of the primary drivers in improved real income in the late nineteenth century was the expansion of markets for agricultural goods underpinning falls in the price of foodstuffs in Europe. This too was largely a result of cheap transport expanding the real resource base of the western European economy. Indeed, the expanding resource frontier in America combined with cheap passenger rates also opened up new opportunities for migrants, which has been argued to have had a significant effect in pulling up wage rates in the poorer regions of Europe such as Ireland, Norway, and Italy.[14]

2. SEVEN LONG-RUN PROPOSITIONS

MODERN GROWTH IS CAPITAL-DEEPENING DEVELOPMENT

By the second half of the nineteenth century, observers of the economy realized that they had lived through an epochal change: as popularized by Arnold Toynbee in the English language with a series of lectures in 1884, an "Industrial Revolution."[15] Although they worried that coal-based growth would be as finite as the resource itself, people now projected the expectation of rising per capita income far into the future. This was new. Equally, it had become clear that the industrial age had introduced novel forms of social organization, a phenomenon we have come to call capitalism, although that was not a term employed by its most famous analyst, Karl Marx. In the traditional narrative of this change, the new technology employed required

---

[12] Alternatively, if idle resources were present, then traditional carriers, such as mules or horses or men, could have been employed relatively cheaply, because they were already effectively being paid a subsistence wage; they were after all alive, so this must have been the case, but not fully exploited. This would exaggerate the "social saving" calculated on the assumption that all resources were being efficiently used. If there was unemployment, then the gains from the new technology were not really so great.

[13] Cronon, 1991; specialization encouraged by transport improvement had similar effects. Caron, 1983, 45–47.

[14] Williamson and O'Rourke, 1999.

[15] Toynbee, 1884; Deane and Cole, 1962, 40; Wrigley, 2010.

large-scale investment, and tight organization of work processes on large-scale sites. Workers were separated from control over the means of production, as small-scale artisanal production became less feasible. In fact, then as now, small businesses predominated in the economy. Neither was "capitalism,"—if by that we mean the organization of production such that owners of capital set to work laborers who have no other means of subsistence—by any means novel.

Yet the industrial revolution did bring something new in regard to capital: each unit of output had a proportionally greater input of capital in its production, becoming more and more likely to depend on the fixed inputs of machines, the buildings that housed them, and the infrastructure that facilitated their operation. This is a *biased* technological development, meaning that the economy using the new technology does not simply employ equal proportions of resources (energy), capital, and labor to the previous economic structures, but requires relatively more of one or more of the inputs. The increase in the relative input of capital depended on the costs of the raw materials to produce that capital, and the elastic supply of energy to keep it running, but above all on the most important macro-innovation of the period, the steam engine, which shifted the economic possibilities for combining factor inputs, and gave a biased technical change in capital-deepening direction.

Technically, energy is converted by both capital and labor into useful work in the economy. But the ceiling for the energy employed directly by labor is the food that can be consumed by each worker. Capital has no such ceiling, or only that imposed by current technology. Thus, in the nineteenth century, capital-deepening production tended to mean energy-deepening production too. In some countries, and at an aggregate level, this also meant more energy-intense production. The cost of energy was a major consideration in investing in new capital, while the cost of energy consumed by labor is subsumed in the wage. It is important to remember that we are talking here about the ratio between the different inputs into the production of a given output. The "bias" was toward energy use and away from labor in a *relative*, not an *absolute*, sense. Capital- or energy-deepening development might well lead to a greater employment of labor and a larger population; but the increases in capital and energy consumption are proportionately greater. This is the trend that we see, illustrated in table 7.4.

Labour inputs in Britain rose under 50 percent between 1856 and 1913. Capital, energy consumption, and GDP all rose more than 200 percent.[16] The acceleration in Germany was even greater, industrializing from a more traditional base in the 1850s. In contrast we can see how Italy languished in premodern economic patterns at the start of the early 1870s and followed a less energy-deepening path as modern growth began thereafter. While the

[16] Calculated from Warde, 2007; Feinstein and Pollard, 1988 ; Matthews et al., 1982.

TABLE 7.4

Ratio of Energy Consumption and Capital to Labor (ratio in 1856/61 = 100)

	Britain		Italy		Germany	
	E/L	C/L	E/L	C/L	E/L	C/L
1856/61	100	100	100	100	100	100
1871/3	160	149	93	105	161	136
1911/3	213	222	138	172	395	269

Sources: Britain: capital from Feinstein and Pollard, 1988, labor from Feinstein and Matthews, 1983, 64–65; Italy: capital from Rossi et al., 1993, and Ercolani, 1969; labor from Daniele and Malanima, 2012; Germany: capital from Hoffmann, 1965, 253–54, labor from Warde, 2013, and Hoffmann, 1965, 204–5.

capital requirements per worker could be paid for in a few months' wages around 1800, by the end of the century industrializing nations such as Hungary saw the ratio climbing to several years.[17]

Capital deepening is not a contested idea, but the idea of "biased" technical change remains controversial both in modern economics and its application to the industrial revolution.[18] For those who wish to engage in these theoretical debates in more detail, a technical appendix is provided explaining our view.

CHEAPER ENERGY STIMULATES LABOR SAVING

As we have seen, labor and capital are really supplied in a bundle with energy. Neither can function without it. But during the nineteenth century, *fossil fuel* energy became and stayed cheap while wages rose. The overall price of energy, but in particular the price of thermal energy, and the price of labor diverged. In part I we have already seen how high nominal wages relative to energy costs encouraged mechanization within England. With declines in the price of energy and capital goods associated with the new coal-iron-steam development, labor became relatively more expensive without having become, in itself, more productive (i.e., irrespective of whether it was augmented by greater knowledge, skill, or human capital). This made energy-deepening development more attractive, and promoted further expansion of coal-using technology in preference to human labor.

In England, the startling shift in the relative cost of energy and labor occurred in the 1820s and early 1830s. Before this date, energy prices and

[17] Pollard, 1981, 221.

[18] For modern advocates of this view, see David, 1975 and Allen, 2009.

labor prices had risen roughly parallel for centuries.[19] This is hardly surprising, given that so much of the cost of coal came from the expense of transportation, itself linked to the wage level or the cost of animal fodder. Then this link was broken. The divergence came a little later for Germany, and was briefly arrested by economic upheaval in the 1870s. But the trend is unmistakable. A similar process can be observed for Italy at a later date. Before the 1870s, coal prices and wages moved in parallel. In that decade coal prices fell dramatically, and wages began their relative rise (see figure 7.3).

The long-term price trend in favor of more energy-deepening and labor-saving production is clear. This does not necessarily explain, however, why firms at any given moment might favor labor- as opposed to capital-saving innovation.[20] We can suggest two reasons for this trend. First, the emergence of the macro-innovation of steam engines and the emerging development block around it employing new machinery entailed a kind of "lock-in," as engineers were constantly presented with technical challenges and opportunities for efficiency gains by micro-inventions or "learning by doing" with the technology at hand. These efforts gave a fairly continuous stream of efficiency gains to mechanization that encouraged its further advance, not least because of constant localized pressures of "market suction": an improvement in one process created demand pressures on other mechanized processes that required innovation to keep up.[21] As competitors employed more advanced technology, the incentives grew as an investment cycle went on to catch up or leap ahead in the next round of investment.

Second, there is also a basic asymmetry between labor- and capital-saving innovation. Labor-saving innovations do not *necessarily* consume more energy, although this was often the case in the coal-consuming first industrial revolution. But labor-saving does usually imply technology as a substitute for human work.[22] The greater scale of operation often associated with steam engines also led to a greater specialization in the application of labor, although not necessarily higher levels of skill. As tasks in engineering such as cutting, grinding, and polishing came to be done by engine-driven machines, the labor force was divided into machinists dedicated to each task,

---

[19] This divergence is most notable of course in places distant from coalfields, where prices fell steeply. But it was also present in the major industrial cities and even on the coalfields themselves, where wage rates rose faster than the very modest rise on coal prices. Before the 1820s wage rates in Britain were not yet significantly influenced by modern growth. Allen, 2009, 419.

[20] In neoclassical theory, in perfect competition firms add inputs of capital and labour until the marginal return from each unit of input is identical at the margin, so the incentive to economise on each is equal. However, in a dynamic economy with price trends constantly being driven by factors exogenous to the firm we can doubt whether such conditions ever held. Firms tended to face higher wage bills than capital costs and may have made the straightforward assessment that in absolute terms there was always more to gain from cutting labour costs than capital costs if the productivity gain in each was equal.

[21] See David, 1975, 80–84.

[22] Of course organizational changes in the workplace may also improve labor productivity.

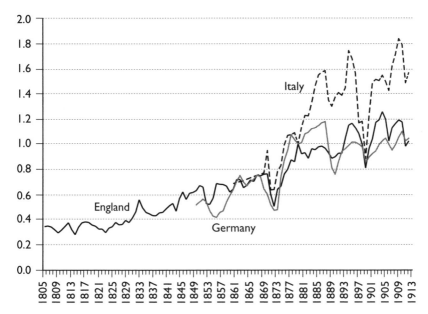

Figure 7.3. Ratio of wages and coal prices in London, Germany, and
Italy (1 = 1880)
Source: London: coal prices from Mitchell, 1988 and wages from Officer, 2008;
Germany: coal prices from Jacobs and Richter, 1935, table C.1; Italy: coal
prices from ISTAT, 1958; wages from Malanima in www.paolomalanima.it
(Italian economy).

rather than being made up of artisans who performed a range of operations
with hand tools. This created a unidirectional dynamic toward raising productivity by more mechanization and specialization, and made substitution
in a reverse direction, back from capital to the use of more labor, less and
less likely.[23] Once people had become trained in managing very particular
machines, they were not likely to be used for something else, or return to a
less specialized set of tasks. Hence the long-term dynamic of mechanization,
once set in motion, tends to continue toward greater capital-deepening so
long as there are not severe bottlenecks in the supply of engines and machines.[24] Equally, as economic growth promotes rises in wages across the
whole economy, over time more capital-intensive industries are favored and
tend to grow more rapidly (assuming there is demand for their goods).[25]

[23] A range of recent studies suggests the elasticity of substitution between capital and labor
in early industrialization may have been as low as 0.2; Allen, 2009, 425–26.

[24] If the cost of energy stays lower than other costs, a shift in an economy toward more
energy-intensive production will also raise total factor productivity, as it is effectively lowering
the costs of production; see Stern, 2010b, 31.

[25] On this last point, see Ruttan, 2001, 117.

GREATER POWER EQUALS HIGHER SPEEDS EQUALS GROWTH

We are familiar with the idea that modern society is an accelerated society, one that is always racing, a "hot"and not a "cold" society (in the case of domestic heating, this is literally true). Modern technology works fast. It was not just the capacity to move things and work machinery that grew, but the pace at which it operated. These advances were highly dependent on the availability of energy, as well as on the ability to concentrate power in machines that could be larger, more precise, and accurate. In turn, and necessarily, these machines used fuels with a greater energy density (joules/kg). Concentrated power expanded the range of possible services and tasks in the economy. But by allowing work to be done more quickly, it also greatly expanded the range of uses of people's time, which by itself could not be expanded any more than the number of hours in the day.

This great acceleration is a key aspect of the benefits of mechanization. It was not just the case that it became cheaper to move goods and people. It also meant that turnover could become higher. A journey by coach from Paris to Calais took forty hours in 1815. By 1914, the train took little over three hours.[26] Equally, shortened journey times meant that more remote regions could become integrated into the growing economy, a process that had a profound influence on regional specialization in agriculture where products were perishable, for example. Some of these time gains would have been captured in the price of travel, so the real decrease in the basic cost of transport is underestimated if we look at transport costs per kilometer. The lower costs of new transport technology would have been countered to some degree by the fact that people would pay a premium to get things done so much more quickly. But not all of this time windfall would be incorporated into the cost of travel.

Speed was not just a matter of reducing the "tyranny of distance." Mechanization also meant acceleration of work. It was not that machine technology simply allowed one to produce goods at the same rate as before, but also that it used fewer people.[27] The trend was to produce much more in the working day, expanding output. For instance, in America, the application of steam power and machine technology to manufacturing plows reduced production time from 118 man-hours to just 3.75.[28] It was as if time itself had been stretched in the world of machines. As a consequence, the output per worker also rose.

As capital and energy had an elastic supply, it was labor that became relatively scarcer (there is of course more to human labor than muscle power,

---

[26] Fontana, 2006, 208; see also Leunig, 2006.

[27] Indeed, as Marx famously pointed out, mechanization did not necessarily reduce the length of the working day, but implied a greater intensity in the work experience.

[28] Atack et al., 2007, 187.

but the number of brains are still limited by biology and demography). For a person, the day had not been stretched; it lasted as many hours as before, and the scope for doing more in that time simply by human endeavor alone, without the assistance of technology, remained limited. Indeed there was a tendency, especially in the more advanced countries, to shorten the working day. Yet the demand for the services provided by people grew. This has further driven a relative price increase in labor or, in other words, further driven up wages relative to capital and energy costs. However, the possibility for substitution between labor and capital varied considerably among branches of the economy. Even if workers in particular enterprises do not become more productive, their wages are set with reference to the general wage level in the labor market and hence the productivity gains of technological advance have been spread even to those areas where there has been relatively little change in capital and energy inputs. Even those working in the most plodding and traditional activities have benefited from the revolution in speed, so long as they have not been forced out of business altogether.[29]

STRONG COMPLEMENTARITY BETWEEN ENERGY AND CAPITAL

The most important aspect of capital was machinery; we would not expect greater provision of dwelling-houses to make any difference to the productivity of the economy. It was mechanization that reduced relative demand for labor.[30] During the first industrial revolution machinery prices fell, and diverged from wage trends even more than energy costs. This is because the greatest cost in making machinery was metals, which as we have seen in chapter 6, became very much cheaper due to coal-smelting. The risk from rapid mechanization might have been that this generated market suction, pushing up coal prices, especially as a very large proportion of the coal mined was consumed by the iron industry in countries like Germany and Britain. Supply, however, was equal to the task. The second half of the nineteenth century was the golden age for the coal development block. As we can see in figure 7.4, the ratio of prices of machinery and coal moved in the opposite direction to that of labor and coal (shown in figure 7.3).

If capital is becoming relatively cheaper compared to fuel (albeit partly driven by developments in the energy economy), might we not also expect that capital substitutes for energy? To some degree this seems to be the case; the capital-deepening economy was, in many branches, a more

---

[29] Ruttan, 2001, 8–13.

[30] Indeed there is something to be said for the first English dictionary definition of the Industrial Revolution, from 1926: "rapid development of industry owing to the employment of machinery." Cited in Griffin, 2010, 8.

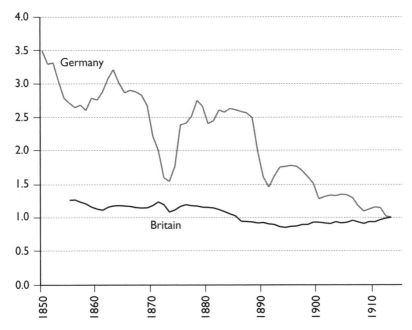

Figure 7.4. Ratio of machinery and coal prices in
Germany and Britain (1913 = 1)
Note: British coal prices are an unweighted
average of pithead and London prices. British prices
are for plant and machinery, German for machinery only.
Source: Church, 1986, 53–54; Feinstein, 1972, table 63;
Hoffmann, 1965, 572–73, 607; Jacobs and Richter, 1935.

energy-efficient one.[31] Nevertheless, despite the fact that steam engines became very much more economical in their use of coal during the eighteenth
and nineteenth centuries, and that highly efficient processes such as Neilson's hot-blast in iron-making were very attractive in markets where fuel
was relatively expensive, the trend during the first industrial revolution was
for energy consumption and capital to be complementary. Even in industries where wage costs were a comparatively small part of total costs (for
example in pig iron smelting as opposed to textiles), advances were far more
labor-saving than capital- or energy-saving.[32] In turn, capital formation was
much more rapid in the "modern" and more energy-intense sectors of the
economy. In Britain the share of net capital formation in the "modern sectors" climbed from 11.4 percent of the total in the 1790s to 46.1 percent
in the 1850s. If we remove land and dwellings from this calculation, the

[31] See the discussion in Stern, 2010b, 10–29.
[32] Allen, 2009, 221.

advance is from 35.9 percent of the total (indicating the already relatively developed nature of the British economy before 1800) to 65.6 percent.[33] Overall, industrial output saw a relative shift toward capital rather than consumer goods.[34]

A New Distribution and New Horizons for Knowledge

Obviously new technology required inventors, operators, and in some cases theoreticians who collectively had the requisite skills to conceive, construct, refine, maintain, and put into effect new equipment and techniques.[35] But economies had always required what has come to be called "human capital," tacit and explicit forms of knowledge and capabilities that allow them to generate income and strive for well-being, just as societies have always required "social capital" to function: trust, personal networks, and institutions to facilitate exchange, and indeed a degree of faith in the future.

The question for us is, did any of these forms of "capital" become qualitatively different during the first industrial revolution? In other words, was there a *biased* development in which these factors became relatively more important? Clearly, technical advance led to societies, collectively, having knowledge of many more processes and possibilities. No one would have attempted to generate higher future incomes from technological advancement if they did not expect ingenuity to win reward, whether pecuniary or in esteem. In this sense the discourse of "improvement" that emerged more markedly from the seventeenth century, and the culture of enlightenment, played their part in generating the conditions for advance; most notably, of course in urban centers and among well-connected groups with money to invest, in other words, those who had already profited from generations of more gradual economic advancement.[36]

It is harder to determine how this knowledge was distributed and assess its contributions to adding value in the economy. Unfortunately, metrics sometimes used for human capital are inappropriate for nineteenth-century society. General literacy rates are only very roughly equated with income in the early modern period and nineteenth century. A lifetime of Bible-reading did not necessarily bring any gains in metallurgical technique, for example, and most of the general skills of the workforce were learned "on the job," "by doing." The advance of technical manuals and publications of leading engineers such as John Smeaton may have made some difference, although tireless personal advocacy and working may have been as influential as

---

[33] Calculated from Wrigley, 2010, 200–3.
[34] Schön, 1988; Gustafsson, 1996, 208.
[35] Mokyr, 2002.
[36] Warde, 2011; Mokyr, 2009.

anything they wrote.[37] While much of western Europe introduced compulsory elementary schooling in the nineteenth century (if not before), and set up academies for the promotion of navigation, engineering, mining, arts and sciences, to name only a few, it is less clear whether this was the consequence rather than the cause of growth, and in any case, only a tiny proportion of the population attended them. These institutions would prove important for the future and provide key skills during the second industrial revolution, but their role in earlier developments appears marginal.

There is no doubt that, as has been detailed in the previous chapter, breakthroughs in knowledge and the dissemination of ideas and skills were required for the combination of new technologies and techniques that built the development block of the first industrial revolution. In this sense the modern economy was indeed a "gift of Athena," among other things. Knowledge of scientific developments, whether acquired through formal educational institutions or not, was essential for the long-term development of the steam engine and the chemical industries.[38] Robert Allen has argued for the importance of expertise in clock- and instrument-making for promoting early mechanization, and the everyday maintenance of increasingly complex machinery required similar skills.[39] Yet whether the new coal economy required a more general enhancement of human capital, as did subsequent energy regimes, is more open to question. Indeed, some new developments in capital and mechanization were explicitly introduced to break the power of skilled male laborers and permit a wider use of child and female labor.[40] Econometric studies have come to rather varied results depending on assumptions made about how human capital should be measured.[41]

Clearly many key services that oiled the wheels of commerce and exchange required literacy, knowledge of the law, and mathematical skills. There is little doubt that humanity's stock of useful knowledge was expanding, just as human numbers themselves were growing. What we can state more clearly is that there was a changing distribution of expertise and knowledge, and increased levels of specialization across the economy, whether presented by a career researching chemistry, or becoming highly proficient in operating a particular kind of printing press. As specialization and disciplinary expertise advanced, it provided greater incentives for those individuals to expand their useful knowledge, more so than in the wider but shallower expertise

---

[37] Mokyr has attempted quantification of publications on particular subjects using online book catalogs, and it is clear that technical journals had a wider circulation at this time. Mokyr, 2009, 47.

[38] Mokyr, 2002, 28–118; 2009, 30–144; Kleinschmidt, 2007, 93–96.

[39] Allen, 2009, 204–6, 243–44.

[40] Evans and Rýden, 2007, 260–5; Humphries, 2011, 24–25.

[41] Prados de la Escosura and Rosés, 2010, 11–12; Allen, 2009, 423; Schulze, 2007, 203; Le et al., 2003.

of the artisanal milieu. But one can also point to examples of de-skilling as advances in education across the broader sweep of society. The net balance is more difficult to weigh.

THERE ARE LIMITS TO PER CAPITA GROWTH WITHOUT LABOR SAVING

At the end of chapter 4, we showed, using a simple production function, how the productivity of labor was determined by its combination with capital and natural resources:

$$\frac{Y}{L} = AF\left(\frac{K}{L}, \frac{R}{L}\right)$$

where Y represents the output, L, K, and R respectively labor, capital, and resources, and A any technical knowledge or qualities able to increase the efficiency of the system. The knowledge A can augment the value of capital or labor or may represent a quality of the energy carrier itself (such as higher density). Often it is difficult to disaggregate these effects (see appendix A for an example of how it can be done). In most of Europe in the pre-industrial period the trend in labor productivity appears to have been downward; capital and resources per worker were falling, and technical progress was not fast enough to counteract this trend. Even in the early years of the industrial revolution, developments in the economy were only able to stabilize the capital endowment per worker and wages rather than actually expand them. But by the 1820s, the long-run process of modern growth was in train in parts of the continent. The coal-iron-steam development block brought declines in the price of resources and capital goods relative to labor, which allowed the rapid expansion in their use and the resources available per laborer, in other words, labor-saving. Without these labor savings, the level of consumer demand for manufactured goods and services could not have been raised to any great degree.

THERE ARE LIMITS TO GROWTH WITHOUT LAND-SAVING

We can take a much more basic view of the importance of coal and energy transition that is not based on the calculation of economic *values*, but on the simple ecological constraints of the amount of energy available. If there was no coal, how much wood might have been required to power an industrial revolution? An answer provides an indication of the physical limits to the traditional energy regime.

TABLE 7.5

Counterfactual firewood requirements for Europe with no coal

	Actual energy consumption		Counterfactual if no coal		
	Percent Firewood	Percent Coal	Firewood equivalent (million m³)	Land Area required (million km²)	Percent of Total Land Area
1850	58	42	388.4	1.29	58
1870	23	77	698.8	2.53	96
1900	5	95	1492.9	5.28	201

Note: At 1850, the dataset covers England and Wales, France, Spain, Sweden, Netherlands, and Germany. At 1870 and 1900 it additionally covers Italy and Portugal.

Let us assume then that wood could have replaced coal at any given date, combined with the assumption that it would have been used just as efficiently as coal was to produce income (as coal technology became much more efficient over time, this would equally have been required of wood-burning technology, assuming it could have provided the same kind of output). We can examine both the amount of wood required and how this relates to the actual area of woodland available to Europeans during the nineteenth century (remembering that wood imports from other continents were very small at this time; an international market for firewood on any scale has never existed; and that these figures dwarf the international timber trade of the age, when we remember that any firewood supply to major population centers would have had to be transported considerable distances).[42] These estimates are made on the somewhat generous basis that European woodland would have produced on average some 3 m³ of firewood per hectare per year (table 7.5).[43]

[42] For comparison, before the First World War, the United Kingdom imported almost all of its timber consumption, and repesented a much larger market than any that had previously existed. None of this was used for firewood, but met construction needs. At that point it imported around 14 million m³ of wood per year, predominantly from the Baltic and Russia; less than 1 percent of the counterfactual level of demand calculated above. Iriarte-Goñi and Ayuda, 2012.

[43] Nineteenth-century wood yields were often considered to be closer to 1 to 1.5 m³ per hectare. While individual woodlands (as with fields) could achieve much higher yields, especially if coppiced: 3–4 m³ per ha across relatively large areas, although large parts of Europe would not have been suited to this usage or level of output. In any case, even a substantially higher yield would have required improbably large areas of the continent to be wooded, and exploited at their highest sustainable rate. This would also exclude the use of timber for any other purposes. On wood yields, see Warde, 2006.

TABLE 7.6
Hectares of soil theoretically needed by the European population to meet energy
requirements in 1750, 1900, and 2000, using the same energy carriers as in 1750 at
the same efficiency (Europe without Russia)

	Per c. Mj* Per day	Per c. Toe per year*	European Population (millions)	Land per c. (ha)	Total land (million ha)
1750	63–84	0.55–0.73	121	1.75	211,750
1900	157.3	1.37	295	4.50	1,330,000
2000	423.0	3.7	523	11.00	5,800,000

* Mj: Megajoules; Toe: Tons Oil Equivalent (1 Toe = 10^7 kcal).
Sources: Malanima, 2003 and 2006a.

Already by 1850 thermal energy requirements would have required woodland to cover 58 percent of the land in the sample to be entirely used for firewood. This was undoubtedly well above the actual forested area at a time when, coincidentally, 58 percent of thermal energy supply did come from firewood and 42 percent from coal. By 1870, as coal became increasingly dominant, nearly the entirety of western and northern Europe would have had to be covered with woods to supply its energy needs, and by 1900, double the total land area. In the regions of highest demand the energy demand was far and away above the local capacity of the land to supply it: in England and Wales, already needing nearly five times the land area by 1850 and more than fourteen times by 1900. Germany moved from requiring around a third of its land area in 1850 (approximately the total actually wooded at the time) to more than three times the total land area by 1900. By the 1870s, such levels of wood supply would have been a physical impossibility, even if we could suspend the normal operations of economics.

We can expand the same exercise to cover the whole "organic economy" and longer growth of population and energy consumption in modern times. A simple calculation shows that, if the energy system had been based for the last 250 years on the same sources exploited in 1750—assuming the same land productivity—the need for fertile land would have grown to more than three times the entire surface area of Europe in 1900 and to ten times that area in 2000 (table 7.6). Alternatively, the land of Europe would have had to become almost thirty times more productive without the benefits of modern fertilizers, or the use of "organic" energy in generating income would have had to become more efficient to the same degree to maintain the population at modern levels of income while using the energy base of 1750.

3. ENERGY INTENSITY AND ECONOMIC STRUCTURE

FORWARD AND BACKWARD LINKAGES

The dynamics of the new development block can be illustrated through examining what economists call "forward" and "backward" linkages. These trace the influences that developments in one area of the economy have on others: in the case of backward linkages, how developments in one process influence the demand and supply of *inputs* into that process, and in the case of forward linkages, how developments in the *output* of one sector lead to changes in the inputs in another. Tracing these relationships helps us understand the interdependencies of the development block. For example, we have already seen how new iron-making techniques using coke instead of charcoal have a backward linkage to coal mining, because demand for coal may rise significantly. At the same time, this allows iron to be produced far more cheaply, creating a forward linkage into the supply of machinery made out of iron, and the capital costs for industries that use this machinery. It is out of such linkages that development blocks are formed.

The railways in the nineteenth century provide the most spectacular example of forward and backward linkages, although it is a characteristic of a development block that no single element, even such a major technological breakthrough, can catapult an economy into rapid growth: it is the power they have *in combination*. The steam locomotive was of course a British creation, but its potential was immediately widely recognised (if not universally; Austrians persisted in building a horse-drawn railway over two hundred kilometers long as late as 1836).[44] In every one of the European "successor" countries the first rails and locomotives were imported, providing a very considerable boost to British engineering. It was not until the mid-1850s that Germany began to emancipate itself from dependency on imports. Later, Italy and France took the same course, producing their own equipment.[45]

Frequently it was not the initial construction of the railways, but the need for their continual maintenance and updating of the stock that provided a major stimulus to domestic industry. Demand from the railways accounted for 25–33 percent of the output of machinery, and 11–12 percent of total iron and steel output in France, 1830–80. In Germany, consumption levels were even higher between 1840 and 1859, when between 16 and 26 percent of all domestic iron consumption, and up to 37 percent of production, went to rails alone.[46] The concentrated demand from first textile machin-

[44] Pollard, 1981, 202.

[45] Fenoaltea, 1983, 67–8; Fremdling, 1983, 123–4.

[46] Belgium's modern iron industry similarly took off and freed itself from dependence on imports in response to the huge demands of constructing a national rail network from 1834;

ery and then railways provided a scale of market that justified the much greater capital investment required for the coke-smelting of iron and more advanced refineries, even if at first their market share remained lower than the more diffuse traditional markets such as for agricultural tools.[47] The specific requirements of quality rails and equipment were a stimulus to innovation and new techniques, such as the spread of the Bessemer steel-making process. In France, 83 percent of high-quality steel went to the railways in 1879.[48] With these "backward linkages," the supply-side innovation of the locomotive on rails pulled up connected industries in its wake as people rushed to enjoy its benefits.

But the most important kind of linkages were "forward linkages": the services provided by the rapidly expanding transport sector itself. And in the case of steam, people and goods did not just move greater distances. They moved over them quickly, and hence paying for a railway ticket really was a way to buy more time. This effectively brought new resources into the economy: trains effectively lengthened the day for those who used them.

The ability to transport cheaply and in bulk over water and especially over land brought wide benefits, not least in the delivery of coal itself. The coal trade thus came to be one of the key users of the railways, and instrumental in expanding traffic. In England, coal shipments accounted for 30 percent of the receipts for rail freight by 1870. Even in Italy, coal was easily the single product that provided the greatest weight of shipments, and accounted for nearly a quarter of the total in 1911.[49] In the Ruhr, it cost 40 *pfennig* to cart a tonne of coal one kilometer in 1840, but the price by train was less than half this; by 1850 it was a mere 2 *pfennig* per ton! Freight rates in Germany were 13.6 *pfennig* per ton-km in 1845 but less than a third of this figure by 1880.[50] Any energy-intense industry had its costs slashed. Falls of similar magnitude were repeated everywhere. The huge surge in the use of transport that came with the railways shows that demand was highly price-elastic. Thus the inter-linkages between coal and rail were not simply about the affordability of the fuel for the new technology, but the market-widening effects in providing cheap coal.

Caron, 1983, 37. Comparable impacts are found in Italy; Fenoaltea, 1983, 68–69; also, in Germany railway demand more than doubled that from the large agricultural sector from the 1840s–60s, although with the expansion of agricultural machinery the latter still accounted for between one-third and one-fifth of total demand, an indication of the importance of the boom in iron production to supply from the primary sector. Similar effects can be observed in Hungary. Fremdling, 1983, 125; 1975; Tilly, 1996, 102–9; Milward and Saul, 1977, 443; Pollard, 1981, 239; Berend, 1996, 281.

[47] Milward and Saul, 1977, 329–30; Herrigel, 1996, 77; Pieremkemper and Tilly, 2004, 58–64; Gross, 1973, 267.

[48] Caron, 1983, 39.

[49] Hawke, 1970, 73, 174. Mineral freight took 40 percent of the receipts and 75 percent of this was coal or coke. By weight or volume the share would be much higher.

[50] Fremdling, 1983, 132–33.

Forward linkages meant that even in relatively far-flung outposts of coal's new empire like Italy, heat-intensive industry could expand. At first the new Italian industries using coal served largely domestic markets, unable to compete with the world leaders. The peninsula saw a great surge in the production in metallurgy, paper, bricks, glass, cement, but above all engineering and chemicals between 1878 and 1911. This would provide the basis for Italy's strong performance in light engineering during the twentieth century. Trains were also essential to the spectacular advance of the chemical industry, which centered on agricultural fertilizers. These were delivered to market exclusively by rail. Thus, although the Italian industrial sector grew little as a proportion of the economy, it underwent radical restructuring.[51] Over time, import substitution took place, and these economies were able to develop some specialist sectors that employed the new technology for local uses.

The effects of cheap capital and energy can also be illustrated with a simple "input-output" model, as has been estimated for the British economy in 1841.[52] The price of iron in Britain in the 1830s was about 40 percent of the 1780s level.[53] We can get a sense of the effects of this price decline by inserting alternative price data into the input-output model, assuming that the revolution in iron production making it relatively more cheap had not occurred. If iron in the 1830s had been 150 percent more expensive, the cost of metals for the economy would have been nearly £30 million instead of the approximately £12 million it was in 1841. Both these figures are fairly small shares of GDP at the time. But as the metal input accounted for most (c. 80 percent) of the cost of metal goods, these in turn would have cost £33.2 million to produce instead of £15.2 million. In turn, about half of metal goods went into investment as machinery.[54] These would have cost nearly £17 million instead of the £7.7 million they did in 1841.

Thus investment in machinery would have been substantially more than twice as expensive as it actually was, even at this relatively early stage of the great advances achieved in the nineteenth century. Costs would in all probability have been much higher, as it is hard to believe that charcoal-smelted iron could have seen output expansion without very significant *rises* in its price.[55] The knock-on effect would be to increase the cost of power and

[51] Zamagni, 1993; Fenoaltea, 1983, 77–78. In Italy's case the expansion of steam power seems closely linked to the cheapening of coal after about 1870. Italy had virtually no steam engines in industry in 1861. Pollard, 1981, 230.

[52] Horrell, Humphreys, and Weale, 1994.

[53] In fact there was considerable local variation and various qualities of the product, not least the distinction between pig and bar iron, so this can only be an approximation. Hyde, 1977.

[54] So closely are these prices linked that historians have taken the price of iron as a proxy for the price of machinery. See Hoffmann, 1965.

[55] Calculations made from data in Horrell, Humphreys, and Weale, 1994, 547. See the related critique of the social savings approach above.

transportation, making resource use more expensive. Even if these are still small sums relative to GDP, what matters for producers is *marginal cost*. More expensive machinery and resources would have led to less capital investment, lower labor productivity, and lower wages. In such circumstances, it is likely that economic growth would have done well indeed to match the rapid population growth of the nineteenth century.

Such considerations by no means exhaust the inter-linkages. It has been claimed, for example, that the vast investment sums required for railway construction, and the speculative enthusiasm these generated, played a significant role in the development of financial institutions and the equities market in several parts of Europe. Certainly these investments became a very large part of capital formation, playing a dominant role in many countries in some periods. Urbanization, often closely linked to the adoption of fossil fuels, brought large concentrations of people and knowledge, the "economic density" often credited by economic geographers with "spillover" effects promoting specialization and growth.

ENERGY SAVING VERSUS ENERGY EXPANSION

Modern energy history has been a battle of countervailing pressures. Ever since the first power machinery was invented, people have sought to get more out for less input. The efficiency gains over time have often been spectacular, and so have the energy savings. Yet the fossil fuel economy also made a vast stock of energy available to society at a relatively cheap price. At the same time, new power technology has opened new possibilities and a great range of new activities. These two forces combined have promoted the expansion of energy use. The overall balance sheet of the energy economy, the end result by which energy consumption rises or falls, can be imagined as the outcome of the race between saving and expansion.

Different economic activities have, of course, very different energy intensities. Heat-intensive processes, such as smelting in furnaces, are far more demanding of energy than those using fuel simply as a source of motive power, especially as more efficient steam engine technology was developed. In turn, branches such as retail premises that only consume fuel to provide some warmth and light put even fewer demands on energy supply. Thus the structure of the economy will affect its capital and energy intensity.

We can now flesh out this analysis. Table 7.7 shows the energy intensity of various activities in the British economy around 1870. The most voracious consumers of energy were the chemical industry and the utilities. They were only a small proportion of national income—no more than 2 percent in 1870—but nevertheless key aspects of modern life in the provision of industrial raw material, light, clean water, and power. Next was iron. Collieries themselves were very energy-intense. It might seem trivial to say that

TABLE 7.7

Energy and Labor Intensity by Branch in England and Wales, 1870 (tons of coal per £1000 and workers per £1000 output at 1913 prices)

Branch	Coal Intensity	Labor Intensity
Agriculture	4	16.4
Mining	137	8.4
Iron and steel	281	4
Textiles and clothing	48	20.8
Food, drink and tobacco	31	20.7
Gas and water	1213	5.3
Transport	67	8.8
Chemicals	479	N/A

Source: Calculated from BPP, 1871; Feinstein, 1972; Deane and Cole, 1962.

to produce a lot of coal you need a lot of coal, but of course it is not: this is a condition of having an elastic supply of energy in the economy more generally, and thus was a great advantage to Britain, Germany, and Belgium. Energy extraction is energy-intense.

Precisely because of the presence of both forward and backward linkages, the twin processes of saving and expansion cannot be considered in isolation. It was recognized by Jevons as early as the 1860s, while contemplating the new coal economy, that energy savings could themselves lead to the expansion of energy consumption. The effect of increased efficiency was to make the good or service provided cheaper. This fall in price had a forward linkage that stimulated demand and that increased demand that in turn cascaded down through backward linkages to stimulate further production. Efficiency is, after all, getting the same for less and this in turn promotes greater consumption, although not necessarily of the same kind.[56]

Trends in energy intensity, the measure of the process of "energy saving" in an economy, differed significantly between countries. In most countries, especially those in the south, energy intensity remained quite stable over the nineteenth century. British energy intensity rose in the first half of the century, but declined slightly after the mid-1870s. Sweden's energy intensity was remarkably high, but fell over the nineteenth century primarily because of the introduction of much more efficient domestic heating, and to a lesser

[56] Jevons, 1866; Ayres and Warr, 2008; Hanley et al., 2009.

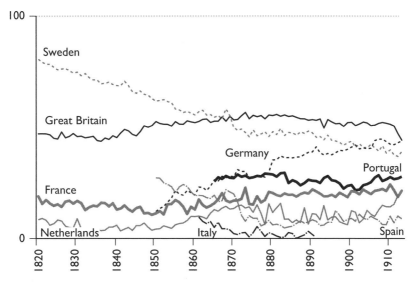

Figure 7.5. Energy intensity, 1820–1913 (MJ / GDP in 1990 $). Log scale. *Source*: See www.energyhistory.org.

degree efficiency improvements in iron industry and in agriculture.[57] Germany's intensity rose.

Countries thus did not follow a standard pattern in the development of energy intensity over time.[58] For the most part, countries stayed within a range, and a level, that was already established by the mid-nineteenth century. From the middle of the nineteenth century most countries saw very modest falls, but in Germany, energy intensity rose rapidly to British levels.

There was thus energy saving in nearly all of the countries, but expansion won out. Table 7.8 presents a more detailed Commoner-Ehrlich decomposition of the drivers of energy consumption in our sample countries. In nearly all cases population growth outpaced any efficiency savings, with the exceptions of Sweden and Spain. Increases in income per capita also had a positive effect on energy consumption, pushing it upward, and in nearly all cases a larger effect than population growth. If these population and income changes had operated without any changes in the efficiency of energy use, then northern Europe would have seen general increases in energy consumption of more than 2 percent p.a. across the period, and southern Europe between 1 and 2 percent p.a., reflecting the more rapid growth of population and income throughout most of the north.

[57] Kander, 2002
[58] See Gales et al., 2007.

TABLE 7.8

Annual growth rates (%) in Population, Income per capita, Energy Intensity, and Total Energy Consumption, 1856–1913

	GB	Sweden	Netherlands	Germany	Italy	Spain	France	Portugal
Population	1.15	0.75	1.13	1.08	0.66	0.46	0.11	0.66
Income per cap	0.93	1.81	0.89	1.56	1.19	1.00	1.31	0.45
Energy Intensity	−0.29	−0.76	0.56	0.97	−0.65	−0.58	0.21	−0.07
Energy	1.80	1.80	2.58	3.61	1.20	0.88	1.63	1.04

[1] Italy from 1861–1913.

In Britain, already a mature industrial economy by 1870, technical improvements such as the increasing use of the high-pressure steam engine led to modestly energy-saving growth, while energy consumption, population, and income expanded at a greater rate than these savings. Jevons was thus a sharp observer of his times, writing in the mid-1860s. In southern Europe and Sweden, it was efficiency savings in the use of traditional carriers which created an energy-saving effect, and decelerated the rate of growth of energy consumption that was being driven by income growth and more modest population expansion. But as we shall see, this growth leaned upon imports from more energy-intense economies and by the end of the period was already reaping the gains of the second industrial revolution. In contrast, Germany and the Netherlands saw rises in energy intensity which compounded the general tendency toward expansion and led to extraordinarily high rates of growth in energy consumption: nearly 3.7 percent sustained over six decades in the case of Germany.

DIVERGENCE AND THE INTERNATIONAL DIVISION OF LABOR

Differences in energy consumption and energy intensity are explained by and reflect differences in the structures of economies. Over the longer term, most regions of Europe could share in roughly the same technology, even if sharing information and technique could be a protracted process, often requiring the migration of skilled individuals.[59] But where energy was cheapest, the structure of the economy was such that energy-intense sectors were proportionally very large, making for a high level of total energy consump-

[59] See chapter 6.

tion and a high level of intensity. Where energy was more expensive, these more energy-intense sectors remained modest in size, although key for overall development. Germany underwent a structural transformation to an energy-intense economy after 1850, a process Britain had already undergone in an earlier period. It so happened that these energy-intense sectors were also the core of the new industrial development block.

The level of energy intensity reflected what was economically possible in different parts of Europe. An industry that was highly energy-intense needed to be situated where fuel supplies were cheap both to survive international competition, and be seen as a viable investment in the first place. Not every single one of such industries had to be right on top of a coalfield, although it was a clear advantage if they were. What was ideal was the ability to combine the supply of raw materials from nearby sources, as did the copper industry of southern Wales, iron-making in lowland Scotland and Teesside in England, and iron production in the Ruhr region of Germany. By 1870, Britain produced more than half of the pig iron in the entire world, and 43 percent of the steel. After this date Germany and the United States caught up rapidly, partly through highly effective integration of the different stages of production, recycling of hot gases, and the exploitation of waste products such as phosphorous-rich slag from steelmaking as agricultural fertiliser.[60] But no country without direct access to both these mineral and metallurgical resources could hope to compete. Coal-rich regions became the centres of key heat-intensive industries, especially metallurgy, heavy engineering, and aspects of the chemical industry that often used coal by-products. As well as the coalfields of Britain, and the Sambre-Meuse and Ruhr regions of northwest Europe, by the First World War great industrialized concentrations had arisen in the Czech lands and after railway development from the 1880s, the Donets basin in Russia.[61] This in turn encouraged the development of expertise in the kinds of capital equipment required, becoming suppliers of machinery when cheaper transport facilitated the spread of energy-intense techniques. While steam shipping eventually would come to predominate in the merchant fleets of all European nations, only Britain and Germany could afford to construct the fleet domestically. Scandinavia and Mediterranean Europe imported a large proportion of their fleets second-hand, a share as high as 88 percent in Italy in 1914, as well as sticking with sail ships much longer.[62]

Areas where energy was expensive opted for much less energy-intense forms of industrialization, and generally their industrialization also came late. New technology was only adopted when its efficiency had improved to such an extent that the effects on overall energy intensity were small.

[60] Broadberry, 1997, 165; Kleinschmidt, 2007, 20.
[61] Pollard, 1981, 225, 241, 247; Munting, 1996, 333.
[62] Milward and Saul, 1977, 176; Cafagna, 1973, 314.

TABLE 7.9
Sectoral share of coal consumption in Britain 1800–1870 (%)

	Mining	Iron	Other Industry	Transport	Gas	Agriculture	Domestic
1800	12	12	39	0	0	0	37
1830	13	19	29	0	0	0	39
1850	12	27	33	4	2	0	23
1870	11	28	32.5	4	4	0.5	20

Source: Flinn, 1984; Church, 1986.

Advances tended to come in light engineering, textiles, and more special-ist capital goods. Sweden is a case in point. Here, early industrialization actually led to a *decline* in the energy intensity of the industrial sector. The diversification of industry away from iron smelting and a partial switch to coal lowered fuel consumption per unit of output.[63]

These divergent experiences are clear if we compare the share of coal consumption taken by each sector, illustrated in tables 7.9 and 7.10. We must remember, of course, that per capita level of coal consumption was very much higher in Britain. Even in the 1870s Swedish consumption was dominated by domestic households, partly from foreign coal imported to the port cities, and in part from localized domestic coalfields in the south. But the overall scale of consumption was very small. In contrast, the house-hold share of British consumption shrank quite rapidly after 1830. Between 1830 and 1870, as British consumption shot upward, industry took the li-on's share of this growth, two-thirds in total. In both periods well over half of this industrial growth came from coal consumed making one single com-modity: iron. We can also observe that the mining sector itself consumed a large and steady share, almost all in collieries.

In those countries without the combination of coal and iron ore, it was the introduction of railways that directly promoted growth in coal con-sumption. Transport accounted for only a small amount of the growth of coal consumption in Britain, and was less than a tenth of total consumption in the early twentieth century, even with an extensive railway network and the mighty merchant marine of Victoria's empire. This low share for trans-port was almost precisely the same as Belgium, another coal-rich country. But in Sweden, railways accounted for 39 percent of the expansion in use in 1850–70, and industry only 16 percent. In Italy transport was the largest consumer.[64] In those countries, coal was still so expensive that only custom-

[63] Kander, 2002, 82.
[64] Kander, 2002, 202; Church, 1986, 30; Laffaut, 1983, 213.

TABLE 7.10
Sectoral share of coal consumption in Sweden 1850–1870 (%)

	Mining	Iron	Other Industry	Transport	Gas	Agriculture	Domestic
1850	0	0	13	30	0	4	53
1870	0	0	9	37	6	8	40

Source: Kander, 2002.

ers that were willing to pay a premium for the energy density of coal would consume much of it.

Table 7.11 shows the steady progress toward industrialization of a number of European economies in 1870 and 1913. We can also see the increasing divergence of north and south, especially by the later date.

What a simple sectoral breakdown does not show is the *scale* of production in each sector in each country. To show the real benefit each inhabitant

TABLE 7.11
Sectoral shares of national income, 1870–1913 (1913 prices)

	Primary	Industry	Transport & Services
1870			
Britain	14	34	52
Sweden	50	17	33
Italy	54	17	29
Spain	38	19	44
Germany	38	32	30
1913			
Britain	6	39	55
Sweden	25	40	35
Italy	39	23	38
Spain	28	27	44
Germany	23	45	32

Sources: Britain from Feinstein, 1972, with adjustment of 1870 figure to account for the more agricultural economy of Ireland being included in his total for the UK. See also Matthews, Feinstein, and Odling-Smee, 1982, 222–23; Sweden from Krantz and Schön, 2007; Italy from Malanima, 2006, 132–33; Spain from Prados de los Escosura, 2003; Germany from Hoffmann, 1965, 33.

TABLE 7.12
Per capita sectoral production, 1913 (1990 $)

	Primary	Industry	Transport & Services	Total GDP per capita
Britain	309	2009	2833	5150
Sweden	774	1238	1084	3158
Italy	1000	590	974	2564
Spain	576	555	904	2035
Germany	839	1642	1167	3648

Source: See table 7.11; Maddison, 2003.

(on average, of course) gained from this distribution of economic activity across the continent, table 7.12 allocates the income from each sector on a per capita basis. It is important to stress that these are not measures of productivity, because we are not examining output relative to the workforce in each sector, but the output relative to the total population.

Thus we see that while in 1913 Sweden's industrial sector was the same size relative to its own economy as that of Britain, its industrial output per head was only 62 percent of that achieved by the European leader. Indeed, British per capita industrial production, in only one sector, was roughly the same as Spanish per capita GDP! The lead of Britain in services and transportation was even greater. Although agricultural production provided less value to each Briton than was the case in neighboring nations, the gap was not nearly as large as one might expect given the very small share of agricultural production in national income. Agriculture on the island was highly productive relative to quite modest inputs. But the British population was very heavily dependent on imports for its food supply, a situation made possible by its manufacturing and commercial prowess.

The distribution of resources was a powerful force in creating an international division of labor among economies. As can be seen in table 7.13, this divergence was very marked in energy regimes. Around 1820, the largest consumer of energy used only about four times more energy per person than the smallest, and nearly all countries fell in a narrow range. By 1910, the dispersion was much wider, and the largest consumer consumed over eight times more than the smallest. Figure 7.6 illustrates the startlingly different balance of different carriers within each economy, despite the common trend toward increased use of coal by the second half of the nineteenth century. Traditional carriers remained dominant in the less energy-intense countries.

We should not view each country in splendid isolation, as if they represent alternative and equally possible paths to modern economic growth. This was not the case. Even an industrial powerhouse like Britain, that was so suc-

TABLE 7.13
Per capita energy consumption (GJ per person)

	England & Wales	Sweden	Netherlands	Germany	Italy	Spain	France	Portugal
c. 1820	60	43.3	21.8	16.0	18.0	20.2	18.1	18.4
c. 1850	89.4	35.4	24.9	18.0	18.0	20.2	21.1	18.4
1880	134.4	39.0	40.0	43.2	17.6	18.5	35.3	19.2
1910	152.8	58.1	49.2	86.3	22.3	22.7	54.0	22.0

Sources: See www.energyhistory.org. As no data are available at the earliest date for Italy, Spain, and Portugal, the earliest extant data are used.

cessful for a time in out-competing its neighbors in the production of some highly important goods, albeit a relatively narrow range of them, needed centers of productive success elsewhere; not least to generate demand for its leading sectors, which were heavily dependent on exports. By 1851 Britain exported over 60 percent of its cotton, 25 percent of its wool, and nearly 40 percent of its iron. If these exported goods alone were removed from the national energy account and attributed to the countries where they were actually consumed, British energy consumption would have been approximately 12 percent lower. This figure, which itself should be treated as a minimum, is certainly too small to produce a major convergence between the exporters and importers of energy-intense goods, but begins to give a sense that interdependencies could operate on a considerable scale in quantity as well as the qualities of the goods (such as steam engines) traded.[65] Britain and Belgium could benefit from the export of machinery, although this in part sowed the seeds for the demise of the division of labor that so benefited them. In France the catch-up was rapid and the country was producing nearly all of its own steam engines and locomotives by the mid-1840s, moving to becoming an exporter itself. In some cases, this international division of labor was also promoted by major capital flows, especially toward important suppliers of raw materials in the New World and Scandinavia, or eastward from France, Germany, and Austria into Poland and Hungary.[66]

Equally, countries that pursued less energy-intense paths to growth still required the expanding markets of the new economic order. Italian industrial centers were not very energy-intense but they could not have existed without the prior development of Britain. The Baltic countries exported raw

[65] As yet, no historical work on energy embodied in trade has been undertaken. Estimates of coal consumed in the exported industries from Church, 1986 and British Parliamentary Papers, 1871.

[66] Crouzet, 1996, 43; O'Rourke and Williamson, 1999, 235–37; Pustuka, 1992; Pollard, 1981, 226; Berend and Ránki, 1979, 1982; Munting, 1996, 337.

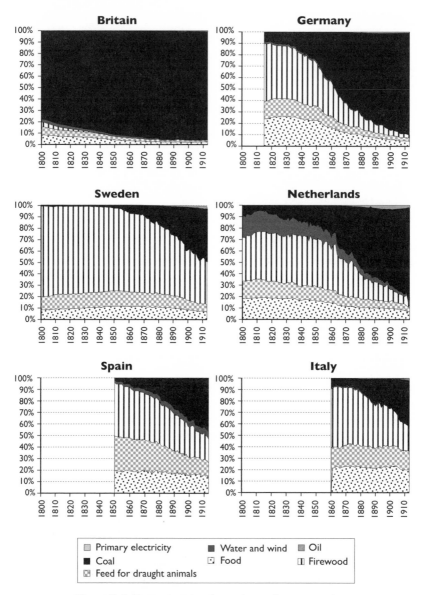

Figure 7.6. Energy carrier shares in total consumption

materials, especially forest products and foodstuffs to Britain. The tenfold expansion of softwood exports from Sweden depended on a range of linkages in the new economy for expanding trade in this traditional product. Steam power cut freight rates, while coal imports to Sweden increased demand for heavy freight on the return voyage. Sawmilling became steam-driven and used new cheap iron technology.[67] In turn, Britain supplied semi-finished products like pig iron to continental industry for finishing. These paths were different but interdependent, and "late-comers," as Gerschenkron insisted, had their destinies shaped by those who had industrialized before them. Even at the very end of the nineteenth century, Britain was remarkable for its ability to produce its own semi-finished and intermediate industrial goods and machinery, importing raw materials or finished goods; while intermediate goods like metals, yarn, and the machinery to process them made up a much more considerable share of manufacturing and industrial imports for other European countries (see table 7.14).[68]

For some areas, regional specialization meant avoiding the heavily mechanized sectors, where it was hard to compete with the British, and maintaining more labor-intensive development. Hungary, as an agricultural producer, developed its milling technology and agricultural machinery. Food processing used 60 percent of the nation's stationary steam power in 1884. In Switzerland, both the watch and cotton industries combined high levels of skill and traditions of innovation in niche markets with a balance of costs that militated against heavy capital investment. However, Switzerland exemplifies the fact that while some economic successes used little energy themselves, they still relied either on the new cheap transportation (such as tourism) or the general growth of incomes in bigger economies to provide a market for their exports. And even in this case, coal made up no less than 78 percent of primary energy consumption when statistics first become available in 1910, making it comparable to the development of other economies depicted in figure 7.1.[69]

For all the integrative benefits of transport technology, and the revolution in speed, the benefits of industrialization were still unevenly distributed.[70] This was also true *within* countries as well as between them. While for convenience of comparison we employ national statistics, in reality industrialization was a regional phenomenon. The hot spots of industrialization tended to be favored regions that could combine a range of resources with access to markets, such as Alsace in France, the Ruhr in Germany, and Lancashire in England. These regions attracted migrants and investment and could drive the structural transformation of the national economy. Other regions or countries showed more "balanced" growth and less structural change, but became dependent on the products of the core regions, especially

[67] Milward and Saul, 1977, 484–85; Pollard, 1981, 221; Gustafsson, 1996, 213; Cameron, 1985, 19.

[68] Backwardness in itself cannot determine the course of economic development, however, as we argue that the pattern of capital investment and specialization is determined by relative access to resources, among other things. Gerschenkron, 1962; von Tunzelmann, 1995, 70–72.

[69] Berend, 1996, 280–83; Fritzsche, 1996, 136; von Tunzelmann, 1997, 158; Milward and Saul, 1977, 224, 458, 464.

[70] Ruttan, 2001, 19.

TABLE 7.14
Share of goods in imports of industrial products, 1899 (%)

	Metals	Machines and metal goods	Chemicals	Textiles: Yarn	Textiles: cloth	Textiles: clothing	Semi-finished manufactures	Finished manufactures
Britain	8	6	8	5	23	15	12	23
Germany	13	13	10	34	11	4	4	12
Italy	17	22	14	10	15	3	5	14
Sweden	19	24	5	19	14	5	5	10

Source: Maizels, 1963.

for capital goods. Berlin and the cities of southern Germany developed specializations in machine-making, building a mutual dependence with the heartlands of coal and iron-smelting.[71] Proximity to water became less important than in the pre-industrial economy, but landlocked regions without their own coalfields still labored at a great disadvantage. Given the uneven distribution of energy sources and other essential resources, a distribution far less even than the distribution of vegetable products in the pre-industrial world, we should hardly be surprised that we find a story of different paths taken, of leaders and laggards. In much of Europe transport and coal were still expensive, and short-haul journeys for many products in a country like Italy were still most cheaply done by cart.[72]

4. CONCLUSION

The Industrial Revolution, and the role that energy played within it, was the continuation of tendencies we have already identified in the first part of this book, toward the saving of land and labor in the economy. The drive toward mechanization facilitated by new power technology and smelting techniques maintained the pattern of development where capital-intensive techniques meant higher labor productivity and higher wages meant more demand for fixed capital in order to replace labor, because of continual relative falls in the price of energy and capital. Higher wages also meant higher demand for industrial products and services, further promoting expansion in these sectors. A transport revolution linked to this technology dramatically lowered the price of transport, especially for bulk goods. Having begun in England, the process spread over the continent of Europe and to the eastern United States. A continuing "race" emerged between energy-saving technology and the energy-expanding tendencies of the development block, with varied regional results depending on economic structure. At the same time, we see continued expansion in demand for traditional energy sources, driven by population increase and continued investment because of high relative returns, promoting further industrialization of work processes and agriculture. Nevertheless, expansion in traditional energy carrier use was unable to keep up with population growth. The new industrial economy did not make for even development or a set pattern of change in the energy economy, but rather processes of divergence: a new international division of labor that varied over time according to local resource endowment, technical expertise, and consumer demand.

[71] Pollard, 1981; Van Zanden, 1996, 79; Borchardt, 1973, 139.
[72] Toniolo, 1983, 227.

PART III

The Second and Third Industrial Revolutions

Astrid Kander

CHAPTER EIGHT

ENERGY TRANSITIONS IN THE TWENTIETH CENTURY

1. THE RISE OF OIL AND ELECTRICITY

THIS FINAL PART OF THE BOOK examines the rise in energy consumption in the twentieth century and the breakthrough of oil and electricity. These developments display similarities and differences with the previous century, that of the first industrial revolution, where coal came to dominate the scene and released the economy from the constraints of the organic economy. Rather than speaking of one industrial revolution, or *the* industrial revolution, and one big energy transition (from traditional, area-restricted resources to modern fossil fuel energy resources), we will use the idea of a second industrial revolution (related to oil and electricity) and a third industrial revolution (the microelectronics revolution, also related to electricity). This helps us to distinguish several distinct technological shifts and energy transitions within the realm of the larger modern energy transition. The new energy carriers, oil and electricity, changed the relative positioning of European countries. It was no longer such a great advantage to have domestic coal resources. New, more peripheral, countries made progress based on their domestic natural resource advantages, primarily hydropower, while one of the major new carriers, oil, became largely imported from outside the continent.

These transitions were also, importantly, to *higher quality* energy carriers, which allowed a related increase in economic efficiency of energy use. Coal use did not become relatively less important because it became scarce, but from new possibilities opened up by technological change. Explaining these processes and their consequences is thus the core focus of this part of the book. We will examine in particular the reasons for the stabilization of per capita energy consumption from the 1970s onward, which was portrayed in figure 1.1. What has driven this discontinuity in energy consumption will be a major theme in the next three chapters.

The modern energy transitions of the twentieth century did not imply that traditional energy (food, fodder, etc.) was phased out; instead there was a great expansion in agricultural production and energy supplied from areal resources. This was enabled by the use of fertilizers and pesticides, which required large inputs of fossil fuels.[1] However, the growth of traditional

[1] Madison, 1997.

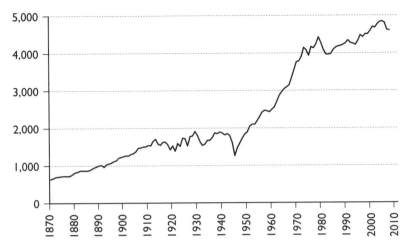

Figure 8.1. Total energy consumption in Western Europe,
1870–2008, in PJ. See www.energyhistory.org.

energy carriers was much slower than the rise of the modern energy system,
so the structure of energy consumption changed profoundly, with oil and
electricity taking on larger shares.

THE RISE OF ENERGY CONSUMPTION

The increase of energy consumption in the twentieth century is less smooth
than that of the nineteenth century, and clear phases of expansion can be
discerned (see figure 8.1). The first expansion took place between 1870 and
1910. During this period the second industrial revolution gradually began
to make an impact on energy systems, but the major driver was still increasing coal consumption resulting from the general dissemination of the
development block of the first industrial revolution. This was a period of
economic integration in Europe that boosted both energy use and GDP. In
the following periods of disintegration and World War between 1914 and
1945, economic growth was lower and total energy consumption hardly
grew at all. The World Wars also saw efficiency improvements in energy
use, stimulated by the import restrictions for coal, and interestingly, the efficiency gains were not eaten up when the Wars were over. This suggests that
innovation took place and not just temporary energy savings; the wars and
their aftermath prompted the use of more modern and efficient capital. A
renewed period of globalization that emerged around 1950, when Europe
became much more integrated with other parts of the world, can be divided

into two parts. Between 1950 and 1970 there was a hitherto unparalleled burst in energy consumption coupled with rapid economic growth, followed by a period of slower growth between 1970 and 2005.

Over the long twentieth century (1870–2000) the use of energy in Europe increased sevenfold. At the same time the population only doubled. This means that in 2000, an average person in Europe had slightly more than three times the energy at his or her disposal compared to an average person in 1870. Not all of this extra energy was experienced directly by people, giving them better access to energy services, such as light, heat, or motion, because much of it was consumed in the manufacturing industry. Nevertheless the changes of the twentieth century brought about a greater impact on people's everyday lives than had been the case for the majority of the population in previous centuries: in the consumption of manufactured products and in final consumption of electricity or petrol. People's lives became much more varied and comfortable. Instead of having long working days, no holidays, rarely being able to travel anywhere, owning few and often drab clothes, eating monotonous food, shivering through the winter, and possessing few goods, by the end of the century a typical European could go to work by an oil-fueled car, work in an office in front of a computer, travel abroad on holidays, own many clothes, eat varied food from all over the world (often putting on too much weight, leading them to try to expend energy in specially designated periods of exercise), and live in a heated apartment replete with goods such as music systems, TVs, and a washing machine, all run by electricity.

Per capita energy consumption also grew at different rates in different periods between 1870 and 2008, closely following the path of total energy consumption, as can be seen by comparing figures 8.1 and 8.2. Between 1870 and the outbreak of the First World War there was a big leap in energy consumption per capita, largely caused by coal. The period of the war and the Great Depression were marked by stabilization in the levels of per capita energy consumption. In the 1950s there was another big leap in per capita energy consumption, to be followed by a slowdown after the 1970s up until the present. Clearly something changed from the 1970s, both in terms of total and per capita energy consumption.

The expansion in energy consumption was unevenly distributed among nations. In Western Europe, England had taken the clear lead in this expansion, and in 1870 its energy consumption per capita amounted to 130 GJ, not to be matched by any of the other countries in our sample (see table 8.1). The second largest consumer—Germany—only consumed a quarter of the British amount, similar to Swedish and Dutch consumption. France was slightly lower. The southern European countries, with a warmer climate and lack of abundant, cheap energy sources, had a different industrial structure and lower energy consumption. Over the twentieth century Sweden and

Figure 8.2. Energy per capita in Western Europe, 1870–2008, in Giga Joules
Source: www.energyhistory.org.

TABLE 8.1
Energy consumption per capita in Western European Countries, 1870–2005, in GJ

	England & Wales	Germany	Sweden	Netherlands	Spain	France
1870	118	33	37	36	19	29
1910	153	86	58	49	24	54
1950	152	89	82	62	27	68
1970	180	160	179	139	55	122
2005	170	152	181	191	130	133

Source: See www.energyhistory.org.

the Netherlands caught up with English per capita energy consumption, ending up with slightly higher levels by 2005. Germany, Spain, and France remained below the English level.

By 1870, Europe had set out on a path of heavy energy use, matched only by the United States and Canada (who used more energy per capita). These "western" countries were exceptional in world terms.[2] While some other countries in the world have clearly caught up with Europe in per capita energy consumption, others still lag behind. In 2003, Japan

[2] Henriques, 2011.

TABLE 8.2

Decomposition of energy into two scale effects (population and income per capita) and an energy intensity effect, Western Europe 1870–2005 (%)

	E	p	y	ey
1870–2005	1.5	0.5	1.7	−0.8
1870–1913	2.2	0.8	1.3	+0.1
1913–1950	0.2	0.3	0.8	−0.9
1950–1970	3.6	0.7	4.0	−1.1
1970–2005	0.7	0.3	2.0	−1.6

Source: Own calculations based on the data in www.energyhistory.org.

was slightly above the European average with its 185 GJ per capita. On the lower side of the spectrum we find developing countries like China, which used 40 GJ per capita, India at 15 GJ, and the poorest African countries that only consumed 1 GJ.[3] Electricity consumption—a high-technology product and indicative of development—is especially unevenly distributed across the world. In 2000, the richest people in the world consumed 10 MWh each, while some two billion people had no access to electricity at all.

DECOMPOSING THE ENERGY GROWTH

By employing the Commoner-Ehrlich identity we can decompose the energy consumption into the effects from population increase, income increase, and energy intensity changes (see chapter 2). The results for the period 1870–2005 are given in table 8.2.

There is no doubt which scale factor was more important in the long run. Changes in income per capita played a role that was three times as large as the population factor over the long period 1870–2005. A growth in scale of the economy (p and y) needs to be balanced by declines in energy intensity (e_y) in order for energy consumption (e) to stay constant. Such a balancing out of the scale effects very rarely takes place. If we look at table 8.2 we find that the only period where energy consumption stayed fairly constant (growing by as little as 0.2 percent annually) was 1913–1950, which encompassed two World Wars and a long economic recession in between. In this period, energy intensity declines managed to counterbalance the weak income increase, but not entirely to offset the population effect as well. In

[3] Smil, 2008a, 258.

the period 1950–1970, when energy consumption increased the most (by 3.6 percent per year), this was largely driven by increases in income.

The most rapid drop in energy intensity was in the final period: 1970–2005, when energy intensity fell by an annual average of –1.6 percent. With an income increase that was 2 percent per year and a population increase of 0.3 percent, this was still not sufficient to keep energy consumption constant, but the rate of increase was modest compared to the golden decades of 1950–1970. Again we notice that the period after 1970 is different when we examine the relationship between energy and the economy.

Oil and Electricity Expansion

While the energy expansion of the nineteenth century was mostly a story of coal, the expansion in the twentieth century was above all the story of oil and electricity. Oil started to be used in Europe around 1860, but only in small quantities. Until the turn of the century, oil's share of the total was less than 1 percent of the primary energy needs of Europe. The first real phase of expansion took place in the interwar period, when oil reached 10 percent of the total. Still, the most conspicuous increase of oil consumption—the real breakthrough—did not take place until after the Second World War. Coal remained the basic energy carrier well into the twentieth century. Introducing a new energy carrier on a large scale is not simply a matter of relative prices of the new and alternative fuels—although relative prices play a crucial role for stimulating transitions. Changing or constructing the capital equipment and infrastructure related to a particular energy carrier involves large costs. In the case of heavily coal-using countries or sectors, large investments were sunk in coal-using technology and it remained a relatively cheap fuel, discouraging a widespread switch to oil: evidence of path-dependence and rigid structures related to energy systems. Even in those countries where the coal share of total energy consumption was relatively small, it took time before the situation was ripe for a major switch toward dependency on oil imports. Even in the United States—the country of oil discoveries and exports—coal remained the largest provider of primary energy until 1950, when it was surpassed by oil. The oil transition was a long process in the United States, stretching from 1850 to 1970, without any dramatic leaps. In contrast in Europe, with its mix of coal-using infrastructure and dependency on oil imports, the oil transition was more abrupt. For almost one hundred years the oil share rose incrementally, and then exploded during the "golden decades" of the 1950s and 1960s, when cheap oil flooded European markets and the oil share rose from 10 percent to 50 percent.

Electricity was the second main energy carrier that increased its share over the period 1870–2005. In figure 8.3 only that part of electricity which was produced by non-thermal sources (mainly water turbines and later

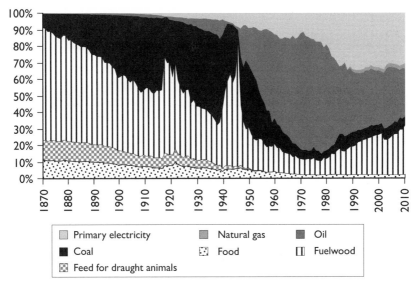

Figure 8.3. European energy consumption,
1870–2009, shares of energy carriers (%)
Sources: www.energyhistory.org.

nuclear power) is counted in our series, in order to avoid inconsistencies in aggregating total consumption, and double counting.[4] We call this primary electricity. This method does not show the increase in *final* electricity consumption, but even the restricted indicator of electrification used here shows a substantial increase, especially from the 1970s onward when nuclear power was being used in some countries.[5]

Natural gas was another main energy carrier that grew persistently from the 1970s. This was a less generalized phenomenon, and mainly occurred in countries like England and the Netherlands, where large reserves of natural gas were found offshore. However, their switch from oil and coal to natural gas was large enough to affect the overall European picture (see figure 8.3).

Figure 8.4 shows the diffusion of oil in different European countries. It is striking that despite variations there is a very uniform pattern of a phase of expansion in the interwar period followed by a big surge in use right after World War II.

---

[4] It would be a logical mistake of "double" counting to include both the fuel used to produce electricity and that electricity itself.

[5] The full amount of electricity, including the share produced from fossil fuels, will be accounted for when we deal with final energy consumption or the changing quality of energy in the following chapters of the book.

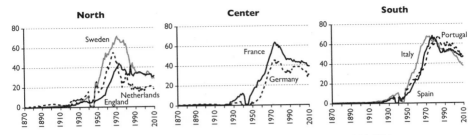

Figure 8.4. Oil shares in different countries, 1870–2009 (%)

The big shift occurred in a very narrow time period, much more so than the earlier coal transition. All countries show a decline in oil shares in the decades since 1970. We do not find a similar clustering of countries in groups with the oil diffusion as we did for coal in the nineteenth century. Coal remained important in Germany and England, an example of the "persistence of the old."[6] The Netherlands had a remarkable adoption rate of oil until World War II, while Sweden and Italy show the most impressive adoption rates between 1945 and 1960. Spain and Portugal were latecomers in the oil race and, along with Italy, saw oil retaining a high share of total consumption after the price shocks of the 1970s. Following a high peak, Sweden made a striking turn away from oil. The least oil-dependent countries at the end of the period are the Netherlands, with only 20 percent stemming from oil, and Sweden and England at some 30 percent.

New Conversion Possibilities

Oil and electricity are two new sources of energy that are very different from each other. Raw oil is a fuel, found directly in nature, and can be characterized as a primary energy source, while electricity is always a secondary energy source, produced by means of some primary energy source, such as flowing water, blowing wind, burning fuels, or nuclear reactions. Electricity is useful for most kinds of applications. It is extremely flexible at the point of consumption; it can be used for light, motion, heat, and information conveyance. It can be converted into many different kinds of energy services for people. Raw oil is also refined, but only in the sense that it is split up into different components, such as gasoline and diesel oil. It has not gone through any fundamental change from one mode of energy to another. An innovation that brings new conversion possibilities for energy is a good example of a macro-innovation.

[6] Edgerton, 2007.

In the first industrial revolution, the most important macro-innovation was the steam engine, which enabled the conversion of heat energy into mechanical energy. In the second industrial revolution, a main innovation was another motor—the internal combustion engine—which does the same kind of conversion, from heat to motion, but using liquid or gas fuels. The internal combustion engine can in this sense be regarded as a meso-innovation—a continuation of the steam engine. This motor had many advantages over the steam engine and became more widespread throughout society. In addition, another path-breaking step in energy conversions was taken during the second industrial revolution: the transformation of mechanical energy to electrical energy. Electrical energy is generated from mechanical energy through a generator, and can be used for mechanical movement again with the assistance of a motor (see figure 2.1). The twentieth century meant an increased variety of both energy carriers and energy converters as compared to the nineteenth century.

Innovations in Cracking Oil

A series of innovations in "cracking" oil, thereby changing the final mix of oil products, was crucial for being able to utilize the oil for different purposes, one of them being as fuel for internal combustion engines. Crude oil is a complex mixture of hydrocarbons, ranging from light liquids, to reddish-brown fluids, to black tar.

Crude oil must be refined to produce different final oil products, such as kerosene, gasoline, diesel oil, LPG (Liquefied Petrol Gases) and heating oil. The problem of separating the crude oil into different fractions had already been studied during the eighteenth century. For instance, a German doctoral thesis in 1734 dealt with the distilling of lighter fractions of crude oil.[7] The problem was beginning to be addressed in a scientific manner, but took some time to be commercialized.

Part of the crude oil consists of asphalt, and a fairly substantial amount (some 10–20 percent) is used as industrial feed stocks to produce plastics and chemicals. Whether or not to include asphalt and feedstock oil in the energy use is a matter of choice. The easiest way is to include it, because of the way national energy statistics are organized, but from an analytical perspective it is preferable to exclude it, since this is not energy in any common sense of the word. Throughout this book we have therefore chosen to exclude feedstock from our energy calculations.

Of particular interest are the components refined from crude oil that are used by the transport sector: gasoline, aviation fuel, diesel oil, and bunker oil. These fuels can to some degree be turned into one another, but not fully.

[7] Forbes, 1958, 5.

In the cracking processes a heavier fuel (having longer chains of hydrocarbons) can easily be turned into lighter products, but the reverse cannot be done. Ever since William Burton introduced thermal cracking of crude oil in 1913,[8] it has been the practice that gasoline was maximized in the output of refineries, because of the high demand for it from cars and its resultant high price. However, this has recently changed with the rise in popularity of diesel oil both for cars and trucks, and with the use of oil for electricity generation in some developing countries (those rich in oil). As a consequence, diesel production is currently maximized in the refining processes, but there are still limits to how much of the raw oil can be turned into diesel. The growing demand for diesel, and rather inelastic supply, is apparent in the relative increase in the price of this fuel compared to gasoline in recent years. The more energy-efficient diesel engines run the risk of becoming less popular with this increase in price. The problem of balancing diesel and gasoline consumption with supply is today partly solved through geographical differences in demand. There is greater consumption of diesel in Europe compared to the United States, which means that the surplus diesel production from the United States is shipped to Europe, and on the return journey the ship brings gasoline. If diesel-powered cars become more popular in the United States, this geographical balancing act will no longer be possible.

The Discovery of Oil Fields and the New Geography of Energy Supply

Crude oil is a natural resource that is found in widely dispersed locations across the Earth, even though in quantitative terms the global distribution is highly skewed, with the Persian Gulf dominating with nearly 30 percent of all giant oil fields. The recognition of potential uses of crude oil began many centuries ago and can be seen from examples such as the word "naphtha" being 4,000 years old, or the use of asphalt and oil for illumination on Sicily 2,000 years ago.[9] The Arabs used asphaltos to caulk their ships in the sixteenth century (when Europeans used pitch refined from wood) and the ability of petroleum to clean wounds was recognized early, but not much used.[10] The ancient oil-producing areas of Europe were mostly in the center of the continent: Galicia in Poland, Alsace, and northern Italy, and production was small.[11] It was in Eastern Europe that crude oil extraction expanded, with Galicia and Romania in particular standing out as areas of production. The French had the most advanced oil drilling technique in Europe in the 1840s

[8] Smil, 2005, 128.
[9] Forbes, 1958, 2.
[10] Forbes, 1959, 49.
[11] Forbes, 1959, 92.

and 1850s, but despite this France failed to experience a breakthrough in oil drilling, for the simple reason that it did not have much oil. In England, the first attempts to produce oil from coal was in 1848 by James Young, intending to use it for illumination. Coal oil was abandoned as crude oil was being imported from the United States by the early 1860s. Some minor domestic production of oil took place on the south coast of England early on, but the big expansion came only after offshore oil was found in the North Sea in the 1950s.

The Baku field in Azerbaijan gets credit for the world's first drilled oil well, and by 1873, ten small refineries had been constructed in this region. Yet it was in the backwoods of Pennsylvania that the ancient tradition matured, and the United States became the clear leader in the world market for oil. The epochal Drake discovery well was completed at Oil Creek in 1859 and quickly stimulated additional drilling. Exports started to Europe in 1860, and the United States was clearly the dominant oil producer in the world by 1865, with 2.5 million barrels per year, Canada second with 110,000 barrels, and the Russian Empire third with 67,000 barrels (largely from Azerbaijan).[12] The production within Europe only amounted to 36,000 barrels in 1860 and had increased to 2.9 million barrels in 1880, but this was insufficient for meeting rapidly growing demand.[13] In the first decades of the oil expansion (1860–1890), producers and refiners largely concentrated on kerosene for lamps, but after 1890 the industry was transformed trying to meet new demands for gasoline, fuel oil, and lubricants.[14]

Oil changed the geography of energy supply. Countries that were rich in coal were not always rich in oil, and vice versa. Britain and Germany were the two largest coal-producing countries, but they did not have any viable oil reserves onshore. In 1900, the world production of oil was dominated by Russia and the United States (see figure 8.5). Europe produced in total less than 10 percent of the output of the United States, but its consumption was large, and Western European countries imported all their oil.

The United States was dominant in the provision of oil to the world for a long time, but competitors emerged from the Middle East, Latin America, and other parts of the world. In Latin America early oil discoveries paired with low economic development meant that coal never gained any important role at all; most countries went directly for oil.[15] Between 1950 and 1975, the Middle East increased its world market share rapidly, partly under the lead of foreign, especially American and British, oil companies, but lost its prominent position in the world oil market in the 1980s.[16] Presently

[12] Owen, 1975, 12.
[13] Forbes, 1959, 107.
[14] Nash, 1968, 2.
[15] Rubio et al., 2010.
[16] The Anglo-American Oil Agreement of 1944 defined mutual interests in the Middle East and provided for collaboration in the construction of new pipes. See Nash, 1968, 177.

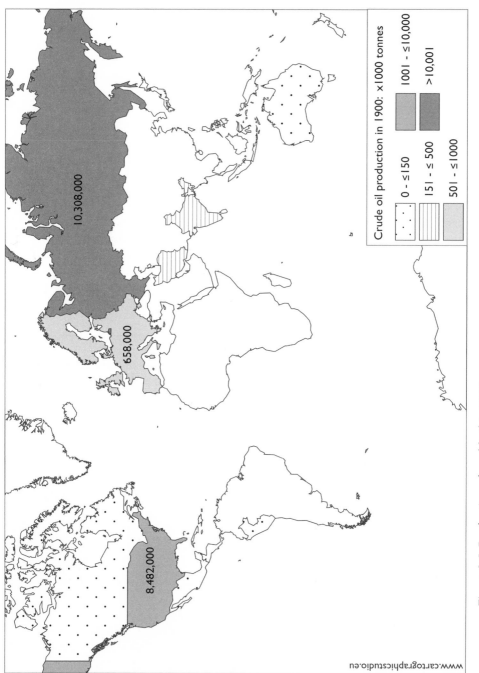

Figure 8.5. Production of world oil in 1900
Source: Annelieke Vries-Baaijens has produced the map based on figures in Etemad and Luciani, 1991.

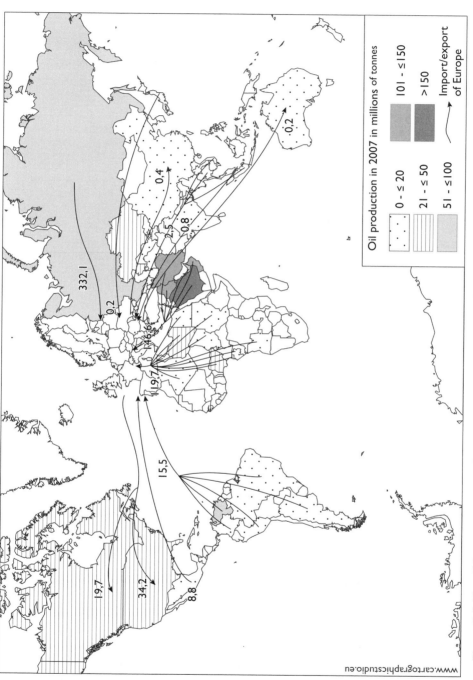

Figure 8.6. Net oil imports to Europe from various world regions in 2006, in PJ

Source: Based on figures in BP Statistical Review of World Energy, June 2008. Map produced by Annelieke Vries-Baaijens.

Oil production in 2007 in millions of tonnes

0 – ≤ 20
21 – ≤ 50
51 – ≤100
101 – ≤150
>150

Import/export of Europe

www.cartographicstudio.eu

there are several major providers of oil, including European countries such as Britain and Norway, who produce from offshore sites and export some production to the United States. The two largest oil-producing countries in 2007 were the Russian Federation and Saudi Arabia with 12.6 percent of world oil production each, while the United States was third with 8 percent. The location of oil supply and sites of consumption of oil do not match each other well. This is different from the case of coal, where the consumption and production generally occurred in closer proximity. Europe as a whole could be self-reliant with coal, but not with oil. The large oil consumers in 2007 were the United States (23.9 percent of the world consumption), Europe (24 percent), and China (9.3 percent), and all of them are far from self-reliant on oil.[17] While a coal trade took place within Europe, and the rich countries had easy access to coal, the oil trade takes place on a world scale between countries of very different political systems, cultures, and levels of development, some of them very unstable, which raises concerns about how to secure energy supplies in Europe. The net flows of oil into Europe from all over the world are portrayed in figure 8.6. The main providers of European oil are Russia (332 PJ), the Middle East (147 PJ), and Africa (120 PJ).

OIL AND POWER TO THE PEOPLE

Oil has empowered people simply by equipping them with more powerful machinery, which has contributed to rising incomes in the twentieth century. People are generally much better off with oil than they were before. Still, the incomes are not evenly distributed among nations or among individuals. Income inequality fell within European countries between 1900 and 1970, as an effect from wider education and tax redistribution within the welfare states, but has risen again since the 1980s.[18] Oil states are known for extremely unequal income distribution and for not thus far using these natural resources to develop diversified economies or widely spread benefits in terms of income and education, as England and Germany eventually did on the basis of their coal. One explanation for this may be that the firms of early industrializing countries in Europe received a natural protection from competition, because coal was bulky and expensive to transport long distances overseas and thus gave sheltered conditions for infant industries close to the coal sites. This was completely different from the case with oil, when internal combustion engines in big oil tankers and pipelines quickly reduced the advantages of proximity to the oil wells. In this new situation, the presence of large oil or other resource reserves has sometimes been con-

---

[17] BP, 2008.

[18] Persson, 2010; see update on: http://www.econ.ku.dk/europe/Updates/UpdatesChap11.pdf.

sidered by economists as having a negative effect on economic development, encouraging dependence on the resource rents and reducing other investments, the so-called Dutch disease.[19]

However the oil transition and new geography of energy supply did not only affect economic power, it had an impact on geopolitical power and democracy in Europe and the wider world too. The new channels of carbon energy flows that were created through oil did not place as large power in the hands of workers as had been the case with coal (see chapter 6).[20] Many fewer workers were needed on the oil fields, and they were not working as experts underground like the coalminers, but rather on the surface, where they were easier to supervise and manage. This gave the workers less power in relation to the owners and managers. Furthermore, the global oil trade through international shipping and pipelines meant that oil provision was much less site-dependent than coal had been. Oil tankers often did not know their final destination when they embarked on a trip, but waited for orders of where to go. This made the trading scheme look more like a spider's web, or a grid, than like linear routes between pre-defined destinations. Shipping companies could easily avoid labor regulations and democratic rights by resorting to international registration.[21] Oil was often shipped through specialized ports and refining centers, independent of dockers and longshoremen. Because of the fewer workers involved in oil extraction and transport and much more flexible oil provision, striking oil workers in the Middle East were far less powerful than striking coal workers had been before. The workforce was more international, and the delivery to final consumers more dispersed through smaller haulage companies. Oil workers could do much less harm to the total economic system than coal workers and hence could not press demands so easily.[22]

The coal-based economy of the first industrial revolution helped concentrate the workforce in fewer locations and gave economic leverage to workers' organizations, shaping political struggles within nations. In contrast, many of the developments of the energy economy of the twentieth century have been more diffuse, but have increased expectations of consumer choice and mobility. The workforces essential to the system are small, highly skilled, and often well remunerated (in oil refineries or power stations),[23] and political leverage has been given to those in a position to shape overall networks of distribution: oil companies themselves, and the governments of producer states. This has led to widespread cartelization and price-fixing on international oil markets from the 1920s onward, but even so no producer

[19] Barbier, 2007.
[20] Mitchell, 2011.
[21] Mitchell, 2011.
[22] Mitchell, 2009, 25.
[23] Occasionally power workers have played a significant political role, such as in bringing down the government of Northern Ireland in 1974.

has had enough market power to be able to maintain a sustained grip on international markets, as the aftermath of the 1970s crises has demonstrated.[24]

The Impact of Electricity on Primary Energy Systems

The per capita consumption of electricity increased rapidly over the century (see table 8.3). It is apparent that the rates of electrification differed substantially among countries. Sweden had an extraordinary rate of adoption, similar to the rates of the United States. The UK was second and Germany close behind, with diffusion in the Netherlands and France coming a little later. By 1980, the UK, the Netherlands, and France had converged completely, and France has subsequently increased per capita electricity consumption much more, probably as an effect of its nuclear program. The Netherlands lagged behind in the 1980s and 1990s. Southern Europe was much slower to adopt electricity, and in 2000, Portugal was at the per capita level of Sweden fifty years earlier. Italy expanded electricity use earlier than Spain, but by1980, Spain had passed Italy and overtaken the Netherlands in 2000.

While the final destination of crude oil is quite flexible (petrol for cars, aviation fuel, heating oil, etc.), there is no good substitute for crude oil. Electricity, on the other hand, is flexible both in its production and its consumption. We can say that the electricity system is modular. Modularity means that the system can be analyzed as separate modules and that each module can be replaced by a set of alternatives. At the consumption module it means that many different technical devices can be plugged into the wall and be run on electricity. At the generating module, it means that any primary energy carrier can be utilized to produce electricity; coal, oil, hydropower, natural gas, nuclear power, wind, and biomass are the most common ones. This opens up possibilities for divergence in primary energy supply as electricity becomes a larger share of the total consumption. The diversification in primary energy supply after the 1970s is illustrated in table 8.4.

The *final* energy portfolio for Europe is different from the primary energy supply of course, with a larger share of electricity (see table 8.5). Final electricity made up 11 percent of total final energy consumption in Europe in 1973, and this share had increased to 19 percent in 2006, which exemplifies the growing importance of electricity as an energy carrier throughout the century.

The diversification in primary energy supply after 1970 was of course not only related to the modularity of the electricity system, and growing importance for electricity as an energy carrier, but also to different patterns of substitution away from oil in the wake of the crises of the 1970s.[25] Oil had

---

[24] Adelman, 1995; Parra, 2004; Vietor, 1984; Mitchell, 2011.

[25] Parra, 2004.

TABLE 8.3
Electricity per capita, 1900–2000, in European countries and in USA, kWh/cap

	UK	Germany	Netherlands	Italy	Spain	France	Portugal	USA	Sweden
1910	47	43	na	37	18	26		267	145
1920	127	149	104	108	45	90	17	529	442
1930	397	322	313	264	111	405	38	927	834
1940	608	534	426	441	140	504	60	1356	1353
1950	1301	979	734	528	247	790	111	2553	2582
1960	2529	2094	1438	1149	612	1579	368	4673	4631
1970	4256	4000	3134	2225	1670	2771	874	7997	7504
1980	4836	5989	4580	3337	2930	4578	1549	10339	11624
1990	5338	7106	4344	3756	3881	7026	1928	10766	17058
2000	6585	6952	4807	4899	5484	9105	2893	11335	16354

Sources: Mitchell, 2007 for electricity and Maddison, 2001 for population. 1950–1990 German figures refer only to West Germany.

TABLE 8.4
Diversification of primary energy supply after 1970 (%)

	Oil		Coal		Natural gas		Primary electricity		Traditional energy	
	1970	2005	1970	2005	1970	2005	1970	2005	1970	2005
England	39.4	32.1	50.1	21.3	4.8	38.5	3.1	8.1	2.3	3.6
Germany	52.7	37.9	39.4	25.1	4.0	24.9	1.1	5.6	2.8	6.5
France	58.5	44.9	23.1	7.0	5.1	20.1	3.4	19.0	9.7	8.9
Netherlands*	45.0	19.9	12.1	12.8	39.6	55.4	0.0	3.0	3.2	9.0
Sweden*	71.9	31.8	5.7	6.3	0.0	2.0	11.0	32.5	11.4	27.5
Italy*	69.7	49.5	7.9	7.0	8.6	31.7	4.2	5.5	9.6	6.3
Spain	55.3	51.9	24.1	15.4	0.0	18.5	5.6	7.1	15.0	7.3
Portugal	5.1	47.9	7.7	12.7	0	13.7	7.3	5.7	39.9	16.5

* Denotes that the last year is 2000 instead of 2005. Primary electricity is the electricity that has been generated on basis of nuclear and hydropower and wind power; see chapter 2. Traditional energy is wood, waste, food, and fodder.
Sources: www.energyhistory.org.

TABLE 8.5
Final energy consumption in Europe 1973–2006

	1973 (Mtoe)	1973 (%)	2006 (Mtoe)	2006 (%)
Geothermal	0.05		1.7	0.1
Solar, Wind, Tide	na		1.2	0.1
Coal	173	17	57	4
Oil	591	57	622	46
Gas	108	10	288	21
Renewables & Waste	28	3	62	5
Electricity	115	11	259	19
Heat	21	2	57	4
Total final	1036		1349	

Source: IEA Statistics. Electricity Information, 2008, III, 93.

become increasingly important for electricity generation during the 1960s, and the vulnerability became apparent with the two oil crises of 1973 and 1978/79, when oil prices skyrocketed as an effect of OPEC's attempts to raise prices after some decades of an extraordinary relative decline.[26] The oil price shock effects gave strong incentives to free European economies from their massive oil dependence and develop domestically available sources of energy. Natural gas was found in the North Sea and developed by the UK and the Netherlands already from the 1910s, but the amount of gas pumped increased massively after the oil price shocks, underpinned by a major expansion of the gas pipeline infrastructure (the "dash for gas").[27] Another driver for energy diversification was environmental concerns. It was increasingly recognized by this time that fossil fuels stressed the environment and caused health risks. Acidification, eutrophication, and global warming all resulted from the combustion of fossil fuels.

NUCLEAR ENERGY AND OTHER PRIMARY SOURCES FOR ELECTRICITY GENERATION

Despite the will to diversify energy supply in recent decades, only one completely new energy carrier has affected primary energy: nuclear power. Nuclear power is a non-organic source of energy and depends on uranium

[26] Adelman, 1995; Parra, 2004; Vietor, 1984.
[27] Glennie, 1998.

mines, so its availability is not as hampered by land constraints as organic sources of energy. The largest reason for the diversification of European energy systems after 1970 was related to whether nuclear power was used for electricity generation or not, and to what degree natural gas was used to replace oil generally in society (also for space heating, cooking, etc., not only for electricity generation). Countries like France and Sweden went strongly for nuclear, while the Netherlands for instance adopted natural gas.

The idea of nuclear power is to release the energy in the nucleus of atoms. Einstein had already formulated the idea that physical matter could be converted to energy in the nineteenth century, but nuclear power did not become a reality until the 1940s. Nuclear fission was first developed and used for military purposes, with the appalling results of Hiroshima and Nagasaki at the end of the Second World War. But after the end of the war, research on civic nuclear power emerged alongside military efforts and was focused on electricity generation in the United States. The first U.S. nuclear reactor to produce electricity was a small prototype in 1951, but larger, more commercial ones soon followed. The first-in-the-world nuclear power plant was started in Obninsk, Russia, in 1954, and an overall development of various nuclear reactor concepts was carried out in the Soviet Union: first, thermal nuclear reactors, then fast reactors. In the 1950s, commercial nuclear reactors began to be used in England and France as well (initially all countries that had nuclear weapon programs). Several other European countries constructed reactors in the following decades. There were 437 reactors in twenty-nine countries by 1998.[28]

All nuclear plants today use heat released from the fission of one particular type of uranium, ^{235}U, the only naturally occurring fissile isotope, which means it can sustain a chain reaction of nuclear fission and is suitable for nuclear plants. It makes up a very small share of all uranium in the world (0.7 percent). Other possible usable isotopes of uranium, like ^{238}U, need to be turned into plutonium before the same chain reaction is possible. This means that there are certain limits to the expansion of this source of electricity generation from a resource perspective. There were experiments with fast breeder reactors capable of using ^{238}U instead, which would substantially expand the resource base, but technical problems led to the closure of all these prototypes: in the United States in 1983, in France in 1990, and in Japan in 1995.[29] Also the hope for the IV generation of nuclear reactors of the fast breeder kind, which could utilize plutonium as fuel, currently seems to be receding far into the future.[30]

This potential resource shortage is not yet a grave problem for nuclear power. With current rates of uranium use in the world being relatively static,

---

[28] McNeill, 2000, 346.
[29] Smil, 2008a, 254.
[30] http://www.nirs.org/reactorwatch/newreactors/fastbreeder21710.pdf.

the supplies will last some two hundred years if the Nuclear Energy Agency (NEA) has accurately estimated the planet's economically accessible resources.[31] But it should be remembered that this is with current rates of usage, so clearly this means that only part of the present fossil fuels–based and hydropower-based electricity generation in the world could be replaced by nuclear fission power; otherwise the resource would be used up more rapidly. The escape from resource limitations would be to use some other method or other material. Fusion power (where nuclei are not split but instead fused together) is one such option that would expand the resource base considerably. Although nuclear fusion has been researched for a long time now, it still has not managed to produce more energy than is required to run the fusion reactor itself, so a breakthrough seems distant. Another possibility for expanding the resource base is to use thorium, which is more abundant in nature and can be turned into ^{233}U, another isotope that is fissile.

The use of nuclear power of the fission kind is controversial, because of the inherent risks, from large accidents like the ones in Harrisburg (1979), Chernobyl (1986), and Fukushima (2011), the danger of the proliferation of nuclear weapons, terrorism, and disposal of radioactive waste. Because of these inherent risks, it may be argued that nuclear power is implicitly subsidized to a considerable degree today, since the plant owners normally do not need to buy insurance to cover for risks and in case of accidents, the costs are borne by society at large, both in terms of health effects and direct money costs. This is of course also true for other environmental costs such as particulate pollution from burning fossil fuels that have been a major cause of death since the first industrial revolution, and continue to kill millions each year. Nevertheless, the politics of risk, and demand for regulation or rejection of nuclear power, have proven far more potent. This is doubtless in part due to the way in which external costs are experienced and perceived, appearing more direct and obvious in the case of large nuclear power stations, and being less related to benefits to consumers (in that nuclear power has substitutes, while currently, driving gasoline-fueled cars does not for most people). Risks from fossil fuel are less strongly associated with memorable events.[32] Equally, public debates on safe levels of radioactivity have occurred since controversies over the safety of atmospheric testing of nuclear weapons in the 1950s, and introduced greater public uncertainty into the risks associated with nuclear power, radioactivity becoming understood as a hazard that was both highly pervasive, impossible to measure in everyday experience, and extremely durable. Regulators have, over time, been more trusted to deliver "safe" levels of particulate pollution, although

---

[31] *Scientific American*, 2009.

[32] There have been exceptions, such as the London smog of December 1952, and of course many more oil and coal accidents that have endured in the memory of the localities where they occurred.

fears about urban smogs were a major feature of debate around energy transitions around 1970.

Notwithstanding these factors, nuclear power has been the most substantial among the new sources in quantitative terms, and in some countries like France it is the totally dominant primary source for electricity (80 percent), while in Belgium and Sweden it makes up roughly half of the primary energy used for electricity generation. Nuclear energy was tried for a period in Italy, but all three plants were closed down as a result of a referendum after the Chernobyl accident in 1986, a decision that was reconfirmed in 2011. Germany decided to abandon nuclear power completely within ten years after the Fukushima disaster. In future scenarios provided by the IEA, nuclear energy is expected to stay at the current share of 5 percent of global primary energy supply until 2030, at the same time as the total energy supply increases from 12,000 Mtoe to 17,000 Mtoe, so they assume a growing use, which will deplete the uranium much faster than in the previously predicted two centuries unless alternatives are exploited.[33]

The share of primary energy carriers used for electricity generation in different European countries has varied over time and among countries depending on their natural resource endowment. In the late nineteenth century most electricity was generated by coal or wood, because that was the technology established first, but shortly thereafter hydropower became important in those European countries that were equipped with abundant waterfalls, such as Sweden, Norway, Switzerland, and Italy. The others stuck with coal. The differences among European countries are striking, as seen in table 8.6. At one extreme we find England using nearly exclusively thermal energy (mainly coal and later some fuel oil), and at the other end of the spectrum we find Italy and Sweden relying almost entirely on hydropower. By the 1920s, Italy was more reliant on hydropower than Sweden ever was—having over 90 percent of its electricity generated on this basis. The large height differences found on the numerous streams of the Alps gave Italy a geographical advantage for hydroelectricity. Italy still remains one of the major producers of hydroelectricity in Europe, third after France and Norway.[34] Another geographical advantage that Italy enjoyed from the alpine region was geothermal heat, which was used for electricity generation as early as 1902. Half a century later, New Zealand, the United States, and Mexico also started geothermal electricity production in specific locations.[35] Portugal followed a similar trajectory as Italy, only several decades later, with a large initial share for thermal power and in the 1950s a dramatic switch to hydropower.

[33] IEA, 2006.
[34] Bartoletto and Rubio, 2008.
[35] Smil, 2008a, 255.

TABLE 8.6
Sources of electricity generation 1890–1960 (%)

	England			Portugal		Sweden		Italy		
	hydro	thermo	nuclear	hydro	thermo	hydro	thermo	hydro	thermo	geo
1890	0	100	0	na	Na	32	68	10	90	0
1900	0	100	0	na	Na	60	40	62	38	0
1910	0	100	0	na	Na	68	32	79	21	0
1920	0	100	0	23	77	73	27	96	3	0
1930	1	99	0	34	66	74	26	97	3	1
1950	3	97	0	46	54	79	21	92	5	3
1960	1	97	2	95	5	80	20	88	7	5

Sources: England: Fouquet, 2009, 132; Portugal: Henriques, 2009; Sweden: Kander, 2002; Italy: Malanima, 2006a.

After 1960, the primary energy sources for electricity generation have become more diversified with the introduction of nuclear power, natural gas discoveries in some countries, and the attempt to use more renewable energy sources. Most of the newly installed capacity in electric power generation was based on renewables in the 1990s. Wind energy gained momentum, as well as waste-burning of various kinds. After the 1970s more countries joined the geothermal club, but Italy kept its leading role in relation to the size of its energy system, and produced about a tenth of the global geothermal energy in 2000. Iceland also has large geothermal resources, which they use to produce cheap electricity, utilizing it for aluminum production. In 2004, 15 percent of their electricity came from geothermal energy. In 2010, about twenty-four countries were involved in geothermal power production in the world, and the installed capacity increased by 20 percent between 2005 and 2010.[36]

Despite the attempts to change the electricity system in the direction of renewables, the actual transition has so far been disappointing. On the world scale, two-thirds of installed electrical capacity came from fossil fuels (mainly coal), one-fifth from hydropower, and one-tenth from nuclear power. Only around 1percent was from renewable sources other than hydro (i.e., wind, solar, wood, waste, etc.) in 1999.[37] In Europe the pattern is some-

[36] Geothermal Energy Association. Geothermal Energy: International Market Update May 2010, 4–6.

[37] Johansson and Goldemberg, 2002, 36.

TABLE 8.7
Different fuels in the electricity production of Europe, 1974 and 2006,
TWh and percent

	Coal	Oil	Natural gas	Renewable and Waste	Total Fuels for electricity
1974 (TWh)	525	334	125	2	986
1974 (%)	53	34	13	0.2	100
2006 (Twh)	960	92	621	52	1725
2006 (%)	56	5.3	36	3.0	100

Source: IEA Electricity Information, 2008, III, 90.

what different, with relatively more nuclear and wind power. The share of installed wind power has increased from 2 percent to 6 percent in OECD Europe only between 2000 and 2006. In both 2008 and 2009, more new wind farm generating capacity was added than any other type of power generating plant, including natural gas. Spain and Germany remain the two largest annual markets for wind energy, competing each year for the top spot (2,459 MW and 1,917 MW of new installations respectively), followed by Italy (1,114 MW), France (1,088 MW), and the UK (1,077 MW) in 2009.

The increase in wind turbines is large, but the wind power share still modest. Despite the numerous wind turbines in the European landscape today, they still only produced about one-twentieth of all the electricity we needed in 2010.[38] About 35 percent of the installed power for electricity in Europe is based on renewable energy sources, 50 percent on fossil fuels, and 15 percent on nuclear power. Among the fossil fuels, coal still makes up the lion's share, while natural gas and renewables have substituted the relatively expensive oil to a large degree since the 1970s (see table 8.7).

Before 1970 the sources used for electricity generation were mainly determined on pure economic grounds; the cheaper energy source won. In the second phase—from the 1970s onwards—the choice of primary energy sources for electricity generation has not been based solely on price, but on a wider perception of costs, where the societal costs of health and environmental risks are also factored in, or governmental preferences in the case of nuclear power (where actual costs remain highly controversial). Still, fossil fuels remain a dominant source for electricity generation in Europe today, and nuclear power still plays a major role, so the transition to renewable electricity generation is very far from completion.

[38] Global Wind Energy Outlook, 2010.

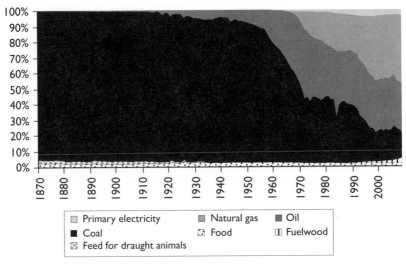

Figure 8.7. England's energy system, 1870–2009
Source: See www.energyhistory.org.

2. OLD AND NEW IN ENERGY REGIMES

REGIONAL DIVERGENCE IN ENERGY TRANSITIONS

The aggregate West European pattern, discernible in figure 8.3, hides big national and regional variations. Three types of economies stand out in particular: the coal economies, the Mediterranean economies, and the Nordic economies, here exemplified by England, Italy, and Sweden.

The major coal economies in western Europe were Britain and Germany (to a lesser degree Belgium). Both Britain and Germany had ample domestic sources of coal, allowing this source to reach a prominent role in their energy systems at an early stage, as described in chapters 5–7. England's surface-level coal seams were more easily accessible and its coal use was outstanding among these two countries. Its twentieth-century energy system is depicted in figure 8.7. Not only were the coal economies special in being early adopters of that fuel, but furthermore the scale of coal consumption reached levels never matched in any of the other countries. In England, coal was totally dominant in 1870, comprising more than 95 percent of the total energy consumption. England was late both in its oil transition and in its adoption of electricity with a non–fossil fuel origin. Oil never reached more than 50 percent of the total energy consumed, which is different from all other European countries (apart from Germany). This reluctance to abandon coal could be regarded as path-dependence. There were clear lock-in

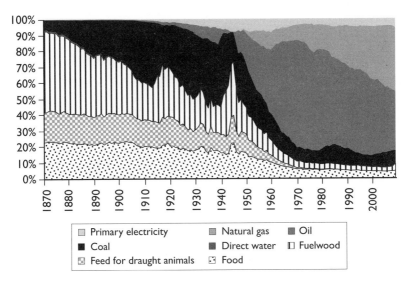

Figure 8.8. Italian energy system, 1870–2009
Source: See www.energyhistory.org.

effects in the form of steam engines, which were costly to replace, and electric power generation and industrial heat processes were based on coal since an early date.

The Mediterranean countries, with their warm climate, did not need so much energy for heating their houses. This had an impact on their energy composition, which was marked by relatively little firewood and coal, and a relatively large share of feed for animals and food for people. Italy did not have any domestic coal and had to import all of its consumption. The coal transition was hence never as profound as in the coal economies. In Italy, coal peaked at some 35 percent in the first half of the twentieth century (see figure 8.8). In the Mediterranean countries, oil came to dominate the scene in the decades after the Second World War, although there were differences, with Spain and Portugal lagging behind Italy.

In the Nordic countries the combination of low winter temperatures and accessible forests led to the consumption of large amounts of firewood primarily for household heating. Hence their energy system looks quite different from all other European countries (see figure 8.9). In Sweden, firewood comprised almost 70 percent of the total energy consumed in 1870, while coal only made up some 10 percent. There was a path-dependent return to firewood in the 1980s—very clear in the case of Sweden, less so in Finland, where peat instead has experienced a revival. In 2000, Sweden had about 20 percent of its primary energy supply from biomass, and uses biomass energy directly in households, in the form of pellets and ordinary firewood, and

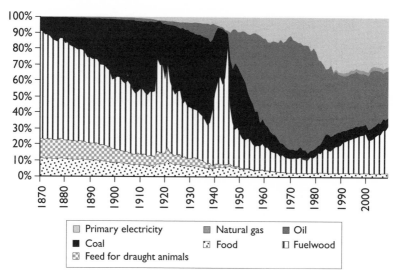

Figure 8.9. Swedish energy system, 1870–2009
Source: See www.energyhistory.org.

in combined heat and power stations, and about half from spent pulping liquor, a waste product used directly in the pulp and paper industry.

A second noticeable feature is the relatively large role played by primary electricity in the Swedish system, based on hydropower and nuclear. The last conspicuous feature is the very small role played by natural gas in the Nordic countries. The weak role of natural gas in Norway and Sweden is not solely explained by small domestic supplies—actually Norway has large supplies of domestic natural gas and has exported most of it to the European continent—but also by institutional factors and path-dependence. The strong state influence in establishing one large technical system—the electrical system—meant a resistance to investing in another capital-intensive network: that of gas.[39]

DRIVERS OF CO_2 EMISSIONS

The energy system determines the amounts of greenhouse gases. The amount of energy used and the kind of energy carriers both have an impact on the emissions of greenhouse gases. We will look into what has so far had the strongest impact on CO_2 emissions in Western Europe. The emissions have naturally increased over the period along with the explosion in fossil fuel consumption (see figure 8.10). There were two periods of particularly dras-

[39] Olsson, 1992, 119–27.

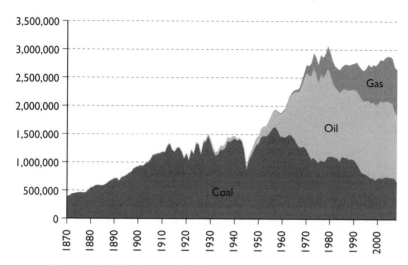

Figure 8.10. The increase in CO$_2$ emissions in western Europe, 1870–2009 by source
Source: Data for the eight western European countries in www.energyhistory.org and own calculations of emissions.

tic increases in emissions: 1870–1910 and 1950–1975. Since 1975, emissions have stabilized or declined slightly.

Was the long-term pattern of CO$_2$ emissions driven by a change in the composition of energy carriers, with a greater employment of low-carbon emitting energy sources, called "decarbonization"?[40] Or was it rather a more efficient use of energy that mattered?

Decarbonization is a popular idea, because it suggests that we can continue to consume huge amounts of energy, if only we switch over to energy carriers that do not cause any net emissions of CO$_2$ into the atmosphere. In theory this is true, but it is important to be critical and realistic about this possibility and how far society has come in this endeavor.[41] The actual reason for most of the decline in CO$_2$/GDP ratio has not been decarbonization, but the decline in energy intensity, as we will demonstrate.

It is of course true that different energy carriers emit CO$_2$ to differing degrees. Basically all energy carriers that contain some carbon atoms emit carbon dioxide (CO$_2$) when they are burned (this also applies to food and fodder combustion at low temperatures in bodies). But it is only fossil fuels that are non-renewable (at least in reasonable amounts of time) that cause *net* emissions of CO$_2$ to the atmosphere. Food, fodder, and firewood do not

[40] Grübler and Nakicenovic, 1996.

[41] See for instance the debate on forecasting overly optimistic decarbonization trends in Pielke, 2009.

TABLE 8.8
CO_2 emission factors for different
fossil fuels, gram CO_2/MJ

Coal	92
Oil	74
Natural gas	56

Source: Levander, 1991, 8.

cause any net emissions, unless land use practices change. If the same land is repeatedly used for the replacement of the consumed food, fodder, and firewood, the same amounts of CO_2 that have been emitted during combustion are absorbed from the atmosphere again by photosynthesis. Therefore the standard procedure for greenhouse gas calculations does not include any emissions from fuels other than coal, oil, natural gas, and maybe peat (although peat is a semi-fossil fuel, and there is an on-going debate on the rate of its natural replacement).[42]

Combustion of all fossil fuels causes some net contribution of CO_2 to the atmosphere, but fossil fuels are not equally bad for greenhouse gas emissions. How bad they are depends on the length of the carbon chains in the molecules, which in turn determine the carbon to hydrogen ratio. The shorter the chains of carbon atoms are, the more hydrogen they are bound up with, and the better the fuel is from a greenhouse gas perspective. The H/C ratio is typically 0.5:1 for coal, 2:1 for oil, and 4:1 for natural gas.[43] So, natural gas made up of methane molecules (CH4) is the best, oil with several different lengths of carbon chains is second best, and coal the worst emitter when set in relation to a a particular amount of energy. The emission factors for these fossil fuels are provided in table 8.8.

The story of energy use in Europe over the "long twentieth century" is one of initial carbonization (see figure 8.11), when coal use rose to its peak in the main mining countries and diffused beyond those as a consequence of the transport revolution based on steam engines; and later, a decarbonization, when coal gave way to more oil, electricity, and natural gas. Surprisingly perhaps, the Western European energy system of 2008 is practically back at the same carbon to energy ratio as it was some 140 years ago! The explanation for this result is that in 1870 a large fraction of the energy carriers (30 percent) did not emit any CO_2 at all. The years between 1870 and 1950 saw a carbonization of the energy system, where fossil fuels (especially

[42] IPCC, 1997, vol. 3, par. 6.28.
[43] Grübler, 2004, 163–77.

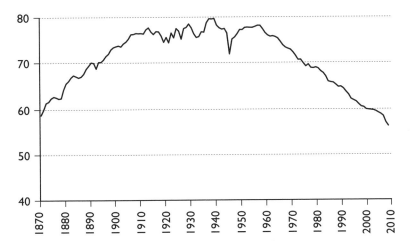

Figure 8.11. Carbonization and decarbonization of the West European energy system 1870–2008, tonnes per Tera Joule (TJ)
Note: Same eight countries as in tables 8.9 and 8.10.

coal) took on a larger role, increasing the ratio from 60 to 80 tonnes per Tera Joule (TJ). With the replacement of coal with oil and later natural gas, there was a decarbonization back to levels of 60 tonnes per TJ.

Not every country in Europe followed this aggregate path of carbonization followed by decarbonization. Finland, for instance, had a relatively stable carbon intensity until after World War II, when the energy mix became more modern and carbon-intense, which meant a fourfold increase in the carbon intensity up until the mid-1970s, followed by a period of modest decarbonization.[44]

In order to understand what were the proximate driving forces behind the increases in CO$_2$ emissions over this long period of time, we will make a similar decomposition as we did for energy intensity. The basic formula for CO$_2$ decomposition is called the Kaya-identity and is written:[45]

$$C = \frac{C}{E} \cdot \frac{E}{Y} \cdot \frac{Y}{P} \cdot P$$

where $C = $ CO$_2$ emissions; $C/E = $ Carbon factor for energy; $E/Y = $ Energy intensity; $Y/P = $ Income per capita; $P = $ Population.

[44] Kunnas and Myllyntaus, 2009.
[45] After the Japanese energy economist Yoichi Kaya. This identity has been used in the reports from IPCC; see Girod et al., 2009.

TABLE 8.9
Carbon emission drivers in Europe, 1870–2008

Variable	Unit	1870	2008	Annual growth rate 1870–2008 (%)
C	1000 tonnes	389,560	2,641,184	1.38
C/E	Tonnes/TJ	58.7	56.2	–0.032
E/Y	MJ/international dollar, 1990 year price level	20.95	6.50	–0.85
Y/P	Thousand 1990 international dollars/capita	2,044	21,694	1.71
P	Thousands	154,940	333,133	0.55

This formula can be rewritten in an additive version, with the respective annual growth rates of the factors above:

$$c = ce + ey + yp + p.$$

The basic information we need for the calculations is provided in table 8.9.

This gives the following result:

$$1.38 = -0.032 - 0.85 + 1.71 + 0.55.$$

Overall, the two scale effects, income per capita and population (Y/P and P), were the main contributors to the increased emissions of carbon dioxide over the period 1870 to 2008, while there was an almost insignificant contribution from the mix of energy carriers (decarbonization) and a strong offsetting factor in the declining energy intensity over the period. The small impact from decarbonization is similar to that found for the United States, where long-term CO_2 emission decline in relation to GDP has been driven by a decline in energy intensity (from technological and structural change) since 1917 (when CO_2 in relation to GDP peaked), whereas the decarbonization of the energy mix was rather insignificant.[46] However, as we have often stressed, the regional picture within Europe is varied. While Italy and Spain conform closely to this pattern, changes in the mix of energy carriers has played a far stronger role in Sweden.[47] These examples demonstrate

---

[46] Tol et al., 2009.
[47] Bartoletto and Rubio, 2008; Kander, 2002; Lindmark, 2002.

Figure 8.12. The CO_2 intensity of Europe 1870–2008,
kg per 1990 international dollar
Source: See www.energyhistory.org.

that the crucial factors for CO_2 emissions look different when all energy carriers are included, and long time horizons are applied. Decarbonization becomes less pronounced when traditional energy carriers are included in the analysis. What matters most in the long run is the decline in energy intensity, meaning that what matters for CO_2 intensity decline historically (figure 8.12) is best understood by analyzing energy intensity. We will return to this in chapter 10.

FOOD CONSUMPTION IN THE TWENTIETH CENTURY

The traditional sources of energy were not phased out during the twentieth century (see table 8.10). Despite falling shares for traditional energy sources in total energy consumption, the proportion remained relatively high in some countries, like Sweden, Portugal and, to a lesser degree, France and the Netherlands. For the coal economies Germany and England, the traditional fuels were already at low levels in 1900 and diminished further in the twentieth century.

The decline of traditional fuels did not normally mean that the consumption of these energy carriers went down in absolute amounts. Rather, there was a slower growth in the use of traditional fuels and an enormous expansion of fossil fuels and primary electricity in total energy consumption.

The share of food in total energy consumption declined. There is a ceiling to how much people can eat (even if affluence means food becomes relatively cheap and easily available), but the same strict limits are not there for

TABLE 8.10
Share of different traditional fuels, in the years 1900 and 2000 (%)

	Firewood/waste		Food		Animal feed		Water/Wind (direct working, not electricity producing)		Total traditional	
	1900	2000	1900	2000	1900	2000	1900	2000	1900	2000
England	0	1.0	2.1	2.0	1.8	0	0	0	3.9	3.0
Germany	4.8	2.4	5.6	2.4	3.4	0.1	0.2	0	13.8	4.9
France	10.6	5.1	8.5	2.7	6.8	0.2	0	0	25.9	8.0
Netherlands	11.8	6.8	9.3	2.2	6.1	0	3.1	0	30.3	9.0
Sweden	43.5	25.1	8.2	2.4	8.8	0	1.0	0	61.5	27.5
Spain	25.8	0.4	15.8	4.3	15.6	0	4.9	0	62.1	4.7
Italy	33.1	2.4	22.2	3.9	17.9	0	0.5	0	73.7	6.3
Portugal	50.2	7.2	17.0	5.6	14.0	0.2	1.2	0.1	82.4	13.1

other types of energy consumption. Food is an energy source which nicely illustrates the fact that value does not depend on the energy content as such, as we stressed in the introductory chapter. The diet has changed away from potatoes and grain (carbohydrates) to meat and dairy products (proteins and fats), with much larger amounts of fresh fruit. Some foodstuffs with very little energy content, like salad, tomatoes, or spices, are very costly, while some basic energy-rich foodstuffs like potatoes and grains are very cheap. Clearly people need energy for their metabolism and in order to conduct work, but they also care strongly about the taste and wider nutritional properties of what they eat. Because of this, and diversified tastes, foodstuffs have become truly globalized commodities and are transported all over the world. Of course, in order to keep the vegetables, fruits, and meat fresh, fast sea-borne and air transportation and energy-consuming cooling systems are necessary.

Since the number of people in Europe grew and they all had to be fed, there was a need to increase food production. This became a particular object of postwar policy after the experience of rationing and shortages during the 1940s. This need was matched through increased land productivity in agriculture, stimulated especially by the use of synthetic fertilizers, pesticides from the chemical industry, irrigation, and biological innovation: in hybrid crops and most recently genetically modified organisms. These innovations were often complementary or interrelated, meaning that an inadequate supply of one of them would hamper the utility received from others.[48] Some of the key innovations were already made in the last decades of the nineteenth century, but subsequent innovations cheapened production and led to a large expansion in their use. Fritz Haber (1888–1934) discovered the possibility of producing synthetic fertilizers by extracting the nitrogen from air, which in the 1910s was developed into the much more energy-efficient Haber-Bosch method, cheap enough for extensive diffusion. Without synthetic fertilizers, the large improvements in land productivity would never have taken place. Small amounts of synthetic fertilizers were used already at the turn of the century, at some 3 kg per hectare, but the exponential increase in the use of synthetic fertilizers took place from the 1950s onward, when petroleum, which was the feed stock for the necessary hydrogen gas, became much cheaper.[49] Synthetic fertilizer use increased from 47 kg per hectare in 1950 to 171 kg per hectare in 1970 and has subsequently fallen to 146 kg.[50] On the world scale, the absolute amounts of artificial fertilizers used increased from about 4 million tonnes in 1940 to 40 million tonnes in 1965 and 150 million tonnes by 1990.[51] Pesticide use has also increased

[48] Federico, 2005, 103, referring to Paul David's explanation of the delay for Britain in adopting the reaper in the mid-nineteenth century.

[49] Morell, 2001, 222–23.

[50] Federico, 2005, 99, table 6.4 figures referring to Europe.

[51] McNeill, 2000, 45.

significantly from the 1950s, peaking in the 1970s, but declining thereafter with the increased awareness of detrimental environmental consequences and regulation.[52]

Biological innovation also has a long history: Mendelev's discovery of the laws of genetics eventually stimulated experimentation and the development of hybrid wheat production in the late nineteenth century. More economically important was hybrid corn, first used in the United States in the 1930s, which improved yields by 20 percent.[53] The prospect of eliminating starvation in developing countries spurred further biological innovation, and led to the development of HYV (High Yielding Varieties). India experienced a tenfold increase in wheat yields in just over twenty years (1960–1980) as a consequence of the so-called green revolution, which combined HYV with irrigation, fertilizers, and pesticides, all of them necessary for the success.[54] The green revolution provides a very clear example of a set of complementary innovations. In the last couple of decades, biological innovation has taken a new step, into actually modifying the genes per se, and not just breeding individuals with desired properties. Genetically modified organisms (GMOs) are much contested on ethical and ecological grounds, but the technology opens up possibilities for increased world food production by making plants that are less drought-sensitive, or are not so vulnerable to harmful pests. The technology is not yet as accepted in Europe as in many other parts of the world such as the United States, Australia, Canada, and Latin America.

Over the period 1880–1993, land productivity increased three times in the UK, and six times in Denmark and the United States. This is when we measure output in terms of value, and involves major structural changes in the composition of what is grown on the land. Over the period 1600–1800, the cereal yields per acre had increased from nine bushels of wheat equivalents to twenty-two bushels in England, the greatest "improver" of this period, less than a factor of three over 200 years.[55] In the following 150 years, wheat yields in Europe rose from 0.86 tons per hectare in 1800 to 1.26 in 1910 and to 1.48 in 1950, i.e., not quite a doubling. Swedish wheat yields took a century to double, between the 1860s and 1960s. This can be contrasted with the much more impressive land productivity increase in the second half of the twentieth century, when fertilizers, HYV, irrigation, and pesticides worked in concert to more than double global wheat yields in just forty years. Wheat yields have trebled in Sweden, Britain, and France since 1945, and have also risen as far in Germany.[56]

[52] Flygare and Isacson, 2003, 219.

[53] Federico 2005, 86.

[54] Schön, 2010, 536.

[55] Wrigley, 2010, 79.

[56] Federico, 2005, 70; Morrell and Myrdal, 2011, 294; Ditt, 2001; DEFRA, 2010; ProdSTAT database of the FAO at faostat.fao.org.

The agricultural land not only has to produce food, but also fodder for draft animals. In traditional agricultures the land required to produce this was often a large share of the total, as we have seen in chapter 3. Generally, fodder for draft animals in Europe was of some importance until 1960, after which it dwindled in the overall expansion of other energy carriers. Still, draft animal use has remained important. The tractor only supplanted horses in northern Europe during the 1930s, and large-scale use of draft power continued in southern Europe right up until the 1960s. As late as the 1980s, about 80 percent of the agricultural fields in developed countries were cultivated by tractors and 20 percent was done by draft animals.[57]

HIGHER QUALITY OF ENERGY AND HIGHER EFFICIENCY IN ENERGY USE

If energy carriers of higher quality have replaced inferior energy carriers, this may constitute an explanation of improved economic efficiency of energy use, because higher quality may have compensated for lower quantity. Relatively less of traditional fuels and more of modern energy carriers could have such a positive effect on economic efficiency of energy use. The price of one energy carrier relative to another indicates how they were evaluated in society. In order for people to pay a higher price for one energy carrier than another, that energy carrier had to have higher qualities, either for specific purposes or by lower costs for dealing with the fuel. Still, prices have certain limitations as quality indicators,[58] and people's assessment of quality changes over time. Generally, the richer a country becomes the more likely its inhabitants are to pay extra to avoid costs in handling the energy. Expressed differently, they put a higher premium on their time. At still higher incomes (also associated with developments in scientific knowledge), external costs to the environment, such as global warming or acidification, will be factored in one way or another (by individual preferences or by governmental management of price structure through taxes and subsidies).[59] Despite difficulties in measuring the quality of energy, we can still safely say that the increasing importance of electricity, for which there were simply no substitutes for many particular uses, and the explosion in the use of the easily handled oil after the Second World War, both contributed to higher average quality of energy consumption in Europe in the twentieth century. This should have had a positive impact on the increasing economic efficiency of energy use (higher energy productivity).

---

[57] Collins, 2009.

[58] If the surplus value that customers get from energy carriers varies greatly, for instance, or when prices are not set on the market; see Kander, 2002; and Chick, 2007.

[59] Kander, 2002, 138–44.

3. CONCLUSION

The story we have told in this chapter is how all the countries of Europe became deeply dependent on fossil fuels during the twentieth century, especially oil, and despite concerted efforts to break this addiction it still has its grip on us in the early twenty-first century. The quantitative account of the energy history of Europe shows this with persuasive force: oil and electricity have increased their shares of energy consumption in Europe, and their absolute growth in consumption has also been great. So, the twentieth century has been a continuation of the energy regime shift of the first industrial revolution; breaking the constraints of the organic economy and setting the forces of modern economic growth in motion, but this time by the use of more advanced fossil fuels than coal (oil and natural gas) and a technically advanced modular energy carrier: electricity. In the next chapter we will see how oil and electricity diffused on European markets, the driving forces within development blocks in the form of market suction and market widening, as well as the consequences of the new development blocks for economic energy efficiency. We will also explore by these means the logic behind the trend break in energy consumption in the 1970s, after which energy consumption per capita stabilized. The century between 1870 and 1970 was in many respects a continuation of the industrial development established with the first industrial revolution, but after 1970 we see a new energy regime emerging with the onset of the third industrial revolution, establishing new relations between energy and growth.

CHAPTER NINE

MAJOR DEVELOPMENT BLOCKS IN THE TWENTIETH CENTURY AND THEIR IMPACTS ON ENERGY

THIS CHAPTER EXAMINES THE IMPACT that the major development blocks of the twentieth century had on the diffusion of new energy carriers and energy use in society. Here we will primarily address the drivers of energy transitions and economic energy efficiency.

The second and third industrial revolutions were each distinguished by major development blocks in the fields of energy and communication. In the second industrial revolution, starting around 1870, but having an impact that lasted over a century, there were two main development blocks: one centered on the internal combustion engine and oil use (henceforth called the ICE-Oil block) and another one centered on electricity (the Electricity block). In the third industrial revolution, taking off from the mid-1970s, the development block around information and communication technology (the ICT block) becomes dominant, with the transistor as its macro-innovation.

We will describe the functioning of the core macro-innovation of each development block and then proceed to its diffusion in society using the concepts of *market suction* and *market widening* introduced in chapter 2, and previously employed in the analyses of coal and steam engines in chapters 6 and 7.

Not only is the choice of energy carriers affected by development blocks, but also the total amounts of energy used in society. The amount is a question of the relative balance of *energy-saving* versus *energy-expanding* properties of the block, and to what degree take-back effects offset the energy savings. This chapter will provide a qualitative understanding of how economic energy efficiency is shaped by these development blocks and how it consequently changes over time.

1. THE ICE-OIL BLOCK

The ICE-oil block, that development block centered on the internal combustion engine (ICE), with oil as a complementary resource, has affected energy use in the twentieth century to a very considerable degree. First we will describe the core technical features of the internal combustion engine, before continuing with a discussion of to what degree oil transition was driven by the relative balance of market suction and market widening. We will then address the resource impact of the block: is it primarily energy-saving or energy-expanding?

What Is an Internal Combustion Engine?

The internal combustion engine is a core innovation with applications in several kinds of machines, used both for stationary work in industry and for transportation. Like the steam engine it transforms heat to motive power. As stressed in the second part of this book, the steam engine was a truly revolutionary step because by converting heat into motion it equipped people with inanimate slaves; machines that could work for them and be fed by non-areal energy sources from the depths of the Earth. The internal combustion engine greatly augmented the initial impact of the steam engine. While steam engines were large and bulky, the internal combustion engine soon developed into a small machine that delivered a large amount of power per kilogram, enlarging the scope for applications. In the internal combustion enginesm combustion takes place *within* the engine, as the name indicates, and is an integral part of the construction and function of the machine. This is unlike the steam engine, where the boiler for combustion and the pistons providing drive are separated from each other. The principal parts of the internal combustion engine are a cylinder with a piston which moves back and forth and a crank shaft that transmits power to a drive shaft, which in turn can be connected to the wheels of a car.

The first internal combustion engines in the 1850s were not very fuel-efficient as they operated at atmospheric pressure (there was no compression before combustion). At best these engines reached only 5 percent thermal efficiency (so 95 percent of the energy value of the fuel was lost). The four-stroke internal combustion engine for which Nikolas Otto (1832–1891) is normally given credit led to the commercial breakthrough of the engine. The thermal efficiency of the Otto engines was much higher, at 11 percent, and already by 1890 some 50,000 engines had been produced and sold in the United States and Europe.[1]

There are two main types of internal combustion engines in use: the two-stroke and the four-stroke engines. A stroke is defined as the movement of the piston from the top position to the bottom position and vice versa. The main difference between the two-stroke and four-stroke engine is how the gas exchange is performed. The two-stroke engine normally has gates in the cylinder wall, which are opened and closed by the piston. The four-stroke

[1] Heywood, 1988, 2.

The Internal Combustion Engine

The principal working of the four-stroke engine is illustrated in figure 9.1.[1] The first stroke is an inlet stroke, where the piston moves from the top position to the bottom position, while the inlet valve is open. Air may be forced into the cylinder by a compressor. The second stroke is the compression stroke, when the piston moves up to the top position and all valves are closed. The third stroke is the expansion stroke and it takes place when the piston again moves toward its bottom position. All valves are then closed and fuel is injected and ignited by a spark plug. The work performed during the expansion exceeds that required for the compression. The net effect results in mechanical work on the crank shaft connected to the wheels. In the last stroke the exhaust valves are open and the exhaust gases are expelled. Then the four-stroke cycle starts all over again. The rotation of the crank shaft is maintained during three of the four strokes (all except expansion) by a flywheel, which is originally started by a starting motor.

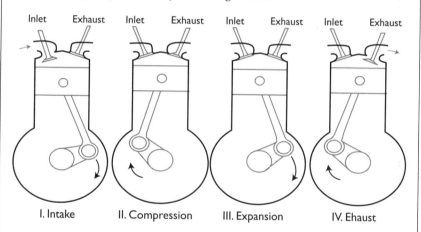

Figure 9.1. The working of the four-stroke internal combustion engine

[1] The figure is drawn by Roland Emanuelsson and inspiration is acknowledged from fig. 1–2 on p. 10 in Heywood, 1988.

engine has valves to control the air inlet and exhaust outlet. Optimization of the control of the valves in the four-stroke engine creates a better basis for controlling exhaust emission compared with the two-stroke engine. Thus, two-stroke engines are mostly used for the very smallest and the very largest power capacities, where emission control is not regulated. The four-stroke engine has become the most widely spread version of the internal combustion engine, suitable for the large share of medium-sized engines, and has proven to be cheap and extremely reliable.[2]

The diesel engine is a version of the internal combustion engine. The principal difference between the Otto combustion engine and the diesel engine is that the air-fuel mix is ignited by compression alone in the diesel engine; there is no need for a spark. As a young student, Rudolf Diesel (1858–1913) learned about the principles of thermodynamics and was stimulated by the challenge to create an ideal Carnot cycle.[3] In such an ideal combustion there would be no energy losses in the transformation of heat to motion. Achieving this ideal combustion proved to be an impossible task, but Diesel still reached much further than his predecessors in achieving a high thermal efficiency with his engine. In 1895 its thermal efficiency was 31 percent, twice as high as all other comparable engines. The high performance of diesel engines continued over the twentieth century, and in 2010, diesel engine efficiency was 40–44 percent, as compared to 30–38 percent for Otto combustion engines. Compound diesel engines in trucks could even reach efficiencies above 50 percent, and the most efficient ones in ships, 55 percent.[4] Their main drawback at this time was the low power to weight ratio and the higher production costs compared to the Otto engine. Diesel engines were suitable for small-scale industry rather than for transport, where weight matters more. Even today diesel engines are mainly used for larger vehicles like ships, buses, and trucks, but are gradually gaining ground in cars due to their higher efficiency.

THE GROWTH DYNAMICS OF THE ICE-OIL BLOCK

The development block around the combustion engine began to emerge in the 1870s. Even though the first uses had been for stationary applications in industry and workshops, the main sector of uptake was transport; first in road transport, later sea and air. Land transportation had historically been cumbersome. This changed with the internal combustion engine and the car, after a long period of development. Indeed, for the development block around the internal combustion engine to come into existence, it was not

---

[2] Smil, 2005, 102: "internal combustion engines . . . should still be a source of admiration if only because these affordable machines, . . . , work so reliably for such long periods of time."

[3] Sadi Carnot (1796–1832) developed the idea that the thermal efficiency of an engine was not due to the fluid or energy carrier used, but due to the difference between the warmest and coldest part of the process. This idea was later incorporated into the general knowledge about thermodynamics.

[4] Information about current efficiencies provided by Professor Bengt Johansson from Lund Technical University, Div. Combustion Engines /Dept. Energy Sciences. Engines in cars are often run at part load with lower efficiency than the maximum. At idling, the efficiency is zero and part load is somewhere between this and the maximum.

sufficient to invent cars, buses, trucks, diesel ships, and airplanes. The new modes of transportation required a new infrastructure with several interconnected components. While steam locomotives required railways, cars, buses, and trucks needed an extensive road network.[5] There had to be widely available filling stations, tire maintenance, auto shops, and available spare parts. These complementarities meant that there were many effects from the emergence of motor vehicles on other parts of the economy, an essential part of the powerful impact of the development block on the economy as a whole. Examples of forward linkages (see chapter 7) are the providers of services for car owners, like gasoline stations, as well as the construction of roads themselves. Among backward linkages are the subcontractors for the car manufacturing industry: fabric manufacturers for car seats, rubber producers, safety equipment like airbags, glass for windows, electronics for steering equipment, etc.

In the more mature phase of the development block we see a transport revolution, just as the locomotives had brought in the nineteenth century, and much more pervasive growth effects from the ICE-oil block. Mobility increased in society. Many more people could commute long distances for work on a daily basis, no longer being dependent on proximity to rail lines. They could take the car to a shopping mall or out for recreational activities, including more remote areas of the countryside; holiday trips were much longer and the world became smaller. Long-distance exchange of goods and people became a more prominent feature of the world economy, especially in the decades after World War II, and the multinational firm became commonplace. This stimulated economic growth, but also led to a large relative expansion for transportation, a sector largely dependent on oil. These new and improved transportation options led to spatial transformations, cut costs across the board for firms and economies, and in many ways revolutionized society.

Oil Transition: Market Suction versus Market Widening

There was, in fact, a period of diffusion in oil use across Europe that started before the ICE-oil development block played any role. During the first half century of diffusion (1860–1910), oil was used exclusively for medical purposes and for light, and consumption was very small.[6] But it was with the development of cars and internal combustion engines that the demand for gasoline began to increase significantly, and by the 1920s kerosene use (for

---

[5] Schipper, 2008.

[6] American troops used petroleum from Oil Creek as a treatment for rheumatism. Also, in other places such as Kentucky, oil was bottled and sold for medical purposes as American Oil. Forbes, 1958, 8.

lamps) was in decline. Gasoline became the main oil product on the market and kept this role for several decades.

There was strong complementarity between cars and gasoline, and thus there was a demand pull, or market suction, on oil from the cars. Still, it took time for this market suction to become strong and for gasoline engines to become the dominant design in cars. The desirability of a flexible motorized mode of transportation had long been recognized, and led to experiments with a number of forms of power: the first cars were driven by a variety of steam engines, electric motors, and combustion engines. A dominant design only emerged after several decades of trial and error. Steam-engine cars, fueled with coal, were popular from the 1830s, but were only disseminated among a still small market in England, France, and the United States. They were heavy, but reliable. Early combustion engines in cars had considerable drawbacks. Karl Benz's famous engine of 1887 was difficult to start and the car had to be pushed up steep slopes. The tendency for the combustion engine to shake and damage the car was only overcome with the invention of the air-filled tires. Before these tires, the cars had to be constructed with bulky suspensions to avoid breakage. Emile Levassor's engine of only 4 hp weighed an enormous 1,000 kg in 1890, thus requiring 250 kg per hp. At the turn of the century, with the introduction of pneumatic tires, the weight of the engine was reduced to 35–40 kg per hp, and ten years later it was down to 7 kg per hp.

The first electric car was produced in England in 1842 and during the 1860s the Frenchman Planté produced a rechargeable lead battery. Electric cars were quieter, simpler, and more reliable than cars with either combustion engines or steam engines, and there were no less than 565 different brands of electric cars (for instance: Bouquet, Doré, Garon, Mildé, Richard and Homard) made before the First World War. In 1899, an electric car surpassed the speed of 100 km/hour, which was considered a sensation. Although winning speed competitions, most electric cars in the early twentieth century were large working vehicles, like fire engines. The main weakness of the electric cars was, and would remain, the battery. In difficult road conditions the electric cars could only travel 30–40 km before the batteries needed recharging.[7]

An important factor for the eventual success of the gasoline-fueled combustion engine seems to have been the international car competitions that took place around the turn of the century. Combustion engines demonstrated their superiority, subsequently strongly influencing both producers and consumers of cars. In the Paris-Bordeaux-Paris race in 1895, for example, many competitors signed up with a variety of steam cars, gasoline cars, and electric cars, accompanied by a great variety of boasts about which vehicle would win. But on the day of the race, only twenty-one cars actu-

[7] Nerén, 1937.

ally started. Out of those, fifteen were gasoline cars, six were steam cars, and *none* were electric! The gasoline cars proved their superiority in the race, and the first prize went to a Peugeot. In the next year's race there were thirty-two cars; only two of them were heavy steam cars that had to be abandoned during the race, because their solid rubber tires broke. The competition made people abandon the prejudice that heavy vehicles were better, and showed quite clearly that light gasoline cars could stand the hardships of a jarring ride at high speed. Between the turn of the century and the outbreak of the First World War, combustion engines became more reliable, and in the 1920s they took the lead and became the dominant design for cars.[8] Although combustion engines were mainly fueled by oil products, the first combustion engine—Lenoir's—was actually driven by coal gas. Coal gas engines were mainly used in France, and also to some degree in Sweden and Finland. Before a dominant design emerged, there were four kinds of combustion engines competing: the carburetor engine, the coal-gas engine, the Hesselman engine, and the diesel engine. The carburetor engine was adapted for gasoline fuel, and together with the diesel engine, were the two winners over time. Gasoline had a much higher energy density than coal gas (nearly 44 MJ/kg, which is about 1,600 times the energy density of illuminating gas), a clear advantage for driving when it is necessary to bring the fuel along on the trip.[9] Both the carburetor and diesel engines predominantly used mineral oil, although the diesel engine demonstrated in Paris at the world exhibition in 1900 ran perfectly well on peanut oil. By then the complementarity between cars and oil was established in a clear manner.

Figure 9.2 shows that design of the first cars often resembled the bicycle (often they had three wheels only and were very light), and how the design has continued to change, until the recent hybrid car, which has both an internal combustion engine and an electric motor.

There are basically two different ways that the internal combustion engine had an impact on the oil transition. The first was through fuel-technology complementarity, or market suction. This simply means that gasoline was a suitable fuel for the internal combustion engine, and with the increasing use of these engines there was an increased demand for the production of gasoline, which affected demand for raw oil extraction, and that in turn provided other oil products as by-products.

This is a clear example of demand-side factors playing the most important role for the oil transition. The other, alternative way, was through the supply side, where market widening of the core technology, especially in transportation, led to lower transport costs and lower prices of the new fuel (oil), so that it was used for wider applications, like heating, where there are

[8] Nerén, 1937
[9] Smil, 2005, 111.

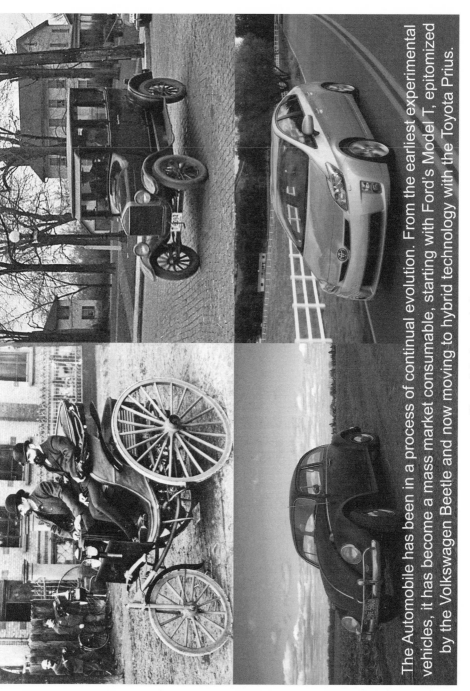

The Automobile has been in a process of continual evolution. From the earliest experimental vehicles, it has become a mass market consumable, starting with Ford's Model T, epitomized by the Volkswagen Beetle and now moving to hybrid technology with the Toyota Prius.

Figure 9.2. Car evolution

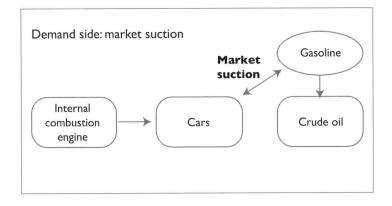

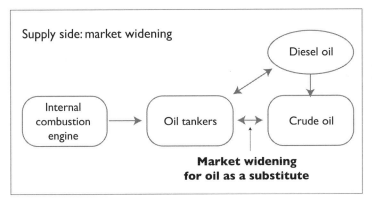

Figure 9.3. Market suction and market widening for oil

always several alternatives. The mechanisms of market suction and market widening are illustrated in figure 9.3.

The upper and lower illustrations of figure 9.3 are in fact very similar. Both of them contain a market suction link, between cars and gasoline in the upper illustration, and between diesel oil and oil tankers in the lower illustration. There is one crucial difference: the arrow between crude oil and oil tankers, in the lower panel, indicating the wider use for oil in society, as a consequence of the improved and cheaper transportation by tankers lowering the oil price.

One method for examining the interplay of market suction and market widening is simply to study the rate of car diffusion in relation to the surge in oil consumption. If those two are strongly correlated, we would be right to conclude that market suction is a strong force. As noted in the previous chapter, the United States had a much more gradual adaptation of oil than Europe, where its use expanded more suddenly after World War II. Is this pattern consistent with the diffusion of cars in Europe versus the United States? The early development of cars took place in Europe. The United States did not make any significant contributions to the early development of the combustion engine and the car, but "put the world on wheels," with the Model-T Ford. Large-scale production on the conveyor belt reduced costs, so that even ordinary workers could afford one. In total 15 million Model-T Fords were produced between 1908 and 1927, and in this period every second car in the world was a Model-T. In 1913, England produced 34,000 domestic cars but there were 208,000 new car registrations, so 174,000 were imported, most of them Model-T Fords. We can compare the massive scale of the Model-T Ford production to the normal car production runs in Europe in the late nineteenth century, where a mere 5–10 examples of most models were produced. The assembly line production methods spread to Europe, where several countries established car industries with large-scale assembly-line production. France took the lead in the new industry, with the brands Peugeot and Renault. By 1913, France produced 45,000 cars, second only after the United States. France was challenged as the European leader in the 1920s by both Germany and the United Kingdom, followed by Italy. Spain and Sweden also established car industries with international importance, but somewhat later, mainly during the 1950s and 1960s.

Production of cars is one thing. Consumption is another. The number of private cars available in different European countries is shown in table 9.1. It is clear that the 1950s and 1960s were decades when the car fleet, in relative terms, increased dramatically. All European countries show at least a doubling in the number of cars both in the 1950s and in the 1960s. The United States only showed an increase of some 50 percent per decade, because the big leap had already taken place between 1920 and 1950. On a very general level, these car diffusion figures thus fit well with the oil transition figures for Europe and for the United States. In Europe, the oil transition was much faster and more abrupt than in the United States. Thus, a simple interpretation of these data suggests that it was the complementarity between combustion engines and oil which made for the oil transition. But this is not the entire story—far from it.

Market widening for oil due to the cheaper transport in bigger and bigger tankers was equally important (if not more) for the great oil transition after World War II. Oil tankers carry oil not in barrels, but in their tanks, which is a much more efficient use of space. In the late nineteenth century only 1 percent of the exports from the United States to Europe went in tankers; the rest was shipped in barrels. In 1906, the situation had changed completely, so that 99 percent of American oil was exported in tankers. The heavy, but efficient, diesel engines were perfect for sea transport, and by 1927 over a quarter of the world's fleet used diesel engines, a share that continued to rise.[10]

---

[10] Juda, 1996, 54.

TABLE 9.1
Number of personal cars in different European Countries, Japan, and the United States, in 1000s, 1920–2000

	United Kingdom	France	Italy	Spain	Sweden	Netherlands	Germany	Japan	USA
1920	187	157	32	na	Na	na	61	7	8,132
1930	1,056	1,109	183	na	104	68	489	48	23,035
1950	2,258	2,150	342	89	252	139	469	48	40,339
1960	5,526	5,546	1,995	291	1,194	522	4,788	440	61,682
1970	11,515	12,900	10,181	2,378	2,289	2,600	15,100	6,277	89,200
1980	14,772	19,130	17,686	7,557	2,883	4,515	25,870	21,544	121,600
1990	19,742	23,550	27,461	11,996	3,601	5,509	30,685	35,152	143,600
2000	25,067	28,060	32,584	17,449	3,999	6,343	42,840	52,738	213,000

Source: Mitchell, 2007.

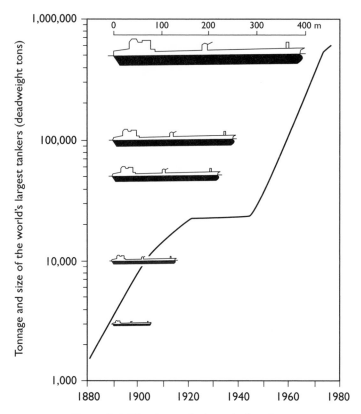

Figure 9.4. The size evolution of oil tankers
Source: Smil, 1994.

Enormous advances took place in oil shipping over the twentieth century, going from relatively small ships with diesel engines, to gigantic ships with large turbo diesel engines (see figure 9.4). An example of a huge oil tanker is *Jahre Viking*, which was built in Japan in the 1970s. The ship is 458 meters long and 69 meters across, and can carry the equivalent of more than 4 million barrels of oil.[11] These enormous tankers require a huge motor capacity, which was sometimes solved by connecting two or four diesel engines serially, but also by making the engines larger, often having cylinders more than a meter in diameter.

The increasing size of oil tankers and their more powerful engines meant that the cost of transporting oil across oceans decreased in relation to the price of the crude oil at the production site. This relative decline of oil shipping costs, clearly visible in figure 9.5, dropped from 50 percent down to

[11] Landau, 2006, 31.

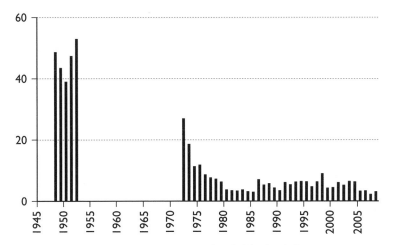

Figure 9.5. Ocean transport cost divided by landed cost
for crude oil, US, 1948–2008, percent.
Note: The oil crises of the 1970s led to price increases
both on oil as such and on the cost of transporting the oil,
but efficiency measures were undertaken, so the ratio of
transport cost to landed cost for crude oil still declined.
Sources: Adelman, 1972, and Zannetos, 1987, for the
early years; Energy Information Administration for the period
after 1972; no values available between 1953 and 1971.

5 percent between 1950 and 2000.[12] Oil cost little more to transport in the
1990s than fifty years earlier (in nominal prices), but the price of landed
crude oil was of course much higher.[13] With the supertankers of today, the
transport of crude oil from the Middle East to Europe sometimes equals
less than 2 percent of the cargo's value.[14] Shipping played a large role in
the global trade revolution. It made sea transport so cheap that the cost of
freight was not a major issue in deciding where to source or market goods.
This opened up possibilities for more usages for oil, also for purposes where

[12] In the period 1953 to 1973, when we lack the necessary data to conduct the calculations
for figure 9.5, we dare say that the ratio declined relatively smoothly. Stopford reckoned the
share to be 30 percent in 1960.

[13] Stopford, 2009, 73–74. See especially figure 2.5 which shows the cost of shipping oil from
the United States to Japan, 1947–2008, in nominal prices. It fluctuates between 0.2 dollars per
barrel to 3.4 in the extreme year 2004, but there is no clear trend. The normal price is between
0.5 and 1 dollar per barrel throughout the period. The price of crude oil increased from 1.5
dollars in 1960 to 50 dollars in 2004, after which the price of oil has risen to over 100 dollars
per barrel. Stopford has assembled his own data for the figure, and unfortunately, no sources
are provided.

[14] Smil, 2010, 172.

there were many substitutes (and hence no strong complementarity) such as heating houses. When we consider the driving forces for the oil transition, the market widening effect for crude oil due to the transport revolution also clearly impacted the oil transition in the 1950s. Thus the internal combustion engine acted both on the demand side and the supply side to enable the oil transition.

The cheap transport of oil overseas has been complemented with improved land-based transportation, also powered by internal combustion engines. Pipelines offer a safe and clean way of transporting oil on land. The United States started experimenting with pipelines in the 1880s, and the world's longest pipeline was constructed between Siberia and Europe in the 1970s.[15] Normally gas turbines of up to 17,000 hp are used to power the pumps on pipelines, and these gas turbines are frequently of the internal combustion kind, although external combustion versions exist too.[16] Lorry transport of oil to consumers has become cheaper as the fuel cost has declined. In combination these two factors have further contributed to the market widening for crude oil.

Further corroboration for the importance of market widening after the transport revolution from the 1950s is found in the distribution of various oil derivates in the consumption. There are many different oil products, suitable for various specific usages. In crude oil a relatively small share consists of gasoline, but with refinement the share can increase. Simply by looking at the distribution of these oil products in consumption, we can get a reasonable idea of how much of the oil was used for cars and how much went into other applications, at least for the twentieth century when gasoline had become the dominant fuel for cars.

In table 9.2 we can see that kerosene, mainly used for illumination, dominated the scene in Sweden until the 1920s, when gasoline for the first time exceeded 50 percent of consumption. After that heating oil gained a prominent role in consumption. Between 1960 and 1980, heating oil was equally important to diesel oil, and each of them was twice as large in consumption as gasoline. We see the price incentives to switch from coal to heating oil in figure 9.6: oil prices fell drastically compared to coal prices after World War II.

In the UK the pattern was quite similar, although we lack figures from before 1938 (see table 9.3). The peak of heating oil usage came earlier in the UK than in Sweden, since the UK had the alternative of natural-gas heating with the expansion of North Sea Gas extraction. Another conspicuous feature of breakdown of products in British oil consumption is the increasing share of kerosene between 1980 and 2005. Most of this is explained by changes in jet propulsion of airplanes in that period, which saw aviation fuel

[15] Smil, 1994, 172.
[16] Scott, 2010.

TABLE 9.2
Share of different oil products, 1900–1990, Sweden (%)

	Kerosene	Gasoline	Fuel oil	Motor oil	Heating oil
1900–1910	99	1			
1910–1920	86	14			
1920–1930	36	64			
1930–1950	9	39	52		
1950–1960	6	17	84		
1960–1980	2	19		38	40
1980–1990	4	37		48	11

Source: Kander, 2002.

shifting from gasoline to kerosene. All in all, the UK confirms the picture of a gasoline-driven expansion until the 1950s, when heating oil became more prominent as a share of the total as a consequence of market widening for oil, itself due to cheaper transport of oil.

In conclusion, between 1910 and 1950, the demand for gasoline from cars was the driving force for the oil transition. But the 1960s was the period of the great breakthrough of oil in Europe, when oil became the main energy carrier in several countries. This surge was driven by a supply push that put cheap oil out on the market, cheap enough to be competitive with coal and coke for heating houses and in industry. This cheapening of oil for European markets was driven largely by a transport revolution for oil with bigger oil tankers, with more and more powerful diesel engines. We see that

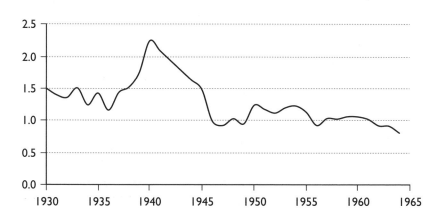

Figure 9.6. The price of heating oil relative to coke, Sweden 1930–1965
Source: Ljungberg, 1990.

Table 9.3
Different oil product shares in the UK, 1938–2005 (%)

	Kerosene	Gasoline	Diesel oil	Heating oil
1938	7	48	27	18
1960	2	21	17	60
1980	7	30	27	36
2005	20	31	43	6

Source: Digest of UK Energy Statistics, 1951–2006.

the internal combustion engine played a crucial role for the oil transition. The form of this importance has however shifted over the century from mainly a demand pull, in the form of market suction, to the supply push, in the form of market widening.

Energy Expanding or Energy Saving

The impact on energy consumption from the ICE-oil block is twofold. First it led to the breakthrough of oil as a dominant energy carrier in Europe, despite the fact that Europe had to import most of its oil. Thus, the development block affected the structure of energy consumption. The second impact is on the total amount of energy used in society. There are always two impacts from a development block on the amount of energy consumed, as highlighted in chapter 2. One is that energy consumption in society increases, there is *energy expansion*, since all the new technological equipment involved needs energy to be produced and must employ energy to function. The other impact is on *energy savings*, as old-fashioned technologies with low energy efficiency are phased out and replaced with more efficient ones. In the very early phase of the development block, when small compact engines replaced steam engines in industry and cars replaced other less efficient modes of transport, like horses or steam locomotives, there was some clear bias toward energy-saving. Later, the huge increase in the number of cars and in new applications for internal combustion engines, like airplanes, meant that the block was clearly energy-expanding, despite continuing improvements in the thermal efficiency of the engines.[17] In the primarily market-widening phase, oil found new areas of use and oil consumption skyrocketed. All in all, over the course of its entire development, the energy expansion was clearly the dominant feature of the ICE-oil block.

[17] For air transportation, the ICE was gradually replaced by jet turbines, which were much faster and more efficient. Smil, 2010, 40.

2. THE ELECTRICITY BLOCK

The Discovery of Electricity

Developments in the generation of electricity relied heavily upon scientific advances, as did the innovations of the second industrial revolution in general. Furthermore, the various innovations in producing electricity were interrelated and complementary to a far larger degree than any previous set of technologies.

Electricity is not visible to our eye and is therefore something abstract to us. Normally electricity is described as the movement of tiny charged subatomic particles (electrons). Each electron flows only a short distance and then transfers its energy to another electron and so forth around a circuit.[18] It is the voltage (energy pressure) that makes all the electrons move in the same direction, and the amount of electricity flowing is indicated by the ampere, which can be imagined as analogous to the width of a water pipe. The unit for electrical flow is the watt and it is equal to the ampere multiplied by the voltage. The watt is the power, the force with which electricity is flowing, and the energy of this electricity is measured as watt hours, i.e., the time the electricity flows also matters for how much electricity is consumed. By this definition, electricity may seem simple to understand. Yet even for experts there is some inherent contradiction in the definition: is electricity the wiggling electrons, or is it rather the high-speed electromagnetic field energy? This electromagnetic wave-energy does not wiggle; instead, it races along the wires.[19] We understand from this confusion that there is some connection between magnetism and electricity, and this has been an essential part of developing electrical technology.

Early experiments on magnetism and electricity led people to suspect some relation between the two mysterious forces, but it took some centuries until this insight was put into commercial applications.[20] William Gilbert (1544–1603) was accredited with being the father of electricity because he discovered that an attracted piece of iron can be magnetized without touching the magnet, just by induction. Gilbert coined the term "electricity" from the Greek word for amber (another material that became magnetic when rubbed).[21] Gilbert spent more than twenty years conducting ingenious experiments to understand magnetism, examining materials he managed to obtain from mountains, mines, and the depths of the sea.[22] Private profits or usefulness were not such important drivers for these early investigators,

---

[18] Galvin and Yeager, 2009, 32.
[19] Beaty, 1996.
[20] Durgin, 1912, 14–55.
[21] Heilbron, 1979, 174–79.
[22] Benjamin, 1898, 266.

and magnetically induced commercial electricity was still far away. Around 1650, Otto von Guericke found that electrical attraction could pass along a linen thread, i.e., that the thread conducts the electricity. This was the first wire-bound electric transmission and important for all future transmissions in electricity systems, but at this early stage still extremely poor in performance.

Somewhat later innovations in electricity resulted from more deliberate intentions to improve people's lives; progress became more rapid in the search for improvements and potential applications. By gaining and applying useful knowledge, people won power over nature.[23] As a first useful application, Benjamin Franklin discovered the electric glow around 1750 and made primitive batteries connected in a series. He also discovered the shared identity of the electric spark and the lightning flash and found ways of leading the lightning to the ground. The motivation for Franklin's experiments was not primarily his private profit, but rather the improvement of others' lives.[24] Another important innovator on the way to making electricity a commercial source of energy was Alessandro Volta (1745–1827), who invented the first generator of continuous electric current, which relied on the contact of dissimilar metals. In 1819, Hans Christian Oersted from Copenhagen carried out an experiment where he made a wire attached to a powerful battery, which then moved a large magnetic needle. This experiment was soon followed up by André Marie Ampére in Paris, who discovered that currents affect each other, so that currents in opposite directions repel and currents in the same direction attract each other. The use of magnetism to close and open electric circuits became a reality with these later discoveries, and is presently a vital part of the design of all electric apparatus.

The Macro-innovations

There is not just one core innovation in the electricity block; rather, it is a set of interrelated innovations, such as the electric motor/generator and transformers. As early as 1830, Michael Faraday developed an apparatus in which the electric current affected only the north pole of a magnet, and thereby made it rotate. This was the first electric motor. Faraday also produced the first electric generators, doing the reverse: producing electricity from magnetism. These electric generators were very important, since producing electricity from batteries was too expensive. The mid-1860s saw the development of the principle of the self-excited generator by Alfred Varley and Werner Siemens, while in 1870 the Belgian Zebobe Theophile Gramme

[23] Mokyr, 2009, 33–35; 2002, 2–27.
[24] Mokyr, 2009, 88.

built a ring dynamo.[25] These two innovations were paramount in the electricity system. Faraday and his followers produced motors and generators for direct current, but these motors were inefficient and unreliable. The standards and performance changed with Nikola Tesla's alternating current (AC) motors in the late 1880s. His was a simpler solution and far more energy-efficient. Today's electric motors with thermal efficiencies of more than 95 percent still basically rely on Tesla's macro-innovation, although subsequent meso-innovations have improved its functioning.

A critical innovation in the electricity system is the transformer. Transformers are ingenious devices without which long-distance transmission of electricity would be impossible, and they became critical in the 1880s.[26] Electricity is best generated and consumed at low voltage, but transmission is best done at high voltage, because it minimizes energy losses. Transformers perform this function. They convert electric current from one current into another, thereby changing the voltage. This is done with virtually no losses of energy. The transmitted electricity is the product of its current and voltage (W=AV), which can be thought of metaphorically as a waterfall, where the same amount of water can be transported either in a wide and short fall, or in a narrow and high fall (the width being the current and the height being the voltage).[27] All transformers work by electromagnetic induction and transform electricity to the appropriate form. At the power station, electricity is produced at low voltage and high current. Then transformers raise this voltage to one suitable for transmission (high voltage and low current). After numerous further conversions in the transmission and distribution network, the power is finally transformed to the standard form utilized for lighting and electrical equipment (low voltage and high current).

THE INTERNAL LOGIC OF SYSTEM EXPANSION—MARKET WIDENING

The electricity block is very knowledge-intensive and has required large investments in research and development. The inventor-entrepreneur Thomas Edison already had a clear awareness of the systemic properties of the development block around electricity. He realized the need for the devices that

---

[25] Mokyr, 1990, 124.

[26] Smil, 2005, 70.

[27] In 1842 the Englishman Joule established the relation between mechanical energy and heat, and later turned to establish the relation between electricity and heat. He showed that every transmission of electricity is subject to a heat loss. The amount of loss is dependent on two variables; one is the amount of current and the other is distance. Current loss is two times the amount of the increase of the electric current, and distance losses are proportional to the length of the transmission lines. That is why it is necessary to transmit electricity at high voltage and low current, something achieved with the three-phase alternating current system in the 1890s.

produced, transmitted, and consumed electricity to develop in tandem and contributed to this himself in several ways: "The problem that I undertook to solve was stated generally the production of multifarious apparatus, methods and devices, each adapted for use with every other, and all forming a comprehensive system." Edison is well known for his inventions in developing the electric lamp, primarily the high resistance filament, but his lighting system also contained a distribution network, with generators and parallel distribution lines. Edison realized that all parts of the electricity system needed to be developed together since they were all dependent on each other, and clearly expressed the systemic properties of electricity: "Improvement of one component in a system will reverberate throughout the system and cause the need for improvements in other components, thereby enabling the entire system to fulfil its goal more efficiently or economically."[28] This idea of interdependence or "reverse salients" in an expanding technological system was a prominent aspect of Thomas Hughes's influential theory of large socio-technological systems.[29] The term "reverse salient" is borrowed from military historians, who use it to refer to those sections of an advancing front that have fallen behind. According to Hughes, "a reverse salient appears in an expanding system when a component of the system does not march along harmoniously with other components."[30] In the theory of development blocks there is a similar concept used for parts that are lagging behind; they constitute "bottlenecks" in the system.

There is an internal logic that drives the expansion of the electricity system. Electricity generation, distribution, and consumption are best performed in a large technical system, because electricity must be consumed immediately. It is a fresh good, a flow, although to some degree it may be stored in batteries or by pumping water up to reservoirs. This feature creates a strong incentive to expand the electricity network and link together different parts of countries and different nation-states over time, improving the chances of finding demand for the electricity produced in the system. This need for balance is sometimes labled "load factor," the measure of the degree to which the system's generating capacity is being utilized. Managing the load factor is an economic force driving the system toward large-scale operation. Another economic force working to increase scale is "economic mix," that is, the advantages of combining several different primary energy sources in the production of electricity within one and the same system.[31] With an economic mix large electricity systems can flexibly operate in accordance with the relative costs for fuels, which vary over time and across countries.

[28] Hughes, 1983, 23.
[29] Hughes, 1987.
[30] Hughes, 1983, 79.
[31] Hughes, 1983, 367.

The endeavor of achieving a large, integrated European system for electricity is a long story, with varying influences from national and international institutions. But the movement has been persistently in the direction of integration and larger scale. The first phase was marked by the integration of consumers and producers in regions *within* countries, for instance connecting the hydropower plants in the mountains with consumers in nearby industries or cities. The 1891 International Exhibition in Frankfurt is generally considered to be the breakthrough for electricity transmission over longer distances.[32] This possibility was especially important for countries rich in hydropower, like Sweden, Norway, and Italy. The geographical conditions for hydropower production and transmission were still somewhat different in these countries. In Italy the suitable sites for generation mainly consisted of small rivers in the northern, Alpine region. Norway had many waterfalls of various sizes, spread out widely across the country, facilitating local production and consumption. Falls were often located at high altitude, which meant that there were no conflicting interests with farmers.[33] In Sweden there were fewer but much larger waterfalls, capable of large deliveries of hydropower. These were located at lower altitudes, in more accessible locations, but also leading to frequent conflicts of interest between farmers and electricity producers in the taming and "industrialization of rivers."[34] France, the UK, and Germany were economically more developed and used coal-fired power stations, even though such plants were quite inefficient at this early time and produced very expensive electricity.

During World War I, when coal supply was restricted, the electrification process sped up in many countries, driven forward by national governments. The economic advantage of hydroelectric plants increased during the war, and many countries issued laws on the exploitation of hydropower during the conflict or immediately afterward. Even countries not directly involved in the fighting faced problems from the expense of importing coal during the war, and consequently tried to intensify their hydropower exploitation.

The economic logic of the system did not give any advantage to building systems solely within national borders, but integrating networks internationally proceeded only very slowly in the interwar period in line with the disintergrative and protectionist economic policies of the time.[35] Still,

---

[32] Hughes, 1983, 131–35, 247.

[33] Millward, 2005, 84.

[34] Jakobsson, 1996.

[35] There were engineers in the interwar period who proposed a truly European electricity network. The Frenchman George Viel outlined an encompassing system for all of Europe with lines going from Trondheim in the North to Naples in the South, and from Lisbon in the West to Bucharest in the East. However, these supranational visions for Europe were too early to be endorsed at the time. Contesters thought that it would be too risky to rely on other countries for basic needs like electricity provision, and rather saw a piecemeal gradual growth of the system, based on small regional networks that combined into national networks, which could in turn be connected with one another.

international integration was not negligible. Border regions between Germany, Switzerland, France, and Italy were interconnected in the early 1920s, and a larger system linked parts of Switzerland, France, and Germany in 1926.[36] Nevertheless, the transmission of electrical power outside national borders remained insignificant compared to the total domestic production.

National governments played a much larger role and took the lead in rural electrification in most countries in Europe from the 1930s onward. Electrification and large investments in infrastructure was seen as a remedy for the great economic crisis of the 1930s. National governments were generally willing to take on responsibility for electrification, partly inspired by the experience of the wartime economy, where governments had proven able to effectively mobilize resources, albeit for destructive purposes. Thus, dirigism—governmental intervention—was the favored road for European nation-states, with governments assuming the role of owning and developing hydroelectric plants, and constructing national grid systems.[37] Even so, the process of national integration of electricity systems was slow. A fully national network that was centrally managed emerged only in Britain before 1939. But all the high-tension networks were publicly owned by the Second World War.[38] In the 1890s, the load / capacity utilization in the UK for electricity was about 10 percent, and had increased to 16 percent in 1929, but had reached an impressive 84 percent by 1939— which is a clear demonstration of the virtues of the national grid.[39] Sweden had much to gain from a unified system, connecting the northern rivers with south consumers, and was the second country in Europe to develop a national network, achieved from the mid-1930s.[40] In 1938, power lines connected Porjus, in the north, to Malmö, in the south.[41] Portugal only decided to create a national integrated grid in 1944, and the decision would take decades to be realized. Portuguese electricity prices were high in international comparisons.[42]

Electrification had reached almost every corner of the densely populated countries of Western Europe by the mid-1930s. In countries like Denmark and the Netherlands, 100 percent of the population lived in electrified areas. Other developed countries close to this figure were France with 96 percent and Italy with 93 percent. In the more geographically dispersed populations of Germany, penetration was only 78 percent, with Spain and Portugal at 87 percent. This could be compared to a mere 70 percent in the United States at this time, motivating President Roosevelt to create the Rural Electric Administration in 1935, bringing electricity to rural areas at a reasonable

[36] Lagendijk, 2008, 40–42.
[37] Berend, 2006.
[38] Millward, 2005, 139–41.
[39] Hennessey, 1972, 15, 40, 50.
[40] Millward, 2005, 133.
[41] Kaijser, 1994, 169.
[42] Henriques, 2011.

price.[43] Only a few central European countries like Austria and Hungary had figures below the United States, but for Eastern Europe the situation was much worse: only 30 percent of Poland's population had access to electricity, and in Bulgaria and Romania it was only slightly more than 20 percent.[44] Households' access to electricity did not correlate with the overall ranking of which countries were the largest electricity consumers. This was more closely related to the electrification of industry, and the United States was the leading country in electrification measured this way. In both Italy and Sweden, more than 75 percent of electricity was used by the manufacturing industry; the number in Spain, Germany, and France was more than 65 percent.[45]

The pan-European integration of the electricity network was a postwar phenomenon. The Marshall Plan for rebuilding Europe after the Second World War involved investment funds for electricity plants and networks. The intention was to make better use of the existing plants by uniting them into one network, thereby achieving better load factors and economic mix. The increasing amount of available electricity was expected to stimulate industrial activity and bring economic prosperity. The idea of connecting the underdeveloped East with the more developed West of Europe was also an important part of the package. To begin with, the Americans wanted European countries to co-own power plants with each other, but this objective had to be abandoned: national sovereignty was too strong. Still, an important step toward a European electricity network was taken by the OEEC Council in 1950, when the agreement to form the Union of Electricity Producers of Western Europe (UCPTE) was signed.[46] UCPTE accomplished an alignment of the systems, regulated the networks to operate at 50 Hz, and worked together to ensure a sufficient reserve capacity for the entire network. There was still no supranational body controlling the system; it was based on national and regional bodies. Another union was formed in Scandinavia at this time; and a similar network operated in Southern Europe, including Spain, Portugal, and France, but collaboration within Eastern Europe proved difficult to achieve.[47] Finally, in the 1980s, the interconnection of Western and Eastern Europe was improved. After the fall of the Berlin wall in 1989 it took some time for an actual infrastructural integration of electricity networks to come about: eastern and western Germany were linked together into one electricity network only in 1995.

The European Coal and Steel Union, founded in 1951 and leading up to the European Union (EU) in 1992, did not initially put much emphasis on the integration of the energy sector, apart from its interest in promoting

[43] Landau, 2006, 37.
[44] Hausman, Hertner, and Williams, 2008, fig. 1.6, 28.
[45] Hausman, Herrtner, and Williams, 2008, table 1.3, 28–29.
[46] Lagendijk, 2008, 146.
[47] Lagendijk, 2008, 153.

nuclear energy.[48] Not even with the oil crises of the 1970s, and the realization of the risks inherent in too high a dependence on imports of Middle Eastern oil, did the organization act to secure energy supplies more generally. The international integration of electricity networks within the EU has proceeded much more rapidly since the 1990s, with the prime goal of building a functioning internal market within Europe; the liberalization of electricity markets has been one important part of this process. In 1999, the European Transmission System Operators was set up with its main task being to harmonize conditions for the international trade of electricity. In 2004, the common European electricity market was opened to all non-household consumers and in 2007, for households too. These unifying activities meant that in 2004, when the EU was extended eastward with ten new members, 90 percent of those countries were already provided with electricity from the core EU states. Thus today the electricity system has come a long way toward fulfilling its inherent economic logic of integration and large-scale operation.

A large electricity system needs large investments in fixed capital and thus can only be undertaken with substantial financial power, or guarantees. In the late nineteenth century and early twentieth century, financial capital for the introduction of electricity was assembled by multinational enterprises and financial institutions outside of the electricity utilities.[49] This effort involved extensive cross-financing across Western Europe borders, as well as drawing in funds from the United States. Electricity utilities could not finance their investments on their own, but those with a good reputation could obtain funds without being subject to foreign ownership and control. Some countries in Western Europe thus managed without little foreign control and ownership, for instance Great Britain and Switzerland, with 1–2 percent and 10 percent respectively of their electric systems owned by foreigners in 1913—aided of course by their own relatively large domestic financial sectors. The ownership situation was remarkably different in Eastern Europe, where in 1930 Bulgaria had 90 percent of their electrification owned and controlled by foreigners, and Greece, 85 percent.[50] In the postwar decades nation-states took over more and more of the ownership and financing investment of electric utilities, so by 1970, foreign ownership and control had ceased entirely all over Europe. In the 1980s a shift back to more foreign ownership took place, along with privatizations when government-owned electric utilities were being criticized for being unreliable and costly.[51]

[48] Lagendijk, 2008, 205.
[49] Hausman, Hertner, and Williams, 2008, 37.
[50] Hausman, Hertner, and Williams, 2008, 31.
[51] Hausman, Hertner, and Williams, 2008, 267.

The technical developments in electricity generation and transmission, with advantages in large scale, meant cheaper electricity, paving the way for wider consumption. In other words, the logic of the system has stimulated market widening for electricity. Around the turn of the nineteenth century it took 25 units of primary energy to produce one unit of electricity in a coal-fired plant, an efficiency of 4 percent, which means that electricity was very expensive. One hundred years later it only took 2.5 units of coal to produce one unit of electricity. That means that the technical efficiency had become ten times higher, and the price could be reduced to 10 percent of the earlier level simply because of this improvement.[52] In addition, there were many innovations in transmission that led to further declines in electricity price relative to coal. In 1892 the price of electricity in Sweden was 282 times higher than the price of coal, and in 2000 it was only three times higher, so the relative price in 2000 had gone down to around 1 percent of its 1892 value! Expressed in constant prices for 2000, in Britain the price of electricity was 120 pence per kWh in 1900 and 6 pence in 2000, a fall of 95 percent in real terms in one hundred years.[53] Table 9.4 demonstrates the real price decrease of electricity in the UK and Sweden, i.e., it shows the price of electricity divided by the consumer price index for each country. The relative price fall was rather similar in the long run. In the period 1893 to 1990, the British real electricity price went down 97 percent and in Sweden it went down 98 percent. One factor behind this change in the relative price of electricity is innovation connected to the expansion of the system. The majority of those scale advantages were already reaped with nationally integrated grids, and we see that the most drastic price decreases took place before the 1970s, when there was not yet a European market in place.

THE USAGE OF ELECTRICITY

The falling price of electricity stimulated new applications that led to a revolution: society was transformed. Today almost everything we can think of is run by electricity. It lights cities, powers transportation, and runs our communication system, whether low-tension electricity for telephones, or the Internet that connects the entire globe. Electric motors are used for heavy mechanical work such as rolling out steel or grinding grain, and also for light work like diagnostic equipment at hospitals or opening doors on trains. Even cars—part of the other major development block of the second industrial revolution—now usually have several electric motors for running air conditioners, operating windows, CD players, and so on. The historical process of electrification is best studied by tracing the development of

[52] Of course, we must also account for the capital costs of generation.
[53] Fouquet, 2008, 314.

TABLE 9.4
Real price of electricity in UK and Sweden in
1882–2000, benchmarks between 1882 and 2000,
pence per kWh, price level 1900

	UK	Sweden
1882	4.2	Na
1893	3.3	2.8
1898	2.1	2.4
1912	1.5	0.93
1921	0.41	0.75
1930	0.31	0.54
1940	0.20	0.47
1950	0.13	0.23
1960	0.11	0.19
1970	0.094	0.083
1980	0.11	0.075
1990	0.093	0.058
2000	Na	0.068

Sources: For Sweden: Kander, 2002; CPI for Sweden
Edwinsson and Söderberg, 2007: Consumer Price Index
1290–2006, Sveriges Riksbank. http://www.historia.se/,
currency converters, see Edwinsson, http://www.historia.
se/. The currency conversion is here made according to the
exchange rate in year 1900, when one pound=18.25 SEK.
For UK: Hannah, 1979, 429–31, National Statistics UK.

applications and can be generalized as consisting of two phases with different features: one early phase and one later phase.

The Early Phase

The first commercially viable uses of electricity were for light, communication using telephones, and for industrial plants where the electric motor replaced steam engines. The production and consumption of electricity was still largely confined to cities at this early phase. Electric light developed during the nineteenth century from arc lamps to incandescent lamps. In 1809, Davy demonstrated the electric arc, which consisted of 2,000 cells of batteries and two points of charcoal (one positive and one negative pole), which when brought close together produced a stream of light between them. The stream of light had the form of an arc, broad in the middle and tapering toward the poles, thereby its name. One problem with these early arc lamps was the enormous heat they produced, and another was the considerable size of the battery required. Parallel to the development of arc light was the development of incandescent light. The principle for this was that any conductor of electricity would glow if heated enough unless it was burned up. The trick was to find materials that would not burn up. In the 1820s, attempts with platinum succeeded in giving light for only a couple of seconds, until it was destroyed. This challenge stimulated experiments with vacuums in lamps, as the absence of oxygen prevented combustion. Experiments with carbon strips that were made to glow continued for another thirty years. Edison then solved the problem of continuous electric light from incandescent lamps by arranging the lamps in parallel and replacing the carbon by carbonized cotton thread, which in 1879 could burn for forty hours, much longer than any previous lamp. Only a year later Edison discovered bamboo filaments, and these would become the dominant design for nine years, until they were abandoned for more artificial filaments with cellulose threads. Electric lighting now reached the cities, but rural areas still had to rely on old technologies for light, such as kerosene lamps, fires, and candles. The final dominant filament design was established with Wolfram and Vacuum lamps in 1913, boosting the popularity of electric light.

Low-tension electricity was used in communication. To use electricity to transmit signals that could be readily transformed into words was an idea already found in the sixteenth century, but experiments to produce it began in the mid-eighteenth century and in 1837, it was discovered that the ground could be used for the return circuit, so that only one wire was necessary to create a closed circuit. In the same year, Samuel Morse demonstrated his first telegraph, which coded all words to numbers. In the 1840s, different cities and continents could communicate almost in real time, which meant hours and minutes rather than months and days for messages to pass back and forth.[54] During the 1840s, the telegraph system grew rapidly in Great Britain and in the United States, driven by business, but the expansion on the European continent was slow and it was not until the 1850s, led by military and governmental concerns, that telegraphs were constructed in continental Europe. The telegraphs were considered to be primarily of military interest and were initially only opened up for the public to use in order to raise finance for their maintenance and expansion.[55] Drastic reductions in the price

[54] Fontana, 2006 , 219.
[55] Kaijser, 1994, 112.

of international telegrams led to a tenfold increase of telegrams transmitted over forty years, again a market-widening effect from lower price.[56]

Once the telegraph had been established, the telephone was not long coming. There were difficulties to be overcome, such as to maintain the quality of the sound during transmission, but in 1876 Alexander Graham Bell demonstrated the first successful telephone. The Bell telephone, however, was incapable of transmitting sound over longer distances. This required stronger electric currents, which was achieved by Hughes and Edison independently in 1878, using a transmitter. The variations in the transmitter resistance produce great fluctuations in the current and enable the transmission of all the subtle variations in a speaking voice. At first the telephone had entirely different applications than the telegraph and the two were not competitors. Telephones were for oral communication over short distances, and telegraphs for written messages over long distances. When improved technologies allowed city telephone networks to be developed into regional systems, the telegraph was outcompeted and soon vanished. In many cases telegraph companies turned into telephone companies, after initial resistance to the new technology.

By 1900, Canada and the United States had higher telephone intensity in relation to their population than Sweden, but in a European context Sweden was outstanding, having many more telephones than the economically more advanced Britain.[57] The rapid spread of telephones in Sweden was encouraged by competition between the American-owned Stockholms Bell Telefonaktiebolag (founded in 1880), and the Stockholms Allmänna Telefonaktiebolag (founded in 1883), leading to falling prices for telephones and market widening. In 1885, there were 5,000 telephones in Stockholm, more than in any other city in the world.[58] Telephones were largely an urban phenomenon and part of the early development block around electricity.

The factory system of the first industrial revolution, with one big steam engine that operated several individual machines through a complex system of shafts and belts in the roof of the factory, had many inconveniences that were eventually overcome with electric motors. The old system was noisy, dirty, and had the major constraint that all the machines had to operate at the same speed. Often if one unit broke down the whole factory had to stop working until it had been repaired. The central power source was connected to all the mechnical machinery in the whole plant, and power was distributed between the floors of large plants through holes in the ceiling. At first, electric motors in industry did not revolutionize this organization, because they simply replaced the central power source (the steam engine) and did

---

[56] In Sweden the number of telegrams was 200,000 in 1860 and 2.5 million in 1900; Kaijser, 1994, 109.

[57] Foreman-Peck, 1992.

[58] Kaijser, 1994, 115.

not provide any greater flexibility. The complex system of shafts and iron belts in the factory remained, and electric motors did not fundamentally improve productivity in factories, although they improved working conditions because they were quieter and did not emit smoke. Real and wide productivity effects in the economy were reaped later when the emergence of electric group drive and single drive reorganized factories.

Householders became increasingly interested in using electricity as the price fell. The first electrical household device was the electric iron. This was much cleaner and easier to use than the old iron, which was either heated on the gas or wood stove, or had a container with glowing coal attached to it. This electric iron was an innovation that was primarily a modification of something already existing, so we may call it a meso-innovation. It led to substitution away from the old type of iron, but was not something brand new. The second popular device was the electric stove (introduced in 1905 by General Electric in the United States) that competed with gas stoves for quite some time. Electric light had already won the battle over gas light at the turn of the century, but using electricity for heating a stove was for a long time too expensive. It was not until in the 1920s that electric stoves were introduced on any scale in the homes in Europe. In Britain, electric cookers swiftly followed the introduction of gas cookers, stimulated by the falling electricity prices in the 1920s, but did not take off in use until the 1930s and 1940s.[59] In 1936, only 6 percent of households used electric stoves, but by 1948 the figure was 19 percent.[60] Electric stoves were also merely a substitute for the older wood or coal stoves; they did not provide a fundamentally new service.

The Later Phase

In the second phase of the evolving electricity block, electric motors were used in a new, more flexible fashion, allowing them to diffuse across factories and society. Factory organization changed and productivity increased when the factory shifted to the electric group drive, having one electric motor for a set of machines, and even more so when every machine was equipped with its own motor: the unit drive, often integrated inside the machine.[61] This increased flexibility of work was highly economical, because selected equipment in the factory could easily be started up or shut down, depending on need. Group drive and unit drive also meant fewer energy losses, because of less mechanical friction in the system with fewer belts and less shafting. Previously extensive power lines had meant that large amounts of the energy

[59] Fouquet, 2008, 84.
[60] Davidson, 1986, 71.
[61] Devine, 1983.

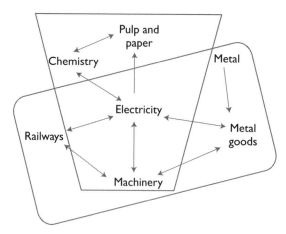

Figure 9.7. Two partly overlapping development
blocks around electricity

was lost in the form of waste heat. There were many arguments about the
pros and cons of the group and unit drives, and both systems competed from
the 1890s; but the shaft-line electric motor system was gradually replaced
by group drive from the 1890s, and the unit drive had its breakthrough in
the 1920s.[62] The latter date was when factories really changed and electricity demonstrated its potential to transform industrial production.

In this second phase, electricity began to have a wide impact on manufacturing industry in general, but was still more important for some branches
than for others.[63] Some branches of industry moved much more in line with
the general electrification of society, which is observable in the production
values (value-added) of these branches. A pioneering study that tried to pin
down the demarcations of development blocks in Swedish industry found
that there were two partly overlapping development blocks centred around
electricity (see figure 9.7).[64] The method to identify the development block
was the combination of two criteria: value added of sectors within a development block should share common long-run time trends (which need not
be linear) *and* be linked to each other with mutually reinforcing links.[65] This
definition comes naturally from the theory of development blocks, which
states that sectors within a development block are strongly dependent on
each other, so that complementarities are a basic feature.

[62] Group drive was a major form of electric drive through World War I and was vigorously
defended as late as 1926. Yet some individual factories installed unit drive already in the 1890s.

[63] Harberger, 1998; David and Wright, 1999; Crafts, 1999.

[64] Enflo et al., 2008. This study uses methods similar to those of Greasley and Oxley, 2007,
2010.

[65] The direction of Granger causality should go both ways.

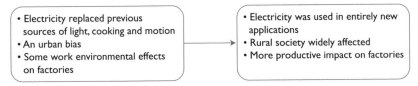

Figure 9.8. Two phases of electrification

Household electric appliances diffused quickly from the 1920s. Many of these products were new, not just substitutes for old ones. Vacuum cleaners arrived on a large scale in the 1920s (after the first Hoover was manufactured in 1909). Although they were labor-saving, they also had the effect of raising standards of hygiene, so women still spent a lot of time cleaning.[66] Another laborious task, that of laundry, was made much easier with the introduction of electricity in homes and the development of washing machines. A fully automatic electric washer, with internal water heating and centrifugation, was a complex machine and was first introduced in 1939 in the United States and reached Europe after the War. Washing machines were very expensive and therefore common washing rooms with a washing machine were introduced in many apartment buildings.

Refrigerators were also introduced after the War in Europe, while the rapid diffusion of freezers occurred in the 1960s. Electric dishwashers and microwave ovens were part of the development of homes during the third industrial revolution, from the late 1970s, because they needed more advanced microelectronics and a merger of electrical engineering and ICT (Information and Communication Technology).

In conclusion, it is possible to discern two phases of the development block from the consumer side (see figure 9.8). In the first phase electricity was introduced in the cities, initially as a substitute for other energy sources for specific applications such as light and cooking. Electric motors were simply used in place of the old the steam engine, and did not revolutionize the way factories were organized. In the second phase, which is more dynamic in its impact on society, there was market widening for electricity due to drastically falling prices, and there was a much greater influence on infrastructure. Trams and rails were electrified, and factories made better use of the organizational changes made possible by group and unit drive of machines. Electricity production increased in line with production in those manufacturing industries that were major users of electrical power. In that second phase the number of new applications of electricity widened greatly, a development that has continued throughout the century.

[66] Hagberg, 1986, 32–47, 226.

Impact on Energy Consumption

Electricity has the propensity both to increase energy use and to improve the efficiency of energy use. Compared to the ICE-oil block, where in the long term the energy-expanding property clearly has been much stronger than the energy-saving one, the electricity block has had a relatively stronger tendency to save energy. Nevertheless, the net balance has still been toward expansion.

The energy-saving effect from electricity has been explored empirically. In the breakthrough period of the electric motor in industry (1890–1920) there was a general surge in American total factor productivity (TFP) as well as energy productivity. Electrification changed the organization of machines in the factories in a way that improved productivity, and reduced energy losses. In addition, electric light made it possible to work longer hours in the factories and so improve the utilization of capital and overall productivity.[67] Similarly, evidence points to efficiency effects in Sweden, especially in industries that used electricity for multiple purposes.[68]

But at the same time as electricity enhances energy productivity and overall productivity, thereby saving energy, electrification also stimulates growth of electricity-using sectors and the economy in general, so in the long run electrification still means that energy use expands in society. In relation to the three rebound effects laid out in chapter 2, what is certain in the case of the electricity development block is that the money saved on the electricity bill will be spent somehow, and some of that spending will go to electricity and other goods that need energy inputs, and some will be invested for future growth. The choice of what to buy with the saved money depends on the price elasticity of demand for various goods and services. If we count all the rebound effects, including the economy-wide effects and economic growth, which is boosted by the electricity development block, then this block is also, certainly, primarily energy-expanding. If we restrict ourselves to the direct and indirect effects, and overlook economic growth, the block may be largely energy-saving.

3. THE ICT DEVELOPMENT BLOCK

In the 1970s, a new development block took off, marking the beginning of a third industrial revolution: the Information and Communication Technology (ICT) or the Microelectronics revolution. With the ICT development block the function of knowledge in society has changed. Knowledge has always been important for changing societies and making economies

---

[67] Schurr and Netschert, 1978; Devine, 1983; David, 1990.
[68] Enflo et al., 2009.

grow, but in different ways. While the first industrial revolution had little formal scientific base, and was highly dependent on trial and error undertaken by manufacturers and artisans, the second industrial revolution relied on a formalized, disciplinary approach to science. In Joel Mokyr's words: "The first industrial revolution created a chemical industry without chemistry, an iron industry without metallurgy, and power machinery without thermodynamics."[69] The second industrial revolution on the other hand meant technological progress increasingly driven by people with a formal scientific training. Still, this scientific knowledge was not so easily accessible, and the knowledge needed to be inculcated in the individual humans. This meant that the individual innovator or some close partner had to be in command of the relevant knowledge.

The third industrial revolution with the ICT block means that theoretical knowledge is increasingly being codified and used for innovation in technology.[70] As knowledge is stored in computers and is largely openly accessible to users, it does not need to be "stored" in people's heads or in less easily accessible texts and manuals. This does not mean, of course, that people are less knowledgeable, but that the knowledge base open to each person can greatly expand. Perhaps even greater than the increased access to knowledge is the acceleration in processing power. Machines do the information processing for us, reducing the everyday need for calculating skills. This creates new demands: competence in utilizing this stock of knowledge in a purposeful way, to set up appropriate forms of processing and calculations, and not be overwhelmed in the information flow. The requirement for training and education, and synthetic and analytical rather than factual knowledge, expands. This paradoxically puts higher demands than before on people's competence to cope with the expanded base of technology (and software), information, and knowledge than before. It has stimulated the expansion of higher education, university education becoming more and more important, and furthermore the complexity of the knowledge has driven a closer collaboration between universities, industry, and government for the successful promotion of activities leading to growth.

First we will outline the main characteristics of the ICT-block and its diffusion in society. The core innovation of the ICT-block is the transistor, also known as the semiconductor, but the development block around the semiconductor could not have emerged without a whole complex of related innovations in computers and electronic control, and it is this wide range of technologies that is at the heart of the microelectronics revolution.[71] We will then discuss the impact on energy use. The ICT development block is more energy-saving than any of the two central development blocks of the second

[69] Mokyr, 1999.
[70] Bell, 1980, 501.
[71] Molina, 1989, 2.

industrial revolution. But the degree of energy savings can still be questioned, because obviously the block also stimulates electricity consumption.

THE TRANSISTOR AS THE MACRO-INNOVATION

Advances in physics were necessary prerequisites for the invention of the transistor, which is the key innovation of the microelectronic revolution: the discovery of electrons (Thomson) and the atomic nucleus (Rutherford) eventually led to what is now labeled quantum physics, with contributors like Planck, Einstein, Bohr, and Heisenberg. More than most innovations, the transistor was born out of scientific discoveries, rather than being based on technology and aided by science.[72] The transistor, also known as the semiconductor, is most familiar to us as the computer "chip," which is in practice millions of miniaturized transistors that are integrated in a circuit (see figure 9.9).

The transistor functions through the movement of electrons from one layer (band) around the atomic nucleus to another. In this process, electricity is released or stored, depending on the direction of movement. An electron always strives to have as low energy as possible, to be close to the positive nucleus, but with energy added it can jump outward to an outer energy level. When it makes this jump it leaves a hole that can be filled by another electron, which leaves another hole, and so on. This is how a current is created.

The Bell telephone company played a crucial role in the development of the transistor. It had a monopoly position in the telephone market in the United States, earning large profits, and accumulating the financial muscle for large-scale investment in research and development. The transistor was invented in 1947 by a group of Bell researchers: Bardeen, Brattain, and Shockley, who received the Nobel Prize for their work in 1956.[73] The transistor allowed the making of much higher quality telephone switches than the previous technology, the vacuum tube.[74] The vacuum tube was beset by a number of problems, namely its limited life-span, large consumption of electricity, high price, fragility, difficulty to miniaturize, and the necessity to warm it up before using it. The transistor on the other hand was sturdy, cheap, long-lasting, and amazingly easy to miniaturize.

Bell was interested in rapid diffusion of the new technology and was also under investigation for monopolistic behavior; spreading their new knowledge through symposia and liberal licensing was a way of gaining goodwill.

---

[72] Molina, 1989, 151.
[73] Braun, 1980.
[74] Brooks, 1976; Mowery, 1983.

The Vacuum Tube: Crucial to the development of the electronics especially the diffusion of radio, butits role was limited as transistors were smaller and more efficient.

The Transistor: A single transistor. The three metal leads are the Base, Collector and Emitter.

The Modern Integrated Circuit: This highly magnified picture of the AMD Six Core Opteron shows the 904 million transistors packed in an area of 346mm² (about the size of a typical postage stamp).

Figure 9.9. Transistor evolution

This became common practice for the industry as a whole.[75] Bell also won strong support from the military. The electronic valve had proved unreliable in the Korean War, so the military put substantial efforts into increasing the supply of transistors to reduce their costs and improve performance. The military used the transistor's high-power radio frequency abilities in radar and hand-held two-way radios. Apart from injecting large amounts of money into R&D and setting up pilot production plants, the military was important on the demand side too, by procurement according to specified military needs, ensuring a market for the products.[76]

FROM MARKET SUCTION TO MARKET WIDENING

The microelectronic development block was shaped by social forces, especially in the United States, which took the lead. During the Second World War there were converging interests that helped the important actors in developing crucial technology to collaborate and promote the development block. In the words of Molina: "Under favourable socio-historical pressures or galvanizing forces such as war and competition, it is possible to suggest that those social forces whose overriding interests are complementary

---

[75] Molina, 1989, 49.
[76] Wilson et al., 1980; Utterback and Murray, 1977, 3.

will tend to converge into systemic interactions reproducing and advancing the interests of each. (. . .) The second world war exemplifies the formation of a complex of social power crystallizing the converging interests of government, the military, science and capital under the impetus of war."[77] The federal government played a critical role in financing research and development, while many different industrial companies participated in the development of the Block, by producing complementary gadgets. The military played a crucial role in the development of the transistor into integrated circuits. With air warfare becoming increasingly important, there was a need to invent compact, small devices that could be integrated in aircraft. This was followed by the Cold War, and the emergence of the space race and a shift toward missile-based strategies, compounding the need to develop much smaller and more compact transistors. These competitive political pressures stimulated miniaturization programs and eventually led to the invention of the integrated circuit. The semiconductors became smaller and cheaper: between only 1959 and 1962 their price fell by 85 percent.[78] This rapid price fall continued, widening the market for them considerably (see table 9.5).

Miniaturization, standardization, and lower prices widened the range of applications for the transistor enormously and led to the real breakthrough of the information and communication society. An important early step in the diffusion of semiconductors came in 1971, when Ted Hoff at Intel invented the microprocessor, i.e., the computer in chip format.[79] In a microchip, or a set of miniaturized transistors, there are endless possibilities for the low-voltage electric current to pass, or be blocked. This means that a long chain of binary solutions can be generated, 0 or 1, stop or go. This is used in microchips or computers to transmit information. Huge maps of these simple binary (0,1) combinations have been programmed according to a standardized scheme to mean specific things. For instance, the letter "A" is one unique combination of (0,1). The standardization of computers and their codified language was necessary for the spread of the computers, and even major competitors such as IBM and Apple have eventually moved to making their systems (almost) compatible.

The chips have three main properties; integrative capacity, memory, and speed. All these aspects have been advanced with a rapidity that seems almost unbelievable in retrospect. In 1971, a total of 2,300 semiconductors could be packed together in a microchip the size of a fingernail, but by 1993 an astonishing 35 million semiconductors could be squeezed in the same space. Memory capacity and processing speed have seen similar rapid

---

[77] Molina, 1989, 5.
[78] Braun and Macdonald, 1982.
[79] Castells, 1996, 53.

The Transistor

The transistor utilizes the phenomenon of semiconductivity, or the ability of certain materials to act as both an insulator (that does not transport electricity at all) and a conductor (that transports electricity well). It was discovered that passing a small amount of current through a unique material like germanium containing impurities (and later impure silicon) that material that was normally insulating would become a

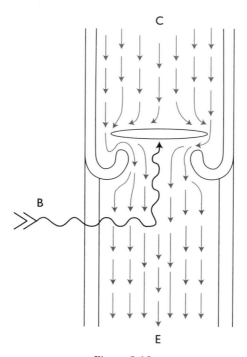

Figure 9.10

conductor. This meant that the germanium could act as an electrical switch, for when a small current was applied to the semiconductor it would allow a bigger current to flow. The process has been likened to a valve controlling the flow in a water pipe; see accompanying figure. The current is controlled by the valve B (called the base) trying to flow from C (the collector) to E (the emitter).

Controlling the current (B) to the base will allow for an increase or decrease in the amounts of current that flow from the collector to the emitter. In this way very small amounts of electricity can control much bigger flows of electricity and thus the transistor can act as an amplifier. A semiconductor has the benefit that the current can effectively be adjusted. It relies on several binary (1 or 0) paths (switches) for the electric current, and enabling logical coding and processing of information. The amplification ability of the transistor was important for the dissemination of the radio and many other electrical devices, but the main use of the transistor has been the more simple ability as an electric switch. When many transistors are linked together in a series, one switch can be used to control many other switches.

developments.[80] Computers have become much more effective, powerful, and yet cheaper.

These developments pose big challenges to economists when they seek to assess the value of computers in society and the role of computer production as a share of GDP. Conventionally, all measures of real growth must deflate away nominal price increases which have no connection to quality increases of the products. This is done by dividing the increase in nominal prices by a price index, which sets the price of every predefined good as constant, thereby revealing the increase in constant prices (or real growth). The "normal" case in economic development is that prices go up and some—but not all—of this price increase will be due to actual improvements in the products. The price increase that has no connection to improvements in quality is called inflation. After proper deflating, to get rid of the effect of inflation, the real growth normally will be lower than the nominal growth. The case of computers is different. With computers the increase in quality is often accompanied not with a price increase, but with a price decrease. So, if this is properly adjusted for, by so-called Hedonic price indices, there will be an even larger increase in real growth than in the nominal growth! Needless to say, it is extremely difficult to establish such hedonic price indices for complex products such as computers with several different quality components, and with new features constantly appearing.[81] It has nevertheless been estimated that the price of computers fell by a factor of 1,000 between 1975 and 2000.[82] This huge increase in quality, at the same time as material require-

---

[80] We are reaching the limits of what silicon could contain in terms of number of semiconductors. In the future, large molecules might do the work that semiconductors do today. This evolving field is called Molecular Electronics.

[81] While this is particularly marked in computers, the same basic problem holds for lots of goods and indeed earlier technology like steam engines. For an overview of price indices and quality adjustments, see Griliches, 1971. For computer development see Berndt, 2001. Ljungberg and Lobell, 2010 show that the growth of the computer sector in different countries will look completely different with Hedonic price indices.

[82] Schön, 2010, 326.

TABLE 9.5
The average price of integrated
circuits ($US)

1962	50.00
1963	31.60
1964	18.50
1965	8.33
1966	5.05
1967	3.32
1968	2.33
1969	1.67
1970	1.49
1971	1.27
1972	1.03

Source: Braun and MacDonald, 1982, 113.

ments go down with miniaturization, is what has led some authors to speak of *dematerialization* of economic growth (see chapter 1).

The microprocessor has found endless applications in society, in consumer products like watches, calculators, mobile phones, video games, and personal computers, but also in smart production systems in manufacturing industry. By providing machines with "brainpower" at low cost, machines could be made smart. It has been suggested that the microprocessor multiplies human brainpower with the same force that the first industrial revolution multiplied human muscle power.[83] The absolutely necessary prerequisite for the impact of microprocessors on society has been the miniaturization of computers. The downscaling in size of the computers is indicated in figure 9.11.

The increase in number of ICT consumer products like personal computers, cell-phones, mp3, CDs, and DVDs, has been very rapid, but uneven in Europe. If we look at numbers of personal computers and Internet access, there are two leading countries: the Netherlands and Sweden, who have even higher levels of use than the United States (see table 9.6). At first the UK lagged behind but it has caught up and in 2007 reached the same levels as the United States. Germany and France are in a middle league, with quite respectable broadband access, but lower figures for computers. Spain and

[83] Perlowski, 1980.

As the transistor decreased in size so did the computer. As more transistors became packed onto a chip the computer became ubiquitous. Once needing vast rooms, now every modern office has computers and computers have become integrated into all aspects of the modern life.

Figure 9.11. Downscaling in size of computers

Italy are far behind the rest of Western Europe. In Eastern Europe the figures are much lower. So the speed with which different countries have joined the ICT revolution has been varied, as was the case with electrification rates in early twentieth century.

Another invention of utmost importance in the ICT-Block is of course the Internet. The Internet originated in 1969 in the U.S. defense industry and was supplemented by the protocol for net contacts in 1974 that enabled the interconnection of several networks. With the Internet the semiconductors have expanded into a truly global network and development block. The United States took the clear lead in developing the Internet, although European scientists from France and the UK made important contributions to it in the 1970s. Some of the key inventions behind the World Wide Web (www) came from CERN (the European nuclear physics research facilities), but it was American entrepreneurs and firms that transformed these inventions into innovations; national and global networks of networks. The scale and scope of the American system contributed to its success. The networks were large enough and the large-scale military funding through the governmental DARPA (Defense Advanced Research Projects Agency) provided the financial means. [84] Yet again we see the significant contribution of a combi-

---

[84] Mowery and Simcoe, 2002.

TABLE 9.6
Spread of computers and Internet in Europe and United States, 1999 and 2007

	Personal computers, per 100 people		Fixed broadband Internet subscribers, per 100 people
	1999	2007	2007
UK	30.2	80.2	25.6
Germany	29.7	65.6	23.8
France	22.2	65.2	25.2
Netherlands	36.0	91.2	33.6
Spain	11.9	39.3	18.0
Italy	19.2	36.7	18.3
Sweden	45.1	88.1	35.9
USA		80.5	24.3

Source: World Bank, 2009, 310, and World Bank, 2001.

nation of the military, government, and industry collaborating to promote the technologies of the ICT-block.

Hardware would not work without software. Innovations in software are almost never patented, because patenting offers poor protection, and thus tracing software innovation is a formidable task. David Wheeler has made a heroic attempt, based on several secondary sources and personal knowledge, and defined some fifty-five really new ideas important for software since the nineteenth century.[85] Wheeler's definition of software innovation is quite cautious, which is why the low number may surprise many. Examples from his list that are well known to most of us are: Word processing (1964), which meant that for the first time text could be edited without having to retype the whole text again; Separating Text Content from Format (1967); Emails (1971–1973); Font Generation Algorithms (1973); spreadsheets (1978); the "domain name system" (DNS) (1984), which allows users to use human-readable names of computers, which the DNS translates into a numeric address. This list only provides a glimpse of the numerous software innovations. With the new possibilities created by the Internet the ICT revolution has diffused worldwide, including the developing countries. Outsourcing of ICT services and development to developing countries has increased tremendously, and India is one of the countries presently hosting many software developers.

[85] Wheeler, 2009.

Microprocessors could contribute to production in the manufacturing industry in various ways: controlling movement of materials, components, and products; controlling process variables like temperature, pressure, and humidity; shaping, molding, and mixing materials; quality control, and organizing the manufacturing process.[86] Typically, when the microprocessor is applied in the manufacturing industry, it turns from being a product innovation to becoming process innovations, affecting the organization of production. From the management side the incentives to introduce microprocessors for process innovations have been complex, including the desire to save on labor costs, the need to expand output, desire to increase quality of production, the elimination of hazardous tasks, and saving on intermediate inputs such as raw material and energy.

The automatic control of machines in industry also depended on the development of numerical control, which means programmed commands encoded on a storage medium.[87] The federal government in the United States made the decision to build up advanced machine-tools capacity soon after the end of the Korean War (1951–1953), in order to stimulate advances in both high technology and the military.[88] They approached industry and gave contracts for numerical control to several large companies, among them General Electric. By the late 1960s, around 20 percent of the new machine tools installed in industry were automatically controlled. Subsequent development of numerical control led to what today is called CIM (computer integrated manufacturing); entirely integrated production systems in industry, entailing engineering, production, marketing, and after-sales-service functions. Financial aspects of the production process, like cost efficiency, are then linked via the computer with factory floor functions, such as materials handling, offering direct control and feedback between the financial and technical sides of the system. This has enabled the flexible manufacturing system, sometimes called lean production (little waste in material and delivery time and little need for storing large inventories).

The Dynamic Impact on Society

The ICT-block is still at an early stage compared to the other development blocks we discuss in this book, which continued to have a large impact for more than one hundred years. The ICT has "only" had a mere 40 or 50 years' of diffusion. Still, the impact on society has already been pervasive. No economic sector is without influence from ICT.

[86] Bessant et al., 1980.
[87] Molina, 1989, 43.
[88] Layton, 1972, 171–72.

ENERGY-EXPANDING OR ENERGY-SAVING?

One effect from the ICT block on the structure of energy consumption is that society uses increasing shares of secondary energy (electricity) as opposed to primary energy (fuels). All ICT equipment runs on electricity. There is no substitute and hence no flexibility in what energy carrier to use.

Whether the ICT block is primarily energy-saving or energy-expanding is much debated. On the pessimistic side, arguments are raised about the large resources need for production of the tiny microchips, with the notion of the 1.7 kilogram microchip, suggesting that the material and water requirements for the production of the tiny chip are still large and maybe even weigh 1.7 kilograms per chip.[89] Another argument suggesting an energy-expanding bias is the economic growth effect: even if every ICT device uses relatively little energy to function, their number is so large that total energy consumption expands.[90] In addition, the turnover of these electronic devices is very high; they swiftly become outdated and are replaced. This stimulates economic growth, but also requires much energy. The optimists stress instead the energy-saving propensities of ICT. The semiconductor technologies are used for "smart" energy solutions: smart buildings, smart appliances, and smart grids that save energy. Sensors are used to measure temperature, geographical position, soil nutrient levels, and sunlight intensity for example; all information that can be used to fine-tune the use of material and energy for particular uses and reduce losses.[91] ICT also opens up options for less paper consumption, and it was believed that computers and email would bring about the paperless office, but the opposite has occurred: printing is easier than ever and paper consumption increases.[92] New trading options and e-bank services reduce the need for travel and for ordinary letters and invoices, and can lead to some energy savings. Digital music and film delivery saves energy by some 40–80 percent compared to physical delivery of CDs or DVDs.[93] These are all direct effects on energy consumption by ICT.

The indirect effects are even larger. The automatization of manufacturing industry on the basis of semiconductors enabled large material and energy savings in traditional industries. A report from the American Council for an Energy-Efficient Economy (ACEEE) has estimated that if the U.S. economy in 2006 still relied on the technologies of 1976, but had expanded at the same rate, it would have consumed 20 percent more electricity than it actually did.[94] The report states: "The powerful connection between semiconductors

[89] Williams, 2002.
[90] Singer, 2010.
[91] Zapico et al., 2010.
[92] Fuchs, 2006.
[93] Weber et al., 2010.
[94] Laitner, 2010.

and energy consumption is more than just unappreciated; it is actually mis-understood by some. Despite the immediate growth in electricity demands to power the growing number of devices and technologies, semiconductors have enabled a surprisingly larger energy productivity benefit in that same period."[95] These large improvements in energy productivity are due both to semiconductors being used to improve thermal efficiency and material flows in traditional manufacturing industries, and to structural changes in pro-duction where energy-lighter branches, such as electronics and pharmaceu-ticals, make up a larger share of the manufacturing industry today than it did in the 1970s.[96] In conclusion, the ICT-block is more energy saving than any of the previous development blocks.[97] This is indicated by GDP increas-ing without much absolute increase in energy from the 1970s, something we will investigate more thoroughly in the next chapter.

4. CONCLUSION

There are clear parallels between the three development blocks when it comes to the manner of their breakthrough with key innovations and their wider impact on society. In the early phase of a development block, the impact on society is rather limited. The very first diffusion for the core in-novation comes in replacing an already existing technology. The internal combustion engine replaces steam engines in industry, electric light replaces other sources of illumination, and transistors are used instead of vacuum tubes in telephones. Next, new appliances open up: cars, trucks, electric mo-tors, and household electric devices and computers. This phase is dominated by market suction. It is not until the key innovation is applied in transpor-tation and communication that the broader impact from the development block comes through, and we have a phase dominated by market widen-ing. When the oil tankers export oil cheaply to Europe, the usage of oil widens a great deal, and oil replaces coal for several uses. As the transport of electricity in grids becomes more efficient, the electricity price falls and electricity can be used for a whole array of new purposes. When the chip is miniaturized and the price falls drastically, the diffusion of computers, microprocessors, and Internet in society explodes. A schematic illustration of this is provided in figure 9.12. The degree of energy expansion versus energy saving differs among the blocks too, as summed up in table 9.7. There is a gradual development from the clearly energy-expanding block—ICE-Oil—to the more ambiguous electricity block—over to the even more energy-saving ICT block.

[95] Laitner et al., 2009.
[96] Kander, 2005; Murtishaw and Schipper, 2001.
[97] Kuhndt et al., 2003.

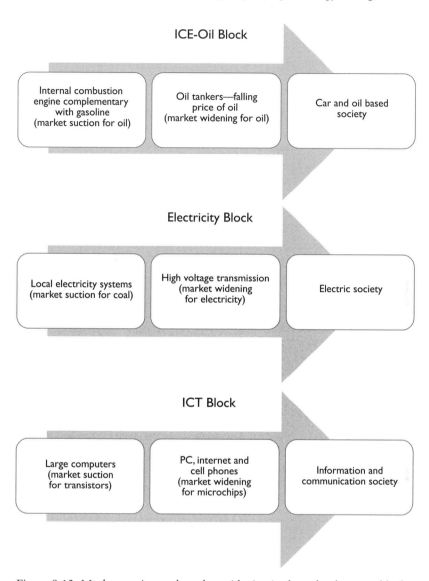

Figure 9.12. Market suction and market widening in three development blocks

TABLE 9.7
Energy saving versus energy expanding development blocks

	ICE-Oil-block	Electricity-block	ICT-block
Overall impression	Energy expanding	Energy saving/ Energy expanding	Energy saving

Unsurprisingly the development blocks overlap in time and space and cannot be quantitatively demarcated in a structural analysis. In chapter 10 we will thus follow up on the question of economic energy efficiency by a quantitative analysis using data of energy intensity at the national scale and its drivers in terms of technical change and structural change.

CHAPTER TEN

THE ROLE OF ENERGY IN TWENTIETH-CENTURY ECONOMIC GROWTH

THIS CHAPTER WILL FOCUS ON the *nature of twentieth-century economic growth with respect to energy.* There has been a degree of convergence in final energy consumption among European nations, while the nineteenth century was a story of divergence. With this in mind, our aim is to examine the interrelations of factors of production, to find the general features of a shared experience of growth, rather than to illuminate the local differences. We seek to understand how factors of production including energy interrelate in a general sense. Nevertheless, we will frequently proceed by investigations on a national scale, mirroring the availability of statistics that make such work possible.

Economic energy efficiency has only doubled in Europe over two hundred years, but the rate of improvement sped up decisively after the 1970s, when the composition of the machine stock changed with more of ICT equipment. We will devote considerable attention in this chapter to analyzing this conspicuous trend break in the relationship between energy and the economy, after which economic energy efficiency increased substantially and energy consumption per capita almost leveled out. We will use quantitative analyses to investigate to what degree this trend break was due to the ICT development block, rather than to a general expansion of the service sector, an explanation most often brought forward to argue for a "dematerialization" of the economy.[1] In other words: was the change driven by a technological shift with its focus in the manufacturing sector, or rather by the transition to the post-industrial society, where people consume services rather than industrial products? In chapter 9 we argued on purely qualitative grounds that the ICT development block of the third industrial revolution was more energy-saving than any of the previous development blocks; and we will argue step by step here that the most credible reason for a steeper decline in energy intensity after the 1970s was the impact of ICT.

The role of foreign trade for driving the economic energy efficiency, with a possible outsourcing of heavy industrial production from Europe to less

---

[1] Panayotou, 1993 for instance suggested that the downward slope of the environmental Kuznets curve was due to the transition to the service economy.

developed parts, will also be addressed in the last section of this chapter. Even though more research is needed on this question, we can state that it did not play a major role at all in the European countries we have thus far subjected to detailed examination. Thus we can categorically state that it was not universally the driver behind energy-efficiency improvements, although it may have played some role in a few countries.

In short, we argue that it was the third industrial revolution that was behind most of the increasing economic efficiency of energy use after the 1970s. The third industrial revolution improved efficiency in three ways:

1. Growth of lighter manufacturing industry, i.e., structural change within this sector with more pharmaceuticals and electronics production that require less energy in relation to its production value than heavy industries such as chemicals, metals, or pulp;
2. Energy savings in the old heavy industrial branches through their adoption of microelectronics enabling the fine-tuning of energy and material flows and reducing losses;
3. Structural shifts toward relatively more services as compared to manufacturing industries, primarily software for ICT and growing shares of business-related services such as banking.

1. DEVELOPMENT BLOCKS AND GDP

The unprecedented growth that took place in the nineteenth century has been surpassed in absolute terms by some distance during the twentieth-century growth (see figure 10.1). We now have a world economy that is about seventy times larger than it was in 1820, when measured by global GDP.[2] Western Europe has increased its economy by a factor of 50 over the same period. The scale of energy consumption has greatly increased as well (about 25 times for Western Europe) and new energy carriers have been widely diffused.

We may think of the development blocks as tides that lift all boats rather than as small waves that ripple across areas of the surface. In other words, that the emergence of development blocks *leads* the global growth waves rather than explains cross-country differences in growth rates. The process by which the tide works is not straightforward or simple. Technology transfer across nations is one important mechanism, resulting in the tendency for income convergence in all the countries that have become an integrated part of the global economy and affected by the development blocks.[3] Of course,

---

[2] The growth of the global economy would look even bigger if we used international traded commodities as our indicator.

[3] Acemoglu, 2009.

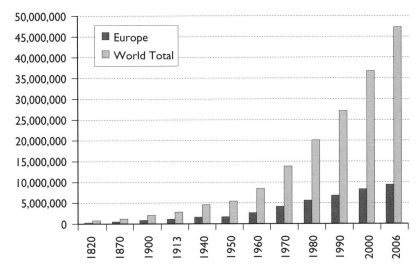

Figure 10.1. GDP in Europe and the World 1820–2006,
million international 1990 Geary-Khamis dollar
Source: Maddison, 2006c.

convergence does not follow completely or immediately.[4] Initially there are
always monopolistic benefits to reap for those that are at the frontier of the
technology shifts, giving scope for income divergence, but later technologies
will be more standardized and cheaper, which will open up for market widening and a subsequent convergence in income.[5]

So development blocks might be expected to diffuse and lead to convergence, but some regions remain peripheral to them. The problem in parts of
the poor periphery, for instance large parts of Africa, is that it is very difficult to reap the full benefits of a development block because it is difficult
to develop the full set of necessary complementarities and institutions. But
it is not mandatory to have a fully fledged development block within the nation itself in order to experience at least some growth and catch-up, because
the benefits can be experienced indirectly through lower prices of imported
capital and energy. Williamson suggests that the spread of industrial revolution worldwide and a catching up of the poor periphery in the critical period
1870–1975 is facilitated by cheap fuel from globally integrated markets.[6]
This view is in line with our view of the diffusion of development blocks,

---

[4] Institutional factors are important to explain deficiencies in growth performance. See for
instance Crafts and Toniolo, 1996.

[5] Schön, 2006.

[6] Williamson, 2011.

with market suction and market widening for oil, outlined in chapter 9. Cheap energy has stimulated global growth in the twentieth century.

Being a pioneer in a new development block should at least give some advantage for relative GDP growth rates, even though there will be catch-up of others. The United States took the lead in all three development blocks of the twentieth century (see chapter 9) and took over economic leadership from Britain at the very beginning of the twentieth century, maintaining it thereafter. This is not, in our view, a coincidence.

2. SEVEN LONG-RUN PROPOSITIONS

Economic growth is commonly defined as growth either in total GDP or in GDP per capita.[7] Here we will focus on total GDP growth, including the effects from population growth, since from the perspective of resource and energy dependency, and associated emissions of pollutants, it is the total scale of the economy that matters. Real GDP growth (Y) (that is, the GDP growth deflated to take inflation into account) is driven by an increase in the number of people (L) doing the work, increases in physical capital in the form of machines and buildings (K), and energy (E) to fuel both K and L.[8] Moreover, technical change in the sense of a more efficient combination of factors of production, has been essential in driving growth. This is usually called "Total factory Productivity" (TFP) and is a measure of all the changes that improve the productivity of the factor inputs. Technical change does not affect different factors of production evenly: over time, labor has been "saved" much more than capital in physical terms; that is, we now use relatively less labor than capital to produce a unit of output than in the past. But since labor has become more expensive and machinery cheaper over time, their cost shares out of total expenditure on production have stayed fairly constant over time, at about 0.3 for capital and 0.7 for labor. As we will show, the constant cost share does not hold for energy; here there was a decline, as cheap fossil fuels entered the energy system, which means that

---

[7] All the value added of products and services that are sold on a market comprise the GDP. GDP growth is consequently the increase in the sum of value added in the economy. It is not the sales values that are added together, because that would vastly overstate the true value of production. All inputs bought from other firms are deducted, when a firm's value added is estimated. Value added = sales value – inputs value.

[8] Inflation—or a general price increase—can distort the picture of growth and greatly exaggerate it. Therefore, GDP must be deflated by a proper deflator and be expressed in constant prices, at the price level and price relations of a chosen base year. These deflators differ between sectors of the economy—agriculture, industry, services, and transport, because inflation's impact on different parts of the economy can be very uneven. We will use this fact in section 3 to analyze the impact of the structural transition to the economy dominated by services on the decline of energy intensity in society.

we need to adjust conventional models of long-run economic growth to accommodate this fact. For those interested in a more technical demonstration of our method, we provide a growth accounting exercise in appendix A to show how energy had a big impact on growth throughout the period, but that this role declined in the second half of the twentieth century.

The main text will however focus on simpler interrelations, i.e., relations between those main factors (L, K, and E) and the output (GDP) as we did in chapter 7. Such relations can be expressed as ratios based on time-series, which provide important insights into what matters for long-run relations between economic growth and energy. For instance, the capital to GDP ratio (K/Y) informs us about to what degree economic growth is based on capital investments. Capital requires a lot of material and energy both for its construction and its use. The capital stock's dependence on energy (K/E) is consequently another ratio of great interest to us. This shows to what degree the capital has become more efficient in its use of energy over time. The third ratio we will devote substantial attention to is energy intensity. Energy intensity (E/Y) is a useful indicator for how much energy (measured by its heat content) is required to produce one dollar's worth of GDP. The lower the energy intensity the better, because it indicates that as a society we are getting more value out of our natural resources.

Strong Growth of Capital Stock and Catch-up with the Leader of Capital-GDP Ratios

The capital stock has grown at the same rate or even faster than GDP. This means that the capital to GDP ratio (K/Y) has either increased or stayed constant since 1870 (see figure 10.2). In the case of the first mover—England, which already had a large capital stock by 1870—there was a stabilization of the ratio, while for some followers with lower levels of GDP at the start date, like Sweden and Spain, there was an increase in the ratio. The most important insight from this is that GDP has not grown at a faster rate than workers have been equipped with machines and buildings. There is no increased efficiency in the way the economies make use of their capital alone. The efficiency gains in labor productivity have been tremendous, and to a large degree this has been an effect from workers getting access to more capital (capital deepening), capital that requires energy to function.[9]

---

[9] Still, all growth accounting since Solow 1956 comes to the conclusion that it is the total factor productivity (TFP) increases that has been responsible for most of growth. This is because of the weights given to the factors of production in the growth accounting as explained in appendix A.

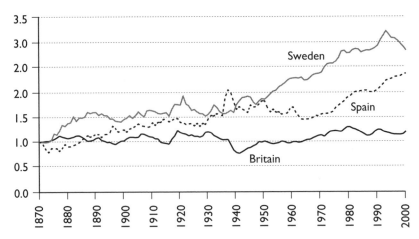

Figure 10.2. Capital intensity of GDP (K/GDP)
in Sweden, Britain, and Spain, index 1870=1.
Sources: Spain: Prados de la Escosura and Rosés, 2010; Britain:
Matthews, Feinstein, and Odling-Smee, 1982, with linear
interpolation for missing values; Sweden: Krantz and Schön, 2007.

The results for Sweden and Spain seem at first glance to disprove one
of the famous six stylized facts formulated by the economist Nicholas Kaldor in the 1960s, who proposed that capital stock remains consistently
three times larger than GDP.[10] The Spanish capital-output ratio increases
2.5 times over the period 1870–2000 and the Swedish ratio, three times.
However, the ratio between absolute size of the capital stock and GDP is
indeed 3:1 throughout the period in Britain, and in the Netherlands between
1900 and 1995 and also in Italy it fluctuates between 2.7 and 3 in the last
two centuries. Especially early industrializers do seem to fit with Kaldor's
stylized fact of a constant K/Y ratio after the first phase of capitalist development has occurred and the economy has reached a reasonable investment
rate.[11] As latecomers, Sweden and Spain started out at much lower levels of
capital in relation to GDP in 1870 and capital investments grew substantially throughout the period. In the case of Sweden the relation was 1:1 in
1870 and about 3:1 in 2000, and in Spain it was 1.5:1 in 1870 and 3.6:1
in 2000. The K/Y ratios have caught up with those of the more advanced
countries, but only after a long delay.

[10] Kaldor, 1960, 1961; Jones and Romer, 2010.
[11] It is a bit odd that Italy, being a late industrializer, also had achieved high capital levels
early on, but presumably this was because of their valuable buildings, making up a large fraction of the capital stock.

MACHINERY INCREASED MORE THAN GDP, LABOR, AND OTHER CAPITAL

Machinery consumes large amounts of energy and is connected to development blocks in a clearer fashion than buildings. Machinery increased much more than GDP and more than the whole capital stock. The increase of Swedish machinery was especially conspicuous in the period 1870–2000. While capital increased three times more than GDP between 1870 and 2000, machinery increased seven times more than the total capital stock! In Spain the situation was similar to that of Sweden. The machinery stock increased four times faster than the total capital stock between 1870 and 2000. This was also true in the more advanced Netherlands, but since machinery started from a higher ratio, it only grew twice as fast as total capital between 1900 and 2000.[12]

Thus economic growth in the twentieth century is a continuation of the capital-deepening trends of the nineteenth century: equipping workers with more machines (see chapters 4 and 7). This is worth stressing, because of the widespread belief that economic growth is largely to do with increases in efficiency and that it therefore does not threaten the environment.[13] This is misleading when it comes to examining the connections between growth, energy, and environmental impact. We think the reason for such a mistaken belief is that there has not been a sufficient focus on capital and energy intensity in the debate; instead, the attention of economists working on growth has been devoted mostly to explaining and integrating into models the large unexplained residual of Total Factor Productivity that seemed to be the main cause of growth ever since Solow's famous work in the 1950s.[14] That growth could be explained by a large rise in TFP, rather than increased inputs in capital, labor, and resources, could suggest a strong "dematerialization" in the economy (see chapters 1 and 2). However, this must assume that technical change was neutral; in fact, the savings associated with rises in TFP are not uniformly allocated to capital and labor in physical terms. We are still moving along a capital- and machinery-deepening path, which generates both a large demand for energy resources and stress on the environment, for instance in the form of global warming. Growth still requires more physical inputs.

Relative price developments have stimulated new ways of combining resources and inputs. Unsurprisingly, labor is the factor that has increased its price the most, far more than the price increase of capital, and it has consequently been utilized less than capital for production in physical terms. The

---

[12] Groote et al., 1996.
[13] Gunnarsson and Andersson, 2011.
[14] Solow, 1956; Aghion and Howitt, 2009.

price of energy has also increased far more than the price of machinery,[15] which leads us to examining the next ratio: capital-energy.

INCREASING CAPITAL-ENERGY RATIO

There is a complementarity between energy and physical capital (machinery and buildings). No machinery can run without energy, and buildings need energy for light, heating or cooling, and ventilation. Still, the relationship is not fixed. Instead we see in figure 10.3 that the capital stock has increased in relation to the primary energy input.[16] One dollar's worth of capital required less energy input (joules) in 2000 than it did in 1870. The capital to energy ratio has increased because of the strong thermal efficiency improvements that have taken place in machinery over this long period, stimulated by dearer energy and cheaper capital. Individual engines have become more powerful. Heating and cooling systems have improved. Electricity generation and diffusion have become more efficient too. Reduced energy losses have acted to lower the "E" factor (primary energy measured by its heat content, in joules) in the ratio.

The capital/energy ratio has increased ten times in Sweden and 4–5 times in England and Spain between 1870 and 2000. It means that, although the growth of the capital stock has followed GDP growth or even exceeded it, this capital stock has increased its energy efficiency. We can thus speak of a *relative* dematerialization. Nevertheless, even in the best case scenario, this efficiency increase has not been quite strong enough to balance out growth in GDP, so energy consumption has still risen, albeit much less after 1970.

ENERGY SERVICES TO GDP—A CLEAR TREND BREAK IN THE 1970S

Consumers do not desire energy. What consumers are looking for is what energy can do for them: the services that energy can provide. This could be light, motion, heat, or information processing (in a computer). The energy actually consumed in directly producing these services (subtracting, for example, the heat generated by a light bulb and only calculating the light) is sometimes called "useful work."[17] A group of researchers have attempted to estimate the average annual efficiency in the conversion from primary energy to useful work, based on different technologies and the composition of energy services in different nations. This is difficult, and generates many

---

[15] Schön, 1995.

[16] There is on the other hand much stronger complementarity between energy services and capital than between primary energy and capital, at least up to the 1970s; see Kander and Schön, 2007.

[17] Ayres and Warr, 2005; Williams et al., 2008; Warr et al., 2008.

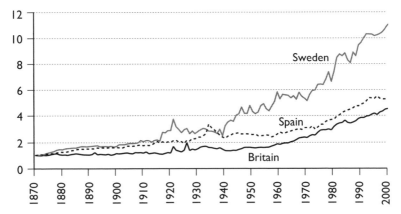

Figure 10.3. Capital to energy ratios (K/E ratios), Britain, Sweden, and Spain, 1870–2000, index 1870 = 1
Sources: Own calculation based on Prados de la Escosura and Rosés (2010); Britain: Feinstein, 1972 (linear interpolation for missing values), Sweden: Krantz and Schön (2007) and www.energyhistory.org.

more uncertainties than in our quantification of primary energy.[18] They find (see figure 10.4) that over most of the twentieth century useful work increased in relation to GDP. Society became much more efficient in transforming primary energy into useful work, and this useful work underpinned economic growth.

However, in the 1970s there is a conspicuous trend break when useful work declined drastically in relation to GDP. What would be the most plausible interpretation of this? Some might argue that it was the oil crises of the 1970s, with skyrocketing oil prices.[19] This explanation is not convincing, because we would in fact expect the opposite effect. A dramatic price increase of oil should have stimulated improvements in the efficiency of conversion from primary energy to useful energy. Then more useful energy would have been squeezed out of the primary energy, and the energy services would have gone up. Instead we find a drop in energy services. This in our view suggests some more profound change: a genuine technology shift. The economy seems to be growing on the basis of something other than energy services after the 1970s.

We propose that the observed decline came from a drastic compositional change in machinery. Machines have become much more efficient in

[18] Basically they assume shared technologies across countries, and consistent efficiency of use within countries, so the difference in the conversion factor is only due to compositional effects from different kinds of useful work being more important in certain countries than others.

[19] Parra, 2004. This book gives a thorough overview of competition and prices of oil since the 1950s. The oil crises of '73 and '79 are extensively discussed.

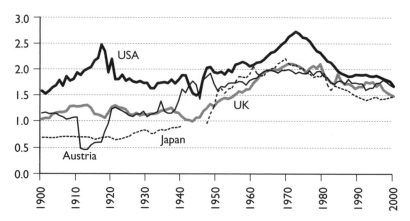

Figure 10.4. Useful work (energy services)
to GDP in USA, Japan, Austria, and UK
Source: Warr et al., 2010.

converting primary energy into useful work (heat, motion, electricity) over time. This is why the ratio of useful energy to GDP increases up until the 1970s at the same time as energy intensity declines. The composition of machinery matters a great deal for how much useful energy is utilized. The impact differs according to the shares of steam engines, internal combustion engines, or electric motors among the total amount of machinery. Computers, in turn, consume far less useful work relative to their value. The drastic and widespread trend break in the relation between useful work and GDP in the 1970s could not have been achieved by energy savings within existing stocks of machinery by micro-innovations. Instead it must be due to something more fundamental in the economy: it was growing more on the basis of something other than increased amounts of useful work and a leading candidate is "information." We are seeing the emergence of the ICT development block.This was manifest in a growing share of ICT capital in relation to overall capital.[20]

Falling Cost Share for Energy

We propose that a country can embark on modern economic growth *because* the cost of energy declines. This is one of the key messages of this book. The cost of energy in relation to GDP is low in modern advanced economies, around 5–10 percent of national income. The lowering of energy prices, as a consequence of past transport revolutions which facilitated the

[20] Warr and Ayres, 2012.

transport of the energy-dense commodities coal and oil across the globe, and improvements in extraction and production technologies of energy carriers like oil and electricity, mean that over the last century energy has gone from being an expensive to a rather cheap commodity. In other words, energy supply has been very elastic.

The cost share for energy declines substantially as a country embarks on modern economic growth based on fossil fuels. In Sweden the energy cost share was as high as 80 percent of GDP in 1800 when the reliance on traditional fuels was still very strong and the ratio had fallen to 20 percent in 1900 (see the growth accounting in appendix A).[21] In England, that went through its fossil fuel transition much earlier; the share was already as low as 6 percent in 1900 and has remained at low levels.[22] The lowering of energy prices was a conspicuous feature of nineteenth-century growth (see chapter 6). The real price reductions of modern energy carriers continued in the twentieth century, but at the same time the composition of energy carriers shifted toward more expensive, higher quality ones.

A falling cost share for energy is not possible in an economy with an elasticity of substitution of unity (known by economists as "Cobb-Douglas" technology) which implies constant cost shares for all inputs. If the price of one factor goes up there will be a movement along the isoquant so that less of that factor is used and the cost share will stay constant. This empirical finding of falling energy costs therefore necessitates adjustments to conventional growth modeling (see appendix A).

Cheaper Energy, but Increased Quality of the Energy Mix

Energy is not a single uniform product. On the contrary, energy carriers have different properties and complement specific technologies to varying degrees. We can therefore say that they have different *qualities*.[23] The quality of a fuel or energy carrier may be thought of as its economic productivity. Some fuels can be used for a larger number of activities and/or for more valuable activities.[24] Generally, carriers for which there are no substitutes are worth more than energy carriers for which there are plenty of alternatives. Oil has a higher value for consumers than coal and firewood, because oil can do things for people that solid fuels cannot, like run a combustion

---

[21] This is when food costs are included and fodder costs too. Food costs are assumed to follow CPI.

[22] Own calculations, available on request. In England in 1900, 95 percent of the energy consisted of coal even when food and fodder are counted. For simplicity, the calculation assumed that the 5 percent that was not coal still had the same price as coal.

[23] Cleveland et al., 1984, 2000.

[24] Stern, 2010a.

TABLE 10.1
Prices of some energy carriers in Spain, benchmarks (pesetas/GJ)

	Imported coal	gasoline	electricity
1913	1.7	17.9	60.3
1925	3.2	18.2	65.3

Source: Prices were kindly provided by Mar Rubio.

engine.[25] But it is not crude oil that can run combustion engines, only certain fractions of it. This means that petrol is worth more than heating oil, for instance. So even within one energy carrier category, like oil, there are great price differences. Petrol can be four times as expensive as heating oil. Electricity is the highest value energy carrier, with almost endless applications. It can power your computer as well as heat your house, and its price is consequently higher than other energy carriers. If we add energy up simply according to its heat content, as we did when we calculated energy intensity, we lose out on all these quality improvements in the basket of energy carriers. The exact relative prices of coal, gasoline, and electricity of course vary among countries, but early in the twentieth century there was a clear ranking between energy carriers that is common to all our countries: electricity is most expensive, followed by gasoline, and then imported coal. Table 10.1 provides one example of price relations in some benchmarks for Spain, which demonstrates this ranking.

Over time different energy carrier prices behaved in quite different ways. Most of them decreased their real price in the twentieth century (that is in relation to the consumer price index, CPI). Electricity prices decreased drastically, while the real price of oil also fell substantially between the Second World War and the late 1970s, only to catch up with the CPI again around 2000. Coal basically stayed on a par with the CPI apart from during the World Wars, when it rose. The price of firewood—a traditional fuel whose supply was much more restricted—rose in price relative to the CPI; see figure 10.5 on Sweden.[26]

In the UK the real price of coal fell in the first decades of the twentieth century, but then stabilized at historically low levels, while the price of oil dropped to a quarter of its 1900 value by 2000 (see figure 10.6).

If we aggregate these results into a weighted price index for energy, we find that despite the introduction of higher quality energy carriers, in general the real price of energy went down in the twentieth century. The price

[25] Reynolds, 1996.
[26] For Sweden this is shown in Kander, 2002.

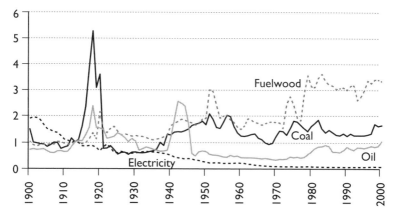

Figure 10.5. The price of coal, electricity, fuel, firewood, and oil divided by the consumer price index (CPI) in Sweden 1900–2000 *Note*: Price levels have been set to 100 in 1913, just like the CPI, so this is not meant for comparing the price levels of different energy carriers. The prices are consumer prices, weighted according to the consumed quantities of various kinds of fuels on the national level. *Source*: Kander, 2002.

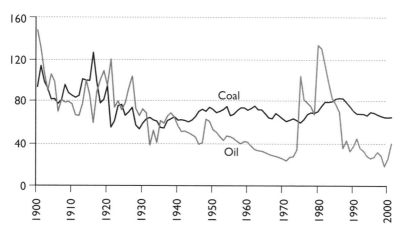

Figure 10.6. Price of coal and oil compared to the consumer price index (CPI) in UK 1900–2001, index 1913 = 100

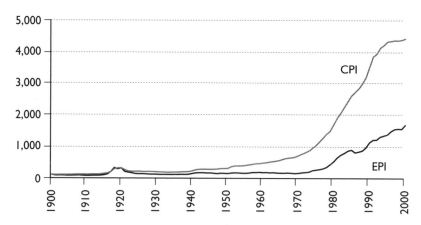

Figure 10.7. Energy Price Index (EPI) and
Consumer Price Index (CPI) for Sweden 1900–2000
Note: The Energy Price Index is constructed as
a Paasche Index with annual links.

of energy increased only one-third as much as the overall inflation rate in
Sweden (see figure 10.7).[27]

There is no perfect method to evaluate the quality of energy carriers, but
prices, although having the drawback of reflecting supply as well as demand
conditions, may with caution be used in the analysis.[28] We can show how
quality has increased by dividing the sum value (in constant prices) of carriers by their heat content.[29] If we do this for the one country where we have a
complete set of price series for all energy carriers—Sweden—we end up with
the results shown in figure 10.8. Calculated this way the average quality of
energy carriers increased by a factor of eight over the twentieth century. If

---

[27] It was nevertheless more expensive than machinery in industry.

[28] Kander, 2002, chapter 5, thoroughly discusses the drawback of using prices. The main
problem is that prices at best can reflect marginal productivity in competitive markets (which
is not always the case for energy), and never average productivity. If the difference between
marginal and average productivity is large, as in the case of electricity, this is likely to underes-
timate the true consumer value. This underestimation has been discussed in the case of the cost
of light by Fouquet, Pearson, 2006.

[29] The value of energy consumed in current prices can be written:

$$EV = \sum_{i=1}^{n} (Eit \cdot Pit)$$

EV is the total value of the energy consumed in current prices, E_{it} the quantity of the different energy carriers in joules and P_{it} is the corresponding price of each energy carrier. The sum
EV includes inflationary increases of energy prices. To get an idea of the actual real energy
increase, we must therefore deflate this volume by a price index for energy to have it expressed
in constant prices instead.

$$EVcons = \frac{EV}{EnergyPI}$$

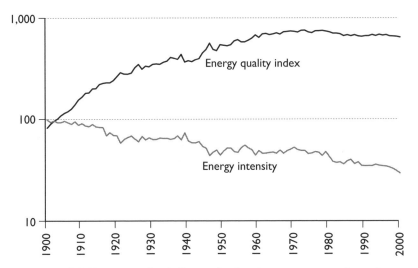

Figure 10.8. Energy quality indicator for Sweden versus energy intensity, 1900–2000, price level 1990, index 1900=100, lin-log scale
Source: Own calculations.

energy carriers of higher quality have replaced inferior energy carriers, this may have contributed to the reduced energy intensity, because higher quality may have compensated for lower quantity.

Indeed, a higher energy quality seems to have stimulated the decline in energy intensity, as seen in figure 10.8. But it cannot be the sole explanation, since the drastic decline in energy intensity since 1970 was not accompanied by a quality increase. So, we see again that the ICT revolution seems to have had an independent role, apart from stimulating more electricity consumption.

FALLING AND CONVERGING ENERGY INTENSITY IN THE TWENTIETH CENTURY

It is frequently argued that long-run energy intensity over the last two hundred years has developed like a belly-shaped curve, or an inverted U-curve.[30] This is based on the idea that when countries industrialize, they

---

EV_{cons} is the energy value expressed in constant prices for the subset energy. By dividing the energy value in constant prices by the aggregate energy quantity we get an indicator of the increase in aggregate energy quality over time, if we accept that prices reflect quality.

$$EQ = \frac{EVcons}{\sum_{i=1}^{n} Qit}$$

[30] Reddy and Goldemberg, 1990, 111–18; World Bank, 1992.

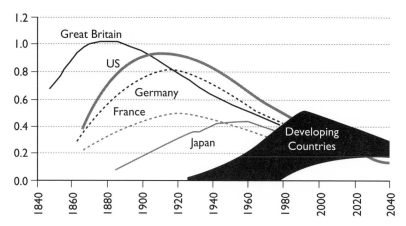

Figure 10.9. The hypothetical relation between energy and GDP
Source: Adapted from Reddy and Goldemberg, 1990, used in
Gales et al., 2007.

use relatively inefficient technologies but later on they became more economical. The pattern is assumed to apply to all countries. According to the
inverted-U model (see figure 10.9) latecomer countries could peak at lower
levels of energy intensity through the adoption of more efficient technology
from abroad.

This optimistic picture has received lots of positive interest and has
stimulated research.[31] It would, of course, be a highly desirable result if the
economy could solve its environmental and resource problems simply by
continuous growth, with less developed countries joining the growth band-
wagon at ever-lower levels of energy intensity. Panayotou in 1993 labeled
the inverted U-curve the "Environmental Kuznets Curve" (EKC), after the
original Kuznets Curve (KC), which had suggested a similar curve for inequality over time with rising incomes.[32] The EKC instead proposes that
environmental degradation shows an inverted U-shape pattern over time
with rising incomes. Energy, with its association to pollution, could serve as
a proxy for environmental degradation, although some energy carriers are
more harmful for the environment than others. We can speak of an EKCE
(Environmental Kuznets Curve for Energy).

In fact this pattern fits well with energy intensity at the aggregate European level (see figure 10.10). During the nineteenth century there was an
increase in energy intensity, and in the twentieth century there was a decline.
However, this was not the case for every individual country in Europe (see
figure 10.11). To illustrate the large national differences within Europe we

[31] Stern, 2004 , 1419–39; Dinda, 2004, 431–55.
[32] Panayotou, 1993; Kuznets, 1955.

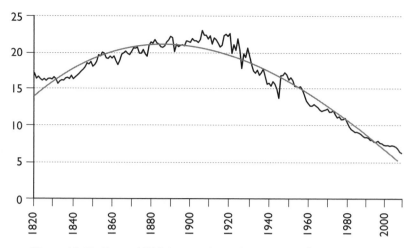

Figure 10.10. Energy/GDP (energy intensity), mega joule per constant international 1990 dollar, in Western Europe 1820–2008

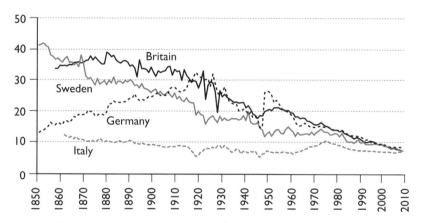

Figure 10.11. Energy intensities of Great Britain, Sweden, Italy, and Germany 1850–2008 (MJ/1990 international dollars)

portray four quite different cases, which are the more conspicuous among our set of countries: Great Britain and Germany (coal economies), Sweden (cold, forest-rich country), and Italy (warm, forest-scarce country). For Sweden, the Netherlands, Spain, and Italy there is no EKCE when traditional energy carriers are included, but rather a long-term decline or more constant levels of energy intensity.[33] For England and Germany there is an EKCE. As

[33] Gales et al., 2007.

these make up a large share of the total Western European economy, they strongly influence the aggregate curve for the continent.

The only country that shows a very clear EKCE over the period is Germany, peaking in energy intensity around 1915.The other "coal country," Britain—the early industrializer—also had an EKCE, but over a very much longer period beginning in the eighteenth century and peaking in the 1870s. Its very high levels of energy intensity have fallen drastically since. The swift increase in energy intensity for Britain between 1850 and 1870 which was suggested by Reddy and Goldemberg is not supported by our data. Sweden shows a dramatic fall in energy intensity over the full period 1850–2005, and the extent of the fall resembles that of Great Britain. However, unlike in Britain, there was never an increase before 1850, so Sweden is clearly an exception to the EKCE hypothesis, with falling energy intensity throughout the whole period. Italy, like several of our other countries (Spain, Portugal, France, and the Netherlands) has a more modest decline in energy intensity, about a 50 percent reduction over the period 1861–2005. These countries started out at much lower levels of energy intensity, so their scope for improvement was not as large in absolute terms.[34] Generally, we can say that countries that had a warmer climate and less need for domestic heating, or were not leading coal economies, never had very high energy intensities. They consequently could not reduce their consumption as much, even with the benefit of technology transfer.

The other conspicuous feature of the long-term energy intensity trend is the strong convergence in levels for all these countries, a pattern that is confirmed also when we include many more countries in our sample (see figure 10.12). This suggests that countries become more similar in their structures or technologies over time, due to technology transfer. It is important to understand the drivers for energy intensity over time and to what degree these forces are common across countries or autonomous. Is international trade significant for the individual country's energy intensity? This will be examined in section 3.

3. ENERGY INTENSITY AND ECONOMIC STRUCTURE

In chapter 9 we argued that the ICT development block of the third industrial revolution was more energy-saving than any of the previous development blocks, and we see that the rate of decline in energy intensities was especially strong after the 1970s when ICT advanced. As we have previously seen, it is commonly thought that this decline in energy intensity is connected to the major structural occupational shift of this period: the rise of the service sector. We will now present an argument that the most credible

---

[34] For a more detailed analysis of energy intensity in Sweden, Italy, the Netherlands, and Spain, see Gales et al., 2007.

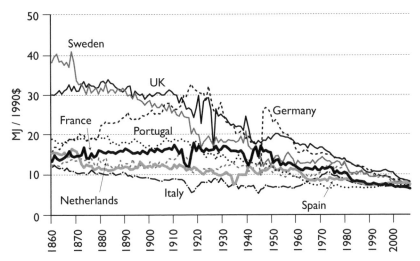

Figure 10.12. Energy intensity for eight Western European
countries, 1860–2007 (MJ/1990 international dollars)
Source: www.energyhistory.org, same figure used also for
Henriques and Kander, 2010.

reason for a steeper decline after the 1970s was not, in fact, the increasing
share of the service sector in the economy, but rather the impact of ICT.

Decomposing Energy Intensity

Energy intensity declined in the twentieth century and we want to understand the causes of the decline. A few words of caution are warranted before
we dig deeper into this problem. In our attempts to understand the drivers behind changes in energy intensity, we must never forget that energy
intensity, although relevant for dematerialization analyses, is only a *relative* measure of energy demands in an economy. It only communicates how
much energy is needed for one dollar's worth of GDP and does not give any
direct information about the *total* (*absolute*) amounts of energy needed for
the economy to function: the total energy consumption. It is of course total
energy consumption that is linked to environmental stress; the environment
does not care about our relative indicators. Energy intensity is nevertheless often used as an environmental stress indicator; the higher the energy
intensity, the worse for the climate (or more accurately, the experience of
ourselves and many other species of the climate).[35] Energy intensity is still

[35] There is a vast body of literature on energy intensity; see for example Ang and Zhang,
2000; Markandya et al., 2006; Nilsson, 1993; Tapio et al., 2007. We must of course not forget

only a partial assessment of resource use and does not give the full picture even of energy demands. Economic growth rates are equally important as trends in energy intensity.[36]

In chapter 8 we decomposed the total energy consumption into the effects from three factors: population increase, per capita income, and energy intensity. The first two factors (population increase and per capita income increase) together comprise the "scale effect" (how much total GDP grows). Here we will investigate the third factor: energy intensity, and decompose it further.

The direct drivers for energy intensity change can be divided into structural (or "between-sector") changes, and technical (or "within-sector") changes. Logically, what is not caused by between-sector changes, must be caused by changes in energy use within each sector. The methodological challenge for all shift-share analyses is to achieve a complete decomposition of changes, without leaving any unexplained residual. In the following calculations we follow the resolution provided by Ang, which satisfies this criterion.[37]

The three factors of "technical change" (within-sector changes), structural change (between-sector changes), and scale are illustrated in figure 10.13. The illustration is meant to convey an intuitive understanding of the three factors behind changes in energy consumption over time.[38]

The upper box illustrates the scale effect: the growth in the size of GDP, which is much larger in 2000 than in 1870. GDP grows as a result of population increase and higher production per capita. The middle box illustrates structural changes. Structural changes in production are illustrated by the changing share of each sector in the total "pie." We see that the transport and industrial sectors are relatively much larger in 2000 than they were in 1870. Industry and transport grow together because they complement each other well; the products from the industrial sector need to be transported to customers. Agriculture is the sector that has declined most over the long twentieth century. This change is an important part of the whole transformation of societies, with growing urbanization rates and fewer people living in the countryside, but also a consequence of the industrialization of agriculture, and has brought with it the possibility of moving labor to other sectors. The most important factor for explaining the decline of agriculture in GDP

---

that there are additional forms of environmental stress apart from global change, like deforestation, water pollution, and loss of biodiversity.

[36] This may seem too obvious to require so much emphasis, but we find that intelligent people sometimes overlook this. For example Radetzki, 1990 argues on the basis of energy intensity changes alone that economic growth is good for the environment.

[37] Ang, 2005.

[38] The illustration is based on empirical data for Sweden found in Kander, 2002. It is worth mentioning that the sector shares are in constant, 1910–12 year prices. With another choice of price level the size of the sectors would differ from this figure, but their relative growth and decline would still be the same.

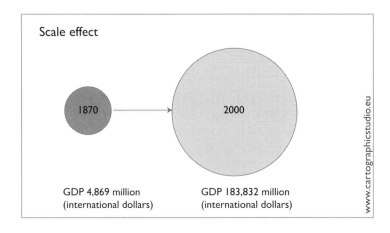

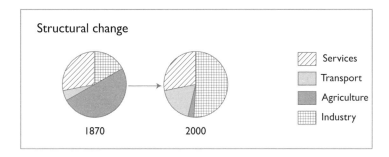

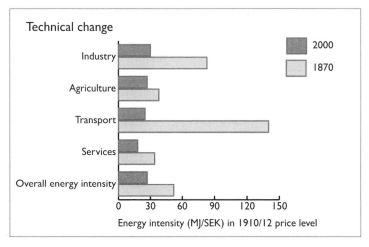

Figure 10.13. Principles of scale, structural and technical change, 1870–2000

is, however, on the demand side: people simply cannot eat endless amounts of food, but they can consume more or less endless amounts of industrial consumer goods and services.

The lower box illustrates technical change (within-sector changes) as measured by energy intensity within each of the four sectors: agriculture, services, industry, and transport. Energy intensity was much higher in transport and industry than in agriculture, both in 1870 and 2000, and lowest in services. It requires more energy to produce manufactured goods or transport these goods than it does to produce haircuts, education, or banking. All sectors experienced falling energy intensity between 1870 and 2000, but the rate of reduction was not even. The reduction in energy intensity between 1870 and 2000 was most impressive in industry and transport, where energy costs were the highest and thereby the incentives to economize on energy the largest. Those were also the sectors that grew the most as shares of GDP.

This poses an intriguing possibility: can the reduction in energy intensity within the sectors (technical change) be strong enough to balance out or even outweigh the between-sector changes (the structural effect)? In that case the industrialization process might mean lower energy demands relative to GDP. Conversely, if the technical change was not fast enough, the industrialization process would mean increasing energy requirements to produce one dollar's worth of GDP. We will investigate how the balance between effects from technical change and structural change evolved throughout the twentieth century and if this changed from the second to the third industrial revolution. Did the third industrial revolution bring about a structural change of a new kind that actually helped to lower energy intensity, so that structural change and technical change for the first time in history co-worked to lower energy intensity? And did this structural change in that case take place in services or in industry?

Drivers of Energy Intensity Change during the Second Industrial Revolution

First we will examine the early phase of the second industrial revolution (1870–1913), a period when the coal and steam technologies of the first industrial revolution were still dominant (see chapters 5–7), but the electricity development block and ICE-Oil block had begun to have some initial impact. The full details of the underlying calculations are provided in appendix B.

In England and Wales energy intensity declined by 7.3 percent in total between 1870 and 1913. The prime driver of the decline in British energy intensity was the savings of energy within the industrial sector. Thermal efficiency increases allowing for more energy services or useful work (heat, light, electricity, motion) in relation to primary energy was behind much of this.

Energy intensity in Sweden decreased from 0.13 MJ/SEK to 0.099 MJ/SEK between 1870 and 1913, which was a more drastic decline of 24 percent. Changes within three sectors (industry, services, and agriculture) contributed to the fall, but in the transport sector energy intensity actually increased initially with the transition from draft animals to mechanical converters of energy.[39] Generally, industry and transport were the two sectors that increased their share of GDP, and since they were the most energy-intense sectors, this structural change tended to increase energy intensity in all industrializing countries at this time. However, the effects from within-sector changes and the decline in the household share of energy consumption outbalanced this, so the net effect was a decline in energy intensity both in Britain and Sweden.

The Swedish decline in this period (1870–1913) was driven largely by changes in domestic heating, and this (as far as we know) is quite exceptional in Europe.[40] However, the declining influence of "households" was more general in Europe in this early stage of industrialization. As energy consumption grows it is largely in the industrial production and in the transportation sector, and thus the relative importance of households declines. So, in other words, the declining share of household energy in relation to the total energy reflects that rapid industrialization sees relatively more energy being consumed in the formal economy and less directly by households.[41] Thus we see that industrialization does not necessarily mean energy intensity increases, if the country consumed large amounts of energy in domestic houses, such as for heating in a cold climate. The same is true for Portugal, where energy intensity fell drastically between 1900 and 1970, presumably mainly as a consequence of a declining share for households.[42]

In Britain the structural effects were even stronger than in Sweden in counteracting the energy-intensity decline from technical change. British energy intensity in the industrial sector was at this time much higher than in Sweden, meaning that even a small increase of the share for this sector had a large impact. The energy-intense English industry, with large shares for iron and steel, was strongly influenced by production for export markets (see chapters 6 and 7).

Most of the impact from the second industrial revolution in terms of energy use and structural effects in the economy took place after 1913, when electrification and motorization had a much greater influence. In the period 1913–1970, energy intensity in Sweden continued downward, by 41 percent.

---

[39] Draft animals are included, with a thermal efficiency of around 10 percent. The early machines that replaced them were even less efficient in converting primary energy into motion.

[40] Cramér, 1991.

[41] The balance between households and the formal economy in the total energy consumption changes later in the twentieth century, when households are equipped with many energy-consuming gadgets, like cars and electric devices.

[42] Henriques, 2011, 111–12.

Industry and transport continued to grow as shares of GDP creating upward pressure on energy intensity, while the energy intensities went down very drastically within the very same two sectors. Energy intensity continued to decline in England and Wales, in total by 32 percent between 1913 and 1950, in line with the Swedish decline on an annual basis.[43] Again the decline was driven by a combination of the technical changes within industry with the household effects, while structural changes continued to play an offsetting role. Thus we see a consistent pattern for the drivers of energy intensity decline throughout the period marked by the second industrial revolution in England and Sweden: the within-sector changes, particularly in industry, combined with the household effect, were strong enough to counteract the structural change of industrialization.

In some southern European countries, as we saw in figure 10.12, the relative strength of the two forces—structural change and technical change—was different, and energy intensity did not fall as much, and even increased in some periods. We lack the necessary sector data to carry out formal decomposition of energy intensity before 1970 for countries other than Sweden and England, but we dare suggest that in some cases, for instance in Italy, a rapid industrialization, stimulated by cheap oil in the 1950s and 1960s, even led to an increase in energy intensity.

DRIVERS OF ENERGY INTENSITY DECLINE DURING THE THIRD INDUSTRIAL REVOLUTION

In the period after 1970, energy intensity in Europe declined faster than it had done before. One idea prominently advanced to explain the rapidly declining energy intensity after 1970 is of a grand structural transformation, sometimes expressed as the transition to the service economy, sometimes as the emergence of a post-industrial society.[44] This was proposed for instance by both Panayotou and Smil, who argued that maturing economies tend to have lower energy intensity. They attribute this phenomenon to the declining importance of energy-intensive capital, generally improved thermodynamic efficiency, and the rise in the importance of the service sector.[45] Production in the service sector is generally less energy-demanding than manufacturing production in relation to the value that is created. However, we find that the transition to the service economy is a less important driver for energy-intensity decline than is normally assumed. It is because in real terms the growth in services is less impressive than when judged from the employment

---

[43] The different benchmarks for Sweden, and England and Wales, are due to practical reasons of available sector disaggregation of energy.

[44] Kahn, 1979; Castells, 1996.

[45] Panayotou, 1993; Smil, 1994.

TABLE 10.2

Growth of service employment and service sector's real share of GDP, and growth of commercial transportation for 11 countries, 1971–2005

	Total Percentage units growth of Service Employment	Total Percentage units growth of real service share of GDP*	Total Percentage units growth of real commercial transport share,
	1971–2005	1971–2005	1971–2005
France	25	9	1
Germany	27	16	0
Italy	25	3	3
Japan	22	6	–4
Netherlands	19	8	–1
Portugal	18	11	–2
Spain	23	2	1
Sweden	19	–1	0
UK	24	14	–1
USA	14	7	1
India	6	22	na
Brazil	29	4	Na
Mexico	22	1	Na

*Commercial Transportation is included here.

Sources: These calculations are based on tables found in Henriques and Kander, 2010.

figures or non-deflated values of production, although its impact is not negligible. A more detailed decomposition of the drivers of change in this period is provided in appendix C.

An analysis of eight developed and three large emerging economies (Mexico, India, and Brazil) shows that the service transition has not been that large when measured in real terms (see table 10.2).[46]

As table 10.2 shows, most countries increased their share of service employment between 1971 and 2005, typically in the range of 18–29 percent, with some exceptions like India (6 percent) and the United States (14 percent). The increase in real service share of GDP was not equally large.

[46] Henriques and Kander, 2010. Similar figures demonstrating a relatively modest growth of the service sector in real terms are provided by Houpt et al., 2010, table 13.3.

Sizable shifts are seen in Germany (16 percent), UK (14 percent), and Portugal (11 percent), but the rest of the sample showed a growth of less than 10 percent in the share of the service sector measured in real terms over thirty-four years, while their employment in services rocketed. The reason why service employment has increased much more than the service sector's share of real GDP is that service production is generally less productive than manufacturing production. It involves many activities, like personal services, where machines cannot easily speed up the work by people. The sector remains relatively labor-intensive, often with the nature of tasks and productivity changing little over time. Nevertheless, service sector wages benefit from productivity increases in the economy as a whole, boosting the size of the sector when measured in current but not constant (real) prices. This phenomenon is known as Baumol's cost disease. [47]

Thus the service transition has not been as large in terms of real output as employment figures suggest and therefore logically must have had a more modest impact on energy intensity, which is also demonstrated more formally in appendix C. If the economic structure within the service sector itself had changed to a greater degree, with for instance more energy-intense activities such as transport taking on a larger role, this would strengthen the argument for only a modest downward impact on energy intensity from the service transition further, because it would have offset any decline from a larger share of employment in labor-intensive work. However, even though transport grew substantially, most car journeys are undertaken by households directly and therefore belong to household energy consumption, not to the service sector. Commercial transportation's share of services (taxis, airplanes, and buses) did not affect energy intensity changes between 1970 and 2005, because commercial transport (unlike private transport, largely cars) hardly changed in this period (see table 10.3). [48] Instead, banking and other financial services, which do not require as much energy, have increased their shares within the service sector. This expansion is linked to the ICT revolution, since these subsectors utilize computers to a large degree.

The strongest evidence that the technology shift of ICT and not a general increase in services was behind the trend-break in energy and growth relations in the 1970s is that we find the main driver to be the manufacturing sector, and more precisely, the change of energy intensity *within* manufacturing industry (as demonstrated in appendix C). This is partly to do with the structural shift within manufacturing industry, which means the breakthrough of new products, and a relative increase of less energy-dependent

---

[47] For a more extensive discussion of this see Baumol, 1967; Kander, 2005; Henriques and Kander, 2010; and Ruttan, 2001.

[48] The subsectors are deflated separately and the price indices used for deflation are annually linked indices, so there is no issue here of the index number problem, which might have distorted the picture if a rougher method was used.

TABLE 10.3
Service sector composition, shares of service sector sum in constant prices, 1971 and 2005 (%)

	1971					2005				
	Wholesale and retail trade, Hotels and restaurants	Transport	Post and commun.	Finance	Public services	Wholesale and retail trade, Hotels and restaurants	Transport	Post and commun.	Finance	Public services
	(50–55)	(60–63)	(64)	(65–74)	(75–99)	(50–55)	(60–63)	(64)	(65–74)	(75–99)
France	20	5	1	37	37	17	6	5	40	31
Germany	25	5	3	30	37	18	5	4	41	31
Italy	26	5	2	33	35	24	8	5	35	29
Japan	25	10	2	28	34	24	6	5	37	28
Netherlands	22	8	2	25	43	23	7	7	35	29
Portugal	43	7	2	26	22	25	5	6	33	30
Spain	31	6	1	25	37	26	7	5	31	31
Sweden	18	9	2	41	29	17	9	6	42	26
UK	24	8	3	27	38	20	7	8	38	27
USA	16	5	2	32	46	20	4	4	41	32

Source: Henriques and Kander, 2010, based on EUKLEMS, 2008 and EUKLEMS, 2009. The numbers in parentheses in the column headings refer to the included sub-sectors in national accounts in the ISIC – Rev3 values.

subsectors in industry, such as pharmaceuticals and electronics.[49] It also was an effect of the more efficient control of material and energy flows through the use of computers, such as electric-hydraulic drills substituting for pneumatic drills in the mining industry during the 1970s, improving the working conditions in mines, and reducing the need for ventilation and thus energy consumption. In the metallurgical industries improvements in electro-steel processing meant that scrap-metal could be used, which saved material and energy; another energy-saving improvement was that the production process became more integrated, using direct production lines from raw steel to refined steel, without the former cooling down, and thus requiring the reheating of the metal before the final treatment to make steel products. ICT had a similar impact on the pulp and paper industry, allowing the process to be integrated directly from the pulp to the paper, without having to dry the pulp in between, saving energy.

We therefore argue that it was the third industrial revolution that was behind most of the decline of energy intensity after the 1970s. The third industrial revolution affected energy intensity in three ways: (1) lighter manufacturing industry grew relatively more important, (2) fine tuning of energy and material flows reduced losses, and (3) there was a relative increase in services, primarily software for ICT, and more business-related services such as banking.

Real Progress or Just Moving the Problems Around?

Any transition to a service economy, or a lighter industrial structure in general—even a modest one—in the developed world may be due to a new division of labor on the global scale after the 1970s. In a globalized world, integrated by a multitude of exchanges, national production and national consumption is of course not the same thing and countries specialized in exports of heavy manufacturing goods will have higher energy consumption than countries specializing in exports of agricultural goods or lighter manufactured goods. We have already seen the beginnings of such a division of labor in the nineteenth century in chapter 7, and the issue here is what happened to this division of labor in the late twentieth century. Some people suggest, "while we live in the service economy our industrial goods are produced elsewhere."[50] Equally, changes *within* industry, with the rise of light manufacturing such as pharmaceuticals and electronics in the developed world, and a relative reduction in steel and chemicals, may be due to trade

---

[49] In the Swedish case we see a clear effect of this kind, where structural change within the industrial sector led to a decline in industrial fuel consumption by 20 percent and a corresponding decrease in electricity use by 5 percent in the period 1970–87; see Schön, 1990.

[50] Hermele, 2002.

flows. Because global warming is a truly global phenomenon, as the atmosphere knows no national borders, there are no gains to the system from the third industrial revolution if it has just meant a relocation of the sources of hazardous emissions becoming generalized over the globe. The most extreme view is that there is no actual clean-up of production over time at all, only a displacement of negative environmental effects from one country to another.[51] Globalization would be simply a zero-sum gain in terms of environmental damage.[52] We know that globalization has been an ongoing process over centuries, but has been reinforced in recent decades in terms of the share of international trade to GDP.[53] It could therefor possibly explain reductions in energy intensity in developed countries since the 1970s.

Against this dismal view stands the more optimistic position that international trade can even improve the environment. According to the mainstream idea ever since Adam Smith and David Ricardo there are systemic benefits from trade that have now expanded into a global system, with possible gains for everyone.[54] In this case, trade would have energy-expanding effects, due to economic growth, but also energy-saving ones, as the general rise in efficiency levels and clean technology is transferred to developing countries. Just as with the European history we have traced, the net balance of these forces would have to be determined empirically. Optimally this should be done for all of Europe, and for individual countries.

This line of research in historical energy studies is fairly new, and more research is needed. Here we will look into the empirical evidence of energy in trade flows for two European countries—the only ones we have the calculations done for so far—and to what degree this possibly could have had an impact on the structural changes driving energy intensity down after 1970. One clarification must be made before we examine the evidence: Europe has been a big net importer of *energy carriers* from the rest of the world throughout the twentieth century.[55] In the nineteenth century, Europe was still self-supplying with coal, firewood, and largely self-supplying with food, but in the late twentieth century huge imports of oil were necessary to fuel the European economy. While 10.9 million barrels of crude oil and another 3 million barrels as refined products enter Europe every day (in 2007), only 2.3 million barrels leave Europe (0.6 as crude oil and 1.7 as refined products), so oil imports are large.[56] But what we want to address here is another and more subtle issue: the *energy embodied in traded commodities* and its impact on the structures of European economies. Then and only then will we

---

[51] Stern et al., 1996; Ekins, 1997; Dinda, 2004; Hornborg, 2011.

[52] Hornborg, 2011.

[53] Kenwood and Lougheed, 1992; Findlay and O'Rourke, 2007.

[54] Smith, 1776; Ricardo, 1821.

[55] That was clearly demonstrated in the map of oil imports (see figure 8.6).

[56] BP, Oil Exports and Imports. One barrel is 159 liters.

be able to judge if there is a sustainable transition to less energy-demanding products in the European economy after the 1970s.

A first indication that trade flows could *not* possibly have played a large role for the declining energy intensity is the falling and converging energy intensities that we already saw in figure 10.12 for Western Europe. In fact we find similar energy intensities for Europe and other regions of the world today, especially when GDP is measured at PPP (Purchasing Power Parity) adjusted numbers.[57] This similarity in levels of energy intensity does not fit with a view where some regions are specialized in heavy, energy-intensive production, and others in energy light production. It rather suggests that the national specialization gets less pronounced over time and that technology transfer is strong between countries. The Chinese success in exports has for instance largely taken place in commodities that have to do with the third industrial revolution, such as electronics, and not in industries processing large amounts of raw materials.[58]

Still, trade may matter on the margin for explaining cross-country differences in energy intensities. The empirical evidence of trade and displacement of energy-intensive industries is mixed, and a further difficulty is that as yet there is no agreement on the best methods for studying this issue. As ever the choice of method should be related to the research question. Much interest in this issue has arisen out of a concern for who is actually responsible for carbon dioxide emissions. Is it the exporting country, which creates the actual emissions when they produce the goods, or is it the consuming country that imports the goods and gets the benefits of consuming them?[59] The appropriate measure for accounting for this moral responsibility is not yet settled.

One method used among researchers today is to simply measure the carbon emissions related to a country's consumption pattern rather than that of its production.[60] The method for investigating this is rather straightforward. The energy used for production in a country is adjusted for the net exports of energy in goods. To calculate the net exports of energy (or CO_2), all the energy (or related CO_2 emissions) that was used throughout the entire production chain for all the exported goods of a country is summed (through input-output analysis) and then the same is done for all the imported goods. The net-export result is then reached by subtracting the second sum from the first.

Although the OECD as a whole is a net carbon importer, results for individual countries vary widely. One study examining twenty large OECD economies found net carbon exports from Australia, Canada, the Czech Republic, Denmark, Finland, Netherlands, Norway, and Poland; balanced

---

[57] International Energy Agency, 2008.

[58] Rodrik, 2006.

[59] Munksgaard et al., 2009.

[60] This is called multi-regional input-output analysis. See Peters et al., 2011.

carbon trade in Hungary; and net carbon imports into other countries, including the United States, Japan, Korea, and all the largest European economies.[61] Individual country studies confirm this mixed situation. For instance, Sweden, Finland, Norway, and Australia are countries that export a lot more energy in goods than they import, and Spain and Denmark both have a fairly balanced trade.[62]

However, there are drawbacks to this consumption-based approach to determine moral responsibility. We think a more dynamic estimate is needed, which includes the foregone emissions on the global level to which trade specialization gives rise.[63] There are two things that affect the net export of energy in goods: (1) the structure of trade and (2) the energy efficiency of production technologies.[64] If trade balance of CO_2 emissions is calculated, a third important impact comes from the energy system of each country: the compositional effect from having zero-emitting energy carriers like hydropower or nuclear can be very large. If a country having a low-carbon energy system trades with another one that is largely dependent on coal, a pure consumption-based model will blame the low-carbon country for all the emissions made in the coal country for producing the import goods of the low-carbon country. But it will not give the low-carbon country any credit at all for all the foregone emissions on the global scene resulting from its exports of clean products to the coal country. Thus the consumption-based method needs to be complemented by a NEGA-emissions calculation, i.e., the foregone emissions should be factored in, in our view.

With our research question here, "Do we have a lighter industrial structure because our dirty industrial goods are produced elsewhere?" we do not want to allocate moral responsibility for emissions to nations. Instead, we want to know if the *structure of trade* impacts our production structure. We will thus disregard the different technologies used to produce the same product in different countries as well as different energy systems, and focus precisely on the flows of products that have a higher or lower energy intensity of production. This means that the technology factor for each kind of commodity is treated as equal for imports and exports, even though we know they are not in reality. The result will then enable us to isolate how specialization in particular products affects the potential energy intensity of countries. How this trade structure affects the distribution of carbon emissions then depends on the choices about the kind of energy in each country. Thus we can simplify the analysis by measuring the trade flows of energy "heavy" and energy "light" products.

---

[61] Ahmad and Wyckoff, 2003.

[62] Munksgaard et al., 2005; Hertwich et al., 2002; Kander and Lindmark, 2006; Mäenpää and Siikavirta, 2007; Sánchez-Chóliz and Duarte, 2004; Lenzen, 1998.

[63] Kander, 2012.

[64] If net-carbon flows is studied rather than net-energy flows, there is a third factor that has an impact: the energy carrier mix, as some energy carriers emit much CO_2 and others, none.

TABLE 10.4
Net-exported energy embodied in goods, Sweden 1970–2000

	Net exported energy embodied in goods, PJ	Net exported energy as percentage of energy consumption in industry; percent
1970	167	29.9
1987	173	35.5
2000	157	29.0

Source: Kander and Lindmark, 2006.

The main results for Sweden and the Netherlands are provided in tables 10.4 and 10.5.[65]

It is clear that both the Netherlands and Sweden were net exporters of energy embodied in goods. In Sweden the share of net-exported energy in relation to total industrial energy consumption did not change much between 1970 and 2000 and thus did not have any impact on the structure of the Swedish manufacturing industry. The shift toward an energy-lighter production structure was in fact mirrored by a shift toward an energy-lighter consumption structure in Swedish society. In this case, the statement that we live in a service economy and our dirty industrial products are produced elsewhere is incorrect.

The net-exported share for the Netherlands was smaller than in Sweden, but it increased over time, so actually international trade counteracted the decline in Dutch energy intensity. Energy intensity would have fallen *more* without trade, not less. Admittedly, the Netherlands is a net importer of embodied energy from non-OECD (developing countries), mainly in the form of machinery and heavy industry. Nevertheless, this trade with developing countries does not *at all* explain its energy intensity decline after 1980, because the net-exported energy as a share of energy consumption in industry actually increased over the period 1980–2005 (see table 10.5). Therefore the trade with developing countries could not possibly have been the reason behind the decline in energy intensity and the transformation of its economic structure during the third industrial revolution. Instead, Dutch people consumed "energy-lighter" products in 2005 than they did in 1980, as a consequence of the third industrial revolution employing ICT.

For a fuller understanding of the impact from trade on the energy intensity decline after 1970, it would be worth investigating the changes in net exports of energy in goods for Europe as a whole, with the same methods as used for Sweden and the Netherlands, and to specifically look into the trade

---

[65] Kander and Lindmark, 2006; de Graaf, 2011.

TABLE 10.5
Net-exported energy embodied in goods, the Netherlands, 1980–2005

	Net exported energy embodied in goods, PJ	Net exported energy as percentage of energy consumption in industry; percent
1980	57	11.5
1995	62	11.6
2005	104	17.8

Source: de Graaf, 2011.

with non-OECD countries and OECD countries respectively. If Western Europe as a whole experienced declining energy intensities as an effect from trade with non-OECD countries, then of course the displacement hypothesis would be persuasive. It also would be of interest to explore the trade impact on energy intensity further back in time, when energy intensity divergence was much larger. The EKCE pattern found for Western Europe as a whole, but not for individual countries (other than Germany and UK) could be explained by trade flows.

Despite the research issues that remain, our results suggest that there is some development and progress taking place in the relationship between energy consumption and economic growth. Especially after the third industrial revolution, a lowering of energy intensities is possible, even when the global division of labor and international trade is taken into account. This has far-reaching implications for our understanding of energy and growth. It challenges the pessimistic narrative of globalization, and suggests that technology shifts may bring about new patterns of consumption across all nations, and profoundly change the interrelations between energy and growth. How far that can help to alleviate the environmental stress from economic growth is yet to be seen. So far the rate of energy intensity decline has not been able to offset the rate of economic growth, even after 1970, so energy consumption has continued to rise, although at a slower pace. But this goal is getting closer: in per capita terms at least energy consumption stabilized, or grew much slower, than before 1970. In order to dematerialize we would need a much larger energy intensity decline from the third industrial revolution over the next decades. And the challenge is large, as many newly industrialized countries in the world, like China and India, are growing fast on the basis of the development blocks of the second and third industrial revolutions simultaneously. These future challenges will be addressed in the concluding chapter of this book.

CHAPTER ELEVEN

SUMMARY AND IMPLICATIONS
FOR THE FUTURE

IN THIS CHAPTER WE WILL FIRST SUMMARIZE the main results of the book, and then move on to a discussion of what we think can be learned for the future. As historians, the first comes rather more naturally to us than the second; and as we are historians, the reader may also accordingly give rather more credence to the first part of this chapter than the second. Nevertheless, we hold two tenets to be true that can inform contemporary debates about energy transition, and the future of economic growth. First, that societies move on trajectories, not perhaps entirely deterministically, but where what has happened in the past bears a strong influence on paths taken in the future. Second, that we can establish relationships between energy consumption and economic growth, but also note that the character of these relationships is not stable over time. These ideas bind together the two sections of this chapter and indicate the value of looking to the past in our need to anticipate the future.

1. SUMMING UP THE BOOK

BREAKING THE CONSTRAINTS OF THE ORGANIC ECONOMY

It is a central part of our argument that pre-industrial Europe faced energy constraints to economic growth, and was set free from these constraints by the adoption of fossil fuels, first of all coal. We find it hard to imagine anything like modern economic growth occurring without this, and we view the transition to fossil fuels both as a necessary condition, and an enabling factor *leading* to modern growth. The energy constraints of pre-industrial Europe had been of two kinds: land area and power. Around 95 percent of aggregated primary energy consumption depended on organic raw materials, requiring vast areas for its production, only achieving what were by later standards low levels of productivity.[1] The only sources for motive power were human muscles, draft animals, and water- and windmills, all with low power. Europe was especially hard hit by these constraints because

---

[1] Of course, England was already escaping from this constraint in the sixteenth century, so even at this early stage the 95 percent total for Western Europe would have been in decline.

of the relatively low land productivity compared to, for instance, parts of east Asia, differences that stemmed from natural conditions like soil quality and climate (temperatures and precipitation). Nevertheless, over the period 1650–1800 the European population doubled, and land availability per capita fell. This stimulated an intensification of land use, and some increase in the productivity of agricultural land, but this was still insufficient to free the economy from its constraints. Instead, the population increase gradually led to a situation where food and wood prices went up and food and fuel consumption per capita fell, since energy supply was unable to meet the rising demand. The two most successful countries of this period, England and the Netherlands, are notable for their lack of dependency on vegetable energy carriers, both using coal and peat; and their ability to generate income out of an extensive commerce, depending on wind and giving access to the raw materials of the Baltic and the Atlantic world. These two countries also saw perhaps the most extensive development of labor-saving devices which also effectively saved land.

The European economy was finally released from its energy constraints by first shifting from "areal" to "punctiform" energy sources: coal mined from seams beneath the surface rather than requiring the great expanses of photosynthesizing plants. In the nineteenth century this transition occurred on a massive scale, raising per capita consumption. Coal saves land, since it is stored solar energy, delivered in a very concentrated form. British coal reserves were relatively shallow and easily accessible, and situated close to large settlements or water facilitating movement of coal, a very major advantage. The dynamic toward coal use already under way in the sixteenth century shifted the population toward the coalfields and set England and eventually Europe on a path toward relatively high energy intensity at an early stage. By itself, this would not have produced modern conditions of growth, but created the context for the emergence of the development block around steam engines that would lead to capital intensive development.

ENERGY AND MODERN ECONOMIC GROWTH

The industrial revolution was the first in a series of technological shifts that has made up modern economic growth and broke with the old organic regime of very low or negligible per capita income growth. During the industrial revolution one macro-innovation, the steam engine, freed the organic economy from another of its constraints: that of low power. We argue that the steam engine is one of the most important innovations in the history of mankind. For the first time in history it was possible to reliably and in a controlled form convert heat to motion, equipping people with inanimate "energy slaves" (machines). Steam engines enabled a large concentration of energy in time and space; they were more powerful than previous sources of kinetic energy and much easier to control. Steam engines saved labor, and initiated a capital-deepening growth path. One worker could be in command of ever greater amounts of power. This capital-deepening growth was almost wholly reliant on fossil fuels and eventually, although by no means instantly, led not just to increased incomes, but set in motion a dynamic that has continued to raise incomes. Coal consumption rose rapidly.

The industrial revolution started in England, as the only country at that point in time where it made sense to develop the steam engine as an economically useful innovation. The first engines had such low thermal efficiency (less than 1 percent) that they could only be placed at pitheads of coal mines, where their fuel was virtually free. Ironically, perhaps, important further innovation in efficiency was driven in the south-west of England, developing the engines for use in valued ore mines, even though locally coal was scarce (yet still very cheap in European terms). The context of a more expensive energy supply and competitive pressure encouraged further innovation in an environment initially created by the cheapness of coal. For the wider diffusion of the engine into factory production, only Britain had the perfect combination of high wages and low energy prices, which stimulated the substitution of labor, at first in the textile industry where such pressures toward mechanization had already been present but had harnessed water power. More broadly, the capital-intense path and diffusion of the steam engine was also facilitated by important developments in iron, to create a first "development block" stimulating economic growth and the further diffusion of coal. Without cheap coal there could not have been cheap iron and steel production, and without cheap iron and steel the costs of capital would have been much higher, with a strong detrimental impact on industrialization. We believe that the commonly used method for assessing the impact of technological change, the "social savings approach," misses the dynamic effects of these processes, as well as underestimating the constraints that afflicted the pre-industrial economy.

Throughout the book we have argued that energy is more important to economic growth than generally believed among economists. One reason for economists thinking that energy does not matter much to growth may be that they stress overall efficiency gains to the degree that they miss the "capital deepening" effect that has had an essential role in raising labor productivity. This has been closely linked to the increase in the use of machinery, depending on cheap energy supplies. Skepticism about the importance of energy is also a reflection of the way models of economic growth are set up, where low-cost shares for energy mean that energy can only play a very modest role in explaining growth, if it is even included in the modeling, which it rarely is. Greater employment, or efficiency in the use of a factor that does not cost very much in the first place, cannot, in these models, account for very much of economic growth.

Alternative models, allowing for biased technical change, may produce very different results, as demonstrated in appendix A, where we show for

TABLE 11.1
Decomposition of energy consumption in Europe 1820–2008, annual growth rates

	Energy consumption	Population	Income per capita	Energy intensity
1820–1870	1.86	0.71	0.83	0.32
1870–1910	2.20	0.79	1.16	0.26
1910–1950	0.51	0.45	0.85	−0.79
1950–1970	3.45	0.72	4.10	−1.39
1970–2008	0.53	0.33	1.98	−1.77
1820–2008	1.54	0.60	1.48	−0.53

one developed country in Europe that energy played the largest role for economic growth up until the second part of the twentieth century, after which other factors became relatively more important, although energy still played a significant role. The economies of the most developed countries now grow more on the basis of information and ICT capital than on capital associated with increasing consumption of energy. Still, many other countries in the world, like China and India, in their process of catch-up with the West, are undergoing the second and third industrial revolutions simultaneously, moving to much more extensive consumption of cars, electric equipment, and computers when these technologies have long been established. Their growth remains much more highly dependent on energy, and global energy demands consequently are still rapidly rising, even though these countries can benefit from the transfer of more efficient technology.

While European GDP grew fifty-five times over the last two hundred years, energy productivity doubled, so total energy consumption "only" increased twenty-seven times. The annual rate of growth in energy consumption was 1.54 percent over the period 1820–2008, while energy intensity declined by 0.53 percent annually (see table 11.1). Generally energy intensity went up during the nineteenth century and declined during the twentieth century. The rate of energy intensity decline varied over the twentieth century, and was highest in the period 1970–2008, when it declined by an annual 1.77 percent.

ECONOMIC ENERGY EFFICIENCY

It took almost one century of modern economic growth for Europe to be set on a course where the aggregate economic energy efficiency actually increased, as shown in figure 11.1. The Coal-Steam-Iron development block

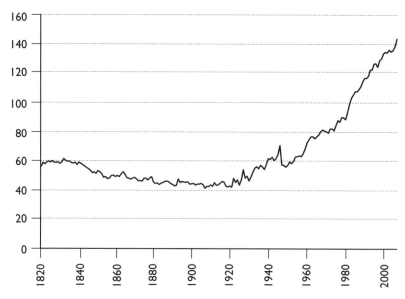

Figure 11.1. Energy productivity in Western Europe, 1820–2008 (GDP/MJ)

was highly energy expanding, indicated both by rapidly increasing energy consumption and by falling energy productivity in the core countries (England and Germany), even though steam engines became very much more efficient over time. The structure of especially the British and German economies underwent such major change in this period when they produced iron, steel, and machinery for the rest of Europe, both in terms of structure and population size, that on balance energy productivity declined in Western Europe.[2]

However, as we see in figure 11.1 there has been an impressive increase in energy productivity during the twentieth century, and this sped up from the 1970s. We argue that the increase in economic energy efficiency in the twentieth century was due to the qualities of the development blocks that dominated economic growth in that period. In relative terms, the twentieth-century development blocks were much more energy-saving than the Steam-Coal-Iron Block of the nineteenth century. While on balance the overall effect of the ICE-Oil Block was still energy-expanding, both the Electricity Block of the second industrial revolution, and even more so, the ICT Block of the late twentieth century, offered much stronger energy-saving options. We show that contrary to the expectations of many, the energy efficiency improvements after the 1970s were not so much driven by the transition to

[2] We may include Belgium among these energy-intense economies, although its aggregate impact was small.

a service economy, but more by the ICT revolution, which affected both the structural composition of the manufacturing sector, and the energy intensity of the old, traditional heavy industries.[3]

It is not yet a settled question to what degree Europe experienced a faster dematerialization after 1970 as an effect from outsourcing of energy-intensive production to less developed countries, and more research is needed. We demonstrate however that certain developed countries, like Sweden and the Netherlands, exhibit strongly falling energy intensities after the 1970s, despite still continuing to be large net *exporters* of energy-intensive goods to the rest of the world. We thus claim that the third industrial revolution is different from previous technological shifts, and did cause real improvements in the energy efficiency of the whole economy. Hence the apparent—although still limited—"dematerialization" in Europe in recent decades is not just a matter of shifting the problems to other parts of the world.

ENERGY TRANSITIONS

Overall the energy system of Europe became much more reliant on fossil fuels in the nineteenth century, and traditional energy carriers declined in relative importance (although they continue to play an important role in absolute terms), as shown in figure 11.2. The coal transition in Europe took place in three geographical "clubs," where distance to coal fields (transportation costs) and economic development played a fundamental role.

In this book we have sought to provide an interpretation of the processes by which energy transitions have occurred in Europe, emanating from the forces of market suction and market widening in development blocks.

In the steam-coal-iron block, the very first stage consisted primarily of market suction between coal and steam engines. Coal is highly suitable as a fuel for steam engines, and is therefore a complementary resource to those steam engines. This created suction on the market for coal, although during the eighteenth century steam engines consumed only a very small part of the total coal supply. Nevertheless they helped maintain its relatively low price as the use of steam engines expanded the number of accessible seams. In the second stage, when steam engines were improved, especially with high pressure engines that were lighter, smaller, and more efficient, they became part of a transport revolution, with railways and steamships. The continued suction on the coal market on the supply side from the more widespread use of engine technology was eclipsed by the market-widening effects from the fall in the price of coal stimulating demand. Drastic price falls made coal widely

---

[3] Of course, this story has varied considerably from country to country, depending on the character of their industrial sector.

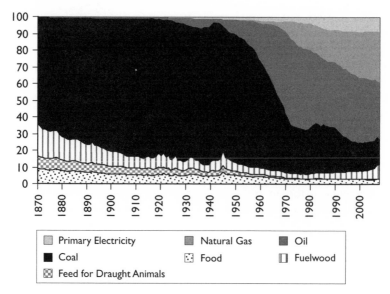

Figure 11.2. Energy consumption shares in Europe, 1800–2009

accessible in Europe. This was a phase of supply push, or "market widening" for coal as a consequence of the development of the steam engines and innovations in metallurgy producing the cheap iron used to construct them.

In the twentieth century, the two big new energy carriers were oil and electricity (although both emerging, of course, in the late nineteenth century). The first uses of oil were, just as in the case of coal, simply replacing another energy carrier (oil lamps replaced candles, wood sticks, or rushlights). Similarly, the first use of electricity was merely substitution (electric light and electric cooking). With the ICE-Oil block, at first market suction between internal combustion engines and oil played an important role in developing the oil market, but after the Second World War, all European countries almost simultaneously experienced a large oil transition as a consequence of market widening for oil. Huge oil tankers (powered by diesel engines) led to drastically falling costs for shipping crude oil and lowered its price on the market. This widened the use of oil from applications without substitutes, like internal combustion engines, to other uses, like low temperature heating of buildings, where there were many substitutes. The drastic price falls of key components of the Electricity Block and the ICT Block have also been essential in the wide diffusion of these technologies in society (market widening) and their revolutionary impact in empowering people.

Transitions were not simple affairs. This helps us address a counterfactual question. We are not deterministic in saying that there needs to be a particular relation between energy and the economy. On the contrary, our argument is indeed that energy and GDP have different relations over time, but this is the effect from the dominant development blocks of the time period. Could we have had an industrial revolution similar to the one we had without coal? If coal for instance had been more expensive, could we not have had a less coal-intensive development and increased the efficiency of renewables more than we did? We have argued that transitions both to fossil fuels and to engines that could transform heat to motion were necessary to the process of modern growth, and that an expansion and improvement in the efficiency of use of traditional energy carriers could not have developed a modern economy, even if there certainly was room for expansion of output within a traditional regime. Indeed, as we show, during the industrial revolution we did substantially increase the absolute consumption and efficiency of traditional energy carriers. But to have anything near the globalized world we see today it was necessary to invent engines that could transform abundant fossil fuels to motive power.

But did that fossil fuel have to be coal? Could we then not imagine development "leapfrogging" to more energy-efficient development blocks (as we have seen emerging, with hindsight)? Could we not have skipped the coal-iron-steam block and jumped directly to oil and internal combustion engines? This seems unlikely to us. We do not think it is likely that the internal combustion engine would have been invented directly without the steam engine first. The same goes for the possibility of jumping directly to using a secondary energy carrier like electricity. Likewise we could not have jumped directly to the ICT block without first having the electricity block in place. To build a development block, various elements had to be in place; resources, the requisite knowledge and technology to exploit them, the right balance of relative prices, and effective transportation networks. In Europe, oil was only present in large quantities far from major sources of demand; Polish Galicia, Romania, or on a much larger scale, the southern Caucasus. Would these regions ever have had the incentive or capacity to develop engine technology, motor vehicles, or tankers out of the circumstances of their pre-industrial economies, exporting this model to other parts of the world (the fields were initially developed for lighting, mimicking the advance of coal gas lighting)? Similarly, in the perhaps more propitious circumstances of mountain-based hydropower in the Alps, Scandinavia or Spain,[4] would we have seen a leap into the necessary transmission networks, batteries, and engines required to operate a manufacturing and transportation network using electricity, especially without the developments in metallurgy and engineering fostered by the coal development block?

Of course, there are many imponderables in the technologies that might have developed should things have been different. It is not so hard to imag-

---

[4] No other regions of Europe have thus far succeeded in developing the large-scale use of hydropower; hitherto, the flows provided by mountain environments have proven essential to extensive use of the technology.

ine, for example, a still coal-fired world running electric cars, even if it is hard to imagine a world of electric appliances in every home and a vast metallurgical industry emerging from mountain hydro-installations in a world without fossil fuels. If we remove oil from the story, we would then not have had cheap diesel ships reducing transport cost to a minimum, and possibly not airplanes unless it became possible to produce high specification liquid fuels from coal (as low-grade ones were produced in the exigency of wartime conditions in Europe). Without the diesel tanker and freighter and the aircraft industry, the world would indeed have been very different and less integrated.

Thus, given the distribution of resources and knowledge in the eighteenth-century world economy, it seems very unlikely that the conditions would have arisen for the development of large-scale use of "alternative" modern energy carriers without coal, even if there is no reason to think that Europe could not have continued on a track of ingenious technological advance that might incorporate some use of energy carriers that would became significant in the twentieth century (albeit with rather lesser incentives for labor saving than the coal-steam-iron block presented).

2. THINKING ABOUT THE FUTURE

Our challenges as global citizens in today's world are indeed large. Multiple challenges in relation to energy exist. There is the prospect of scarcities in key carriers such as oil, with the possibility that we have reached "peak oil" at least in regard to easily tapped reserves of petroleum; and the uneven global distribution of more plentiful reserves of coal and natural gas. Irrespective of balancing supply and demand for the whole globe, there is still much potential for geopolitical tension, and individual nations will want to develop energy regimes with regard to their security. Relatively new or hitherto little used technological options, whether renewable energy sources, nuclear power, or shale oil and gas, are all controversial in different ways given their cost, associated risk, and environmental impact. Currently overshadowing other concerns is the major role the combustion of fossil fuels plays in driving global warming, with potentially catastrophic impacts, most especially in poorer parts of the world. The fossil fuel with the greatest reserves, coal, is precisely the one that presents the greatest risk to the stability of the climate. This presents us with a range of dilemmas and choices, and also with a considerable requirement for urgency in our response; we certainly know as historians that energy transitions take time. But the nature and scale of any transition is a highly contested issue, raising major ethical questions about the distribution of responsibility and costs, moral hazard from unequal exposure to risk, and in the face of reasonable demands for a more equal (and generally higher) standard of living across the globe.

Historians' business—very obviously—is not the future. On the other hand, historians do make the very long-term their business, and also questions of trajectory, path dependency, and the analysis of the consequences of choices, both foreseen and unforeseen. We are often, quite reasonably, asked in our professional lives what implications we think our arguments about the past relationship of energy and the economy will have for the future. In this final section of the book we look to the lessons of the past for our current dilemmas, not to provide predictions or prescriptions, but to highlight issues that a long-term perspective raises, and to consider the consequences if the trends we have identified continue.

LIMITS TO GROWTH

This book is primarily about the relationship between energy and economic growth in Europe. We have seen the figures for the results of two centuries of modern growth; a fifty-five-fold rise in income for Western Europe, and a twenty-seven-fold rise in energy. The two trends are clearly linked, whilst not moving step-by-step. Throughout the twentieth century, and with particular urgency since the Second World War, people have asked: can this growth really continue, especially when built upon finite supplies of raw materials? In the last forty years, most famously since the publication of the *Limits to Growth* report of the Club of Rome in 1972, the primary problem has not been perceived as an end to growth in itself, but the problem of *too much growth*, that will burden us with excessive environmental costs. At the time this was imagined as "pollution" with a particular impact on human health, but today global warming, mass extinction, and crossing the thresholds of fundamental "planetary boundaries" loom as greater dangers.[5] It is now argued that we have entered the "anthropocene," an epoch when humanity have become leading drivers of the fate of the whole earth system, underpinned of course by our energy consumption.[6]

So to return to this question from a historical perspective: are there limits to growth? It is clear that our experience of modernity hitherto, with its capacity for tapping new resources and energy transition, is that limits have not yet been reached and would seem to be a relatively distant prospect.[7] We can, however, shed some light on the consequences of "business as usual" for most of the past century; continuing to generate our energy from fossil

[5] Rockström et al., 2009.

[6] Steffen et al., 2007.

[7] This judgment depends of course on one's perception of "distance." In 1850s' Britain, some considered it highly alarming that coal reserves were predicted to last only another 170 years, a time-span well beyond the concerns of most policymakers today. Nevertheless, this length of time is now only just over two average life-spans in the developed world, and is likely to become less than this as life expectancy rises.

fuels. Given expected rates of income growth and population growth, how much would energy intensity have to fall to keep emissions stable, or lower them to an acceptable target level; and how does this compare with what has been achieved before?

The forecasts by the U.S. Energy Information Administration for world energy use and CO_2 emissions between 2008 and 2035 use the Kaya identity (used in this book in chapter 8) to propose that CO_2 emissions will rise at an annual rate of 1.3 percent, despite energy intensity falling at −1.8 percent per year. This is because per capita income is projected to increase by an annual 2.5 percent worldwide, and population by 0.9 percent per year. Most of this economic growth will take place in the developing world, in non-OECD countries. The impact from decarbonization is not expected to be able to counteract this in any substantial way. The European development is forecasted to be somewhat more sustainable than this and actually lead to an annual decline in CO_2 emissions by −0.1 percent per year (see table 11.2), with a stronger effect from transitions to non-carbon-emitting fuels.

The EIA base their estimate for future emissions up until 2035 on the historical emissions between 1990 and 2008, and we can ask ourselves how these predictions relate to the figures we have been able to provide for the historical development of Europe in this book. First we can note that the forecasts of energy-intensity decline for total non-OECD countries are on the optimistic side, since the rate of decline in Europe has never been that high in any historical period. This does not mean that the prediction is unrealistic, but it will require a stronger positive effect from the third industrial revolution in the following decades than witnessed up until now. On the other hand, such a stronger impact is not expected in their forecast for OECD Europe, where the rates of energy-intensity decline are actually expected to slow down relative to 1970–2008 (where it was −1.77 percent; see table 11.1). Given that energy intensity in many OECD and non-OECD countries has already converged to a significant degree, these divergent predictions seem surprising and inconsistent to us.[8] It would be preferable in our view to base future predictions on long-run historical data and analyses of the underlying causes of change, of the kind that we have provided in this book.

If the EIA predictions will turn out right, this would contribute to very high levels of warming. If we were to reach stabilization of global emissions with the forecasted population increase and income increase, and the predicted decarbonization of energy supply, then energy intensity would have to decline by an astonishing 3.1 percent per year, almost double as fast as in

[8] Some of the non-OECD countries, such as China and India, witnessed a very rapid decline in energy intensities in the 1970–2006 period, while others such as Brazil almost had a flat curve without any reductions, see Henriques and Kander, 2010. The end result is that they converge on levels of 8–9 MJ/1990 international dollars, which is close to the European levels of 6–7 MJ/international dollars.

TABLE 11.2
Decomposition of expected carbon emissions, 2008–2035 (%)

	Population (POP)	Income per person (GDP/POP)	Energy intensity of economic activity(E/GDP)	Carbon intensity of energy supply (CO_2/E)	CO_2 emissions
OECD Europe	0.20	1.60	−1.30	−0.60	−0.10
Total OECD	0.40	1.70	−1.50	−0.40	0.20
Total non-OECD	0.90	3.60	−2.20	−0.20	2.00
Total world	0.90	2.50	−1.80	−0.20	1.30

Source: Calculated based on projections from EIA, World Energy Projection System Plus 2011, retrieved from http://www.eia.gov/forecasts/ieo/table18.cfm. The sums do not completely add up to the CO_2 emissions in these calculations; there is a residual, which is never more than 0.1 percent.

Europe 1970–2008. This indeed cannot be expected to occur just by itself through regular market forces. Political intervention will be necessary.

In the case of physical limits to growth imposed by resource availability that so preoccupied scholars in the decade after the Second World War, we can say again: on a global level, these have not been reached.[9] Local resource exhaustion (as well as simple marginal price increases) is a normal experience that has been resolved by transition, trade, and technological change. Of course, now that the economy has become so much more globalized, the idea of physical limits to growth remains plausible; the number of frontiers of resource extraction has shrunk (at least in a spatial sense), although they are not exhausted. However, the limits of energy per se do not yet seem that close. It is perhaps more likely that other resources, such as valuable metals or fresh water, will become scarce first (although our capacity to obtain these is partly related to processing and transport costs, which would make them an energy question again). What we can observe as historians is that the short period of modern growth, viewed from the totality of human history, or even the very much shorter timescale of settled and urban societies within Europe, is a startling aberration. Over most of our history as a species, per capita income has varied but little. As we have argued in the first part of this book, this experience was closely related to the limited capacity for populations to obtain energy from the areas of land that they could affordably exploit. Given that we also view the prospects for a complete "dematerialization" of the economy to be small, we must suppose that a return to the "steady state" of income, albeit at a historically high level, is to be expected at some point; as the classical economists of the late eighteenth

[9] See for example Ordway, 1956; Putnam, 1953; Political and Economic Planning, 1955.

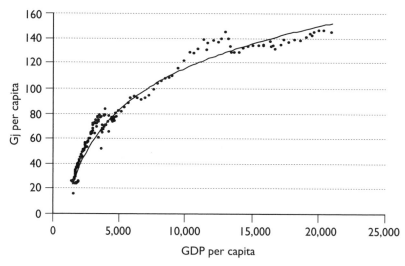

Figure 11.3. Relationship between per capita GDP and per capita energy
Note: The interpolation is done through a log regression. On the vertical
axis we find per capita energy (in GJ), and on the horizontal axis,
per capita GDP in Western Europe in 1990 Geary-Khamis dollars PPP.

and early nineteenth centuries supposed. Viewing the dynamic of modern
growth it is however hard to envisage how this would occur. It is equally
difficult to envisage a millennium of modern growth rates.

What we can say is that even within the short modern era there is no
fixed ratio between energy consumption and GDP growth. Technological
shifts and industrial revolutions have changed the relationship over time.
This in itself indicates that modeling their continuing relationship over only
a short period of time historically speaking (one or two centuries, or less)
using fixed relationships is unlikely to yield much useful information, and
has no reasonable basis in our historical experience. These vary both over
time and in paths that particular countries take, as indicated in figure 11.3,
plotting the historical relationship between GDP per capita and per capita
energy consumption. Of course, these differences partly reflect the fact that
different countries reach certain income levels at different points and with
a different technological mix, but the point about different trajectories remains. Certainly as GDP got higher, so did energy consumption, and we can
be confident that this will continue.[10] But as this is not a linear relationship,

[10] Neumayer, 2004; Huntington, 2005.

but a dynamic and evolving process, we would expect it to continue to be so in the future.

THINKING ABOUT THE FUTURE IN THE PAST

If history teaches us anything, it should teach us to be wary about forecasts; and it also teaches us that only relatively infrequently do we take much notice of whether earlier predictions turned out to be true. Certainly, worrying about energy futures is not something new under the sun.

Fears about imminent shortages of wood have been recurrent in European history, and have sparked lively debate among historians as to the reality of scarcity, or whether such claims were merely a disguise for other interests seeking economic advantage. Predictions, usually made only in a very general way, can be found all over Europe from the late fifteenth century and revived with particular vehemence in the eighteenth century; an age where we can say with some confidence that per capita wood supplies were indeed falling, even if this does not resolve the question of what constitutes "scarcity." As early as 1611, an obscure English pamphleteer and booster for the planting of trees, Arthur Standish, wondered whether (as some said) coal could provide a long-term substitute for firewood. His answer was negative: wood grew back after being felled, but a coal mine, once exhausted, was gone forever. On this logic of sustainability, Standish rejected a future for coal. He was spectacularly wrong, as it turned out; but more from imperfect information than a failing in logic.[11]

This was a precocious observation on the finitude of fossil fuels. In the eighteenth century, economic writers were more likely to note how coal gave Britain an advantage by abolishing the land constraint, but without yet fully grasping the implications of that advantage. The German writer von Justi, for example, noted in the 1750s that "a northern land which has much mineral coal will always, in relation to its other natural endowments, be able to be far more peopled, than another, that is not provided with these subterranean goods of nature, which take up no space on the surface." Relatively soon after this, however, John Williams, a Welsh geologist, was already raising the prospect of "peak coal" in 1789. From then on, predictions would attempt more solid quantification of reserves and rates of consumption. The most famous and influential of a long line of prognosticators of coal reserves in the nineteenth century was the economist William Stanley Jevons in his book, *The Coal Question* of 1865. Jevons was not so much preoccupied with absolute supplies, as with the prospect that the much greater mineral reserves of the United States would lead to it eclipsing the economic

[11] Standish, 1611; Warde, 2006.

lead of Britain as the costs of extraction rose. A Parliamentary commission that examined the question in response to his work concluded that several centuries' of coal remained, although they greatly underestimated future consumption. Current energy predictors should note that Jevons pondered whether oil might become a significant fuel of the future—he wrote just as the Pennsylvania oilfields were taking off—but concluded that there was insufficient information to say anything useful on the issue. He also suggested that a government faced with dwindling coal supplies should at least ensure that it did not also have a very large national debt to bequeath to future generations; an early intuition of the thinking behind ideas of "natural capital" and genuine savings theory.

Once economic growth was clearly linked to the consumption of oil, then the same fears for the future arose. The idea of peak oil was coined in the framework of national energy supplies by the oil industry analyst M. King Hubbert in the 1950s, predicting maximum rates of oil production for the United States between 1966 and 1971. As it turned out Hubbert was right, and government predictions that placed the date of the U.S. "peak" much later were wrong. The future of reserves and the necessity of a transition, partly in reaction to pollution, was a major theme for discussion even before the "oil crisis" began in October 1973. During the 1970s, a very wide range of predictions from inside and outside the industry were made as a response to what was known as the energy crisis, despite the obviously political and at times speculative causes of short-term price spikes. It was then common to predict that serious energy shortages would occur by the 1990s, or in the case of the Saudi oil minister, the necessity of a UN-based "planetary resources mechanism . . . by the year 2000 when shortages are expected to peak."[12]

It turned out that such doomsaying was wide of the mark; oil prices fell and remained at historic lows during the 1980s and '90s. A perception arose that predicting peak oil or fossil fuel shortages (meaning rising prices, rather than no gas at the gas station) was part and parcel of the fossil fuel economy itself (which as we have just shown is true). But the date of the global peak always seemed to regress into the future. Today, there is no disagreement over the existence of the point of peak oil in principle, but some controversy exists over when it will take place and what will be the subsequent effects on the world economy. Some scientists claim that peak oil has already been passed some years ago,[13] while others claim that we cannot see any immediate signs of it, and that we need not worry about oil depletion for many years.[14] The International Energy Agency (IEA) changed its position on the matter between 2009 and 2010, becoming more pessimistic in the 2010

[12] Stork, 1975, 288; Vietor, 1984, 195–99; Parra, 2004, 188; Nemetz, 1981, i.
[13] Zittel and Schindler, 2007.
[14] Smil, 2008b.

press release report and claiming that peak oil had actually already been reached in 2006.[15]

PEAK OIL TODAY

Those who argue that peak oil is here now base their conclusions on the fact that the discoveries of new giant oil fields have declined since the 1960s, and world production of oil has not managed to keep pace with the increasing demand in recent times, resulting in a steep increase in the price of crude oil.[16] If peak oil had not been reached or at least was very close, the large oil producers would have increased production in response to substantially increasing prices, it is argued. Those who do not believe that peak oil is imminent base their argument on historical examples of previous peak oil prophesies that turned out to be wrong. They rightly point to the uncertainties in estimates of remaining oil reserves, and the fact that past innovations in oil discoveries and production have enabled a much higher recovery rate from the oil fields over time, arguing that there is no reason to believe that this kind of innovation will cease. We still think that the evidence of falling rates of new giant oil fields being discovered speaks rather strongly in favor of peak oil being near (if not reached already). And another sign of peak oil is the long-run development of world market price for oil.[17] Since 2008 the real price of oil has risen to around 100 dollars per barrel, levels found in previous price spikes in 1979 or right back at the beginning of the oil industry in the late 1860s. The price is historically high, despite a period of global economic slowdown, and no obvious political causes pushing prices up. Nevertheless the current energy market is clearly in flux, with fracking and shale oil leading to dramatic declines in natural gas and oil prices in North America. This is likely to affect the entire hydrocarbon market.

Not only is the timing of peak oil disputed, but also its consequences. Peak oil does not mean that oil production will cease in a couple of years. Rather, it means that half of the oil reserves has been depleted, which still leaves us with plenty of oil. But that does not imply that oil will last as many years as it took for the peak to be reached, simply because the size of the world economy now being run on oil is massively bigger after the peak than it was before. However, rising oil prices as production levels fall will also

[15] IEA, 2010; 2009.

[16] Smil, 2008b, 117, estimated reserves of new giants about 270 Gb in 1960s and only about 30 Gb during the 1990s. "b" denotes barrels and is the normal way of measuring oil. One barrel equals roughly 159 liters. Just over six barrels of heavy crude oil weighs one metric ton, while 8.5 barrels of lighter crude oil are needed for one metric ton.

[17] Historical Crude Oil prices, 1861 to Present, ChartsBin.com, viewed February 29, 2012; http://chartsbin.com/view/oau.

stimulate innovations and transitions to other energy carriers. More dismal authors claim that the price of oil (and energy more generally) will rise so rapidly after peak oil that the world economy will collapse. Production and transportation will almost cease and violent conflicts over the remaining oil reserves will lead to disasters. New energy carriers will never be able to replace oil, because of oil's prominent position in the world energy system. The line of division between pessimists and optimists in the peak oil debate is clearly linked to their position taken on technological advance and rate of innovation in general. Some extreme peak oil prophets even subscribe to the idea that the rate of innovations peaked long ago, and that the "major technical branches of the world tree of ideas" have already been explored.[18]

In recent years, of course, attention has focused more on the process of anthropogenic global warming and scenarios of climate change related to growth. Curiously, perhaps, most attention has been lavished on the accuracy of the climate models, rather than the economic predictions to which they are related. More reliable energy reserve statistics are collected by the International Energy Authority, founded as a reaction to the crisis of 1973. Although arguments about peak oil remain current, even greater interest is now shown in the question: what kind of conditions in the future might facilitate energy transitions that reduce carbon emissions? And what kind of implications might this have for growth?[19] It is to this debate that we now turn our attention.

3. SOME REMARKS ABOUT THE FUTURE

In full knowledge of the historical tradition of most forecasts turning out to be wrong, we would still like to make some remarks about the future on the basis of our understanding of change in the past.

TURNING BACK TO THE ORGANIC ECONOMY IS LIKELY TO BE COSTLY AND IMPEDE GROWTH AND WELFARE

Current estimates of the costs of transition to a low carbon society range from it being of net benefit to global GDP, while others suggest costs as much as 11 percent.[20] We doubt that these estimates take really everything into account and model the economy in a dynamic way, which obviously is very hard to do. One perspective on the costs of transition is that in pre-

---

[18] Huebner, 2005.
[19] Stern, 2006; Garnaut, 2011.
[20] Tavoni and Tol, 2010; Mundaca et al., 2013; Stern, 2006.

fossil fuel societies of the nineteenth century, the energy costs amounted to half or more of total GDP. This means that at that point in time half of all the efforts that produced some value on the market were devoted simply to providing people with their basic energy needs, and consequently material welfare was not very high. Naturally the situation today is different, because we have a knowledge pool that can partly compensate for natural resources, but there are far more people on earth, and we do not know how far this compensation of knowledge can reach.

The Necessary Technology Shift Is "Against the Wind"

The perspective of industrial revolutions and development blocks driving them suggests that all previous energy transitions have been closely linked to one or two macro-innovations forming the core of the development block. Initially the strong complementarity between an innovation and its related energy carrier drove the transition and stimulated growth. The positive impact on growth and economic welfare continued in the next phase, as transport revolutions, economies of scale, and miniaturization then reduced costs for the new technology, further expanding its societal impact. In other words, there were major economic incentives for the transition once it got under way, at both an individual and societal level; the carrier provided either greater services, improved efficiency, or both, a "win-win" situation where the transition had a following wind rather than working "against the wind." The currently proposed transition to alleviate problems of climate change or fossil fuel scarcity have none of these advantages; they essentially propose to change the primary energy carriers, but not the end services. They are not associated with the revolutions in transportation, connectivity, communication, and scale that have driven the expansion of coal and oil use, and electricity, or even ICT. This suggests that they will not occur from consumer demand or competition on the supply side, but require a re-framing of the markets and infrastructure by which energy is delivered.

The NEGA-Watt Is the Best Watt

We believe that the future must rely heavily on more efficient use of energy; the "NEGA-Watt is the best Watt";[21] (the NEGA-Watt is the negative watt, in other words, the energy saved). This energy efficiency increase may become a reality in the second phase of the ICT development block, in the next fifty years. First we would expect an even stronger impact on infrastructure;

[21] Lovins, 1985.

that ICT will be more integrated in every aspect of transport and communication and in all buildings. A wide range of feasible applications exist already, so called smart houses and smart grids, and many more will be invented over the years. Second, a merger with old, established technologies is likely to take place. The railway system of the first industrial revolution was electrified during the second phase of the second industrial revolution and some ICT is applied to it already, but much more is expected and needed in order to cope with the huge information and operational problems of the railway systems of today. Likewise, the electricity network is not yet well adjusted to the special demands that computers have of absolutely even and reliable current provision.[22] Third, we are likely to see entirely new applications of ICT, maybe in conjunction with emerging technologies like nanotechnology and other materials technology.

However, given the lag in replacement and development of capital, a transition adequate to current challenges should begin now; they are unlikely to be delivered without intervention by a market and financial system rocked by recent crisis. In the long run, too much caution in investment is a false economy. High-tech solutions can and must partly offset the otherwise troubling prospect of a drastic lowering of energy consumption per capita, which could be the consequence of returning to the constraints of the organic economy. Of course, improvements in technical efficiency may need to be complemented by other adjustment mechanisms as well, like changes in values and behavior. The historical record on this count is not promising; there is little evidence of voluntary behaviorial change on a large scale to challenges of scarcity and environmental damage in the past.

WE HAVE TO THINK ABOUT REBOUND AND DYNAMICS IN THE ECONOMY

When we talk about efficiency, we must always return to Jevons: "[It] is wholly a confusion of ideas to suppose that the economical use of fuel is equivalent to a diminished consumption. The very contrary is true."[23] This perhaps stated a case with greater certainty than he could really demonstrate. But the risk of rebound is real. We explained in the introduction that the full direct and indirect effects of rebound are difficult, and perhaps impossible to calculate, although it can be done in terms of specific technologies in particular, limited circumstances. We have found strong evidence that in the case of particular technologies and their associated carriers, efficiency improvement has led to considerably greater uptake and in the long-run rises in energy consumption. This was a strong characteristic of the develop-

[22] Galvin and Yeager, 2009.
[23] Jevons, 1866.

ment block of the first industrial revolution, where great gains in efficiency within energy-intense sectors promoted rapid growth and a structural shift in economic activity in favor of those sectors. If we analyze efficiency, rebound, and the elasticity of demand at only a very localized level, in regard to particular uses of individual technologies, or alternatively, at a "whole economy" level, we miss much of the real dynamics of change. Naturally the dynamics may go in the other way too, so that energy savings from particular technologies may have very far-reaching dynamic effects in the economy, as in the ICT. These issues should be high on the policymaking and research agenda, for both ethical and economic reasons.[24]

Technology Often Develops in Niches and Networks

We stated in the introduction that we were not attempting to write a history of technological inventiveness, but that *innovation* played a major part in our story. How and why did particular innovations gain economic traction, in some cases becoming the core innovations of development blocks? As many others have observed, this takes time. It is only a surprise to those who do not closely examine history that what with hindsight become marvelous and seemingly essential inventions often show a stuttering early progress. Often the potential of prototypes is uncertain, the technology unreliable, repair difficult, and expertise limited. It often requires particular "niche" markets for technological potential to be realized and refinements and learning achieved that allow an innovation that has only very localized advantages to go on to achieve general success.

Equally, as development blocks are put in place, there are many aspects of co-ordination and complementary goods and services that have to be provided at the level of wider networks. The construction of infrastructure, often facilitated or directed by the state, is an obvious example (road, electricity, pipeline networks and so on). The integration of different parts of the production and distribution process, operating with important economies of scale, have historically been highly significant for the establishment of development blocks.

Policymakers would do well to consider what kind of institutional frameworks will foster the kinds of innovation and system-building required to achieve energy transition. Many technologies that subsequently have become key to particular sectors have been reliant on an institutional framework that permitted localized niches for their slow emergence, and some kind of protection, whether intentional or not. Enforcing competition and prying open niches to expose (relative) newcomers to established competitors may not be to our long-term benefit. Equally, a resilient energy transition

---

[24] Sorrell, 2010; Herring and Sorrell, 2008.

may require fostering temporary inefficiencies and allowing a diversity of energy systems. Energy policy always has been, and will remain, a contested area where few major developments have been self-evidently seen as good from the start. In that regard, it would certainly be naïve to expect the future to be much different from the past, and that any particular group of people, or indeed the marketplace (which amounts to a set of institutions favoring innovations that have particular characteristics right now) should be conceded a monopoly on wisdom.

THE ROLE OF ENERGY IN
GROWTH ACCOUNTING

WE WILL DEMONSTRATE IN THIS APPENDIX THAT ENERGY can play a major role in explaining growth in a growth accounting framework, by making only rather modest changes to the basic assumptions usually employed. We will assume less substitutability between production factors and allow for the possibility of biased technical change. The Cobb-Douglas production function formula, which is used for conventional growth accounting, is written:[1]

$$Y = A(L^\alpha K^{1-\alpha}).$$

In this formula Y is GDP, L is labor hours, K is physical capital (machinery and buildings), and A is the so-called Solow Residual, or the total factor productivity (TFP). Alfa (α) is the wage share of GDP. This rests on the assumption that the salary corresponds to the marginal contribution of labor. The TFP growth may be computed as:

$$\Delta A/A = \Delta Y/Y - \alpha\, \Delta L/L - (1 - \alpha)\, \Delta K/K.$$

The factor income shares for labor (α) and capitalists ($1 - \alpha$) respectively are used as weights to model the contribution of labor and capital to GDP under the assumption of constant returns to scale. In growth accounting, it is what grows fast and gets paid more that is attributed with the largest explanatory power. If capital grows at the same pace as GDP (which is normal for developed countries), it will only explain roughly a third of GDP growth in the growth accounting framework, because the weight of capital, judged by its cost share, is usually around this level (0.3–0.4). This means that capital would have to grow three times faster than GDP to "explain" all of it. As a consequence, all conventional growth accounting ends up with a large role for total factor productivity (TFP); what is not explained by more capital per worker (capital deepening) is explained by higher efficiency in the combined use of capital and labor.[2]

---

[1] Solow, 1957, 312–20.

[2] A practical illustration of the growth accounting excercise can be based on these values for the Swedish economy:

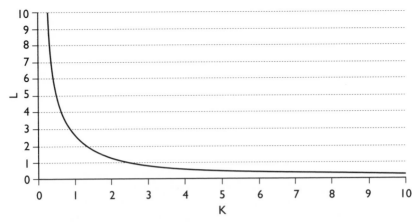

Figure A.1. Substitution possibilities. Cobb-Douglas,
a special case of constant elasticity of substitution with
unitary substitution, sigma (elasticity of substitution) = 1.

For energy to play a more fundamental role in a growth accounting
framework it is necessary to modify the basic assumptions of the model.
One possibility is to edge away completely from the neoclassical idea of
compensation to the factors of production according to their marginal productivity, and allow any kind of weights for the cost share of each factor
as long as the sum of weights is 1 (constant returns to scale), but this can
lead to severe theoretical difficulties.[3] Another possible adjustment, which
we follow here, is to allow restrictions to the degree of substitution between
energy, labor, and capital. A certain amount of energy is always needed, so
it may be better to assume less possibility for substitution than the Cobb-
Douglas framework does.[4] The Cobb-Douglas production function does not
assume perfect substitution, but that the elasticity of substitution is fairly
easy, or unitary = 1; see figure A.1. The farther away from origin one gets the
curve approaches the Y-axis and the X-axis, so there is never any absolute

---

Sweden 18702000 Annual growth rate (%)
Labor 100227(ln(227)–ln(100))/130 = 0.63
Capital stock 10010724(ln(10724)–ln(100))/130 = 3.6
GDP 1003776 (ln(3776)–ln(100))/130 = 2.8
TFP growth = 2.8–0.7*0.63–0.3*3.6 = 1.3

This implies that 1.3/2.8 = 46 percent of Swedish GDP growth between 1870 and 2000 is
"unexplained," or the result of increased efficiency in the use of labor and capital combined.
    [3] Ayres and Warr, 2009, 190–95. Some results of their modeling seem counterintuitive and
unrealistic: the marginal productivity of labor approaches zero when workers are equipped
with more capital.
    [4] Stern, 1997.

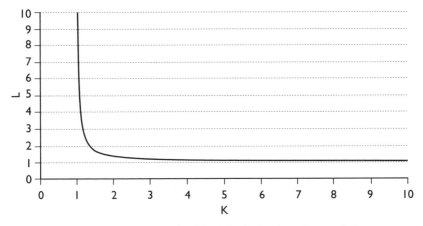

Figure A.2. Constant elasticity of substitution, sigma = 0.4.

minimum amount of one of the factors necessary for production to take place. In principle, substitution options are endless.

With only rather modest changes to this assumption, where a certain amount of one factor will always be needed and substitution options decline even further on the margin, we have instead a constant elasticity of substitution (CES) less than 1 (see figure A.2).

Based on our historical time-series we know that energy made up a much larger cost share of GDP historically in organic economies than it does in today's economies. The cost share of energy in Sweden, a country for which we have all the necessary data (quantities and prices) from 1800 till the present, fell over time (figure A.3). The fall in Sweden is exceptionally large, but it also took place in other countries.[5] This fall is not possible in an economy with an elasticity of substitution of unity (Cobb-Douglas technology), which implies constant cost shares. If the price of one factor goes up, there will be a movement along the isoquant so that less of that factor is used and the cost share will stay constant. Therefore, the extent of the fall from an energy cost ratio of 90 percent of GDP or more in 1800 to close to 10 percent of GDP today, does not at all support unitary elasticity.

A rather simple way of modifying a Cobb-Douglas model, so that it can deal with changing cost shares, is to either assume biased technical change combined with an elasticity of substitution (CES) less than 1 or just an elasticity of substitution less than 1.[6]

[5] Jones, 2002 found that the cost share of energy for the United States between 1950 and 1998 fell by 1 percent per year, but in the period 1971–1980 it actually increased from 2 percent to 7 percent). Smulders and Noij, 2003 find similar trends for Japan, France, UK, and West Germany after 1969.

[6] Arrow et al., 1967.

Figure A.3. Ratio of the value of energy relative to GDP in Sweden, 1800–2000

If the CES is less than 1, changes in the input ratio will no longer exactly compensate for the change in the price ratio (as it does when CES=1), and thereby cost shares may change. If there is in addition biased technical change, the production function curve itself moves in a skewed way, saving more on one factor than the other. This can also cause changes in the cost shares. There is much that speaks in favor of technical change generally being biased rather than neutral.[7]

We set up a model where we allow for a biased technical change (with the possibility of saving more on energy) and where the CES is allowed to be less than one between energy on the one hand and the combination of labor and capital on the other.

We set the capital and labor as one joint factor in order to simplify the model. With these relaxations of the Cobb-Douglas assumption of unitary substitution and neutral technical change, energy will matter considerably for long-run growth in Sweden in a growth accounting framework.[8]

Our model consists of one main equation:

$$Y = \left(\gamma_V^{1/\sigma} (A_L^\beta L^\beta K^{1-\beta})^\phi + \gamma_E^{1/\sigma} (A_E E)^\phi \right)^{\frac{1}{\phi}} \qquad (A.1)$$

Equation (A.1) is a nested CES production function that embeds a Cobb-Douglas function of capital (K) and labor (L) in a CES function of the capital-labor aggregate and energy (E) that determines gross output Y. The approach we follow is thus to perceive energy as an additional production

---

[7] Antràs, 2004; Acemoglu, 2003; Koetse et al., 2008.

[8] In this very preliminary analysis, there is still unitary substitution between labor and capital.

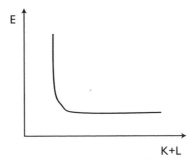

Figure A.4. The two factors of
production in our model

factor.[9] We consequently adjust the GDP measure by adding the value of
primary energy inputs to it, thereby creating a gross *output* measure (rather
than a *value added* measure).[10] In e equation (A.1) substitution options are
expressed as $\phi = \dfrac{\sigma - 1}{\sigma}$, where σ is the elasticity of substitution between energy and the capital-labor aggregate. Sigma (σ) is allowed to be less than one
in this set-up, and then its actual value is estimated on the basis of the data.
The estimation shows that sigma is not quite as low as 0.4 (as in figure A.2),
but definitely less than one. It turns out to be in the range between 0.64
and 0.69 in the Swedish case.[11] The lower the elasticity of substitution between energy and "labor-capital" the greater is the contribution of energy to
growth in GDP at each level of the cost shares. Our empirical results show
that as long as sigma is less than one, the GDP output elasticities of capital

[9] If we are explaining the growth of GDP and using a Cobb-Douglas model, only capital
and labor should be regular factors of production. This is because the value of inputs, such as
energy or raw material, is not really included in the GDP measure.

[10] There are various qualifications of this statement. The value of imported energy is not
included in GDP, neither is the value of subsistence energy (collecting firewood for own use
or growing food for own consumption). However, the value of turning primary energy into
secondary energy, as in the electricity sector or in the oil refineries, is included in GDP. This
means there is no clear-cut optimal method for adjusting the GDP measure so that it includes
the value of energy, but does not overestimate it. We chose here to construct a simple gross
output measure by adding the full cost of energy to the GDP. Optimally we should perhaps
first have subtracted the value added from the refineries and from the electricity industry from
our GDP measure. This was partly attempted in Kander, 2002, where gasworks and electricity
works were omitted, but refineries were kept (being part of the chemical industry and difficult
to exclude). Actually this did not make such a large difference to the size of total Swedish GDP,
so we did not do any downward adjustments of GDP. And in this appendix and in Stern and
Kander, 2011, we do not include secondary electricity. We just added the full cost of energy to
the normal GDP, and got a gross output measure.

[11] For more exact information of the value according to different model scenarios, see Stern
and Kander, 2011.

and labor are in fact less than their cost shares if we assume that the gross output production function has constant returns to scale. In other words there are decreasing returns to scale of GDP in capital and labor.[12]

In contrast to the normal Cobb-Douglas production function there is no common "A" factor for the production factors, i.e., no TFP (total factor productivity). This is because we assume that technical change may be biased and save more on one factor than the other. In the equation there are two augmentation indices: A_L (labor augmenting index) and A_E (energy augmenting index) capturing the productivity increase of each factor. If both AL and AE grow at the same rate there is neutral technical change, so the model does not rule out this option. We do not however take neutral technical change for granted, as the normal growth accounting with TFP does. The model above should not be seen as a complete model of economic growth. It does not incorporate the quality changes of labor (human capital), nor does it model the drivers of technological change endogenously. The impact from the quality increase of energy is however modeled, based on the compositional changes among energy carriers and on their relative price, already laid out in the main text, where the construct of a quality-adjusted energy aggregate was called energy volume.

The model is set up to explore the mechanism whereby energy can constrain or enable growth depending on its relative abundance. It is capable of incorporating a time-varying energy cost share, by allowing a low elasticity of substitution between energy and the other factor of production (labor and capital). Three aspects of energy are investigated: (1) the amount of energy in pure physical terms (in heat units, for instance joule); (2) the aggregate quality of energy carriers; and (3) the energy saving biased technical change (also called energy augmentation). Together all three factors are called "effective energy supply," and are the sum of columns A, B, and C in table A.1.[13] Explaining how the modeling of these three energy factors was done requires many more equations, and we refer the interested reader to Stern and Kander (2011).[14] For this appendix we did a growth accounting instead based on our modeling results, where all columns sum up to the GDP growth rate, reported in table A.1.[15] This was done to allow comparison with conventional growth accounting.

---

[12] This is in terms of the contributions to GDP growth. In terms of the original gross output production function the contributions of capital-labor and energy are symmetric. If we increase capital and labor by 1 percent each and hold energy and the two technology variables constant, GDP increases by less than 1 percent i.e. decreasing returns to scale. If we increase energy also by 1 percent then GDP increases by 1 percent i.e. constant returns. .

[13] Cleveland and Stern, 2000.

[14] In the paper we do not carry out a complete growth accounting, which means that the columns do not sum up to GDP growth rate.

[15] We would like to thank David Stern for taking the trouble of turning the modeling results of Stern and Kander, 2011, into the growth accounting results for this appendix.

TABLE A.1
Growth accounting for Sweden, 1800–2000, with two production factors: energy vs. labor-capital (%)

Column	A	B	C	D	E	F	G
Period	Contribution of Energy (Heat Units)	Contribution of Energy Quality	Contribution of Energy Augmentation	Contribution of Labor (hours worked)	Contribution of Capital	Contribution of Labor and Capital Augmentation	GDP
1800–1850	0.13	0.26	0.61	0.25	0.09	0.0	1.34
1850–1900	0.70	−0.20	1.14	0.35	0.49	0.0	2.47
1900–1950	0.60	0.49	0.34	0.42	0.59	0.62	3.06
1950–2000	0.48	0.10	0.25	0.17	0.80	1.40	3.20
Average 1800–2000	0.46	0.16	0.59	0.30	0.49	0.51	2.51

On average, GDP grew by 2.51 percent per year over the period 1800–2000, and the rate of growth was substantially higher during the twentieth century than during the nineteenth century. The growth rate in the first half of the nineteenth century, before industrialization had taken off, was especially slow at only 1.3 percent p.a. It is clear that the supply of effective energy (columns A, B, and C) has been very important for long-run growth. Between 1800 and 2000, the contribution to gross output from effective energy supply was 1.21 percent, while the contribution from labor and capital and its augmentation was only slightly larger: 1.3 percent. Technical change was on average fairly neutral in the very long run, but with a slight tendency of saving more energy than labor and capital (0.51 percent for A_L and 0.59 percent for A_E). But in the nineteenth century it was clearly biased in the energy-saving direction, and in the twentieth century it was biased to save capital and labor. Labor and capital augmentation did not play any role throughout the nineteenth century. This means that in the nineteenth century all efficiency increase was related to energy and energy-saving technical change was a key factor for growth. Thus, our results show that energy does play an important role in growth, with the adjustment of Cobb-Douglas assumptions to allow for possible biased technical change and a CES less than 1. The high cost shares for energy in the nineteenth century translate into a large impact on growth in the accounting. In the twentieth century, when cost shares for energy are much smaller, the impact is smaller in the growth accounting. Still the cost shares do not simply translate into weights for the factors, due to CES less than 1.[16] In the twentieth century the whole balance between energy and the other factors changes. Capital and labor become more important than energy. Still, in our model, the economy never breaks loose entirely from energy constraints; in the twentieth century it remains constrained by resources.

This model has so far only been tested on Sweden. More country studies are necessary to check whether energy also matters in cases, where the fall in the cost share for energy took place much earlier, and in this period was less drastic, as in England.

---

[16] The model set-up means that the size of the cost shares is not all that determines the impact; limited substitution plays out as a break effect on the weights given to the respective factor.

DECOMPOSING ENERGY INTENSITY, 1870–1970

THIS APPENDIX PROVIDES THE BASIC DATA AND RESULTS for energy decomposition for Sweden and England and Wales between 1870 and 1970. The results are discussed in the main text.

Table B.1 shows all the necessary data for the two benchmarks, 1870 and 1913, for Sweden, and table B.2 gives the equivalent data for England and Wales.

Tables B.3 and B.4 present the results of a LMDI (Log Mean Divisia Decomposition) according to the formulas and methods described in Ang, 2000.

Most of the impact from the second industrial revolution in terms of energy use and structural effects in the economy took place after 1913, when electrification and motorization had a much greater influence. In the period 1913–1970, energy intensity in Sweden continued downward, by 41 percent, and the driving forces are provided in table B.5.

In the latter phase of the second industrial revolution in England and Wales, energy intensity continued to decline, in total by 32 percent between 1913 and 1950, which on an annual average basis is in line with the decline in Sweden.[1] Again, the relative impact from the changes within industry combined with the household effects drove the decline, while structural changes continued to play an offsetting role (see table B.6). Thus we see a consistent pattern for the drivers of energy intensity decline throughout the period marked by the second industrial revolution in England and Sweden: the within-sector changes, particularly in industry, were, together with the household effect, strong enough to outbalance the structural change of industrialization.

---

[1] The different benchmarks for Sweden and England and Wales are due to practical reasons of available sector disaggregation of energy.

TABLE B.1
Energy and value added per sector in Sweden 1870 and 1913

	Agriculture		Industry		Services		Transport		Households		Total	
	1870	1913	1870	1913	1870	1913	1870	1913	1870	1913	1870	1913
Value added	515	800	198	1305	454	1278	39	284	na	na	1206	3667
Share of value added, %	43	21	16	36	38	35	3	8	na	na	100	100
Energy consumption PJ	20	27	16	100	11	27	7	62	99	147	153	363
Energy intensity, MJ/ SEK	0.039	0.034	0.081	0.077	0.024	0.021	0.18	0.22	0.082	0.04	0.13	0.099

Sources: 2002, Krantz and Schön, 2007, value added in constant 1910/12 prices. Industry comprises manufacturing industry and construction, services comprise public and private services and dwelling usage, transport comprises both transport and communications.

TABLE B.2
Value added, sector shares, energy consumption and energy intensity, for England and Wales in 1870 and 1913

	Agriculture		Industry		Services		Transport		Households		Total	
	1870	1913	1870	1913	1870	1913	1870	1913	1870	1913	1870	1913
Value added, constant 1990 international dollars	11	11	28	70	39	85	6	18	na	na	84	184
Share of value added, according to 1913 constant prices %	13	6	33	38	46	46	7	10	na	na	100	100
Energy consumption, PJ	34	34	1942	3817	112	301	180	497	1030	2050	3298	6699
Energy intensity, MJ/1990 international dollar	3.09	3.09	69.4	54.5	2.87	3.54	30	27.6	12.3	11.1	39.3	36.4

Sources: Own calculations based on Warde's new estimates of sectoral energy consumption, Warde's adjustment of Maddison's GDP for UK to fit for England and Wales, the indices of sector shares in constant prices from Groningen's adjustment of Feinstein, and the sector distribution of GDP for sectors in 1913 by Mitchell, slightly adjusted to account for Ireland being more backward than England and Wales. Still, Ireland only made up 10% of UK's GDP in 1870 and 5% in 1913, so our implemented adjustments were not large.

TABLE B.3
Driving forces for energy intensity decline in Sweden, 1870–1913

	Agriculture	Industry	Services	Transport	Households	Total	% of total Impact
Structure	0.93437	1.14319	0.99438	1.08407		1.1514	–57
Intensity	0.98592	0.99086	0.99004	1.01826		0.9848	6
Per capita					0.6881	0.6881	151
Total	0.92121	1.13274	0.98447	1.10387		0.7802	100
% of total impact	33.1	–50.2	6.3	–39.8	150.7	100	

Sources: Same as table B.1. An excel sheet with all the calculations is accessible on demand. The numbers in italics represent percentage change. 1 represents no impact. Values less than 1 mean a declining impact on energy intensity, and values larger than 1 mean energy intensity increasing impact.[1] The bold figures indicate the percentage of the total decline. The total decline was 0.78028–1 = –22 percent. This is thus 100 percent of the impact. The structural impact counteracted this by –57 percent, etc.

[1] For example 0.93437 for structural effect from agriculture should be understood as 0.93437–1= –6.56 percent. The total impact, for example 0.92121 for agriculture, is achieved by multiplying the structure and intensity effect (0.93437*0.98592). Note that it is not possible to first transform the figures written in italics into percentage change and then add these up. Doing that will not result in the total impact, there will be a difference and not a complete decomposition. The figures in bold (percent of total impact) are achieved by transforming the results from the multiplicative version of the Divisa, used above, to the additive version, and cannot be immediately derived from the table.

TABLE B.4
Driving forces of energy intensity decline for England and Wales between 1870 and 1913

	Agriculture	Industry	Services	Transport	Households	Total	% of total Impact
Structure	0.9942	1.0796	0.9998	1.0203		1.0948	120
Intensity	1	0.8699	1.0082	0.9947		0.8724	181
Per capita					0.9708	0.9708	39
Total	0.9942	0.9391	1.0080	1.0148	0.9708	0.9273	100
Percent of total impact	8	83	−11	−20	39	100	

Source and explanations: Same as table B.3. An excel sheet with all the calculations is accessible on demand.

TABLE B.5
Driving forces of Swedish energy intensity decline between 1913 and 1970

	Agriculture	Industry	Services	Transport	Households	Total	% of total Impact
Structure	0.92345	1.07930	1.00302	1.08276		1.08243	−15
Intensity	0.99758	0.87382	0.98496	0.77804		0.66803	76
Per capita					0.8157	0.8157	39
Total	0.92122	0.94312	0.98794	0.84244	0.8157	0.58986	100
% of total impact	15.5	11.1	2.3	32.5	38.6	100	

TABLE B.6
Driving forces of energy intensity decline in England and Wales, 1913–1950

	Agriculture	Industry	Services	Transport	Households	Total	% of total Impact
Structure	0.9972	1.1321	0.9850	1.0114		1.1246	-31
Intensity	1.0046	0.6331	1.0309	0.9848		0.6458	114
Per capita					0.9380	0.9380	17
Total	1.0018	0.7168	1.0310	0.9848		0.6813	100
% of total impact	−0.5	86.8	−4.0	1.0	16.7	100	

THE IMPACT FROM THE SERVICE
TRANSITION ON ENERGY INTENSITY

ONE POSSIBLE EXPLANATION FOR FALLS IN ENERGY INTENSITY in the twentieth century is the transition to a service economy, because service production is generally less energy-demanding than industrial production in relation to the value that is created. This would also offer hope for the future: energy intensity would be lowered as developing economies moved toward a "service transition," following the course of the developed world. We will demonstrate in this appendix that the impact from the service transition on energy intensity decline has in fact been rather modest so far in the developed world.[1]

It is beyond dispute that employment in the service sector has increased drastically over the last few decades and that services make up the lion's share of GDP today. However, this trend bears little resemblance to what happens in real production. As we know, output is always measured as quantities of particular goods or services multiplied by their price. The quantities of services may not have increased their share if prices of services have gone up relative to manufacturing production. This means the service transition might partly be a price illusion.

The reason for the price illusion can be analyzed in terms of "Baumol's cost disease," meaning that services tend to get more expensive than manufactured goods over time.[2] In order to prove this, Baumol used a simple two-sector model of the economy that included the technically progressive sector (roughly speaking, industry) and the stagnant sector (roughly speaking, services). In the technically progressive sector, labor time is a means to achieve an end, so production can be rationalized by equipping workers with time-saving machines. In the stagnant sector, human time is often an indispensable part of the product itself, and labor productivity cannot rise as fast as in the manufacturing sector. In many services, like haircutting, psychological counseling, concerts, etc., the time spent in consuming the service is part of the good itself. Imagine a counselor skipping the listening part of her work, or a concert pianist playing the tune twice as fast, and you

---

[1] A substantial part of this appendix is written together with Sofia Henriques. It has been published in Henriques and Kander, 2010 and in Henriques, 2011, but the section on deflating problems is new.
[2] Baumol, 1967.

will understand why this will not improve their productivity, but rather ruin their performance and undermine the value of their service.

Productivity gains in the progressive sector normally lead to an increase in industrial wages, and consequently, service workers will for justice reasons also demand higher salaries even though their productivity has not risen to the same degree. The result is higher costs for service production relative to manufacturing production. Consequently, the prices of industrial goods go down, in relative terms. Most of us have personal experiences of this kind: going to a concert has become more expensive relative to buying a CD, or going to the hairdresser has become more expensive than buying a razor and cutting your own hair.[3] At the macro level, we find that the price of services goes up more over time than the price of manufactured goods, as demonstrated in sector price deflators (see figure C.1). The higher costs in service production will be passed on to consumers, and prices of services will tend to increase compared to manufactured goods. There is consequently a "cost disease" in the service sector, and if people continue buying services in roughly the same relative quantities as they buy manufactured goods, despite the relatively higher costs, employment will logically have to shift over gradually from manufacturing to services. Thus, the service sector will employ an increasing share of the labor force, and services will become more expensive than industrial products over time. This cost disease may actually be a quite powerful explanation behind what we see: rising shares of employment in services and a rising share for services in current values.

Services are not, of course, universally trapped in low and unchanging levels of productivity. Certain market services have had large increases in productivity; indeed we can speak of the "industrialization" of services both to business and consumers, developing mass markets. This has characterized areas such as transport and telecommunications, wholesale and retail distribution, and banking and finance.[4] Yet the service sector also incorporates areas of much slower rises in productivity, such as hotels and restaurants, insurance and real estate, and community, personal and government. Even with the industrialization of services, as a large fraction of the sector consists of personal services, real productivity gains typically lag behind the manufacturing sector.

This unbalanced productivity increase means that there is an inherent price delusion component in the sector shares, when these are measured in current prices. All sensible researchers use sector values in constant prices,

---

[3] These relative price changes imply that what a rich country can consume more of is what they are productive in producing, mainy manufactured goods; see Ingelstam, 1997. People in general cannot afford to consume personal services more in a rich country than in a poor, because wages for service work are higher in a rich country than in a poor. It is just the relative income level within one country that will determine the relative purchasing power of those personal services.

[4] Baumol et al., 1985; Broadberry, 2006.

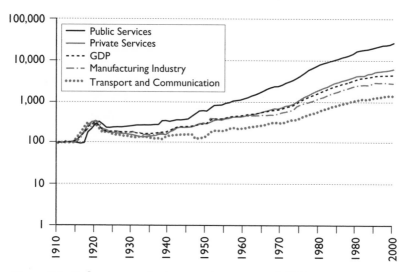

Figure C.1. Deflators, or price increase, in sectors and GDP,
Sweden 1910–2000, index 1910/12 = 100.
Source: Kranz and Schön, 2007. These deflators are implicit in the database
(apart from the period 1800–1950 when they are explicit), and here calculated
by dividing the values in current prices by the values in constant prices.

as opposed to current prices, when they calculate sectoral growth. This is
done to account for price inflation within the sector, which has nothing to
do with real growth.

Figure C.1 shows the long-term price development (price deflators) for
some main sectors of the Swedish economy, as well as for GDP. The price for
public services rises substantially more than the price of GDP does. Private
services increase only a little more than the GDP deflator. Manufacturing
industry increased its price less than GDP, whereas transport and communication, on average, was more technically progressive than GDP and even
industry, and thus its price rose less. Price deflators are used in national
accounts to recalculate values in current prices to constant prices to measure the sectoral growth.[5] This means that when the sectors are measured
in real terms (as shares of GDP in constant prices), the service sector will
have grown much less than if it is measured in current prices or in terms of
employment. The more rapid increase of service prices over other prices, as
shown in figure C.1, is an illustration of what Baumol calls the cost disease
of services.

[5] The simple procedure for transforming numbers in current values into real production is
to divide the values in current prices by the proper sector price deflator. Naturally, dividing the
values in current prices with such different price deflators, as we find in figure C.1, means that
sector growth rates will differ expressed in current prices and in constant prices.

Deflating involves several difficulties. There are four main problems. One has received more attention than others and may be called *the index problem*.

1. The index problem stems from the fact that there is no natural base year for a price index construction. Growth rates may differ with an early and a late price basis if these are far apart in time, as discussed in chapter 7.[6] But this problem can be avoided where the data are available by linking one-year price indices into a chain index, for instance an annual chained Paasche index, or the Fischer price index. Such chain indices are used for the deflators in figure C.1 and in all proper national accounts, and therefore the index problem does not really pose a problem for the growth rates of sectors or of GDP when analyzing modern economies.

2. A second problem is that adding up deflated sectors will not result in the deflated GDP; there will be a residual, and this is therefor called the *additivity problem*.[7] In general this problem is not very large, and can be dealt with by proportional allocation of the residual (a couple of percentage units) to the sectors.

3. A third problem has to do with whether real service production is underrated, especially in public services, where most often a zero productivity increase is assumed. This admittedly is a bigger problem. It implies that if the deflator for services was constructed to account for those productivity increases, of course the real service growth would have been larger, and so would GDP growth per se.

4. A fourth problem is more of a pedagogic kind than a real problem, but it confuses people over and over again. It is that the choice of price level year (not base year, which is changing every year in the chain index), for instance 1950 or 2000, will determine the size of the sectors relative to one another. If we choose 1950 as our price level, then the price relations in that year will determine how large the sectors seem to be in relation to each other. Typically the service sector will look larger compared to the industrial sector with a later price level than with an earlier, because then the service prices are relatively higher compared to industrial goods. This does not however affect our calculations of rates of structural change versus technical change, because the *annual growth* of the service sector (or any other sector, or GDP) will be exactly the same if the price level is 1950 (when services were cheaper and manufacturing goods more expensive than currently) or if it is expressed in the price level of 2000 as long as we use annual linked chain price indices.

---

[6] See also Kander, 2002, appendix B and Kander, 2005.

[7] Lindmark, 2002, is right in pointing to the additivity problem, but has by mistake exaggerated the error effect; it only amounts to a couple of percentage units and in subsequent discussions we have agreed upon this.

We do not propose to count services differently from how they are in fact implicitly calculated in modern national accounts. All we are saying is that the growth of services in real terms is not as big as the growth in values in current figures or employment figures. If services were measured differently (taking better account of their productivity increase, solving the third problem listed above) then they would have grown more and total GDP would have grown more too. In such a different scenario, the impact from the service transition would have been greater for energy intensity decline than it is with the established methods of national accounting.

Using real growth of sectors, we investigate the relative role of within-sector changes (technical change) and between-sector changes (structural change) for the decline in energy intensity in the period 1971–2003 (see table C.1) for ten developed countries, by using a five-sector economy: agriculture, industry, services, transport, and households, as in appendix B. This time the household sector is divided into residential effects and private car effects.

In order to investigate the proximate reasons behind changes in energy intensity, divided into between-sector and within-sector changes, we employ the decomposition method of LMDI (Logarithmic Mean Divisia Index) in the version described in Ang and Zhang (2000) and Ang (2005).[8] This method distinguishes between structural factors (change in the shares of sectors, keeping energy intensities constant) and intensity factors (changes in sector energy intensities, keeping the structure of economy unchanged). The LMDI has been used in a large number of energy studies because of its attractive properties: ease of interpretation, unity independence, and perfect decomposition (i.e., leaving no residual).[9] The elements in the decomposition scheme are as follows:

E = Final energy consumption (= $\Sigma E_i + \Sigma E_k$)
E_i = Energy consumption in economic sector i (Agriculture, Industry, Transportation, and Services)
E_k = Energy consumption in non-economic sector k (Residential, personal transportation)
Y = Total value added (constant prices)
Y_i = Gross value added of sector i (constant prices)
I = Final energy intensity (= E/Y)
I_i = Energy intensity of sector i (= E_i/Y_i)
S_i = Share of sector i in total value added (= Y_i/Y)
D_{tot} = Total energy intensity change
D_{str} = Change of I due to structural effect (between-sector changes)

[8] This method description is identical to the one in Henriques and Kander, 2010.
[9] For a description of the properties of LMDI and comparisons with other methods, see the previous reference and also Ang and Liu, 2007 and Choi and Ang, 2003.

D_{int} = Change of I due to technological effect (within-sector changes)

D_{pcons} = Change of I due to personal consumption effect (non-economic sector changes)

D_{tot} = I^T/I^0 ,where T is the year of comparison (here 2005) and 0 is the starting year (here 1971).

In the multiplicative version we decompose the total energy intensity change into structural effect, technological effect, and personal consumption effects:

$$D_{tot} = D_{str}D_{int}D_{pcons}.$$

D_{str}, D_{int}, and D_{pcons} can be computed as follows:

$$D_{str} = exp\left[\sum_i w_i' \ln\left(\frac{S_i^T}{S_i^0}\right)\right]$$

$$D_{int} = exp\left[\sum_i w_i' \ln\left(\frac{I_i^T}{I_i^0}\right)\right]$$

$$D_{pcons} = exp\left[\sum_k w_k' \ln\left(\frac{E_k^T}{Y^T}\middle/\frac{E_k^0}{Y^0}\right)\right].$$

The weights of the economic and non-economic sectors i and k are calculated in a similar fashion using the logarithmic mean of the energy consumption of the sectors divided by total value added in the numerator and dividing it by the logarithmic mean of total energy intensities,[10] so that:

$$w_{i(k)}' = \frac{L\left(\frac{E_{i(k)}^T}{Y^T}, \frac{E_{i(k)}^0}{Y^0}\right)}{L\left(I^Y, I^0\right)}$$

where the logarithmic mean weight function of two positive numbers is given by:

$$L(x,y) = (x-y)/\ln(x/y).$$

For all the developed countries, except the United States, we use the newly updated EU KLEMS November 2009 release for thirty-two industries.[11] In the case of the United States, we had to use the EU KLEMS 2008, SIC version that covers the period from 1970 to 2005 because the EU KLEMS 2009 release—NAISICS version only goes back to 1977.[12] The reason we prefer the EU KLEMS to other databases is that it separates postal services and

[10] Ang, 2005.
[11] EU KLEMS, O'Mahony and Timmer, 2009.
[12] EU KLEMS; Timmer et al., 2007.

TABLE C.1
Divisia decomposition for Western Europe, United States, and Japan, 1971–2005

	France	Germany	Italy	Japan	Netherlands	Portugal	Spain	Sweden	UK	US
	71/05	71/05	71/05	73/05	71/05	71/05	71/05	71/05	71/05	71/05
Agriculture										
Intensity	1.00	1.00	1.00	1.01	1.05	1.01	1.00	1.01	0.99	0.98
Structure	0.99	1.00	0.99	0.98	1.01	0.97	0.98	0.99	1.00	1.00
Industry										
Intensity	0.78	0.82	0.79	0.66	0.89	1.06	0.90	0.71	0.80	0.77
Structure	0.92	0.87	0.98	0.97	0.92	0.93	0.99	1.04	0.88	0.93
Services										
Intensity	0.84	0.87	1.11	0.97	0.91	1.08	1.08	0.96	0.92	0.88
Structure	1.02	1.05	1.00	1.03	1.02	1.01	1.00	1.00	1.03	1.02
Transports										
Intensity	0.99	0.95	1.00	0.99	1.02	1.06	1.05	0.97	0.98	0.94
Structure	1.04	1.03	1.08	0.96	1.00	0.99	1.06	1.01	1.03	1.00

Total Productive Sector										
Intensity	0.65	0.68	0.89	0.64	0.87	1.22	1.03	0.67	0.72	0.63
Structure	0.98	0.93	1.04	0.94	0.94	0.91	1.04	1.03	0.92	0.95
Sub Total	0.63	0.64	0.92	0.60	0.82	1.11	1.07	0.69	0.66	0.60
Personal Consumption										
Residential	0.99	0.85	0.84	0.99	0.78	0.86	0.96	0.73	0.89	0.84
Personal tr.	0.99	0.98	0.97	1.03	0.97	1.10	1.04	0.97	0.99	0.88
Total										
Intensity	0.65	0.68	0.89	0.64	0.87	1.22	1.03	0.67	0.72	0.63
Structure	0.98	0.93	1.04	0.94	0.94	0.91	1.04	1.03	0.92	0.95
Pers. Cons.	0.99	0.83	0.82	1.02	0.76	0.94	1.00	0.71	0.88	0.75
Total impact	**0.63**	**0.53**	**0.76**	**0.61**	**0.62**	**1.04**	**1.07**	**0.49**	**0.58**	**0.45**

Source: Henriques and Kander, 2010. A value of 1 implies no change; 1.1 a 10 percent contribution for increasing energy intensity; 0.9 a 10 percent contribution for decrease on energy intensity.

communications from commercial transport in the service sector; these factors are very different from an environmental perspective. The benchmarks for 1950 are obtained by linking the EU KLEMS database to the ten-sector database of the Groningen Growth and Development Centre (GGDC).[13]

For the Divisia decomposition, the 32-sector data in 1995 constant prices for the ten developed countries was reduced to four sectors for the years 1971 and 2005 as follows: (1) Agriculture (includes forestry and fishing); (2) Industry (Mining and Quarry; Manufacturing, Public Utilities and Construction); (3) Services (Wholesale, Retail Trade, Hotels and Restaurants; Finance, Insurance, and Real Estate; Community, Social and Personal Services, and Government Services; Post and Communications); and (4) Transportation. This division allows us to focus on the main issue: the effect from the transition to the service economy, where commercial transportation should be separated from the rest of the service sector because of its different energy intensity.

The results in table C.1 clearly show that the impact of structural change was very small when compared with the technology effect, and even the personal consumption effect. The transition to a service sector had a small downward impact on energy intensity in seven of the developed countries (and no impact in the others). The technology (within-sector) effect had the strongest impact on energy intensity declines. Industry played this special role in all cases except Portugal. The impact from what happened in industry was 34 percent for overall energy intensity reduction in Japan, 10 percent in the Netherlands and Spain, and about 20 percent in the remaining countries. Overall, this analysis strongly reinforces our message in this book that it was the ICT revolution, transforming the manufacturing sector, that is behind the more drastic reduction in energy intensity since the 1970s than a general service transition.

[13] van Ark, 1995.

BIASED TECHNICAL DEVELOPMENT

NEW COAL-USING TECHNOLOGY TENDED TO USE MORE energy than old methods of production, and nearly always less labor. This is what is called *biased technical development*: that is, a permanent change by which it is possible to produce any given level of output using a relatively greater amount of capital and lesser amount of labor. This does not simply reflect a change in the price of capital and labor which might induce a producer to have the same amount of output using a different combination of the two input factors, but a technical change that means the range of possible combinations itself shifts.

Figure D.1 illustrates the process of biased technical development. It shows the combinations of capital and labor that can be used to produce given levels of a good with the curve (called an isoquant) Y. In the pre-industrial economy, inputs to production are relatively labor-intensive, and the set of possible combinations of capital and labor to produce a good at cost Y is represented by the straight line (called an isocost line) X_1. As firms want to minimize costs (i.e., be as close to the origin as possible, minimizing capital and labor inputs), they will produce at the point where Y and X_1 intersect, with the capital input K_1 and labor input L_1. Then a new technology arrives which means that goods can be produced with a quite different combination of capital and labor that is much more capital-intensive, and requires fewer inputs overall. In other words, it is productivity-enhancing. The possible combinations of capital and labor shift to Y_2.[1] On this curve, producers could stay at K_1L_1, but could produce much more cheaply at K_2L_2 (this assumes that the relative cost of labor and capital stay the same, so producers follow the isoquant to an isocost line closer to the origin).

However, whether the new technology is adopted or not depends on local cost conditions. Imagine the new technology has to be brought in from a great distance, requires expensive fuel to run it, or needs extensive training of the workforce. These push the actual cost of employing the new technology up to Y_2+t (we are assuming for the sake of simplicity the unlikely scenario that the ratio of capital and labor costs remains constant). In this event, the new isoquant does not allow the producers to leave the isocost line X_1, although production could become more capital-intense, at the combination

[1] Another way of expressing this particular change is that the marginal productivity of capital increases relative to labor in the curve Y_2. For a more technical explanation, see Ruttan, 2001, 47–60.

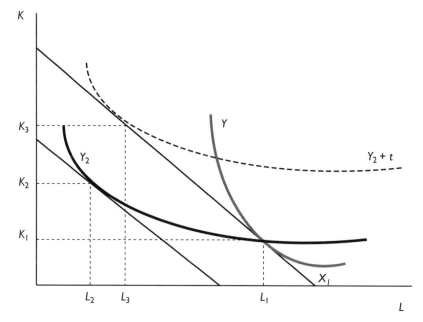

Figure D.1. Biased technical development.[1]

K_3L_3. But there is no incentive to make this move. The new technology will therefore not be adopted, even though it is known.

The industrial revolution can be imagined as the process of shifting from Y to Y_2. However, this simple view can mislead. In reality, the process of substituting between labor and capital in an economy cannot be represented by a continuous straight line or curve. Rather, consumers require a range of different products produced by different branches, whether these goods are acquired domestically or as imports. The ability to substitute between capital and labor varies extensively between different branches of the economy, and is much easier in the circumstances of small-scale production than where large amounts of fixed capital are required to produce any goods at all. A "real" economy is the aggregate of these different branches, each with its own dynamic of substitution (depending on the price of the relevant capital and labor). In practice it is usually easier to switch labor between different activities, although it may take many years to learn to perform a task well. But fixed capital cannot easily be switched. Swords are not easily beaten into ploughshares. Railway lines cannot be turned into sewing machines, and blast furnaces cannot be used to weave textiles.

[1] Similar figures are provided by Allen, 2009, 152, and David, 1975, 66.

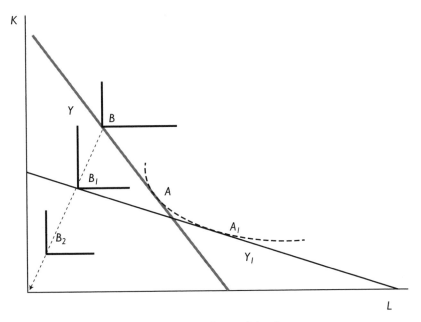

Figure D.2. Innovation and development
under differing technological constraints

Figure D.2 illustrates, in still very simple terms, the problem of substitution. In this case the straight line Y is the isocost line for applying different amounts of labor and capital[2] for a given unit of output in an economy. But what is actually possible in different branches of the economy is illustrated by curves A and B, representing actual substitution possibilities (isoquants) given the current technology. In some branches such as A this is relatively easy, but even here there are limits to the degree to which capital and labor can be economized on: there is a "choke point" beyond which substitution cannot go. In other industries, the situation is far more extreme. The most competitive technology may mean there are very few or even only one combination of capital and labor possible for efficient production. No further additions of capital or labor will make any difference to output, represented by the right-angled line B. Dependence on particular energy carriers, whether coal, wind, or water, might create similar barriers to substitution.[3] The overall balance of capital and labor in an economy is determined by the aggregate effect of these curves, and hence by its economic structure.

[2] This assumes constant costs.

[3] Absolute barriers to substitution are represented by a Leontieff production function. This is more likely to be found the more we look at individual branches or producers rather than on the scale of an economy, which always represents a wide mix of substitution possibilities.

We can hypothesize that investment and innovation will also be shaped by these parameters. In case B, where substitution possibilities are limited no matter what the relative price of capital and labor, there is a strong incentive to seek technological innovation that makes production more efficient, moving the curve toward the origin, say at B_1. This will tend to take the form of new types of capital, and this might be the prevalent form of innovation if an economy has a large number of enterprises of this type.[4] In other words, economies that have already sunk significant amounts of investment in coal-using fixed capital such as railways, locomotives, and steamships will seek to enhance the efficiency of their use, rather than abandon them if they face rising costs. We can illustrate this with a situation where labor costs actually fall relative to capital, that is, a shift from Y to Y_1. In industry A producers simply move along the existing curve to A_1. But this is not an option for industry B. Its products become relatively more expensive and will tend to shrink as a share of national output. To remain as competitive, the only option is to innovate and try to reduce costs within the industry's technological constraints, moving the curve B toward the origin along the dotted pathway.

In an economy where A-type producers predominate, most investors might be reluctant to take the plunge into type-B industries, especially if overseas producers already offer stiff competition. Even if a process of innovation (such as improved steam engine efficiency) moves the B-industries toward B_2, and hence encourages type-A industries to become type-B ones by offering major cost advantages, it may well be that those countries with a greater history of development in type-B industries nevertheless maintain an advantage. In these circumstances, given that all economies need to consume goods produced by both kinds of industries, we would be likely to see specialization along particular development paths. In the long run these are all likely to become capital- and energy-intensive as these factors become relatively cheaper, but the economic structures may remain quite different nonetheless. There will not be convergence, and the changing "bias" in development is unlikely to be internationally consistent.

[4] It is thus not particularly surprising that in an economy moving toward labor-saving, a large number of innovation and patents stress capital- or fuel-saving. See also the discussion in von Tunzelmann, 1997, 113–14.

References

Abel, W. (1966). *Agrarkrisen und Agrarkonjunctur. Eine Geschichte der Land- und Ernährungswirtschaft Mitteleuropas seit dem hohen Mittelalter.* (2nd ed.). Hamburg und Berlin: Paul Parey.

Acemoglu, D. (2003). "Labor and Capital-Augmenting Technical Change." *Journal of the European Economic Association* 1: 1–37.

———. (2009). "Epilogue: Mechanics and Causes of Economic Growth." *Introduction to Modern Economic Growth.* Princeton: Princeton University Press.

Adelman, M. A. (1972). *The World Petroleum Market.* Baltimore: Johns Hopkins University Press.

———. (1995). *The Genie out of the Bottle: World Oil since 1970.* Cambridge, MA: MIT Press.

Aghion, P., and P. Howitt (2009). *The Economics of Growth.* Cambridge, MA: MIT Press.

Agnoletti, M. (ed.) (2007). *The Conservation of Cultural Landscapes.* Wallingford: CABI.

Ahmad, N., and A. Wyckoff (2003). "Carbon Dioxide Emissions Embodied in International Trade of Goods." *OECD Science, Technology and Industry Working Papers* 2003/15, http://dx.doi.org/10.1787/421482436815.

Ajtay, G. L., P. Ketner, and P. Duvigneaud (1977). "Terrestrial Primary Production and Phytomass." In *The Global Carbon Cycle*, B. Bolin (ed.), pp. 1–39. Hoboken: Wiley (for SCOPE).

Allen, R. C. (1999). "Tracking the Agricultural Revolution in England." *Economic History Review* 52, no. 2: 209–35.

———. (2000). "Economic Structure and Agricultural Productivity in Europe, 1300–1800." *European Review of Economic History* 4: 1–26.

———. (2001). "The Great Divergence in European Wages and Prices from the Middle Ages to the First World War." *Explorations in Economic History* 38: 411–47.

———. (2003). "Was There a Timber Crisis in Early Modern Europe?" In *Economia e energia secc. XIII–XVIII*, S. Cavaciocchi (ed.), pp. 469–82. Istituto Internazionale di Storia economica "F. Datini." Firenze: Le Monnier.

———. (2009). *The British Industrial Revolution in Global Perspective.* Cambridge: Cambridge University Press.

———. (2011a). "Why the Industrial Revolution Was British: Commerce, Induced Invention, and the Scientific Revolution." *Economic History Review* 64: 357–84.

———. (2011b). *Global Economic History. A Very Short Introduction.* Oxford: Oxford University Press.

Alvarez-Nogal, C., and L. Prados de la Escosura (2013). "The Rise and Fall of Spain (1270–1850)." *Economic History Review* 66: 1–37.

Ambrosoli, M. (1992). *Scienziati, contadini e proprietari. Botanica e agricoltura nell'Europa occidentale.* Torino: Einaudi.

Anderson, M. R. (1995). "The Conquest of Smoke. Legislation and Pollution in Colonial Calcutta." In *Nature, Culture, Imperialism*, D. Arnold and R. Guha (eds.), pp. 293–335. Delhi: Oxford University Press.

Andrews, T. G. (2008). *Killing for Coal: America's Deadliest Labor War.* Cambridge, MA: Harvard University Press.

Ang, B. W. (2005). "The LMDI Approach to Decomposition Analysis: A Practical Guide." *Energy Policy* 33: 867–71.

Ang, B. W., and N. Liu (2007). "Handling Zero Values in the Logarithmic Mean Divisia Index Decomposition Approach." *Energy Policy* 35, no. 1: 238–46.

Ang, B. W., and F. Q. Zhang (2000). "A Survey of Index Decomposition Analysis in Energy and Environmental Studies." *Energy* 25: 1149–76.

Antràs, P. (2004). "Is the U.S. Aggregate Production Function Cobb-Douglas? New Estimates of the Elasticity of Substitution." *Contributions to Macroeconomics* 4, no. 1: 1–34.

Ark, B. van (1995). *Sectoral Growth Accounting and Structural Change in Postwar Europe.* Groningen: Groningen Growth and Development Centre.

Armstrong, J. (1993). "The English Coastal Coal Trade, 1890–1910: Why Calculate Figures When You Can Collect Them?" *Economic History Review* 46, n. 3: 607–9.

Arpi, G. (1951) *Den svenska järnhanteringens träkolsförsörjning 1830–1950.* Uppsala: Geografiska Institutionen.

Arrhenius, S. (1908). *Worlds in the Making: The Evolution of the Universe.* London: Harper & Brothers.

———. (1987 [1896]). *On the Influence of Carbonic Acid in the Air upon the Temperature of the Ground.* Stockholm: Institutionen för uppvärmnings- och ventilationsteknik, Tekniska högskola.

Arrow, K. J., H. B. Chenergy, B. S. Minhas, and R. M. Solow (1967). "Capital-Labor Substitution and Economic Efficiency." *Review of Economics and Statistics* 43, no. 3: 225–50.

Ausubel, J. H., and P. E. Waggoner (2008). "Dematerialization: Variety, Caution and Persistence." *PNAS* 2, no. 9 (105): 12774–79.

Ayres, R. U. and B. Warr (2005). "Accounting for Growth: The Role of Physical Work." *Structural Change & Economic Dynamics* 16: 181–209.

———. (2008). "Energy Efficiency and Economic Growth: The 'Rebound Effect' as a Driver." In *Energy Efficiency and Sustainable Consumption: The Rebound Effect*, H. Herring and S. Sorrell (eds.). Basingstoke: Palgrave.

———. (2009). *The Economic Growth Engine.* Cheltenham: Edward Elgar Publications.

Bairoch, P. (1983). "Énergie et révolution industrielle: nouvelles perspectives." *Revue de l'énergie* 356: 399–408.

———. (1985). "L'énergie et l'industrie manufacturière entre le monde traditionnel et le monde industrialisé: approche quantitative, 1750–1913." In *Les passages des économies traditionnelles européennes aux sociétés industrielle*, P. Bairoch and A.-M. Piuz (eds.), pp. 171–94. Genève: Droz.

———. (1986). "Le mesures de conversion des énergies primaires. Historique des unités et présentation des coefficients." *Histoire et Mesure* I: 81–106.

———. (1990). "The Impact of Crop Yields, Agricultural Productivity, and Transport Costs on Urban Growth between 1800 and 1910." In *Urbanization in History. A Process of Dynamic Interactions*, A. Van der Woude, A. Hayami, and J. De Vries, pp. 134–51. Oxford: Clarendon Press.

Balderston, T. (2010). "The Economics of Abundance: Coal and Cotton in Lancashire and the World." *Economic History Review* 63, no. 3: 569–90.

Baldwin, C. Y., and K. B. Clark (2000). *Design Rules. The Power of Modularity. Vol.1.* Cambridge, MA: MIT Press.

Banken, R. (2005). "The Diffusion of Coke Smelting and Puddling in Germany 1796–1860." In *The Industrial Revolution in Iron*, C. Evans and G. Rydén (eds.), pp. 55–73. Aldershot: Ashgate.

Barberis, L. (1908). *Lo sviluppo marittimo nel secolo XIX.* Roma: Rivista Marittima.

Barbier, E. (2007). *Natural Resources and Economic Development.* Cambridge: Cambridge University Press.

Barbier, E. (2011). *Scarcity and Frontiers: How Economies Have Developed through Natural Resource Exploitation.* Cambridge: Cambridge University Press.

Bartoletto, S. and M. d. M. Rubio (2008). "Energy Transition and CO2 Emissions in Southern Europe: Italy and Spain (1861–2000)." *Global Environment* 2: 46–81.

Bass, F. (1969). "A New Product Growth Model for Consumer Durables." *Management Science* 15, no. 5: 215–27.

Baumol, W. J. (1967). "Macroeconomics of Unbalanced Growth: The Anatomy of Urban Crisis." *American Economic Review* 57(3): 415–26.

Baumol, W. J., S.A.B. Blackman, and E. N. Wolff (1985). "Unbalanced Growth Revisited: Asymptotic Stagnancy and New Evidence." *American Economic Review* 75: 806–17.

Beaty, W. J. (1996). *What is Electricity?* http://amasci.com/miscon/whatis.html.

Beck, R. (1993). *Unterfinning: ländliche Welt vor Anbruch der Moderne.* Munich: Beck.

Beilby, O. J. (1939). "Changes in Agricultural Production in England and Wales." *Journal of the Royal Agricultural Society of England* 100: 62–73.

Belhoste, J.-F. and D. Woronoff (2005). "The French Iron and Steel Industry during the Industrial Revolution." In *The Industrial Revolution in Iron: the Impact of British Coal Technology in Nineteenth-Century Europe*, C. Evans and G. Rydén (eds.), pp. 75–94. Aldershot: Ashgate.

Bell, D. (1980). "The Information Society." In *The Microelectronics Revolution*, T. Forester (ed.), pp. 501. Oxford: Blackwell.

Benjamin, P. (1898). "A History of Electricity. The Intellectual Rise in Electricity." *From Antiquity to the Days of Benjamin Franklin.* New York: John Wiley & Sons.

Berend, I. T. (1996). "Hungary: A Semi-Successful Peripheral Industrialization." In *The Industrial Revolution in National Context*, M. Teich and R. Porter (eds.), pp. 265–89. Cambridge: Cambridge University Press.

———. (2006). *An Economic History of Twentieth-Century Europe.* Cambridge: Cambridge University Press.

Berend, I. T., and G. Ránki (1979). *Underdevelopment and Economic Growth. Studies in Hungarian Economic and Social History.* Budapest: Akadémiai Kiadó.

———. (1982). *The European Periphery and Industrialization 1780–1914.* Cambridge: Cambridge University Press.

Berndt, E. R. (2001). "Price and Quality of Desktop and Mobile Personal Computers: A Quarter-Century Historical Overview." *American Economic Review* 91: 268–73.

Berov, L. (1996). "The Industrial Revolution and the Countries of South-Eastern Europe in the Nineteenth and Early Twentieth Centuries." In *The Industrial Revolution in National Context*, M. Teich and R. Porter (eds.), pp. 290–328. Cambridge: Cambridge University Press.

Bessant, J., E. Braun, and R. Moseley (1980). "Microelectronics in Manufacturing Industry: The Rate of Diffusion." In *The Microelectronics Revolution*, T. Forester (ed.), pp. 198–218. Oxford: Basil Blackwell.

Beveridge W. H. (1965). *Prices and Wages in England from the 12th to the 20th Century*. London: Longmans (1st ed. 1939).

Barbier, E. (2005). "Natural Resources and Economic Development." Cambridge: Cambridge University Press.

Biraben J.-N. (1979). "Essai sur l'évolution du nombre des hommes." *Population* 34: 13–25.

Biringuccio, V. (1914). *De la pirotechnia*. A. Mieli (ed.). Bari: Società Tipografica Editrice Barese [I ed. 1540].

Bittermann, E. (1956). *Die landwirtschaftliche Produktion in Deutschland 1800–1950*. Halle: Kuhn-Archiv.

Blackbourn, D. (2006). *The Conquest of Nature: Water, Landscape and the Making of Modern Germany*. London: Jonathon Cape.

Blanning, T.C.W. (2002). *The Culture of Power and the Power of Culture: Old Regime Europe, 1660–1789*. Oxford: Oxford University Press.

Bloch, M. (1935). "Les "inventions" mediévales." *Annales d'histoire économique et sociale* 7: 634–43.

Boch, R. (2004). *Staat und Wirtschaft im 19. Jahrhundert*. Munich: Oldenbourg.

Bogart, D. (2005). "Turnpike Trusts and the Transportation Revolution in 18th Century England." *Explorations in Economic History* 42, no. 4: 479–508.

Bogart, D., M. Drechilman, O. Gelderblom, and J.-L. Rosenthal (2010). "State and Private Institutions." In *The Cambridge Economic History of Modern Europe. Vol. 1. 1700–1870*, S. Broadberry, and K. O'Rourke (eds.), pp. 70–95. Cambridge: Cambridge University Press.

Borchardt, K. (1973). "Germany." In *The Fontana Economic History of Europe. The Emergence of Industrial Societies. Vol. 1*, C. M. Cipolla (ed.), pp. 76–160. London: Fontana.

Boserup, E. (1965). *The Conditions of Agricultural Growth*. London: Earthscan, 1993.

Boulding, K. (1966). "The Economics of the Coming Spaceship Earth." In *Environmental Quality in a Growing Economy*, H. Jarret (ed.). Baltimore, MD: Johns Hopkins University Press.

BP (2008). *Statistical Review of World Energy* (June). www.bp.com/statisticalreview.

BP (2012). *Oil Exports and Imports*. http://www.bp.com/subsection.do?categoryId =9037149&contentId=7068599.

Braudel, F. (1966). *La Méditerranée et le monde méditerranéen à l'epoque de Philippe II*. (2nd ed.). Paris: Colin.

———. (1979). *Civilisation matérielle, économie et capitalisme, I, Le structures du quotidien, II, Les jeux de l'échange, III, Les temps du monde*. Paris: Colin.

Braun, E. (1980). "From Transistor to Microprocessor." In *The Microelectronics Revolution*, T. Forester (ed.), pp. 72–82. Oxford: Basil Blackwell.

Braun, E. and S. Macdonald (1982). *Revolution in Miniature: The History and Impact of Semiconductor Electronics Re-explored*. Cambridge: Cambridge University Press.

Bray, F. (1986). *The Rice Economies. Technology and Development in Asian Societies*. Oxford: Blackwell.

————. (1994). "Agriculture for Developing Nations." *Scientific American* 271.

Bray, W. (1968). *Everyday Life of the Aztecs*. New York: Dorset Press.

Bresnahan, T. F., and M. Trajtenberg (1995). "General Purpose Technologies: 'Engines of Growth?'" *Journal of Econometrics*, 65, no. 1: 83–108.

Brimblecombe, P. (1987). *The Big Smoke: A History of Air Pollution in London Since Medieval Times*. London: Methuen.

British Parliamentary Papers (1866). *Reports Received from Her Majesty's Secretaries of Embassy and Legation Respecting Coal.*

————. (1871). *Report of the Royal Commission on Coal Supply.*

Broadberry, S. (1997). *The Productivity Race: British Manufacturing in International Perspective, 1850–1990*. Cambridge: Cambridge University Press.

————. (2006). "Market Services and the Productivity Race 1850–2000: British Performance in International Perspective." *Cambridge Studies in Economic History.* Cambridge: Cambridge University Press.

Broadberry, S., B. Campbell, A. Klein, M. Overton, and B. van Leeuwen (2011). "British Economic Growth, 1270–1870." Working paper, London School of Economics. http://www2.lse.ac.uk/economicHistory/seminars/ModernAndComparative/papers2011–12/Papers/Broadberry.pdf.

Broadberry, S., Fremdling, R., Solar, P. (2010). "Industry." In *The Cambridge Economic History of Modern Europe. Vol. 1. 1700–1870*, S. Broadberry and K. O'Rourke (eds.). Cambridge: Cambridge University Press.

Broadberry, S., and B. Gupta (2006). "The Early Modern Great Divergence: Wages, Prices and Economic Development in Europe and Asia, 1500–1800." *Economic History Review,* II s., LIX: 2–31.

Broadberry, S., and B. van Leeuwen (2010). "British Economic Growth and the Business Cycle, 1700–1850: Annual Estimates." Working Paper, University of Warwick.

Brookes, L. G. (1990). "The Greenhouse Effect: The Fallacies in the Energy Efficiency Solutions." *Energy Policy* 18: 199–201.

Brooks, J. (1976). *Telephone: The First Hundred Years*. New York: Harper & Row.

Brose, E. D. (1983). *The Politics of Technological Change in Prussia. Out of the Shadow of Antiquity, 1809–1848*. Princeton: Princeton University Press.

Brüggemeier, F. J. (1996). *Das unendliche Meer der Lüfte. Luftverschmutzung, Industrialisierung und Risikodebatten im 19. Jahrhundert*. Essen: Klar-text.

Brun, J.-P. (2006). "L'énergie hydraulique durant l'empire Romain: quel impact sur l'économie agricole?" In *Innovazione tecnica e progresso economico nel mondo romano*, Lo Cascio, E. (ed.), pp. 101–31. Bari: Edipuglia.

Brunetti, M., M. Maugeri, F. Monti, and T. Nanni (2006). "Temperature and Precipitation Variability in Italy in the Last Two Centuries from Homogenised Instrumental Time Series." *International Journal of Climatology* 26: 345–81.

Büntgen, U., et al. (2011). "2500 Years of European Climate Variability and Human Susceptibility." *Science* 331 (Feb 4): 578–82.

Burt, R. (1995). "The Transformation of the Non-ferrous Metals Industries in the Seventeenth and Eighteenth Centuries." *Economic History Review* 48, no. 1: 23–45.

Caboara, M. (1998). "Demografia del pianeta Cina." *I viaggi di Erodoto* 12, no. 34: 52–63.

Cafagna, L. (1973). "Italy 1830–1914." In *The Fontana Economic History of Europe. The Emergence of Industrial Societies. Vol.1*, C. M. Cipolla (ed.), pp. 279–328. London: Fontana.

Cameron, R. (1985). "A New View of European Industrialization." *Economic History Review* 38: 1–23.

Campbell, B.M.S. (2003). "The Uses and Exploitation of Human Power from the 13th to the 18th Century." In *Economia e energia Secc. XIII–XVIII*, S. Cavaciocchi (ed.), pp. 183–221. Istituto Internazionale di Storia economica "F. Datini." Firenze: Le Monnier.

Caron, F. (1983). "France." In *Railways and the Economic Development of Western Europe, 1830–1914*, P. O'Brien (ed.), pp. 28–48. London: Macmillan.

Carreras, A. and C. Josephson (2010). "Aggregate Growth, 1870–1914: Growing at the Production Frontier." In *The Cambridge Economic History of Modern Europe. Vol. 2. 1870 to the Present*, S. Broadberry and K. O'Rourke (eds.), pp. 30–58. Cambridge: Cambridge University Press.

Cartier, M. (1985). "Conditions technologiques, sociales et politiques de la croissance démographique chinoise." *Des labours de Cluny à la Revolution verte. Techniques agricoles et population.* Paris: PUF.

Castells, M. (1996). "The Information Age." *Economy, Society and Culture, Volume 1: The Rise of the Network Society.* Oxford: Blackwell.

Chesnais, J.-C. (1986). *La transition démographique.* Paris: Presses Universitaires de France.

Chick, M. (2007). *Electricity and Energy Policy in Britain, France and the United States since 1945.* Cheltenham: Edward Elgar.

Chierici, R. (1911). *I boschi nell'economia generale d'Italia. Loro stima.* Caserta: Tipografia della Libreria Moderna.

Childe, G. (1936). *Man Makes Himself.* London: Watts.

———. (1942). *What Happened in History.* Harmondsworth: Penguin.

Choi, K. H., and B. W. Ang (2003). "Decomposition of Aggregate Energy Intensity Changes in Two Measures: Ratio and Difference." *Energy Economics* 25, no. 6: 615–24.

Chorley, G.P.H. (1981). "The Agricultural Revolution in Northern Europe, 1750–1880: Nitrogen, Legumes, and Crop Productivity." *Economic History Review* 34: 71–93.

Church, R. (1986). *The History of the British Coal Industry. Vol. 3, 1830–1913: Victorian Pre-eminence.* Oxford: Clarendon Press.

Church, R., and Q. Outram (1998). *Strikes and Solidarity: Coalfield Conflict in Britain, 1889–1966.* Cambridge: Cambridge University Press.

Cinnirella, F. (2008). "Optimists or Pessimists? A Reconsideration of Nutritional Status in Britain, 1740–1865." *European Review of Economic History* 12: 325–54.

Cipolla, C. M. (1962). *The Economic History of World Population.* Harmondsworth: Penguin.

Clapp, B. W. (1994). *An Environmental History of Britain: Since the Industrial Revolution.* London: Longman.

Clark, C., and M. Haswell (1967). *The Economics of Subsistence Agriculture.* London-Melbourne-Toronto: St Martin's Press.

Clark, G. (2004). "The Price History of English Agriculture, 1209–1914." *Research in Economic History* 22: 41–120.

———. (2007). *A Farewell to Alms. A Brief Economic History of the World.* Princeton and Oxford: Princeton University Press.

Clark, G., and D. Jacks (2007). "Coal and the Industrial Revolution 1700–1869." *European Review of Economic History* 11: 39–72.

Cleveland, C. J. (2008). "Energy Return on Investment." In *Encyclopedia of the Earth*, C. J. Cleveland (ed.). Washington, DC: Environmental Information Coalition, National Council for Science and the Environment. http://www.eoearth.org /article/Energy_return_on_investment_(EROI)

Cleveland, C. J., R. K. Kaufmann, and D. I. Stern (2000). "Aggregation and the Role of Energy in the Economy." *Ecological Economics* 32: 301–18.

Cleveland, C. J., R. Costanza, C.A.S. Hall, and R. Kaufman (1984). "Energy and the U.S. Economy: A Biophysical Perspective." *Science* 225: 890–97.

Clow, A., and N. L. Clow (1952). *The Chemical Revolution: A Contribution to Social Technology*. London: Batchworth.

Cohen, J. (1995). *How Many People Can the Earth support?* New York–London: Norton and Company.

Coleman, D. C. (1958). *The British Paper Industry, 1495–1860: A Study in Industrial Growth*. Oxford: Clarendon Press.

Collins, E.J.T. (1999). "Power Availability and Agricultural Productivity in England and Wales 1840–1939." In *Land Productivity and Agro-Systems in the North Sea Area, Middle Ages-20th Century. Elements for Comparison*, B.J.P. van Bavel and E. Turnhout Thoen (eds.), pp. 209–25. Turnhout: Brepols.

———. (2009). *Animal Power in European Agriculture in the 20th Century*. paper for the World Congress in Economic History in Utrecht, August 2–August 7.

———. (2010). "The Latter-day History of the Draught Ox in England, 1770–1964." *Agricultural History Review* 58: 191 – 216.

Commoner, B. (1972). "The Environmental Cost of Economic Growth." In *Population, Resources and the Environment*, pp. 339–63. Washington, DC: Government Printing Office.

Cook, E. (1976). *Man, Energy, Society*. San Francisco: W.H. Freeman.

Cornelisse, C. (2008). *Energiemarkten en energiehandel in Holland in de late Middeleeuwen*. Hilversum: Historische Vereniging Holland.

Corona E. (1992). "Cambiamento globale del clima: stato della ricerca italiana." *Atti dei convegni Lincei*, 95.

Costanza, R., L. Graumlich, W. Steffen, C. Crumley, J. Dearing, K. Hibbard, R. Leemans, C. Redman. and D. Schimel (2007). "Sustainability or Collapse: What Can We Learn from Integrating the History of Humans and the Rest of Nature?" *AMBIO: Journal of the Human Environment* 36, no. 7: 522–27.

Cottrell, F. (1955). *Energy and Society: The Relation between Energy, Social Changes, and Economic Development*. New York: McGraw-Hill.

Crafts, N. (2004). "Steam as a General Purpose Technology: A Growth Accounting Perspective." *Economic History Review* 3, no. 4: 67–76.

Crafts, N.F.R. (1977). "Industrial Revolution in England and France: Some Thoughts on the Question, 'Why Was England First?'" *Economic History Review* 30, no. 3: 429–41.

———. (1985). *British Economic Growth during the Industrial Revolution*. Oxford: Clarendon.

———. (1999). "Economic Growth in the Twentieth Century." *Oxford Review of Economic Policy* 15: 18–34.

———. (2003). "Quantifying the Contribution of Technological Change to Economic Growth in Different Eras: A Review of the Evidence." *LSE Working Paper*, No. 79/03.

Crafts, N.F.R., and C. K. Harley (1992). "Output Growth and the British Industrial Revolution: A Restatement of the Crafts-Harley View." *Economic History Review* 45, no. 4: 703–30.

Crafts, N.F.R., and G. Toniolo (eds.) (1996). *Economic Growth in Europe since 1945*. Cambridge: Cambridge University Press.

Cramér, M. (1991). *Den verkliga kakelugnen*. Stockholm.

Cronon, W. (1991). *Nature's Metropolis: Chicago and the Great West*. New York: Norton.

Crosby, A. (1972). *The Colombian Exchange. Biological and Cultural Consequences of 1492*. Westport: Praeger.

Crosby, A. W. (2006). *Children of the Sun: A History of Humanity's Unappeasable Appetite for Energy*. New York: Norton.

Crouzet, F. (1996). "France." In *The Industrial Revolution in National Context*, M. Teich and R. Porter (eds.), pp. 36–63. Cambridge: Cambridge University Press.

Crowley, J. E. (2001). *The Invention of Comfort: Sensibilities and Design in Early Modern Britain and Early America*. Baltimore and London: Johns Hopkins University Press.

Crowley, Th. (2000). "Causes of Climate Change over the Past 1000 Years." *Science* 289: 270–77.

Dahmén, E. (1950). *Svensk industriell företagarverksamhet. Kausalanalys av den industriella utvecklingen 1919–1939. Part I–II*. Stockholm: IUI.

———. (1988). "Development Blocks in Industrial Economics." *Scandinavian Economic History Review* 36: 3–14.

Daly, H. (1992). *Steady-State Economics*. London: Earthscan Publications Ltd.

David, P. A. (1975). *Technical Choice Innovation and Economic Growth: Essays on American and British Experience in the Nineteenth Century*. Cambridge: Cambridge University Press.

———. (1990). "The Dynamo and the Computer: A Historical Perspective on the Modern Productivity Paradox." *American Economic Review* 80: 355–61.

David, P., and G. Wright (1999). "Early Twentieth Century Productivity Growth Dynamics: An Inquiry into the Economic History of 'Our Ignorance'." *Journal of Economic History* 6: 523.

Davids, C. A. (1990). "The Transfer of Windmill Technology from the Netherlands to North-Eastern Europe from the 16th to the Early 19th Century." In *Baltic Affairs. Relations Between the Netherlands and North-Eastern Europe, 1500–1800*, J. Ph. S. Lemmink and J. S. A .M. Konongsbrugge (eds.), pp. 33–52. Groningen: INOS.

———. (2003). "Innovations in Windmill Technology in Europe, c. 1500–1800." In *Economia e energia Secc. XIII–XVIII*, S. Cavaciocchi (ed.), pp. 271–92. Istituto Internazionale di Storia economica "F. Datini." Firenze: Le Monnier.

Davidson, C. (1986). *A Woman's Work Is Never Done: A History of Housework in the British Isles 1650–1950*. London: Chatto & Windus.

Davis, R. (1967). *A Commercial Revolution. English Overseas Trade in the Seventeenth and Eighteenth Centuries*. London: Historical Association.

————. (1979). *The Industrial Revolution and the British Overseas Trade.* Leicester: Leicester University Press.

Dean, J. (1950). "Pricing Policies for New Products." *Harvard Business Review* 28, no. 6: 45.

Deane, P., and W. A. Cole (1962). *British Economic Growth 1688–1959. Trends and Structures.* Cambridge: Cambridge University Press.

Debeir, J. C., J. P. Deléage, and D. Hémery (1986). *Les servitudes de la puissance. Une histoire de l'énergie.* Paris: Flammarion.

DEFRA (Department for the Environment, Food and Rural Affairs). (2010). *Yield and Production Time Series.* http://www.defra.gov.uk/evidence/statistics /foodfarm/food/cereals/ cerealsoilseed.htm

Dejongh, G. (1999). "New Estimates of Land Productivity in Belgium, 1750–1850." *Agricultural History Review* 47: 7–28.

Deng, G. (1999). *The Chinese Pre-modern Economy. Structural Equilibrium and Capitalist Sterility.* London-New York: Routledge.

Devèze, M. (1982). *La forêt et les communautés rurales. XVIe–XVIIIe siècles.* Paris: Publications de la Sorbonne.

Devine, W. D. (1983). "From Shafts to Wires: Historical Perspective on Electrification." *Journal of Economic History* 43: 347–72.

De Vries, J. (1976). *The Economy of Europe in an Age of Crisis, 1600–1750.* Cambridge: Cambridge University Press.

————. (2008). *The Industrious Revolution: Consumer Behavior and the Household Economy, 1650 to the Present.* Cambridge: Cambridge University Press.

Dhondt, J., and M. Bruwier (1973). "The Low Countries 1700–1914." In *The Fontana Economic History of Europe. The Emergence of Industrial Societies. Vol.1,* C. M. Cipolla (ed.), pp. 329–61. London: Fontana.

Dietz, B. (1997). "Wirtschaftliches Wachstum und Holzmangel im bergisch-märkischen Gewerberaum vor der Industrialisierung." November 29, 1995 vor dem *Verein für Orts- und Heimatkunde der Grafschaft Mark im Märkischen Museum Witten.* http://www.lrz.de/~rpf/hardenstein/DIETZ.HTM.

Digest of United Kingdom Energy Statistics, London: Department of Trade and Industry.

Dinda, S. (2004). "Environmental Kuznets Curve Hypothesis: A Survey." *Ecological Economics* 49: 431–55.

Ditt, K. (ed.) (2001). *Agrarmodernisierung und ökologische Folgen: Westfalen vom 18. bis zum 20. Jahrhundert.* Paderborn: Schöningh.

Durgin, W. A. (1912). *Electricity. Its History and Development.* Chicago: A. C. McClurg & Co.

Duvigneaud, P. (1967). *L'écologie, science moderne de sinthèse.* Bruxelles: Ministère de l'Education Nationale et de la Culture.

Eddy, J. A., P. A. Gilman, and D. A. Trotter (1976). "Solar Rotation during the Maunder Minimum." *Solar Physics* 46: 3–14.

Eddy, J. A. (1977a). "Climate and the Changing Sun." *Climatic Change* I: 173–90.

————. (1977b). "The Case of the Missing Sunspots." *Scientific American* 236, no. 5: 80–95.

Edgerton, D. (2007). *The Shock of the Old.* Oxford: Oxford University Press.

Edholm, O. G. (1967). *The Biology of Work.* London: Weidenfeld and Nicolson.

Edwinsson, R. and J. Söderberg (2007). *Consumer Price Index 1290–2006*. Sveriges Riksbank. http://www.historia.se/.

Ehrlich, P. R., and J. P. Holdren (1971). "Impact of Population Growth." *Science* 171: 1212–17.

Ekins, P. (1997). "The Kuznets Curve for the Environment and Economic Growth: Examining the Evidence." *Environment and Planning* 29: 805–30.

———. (2000). *Economic Growth and Environmental Sustainability: The Prospects of Green Growth*. London: Routledge.

Elvin, M. (1973). *The Pattern of the Chinese Past*. Stanford: Stanford University Press.

Endres, M. (1905). *Handbuch der Forstpolitik besonderer Berücksichtigung der Gesetzgebung und Statistik*. Berlin: Springer.

Energy Information Administration, http://tonto.eia.doe.gov/dnav/pet/pet_pri_land1_k_m.htm.

Energy Statistics (1987). *Definitions, Units of Measure and Conversion Factors*. New York: United Nations.

Enflo, K., A. Kander, and L. Schön (2008). "Identifying Development Blocks: A New Methodology." *Journal of Evolutionary Economics* 18: 57–76.

———. (2009). "Electrification and Energy Productivity." *Ecological Economics*, 68: 2808–17.

Etemad, B., and J. Luciani (1991). *World Energy Production 1800–1985*. Genève: Droz.

EU KLEMS Database. *Growth and Productivity Accounts*. www.euklems.net.

Evans, C. (2005). "The Industrial Revolution in Iron in the British Isles." In *The Industrial Revolution in Iron: The Impact of British Coal Technology in Nineteenth-Century Europe*, C. Evans and G. Rydén (ed.), pp. 15–27. Aldershot: Ashgate.

Evans, C., and G. Rydén (2005). *The Industrial Revolution in Iron: The Impact of British Coal Technology in Nineteenth-Century Europe*. C. Evans and G. Rydén (eds.). Aldershot: Ashgate.

———. (2007). *Baltic Iron in the Atlantic World in the Eighteenth Century*. Leiden: Brill.

Evans, C., O. Jackson, and G. Rydén (2002). "Baltic Iron and the British Iron Industry in the Eighteenth Century." *Economic History Review* 55, no. 4: 642–65.

Evelyn, J. (1661). *Fumifugium, or: The Inconveniencie of the Air and Smoke of London Dissipated*. London: Godbid.

Fagan B. (2000). *The Little Ice Age. How Climate Made History 1300–1850*. New York: Basic Books.

Falkus, M. E. (1967). "The British Gas Industry before 1850." *Economic History Review* 20, no. 3: 494–508.

———. (1982). "The Early Development of the British Gas Industry, 1790–1815." *Economic History Review* 35, no. 2: 217–34.

Federico, G. (2005). *Feeding the World: An Economic History of Agriculture, 1800–2000*. Princeton: Princeton University Press.

Federico, G. and P. Malanima (2004). "Progress, Decline, Growth: Product and Productivity in Italian Agriculture, 1000–2000." *Economic History Review* II: 437–64.

Feinstein, C. H. (1972). *National Income. Expenditure and Output of the United Kingdom, 1855–1965*. Cambridge: Cambridge University Press.

Feinstein, C. H., and S. Pollard (1988). *Studies in Capital Formation in the United Kingdom 1750–1920*. Oxford: Clarendon.

Feldenkirchen, W. (1982). *Die Eisen- und Stahlindustrie des Ruhrgebiets 1879–1914: Wachstum, Finanzierung und Struktur ihrer Grossunternehmen*. Wiesbaden: Steiner.

Fenoaltea, S. (1983). "Italy." In *Railways and the Economic Development of Western Europe, 1830–1914*, P. O'Brien (ed.), pp. 49–120. London: Macmillan.

Fenton, R. (2008). "The Introduction of Steam to UK Coastal Bulk Trades: A Technological and Commercial Assessment." *International Journal of Maritime History* 20: 175–200.

Fernández de Pinedo, E., and R. A. Ayo (2005). "British Technology and Spanish Ironmaking during the Nineteenth Century." In *The Industrial Revolution in Iron*, C. Evans and G. Rydén (eds.), pp. 151–72. Aldershot: Ashgate.

Findlay, R., and K. O'Rourke (2007). *Power and Plenty, Trade, War and the World Economy in the Second Millenium*. Princeton: Princeton University Press.

Flegel, K., and M. Turnow (1915). "Montanstatistik des Deutschen Reiches: die Entwicklung der deutschen Montanindustrie von 1860–1912." *Königlich preussischen geologischen Landesanstalt*.

Flinn, M. W. (1984). *The History of British Coal Industry*. Oxford: Clarendon Press.

Floud, R., R. W. Fogel, B. Harris, and S. C. Hong (2011). *The Changing Body: Health, Nutrition, and Human Development in the Western World since 1700*. Cambridge: Cambridge University Press.

Flygare, I. A. and M. Isacson (2003). *Jordbruket i välfärdssamhället, 1945–2000, band 2*. Stockholm.

Fogel, R. W. (1964). *Railroads and American Economic Growth: Essays in Econometric History*. Baltimore: Johns Hopkins University Press.

———. (1993). *Economic Growth, Population Theory, and Physiology: The Bearing of Long-term Processes on the Making of Economic Policy*. Nobel Lecture.

———. (1994). "Economic Growth, Population Theory and Physiology: The Bearing of Long-Term Processes on the Making of Economic Policy." *American Economic Review* 84: 369–95.

Fogel, R. W., S. L. Engerman, R. Floud, G. Friedman, R. A. Margo, K. Sokoloff, R. H. Steckel, T. J. Trussell, G. Villaflor, and K. W. Wachter (1983). "Secular Changes in American and British Stature and Nutrition." *Journal of Interdisciplinary History* 14(2): 445–81.

Fohlen, C. (1973). "France 1700–1914." In *The Fontana Economic History of Europe. The Emergence of Industrial Societies, Vol.1*, C. M. Cipolla (ed.), pp. 7–57. London: Fontana.

Fontana, G. L. (2006). "The Economic Development of Europe in the Nineteenth Century: The Revolution in Transport and Communications." In *An Economic History of Europe. From Expansion to Development*, A. Vittorio (ed.). London: Routledge.

Forbes, R. J. (1956). "Power." In *A History of Technology, II*, Ch. Singer, E. J. Holmyard, A. R. Hall, and T. I. Williams (eds.), pp. 589–628. New York–London: Oxford University Press.

———. (1958). *Early Petroleum History. Part I*. Leiden: E.J. Brill.

———. (1959). *More Studies in Early Petroleum History 1860–1880*. Leiden: E.J. Brill.

Foreman-Peck, J. (1992). "The Development and Diffusion of Telephone Technology in Britain, 1900–1940." *Transactions of the Newcomen Society* 63: 173.

Fouquet, R. (2008*). Heat, Power and Light: Revolutions in Energy Services.* Cheltenham and Northampton: Edward Elgar.

———. (2009). "A Brief History of Energy." In *International Handbook of the Economics of Energy*, J. Evans and L. C. Hunt (eds.), pp. 1–19. Cheltenham-Northhampton: E. Elgar.

———. (2011). *Divergences in Long-Run Trends in the Prices of Energy and Energy Services.* Basque Centre for Climate Change (BC3).

Fouquet, R., and P.J.G. Pearson (1998). "A Thousand Years of Energy Use in the United Kingdom." *Energy Journal* 19(4): 1–41.

Fremdling, R. (1975). *Eisenbahnen und deutschen Wirtschaftswachstum 1840–1879. Ein Beitrag zur Entwicklungstheorie und zue Theorie der Infrastruktur.* Dortmund: Gesellschaft für Westfälische Wirtschaftsgeschichte.

———. (1983). "Germany." In *Railways and the Economic Development of Western Europe, 1830–1914*, P. O'Brien (ed.), pp.121–47. London: Macmillan.

———. (2002). "Regionale Interdependenzen zwischen Montanregionen in der Industrialisierung." In *Die Industrialisierung europäischer Montanregionen im 19. Jahrhundert*, T. Pierenkemper (ed.), pp. 365–88. Stuttgart: Steiner.

———. (2004). "Continental Responses to British Innovations in the Iron Industry during the Eighteenth and Early Nineteenth Centuries." In *Exceptionalism and Industrialisation: Britain and its European Rivals, 1688–1815*, L. Prados de la Escosura (ed.), pp.145–69. Cambridge: Cambridge University Press.

———. (2005). "Foreign Trade-Transfer-Adaptation: British Iron-Making Technology on the Continent (Belgium and France)." In *The Industrial Revolution in Iron*, C. Evans and G. Rydén (eds.), pp. 29–53. Aldershot: Ashgate.

Fritzsche, B. (1996). "Switzerland." In *The Industrial Revolution in National Context*, M. Teich and R. Porter (eds.), pp. 126–48. Cambridge: Cambridge University Press.

Fuchs, C. (2006). "The Implications of New Information and Communication Technologies for Sustainability." *Environment, Development and Sustainability* 10: 291–309.

Gales, B.P.A. (2004). *Delven en slepen. Steenkolemijnbouw in Limburg: techniek, winning en markt gedurende de achttiende en negentiende eeuw.* Hilversum: Verloren.

Gales, B., A. Kander, P. Malanima, and M. Rubio (2007). "North versus South. Energy Transition and Energy Intensity in Europe over 200 Years." *European Review of Economic History* 11: 215–49.

Galloway, P. (1986). "Long-Term Fluctuations in Climate and Population in the Pre-industrial Era." *Population and Development Review* 12: 1–24.

Galvin, R. and K. Yeager (2009). *Perfect Power. How the Microgrid Revolution Will Unleash Cleaner, Greener and More Abundant Energy.* New York: McGraw-Hill.

Garnaut, R. (2011). *The Garnaut Review 2011. Australia in the Global Response to Climate Change.* Cambridge: Cambridge University Press.

Gasparini, D. (2002). *Polenta e formenton. Il mais nelle campagne venete tra XVI e XX secolo.* Verona: Cierre.

Gerding, M.A.W. (1995). *Vier eeuwen turfwinning. De verveningen in Groningen, Friesland, Drenthe en Overijssel tussen 1550 en 1950.* A.A.G. Bijdragen 35.

Gerhold, D. (1996). "Productivity Change in Road Transport before and after Turnpiking, 1690–1840." *Economic History Review* 49: 491–515.

Gerschenkron, A. (1962). *Economic Backwardness in Historical Perspective: A Book of Essays*. Cambridge, MA: Belknap Press.

Girod, B., A. Wiek, H. Mieg, and M. Hulme (2009). "The Evolution of the IPCC's Emissions Scenarios." *Environmental Science & Policy* 12: 103–18.

Glennie, K. W. (1998). *Petroleum Geology of the North Sea: Basic Concepts and Recent Advances*. Abingdon: Blackwell.

Global Wind Energy Outlook (2010). http://www.gwec.net/fileadmin/documents /Publications/GWEO%202010%20final.pdf

Goldstone, J. A. (2002). "Efflorescences and Economic Growth in World History: Rethinking the 'Rise of the West' and the Industrial Revolution." *Journal of World History* 13: 323–89.

———. (2003). "Feeding the People, Starving the State: China's Agricultural Revolution of the 17th–18th Centuries." Paper prepared for the conference in London, September 2003, sponsored by the Global Economic History Network and the Leverhulme Foundation.

Gordon, R. B. (1983). "Cost and Use of Water Power during Industrialization in New England and Great Britain: A Geological Interpretation." *Economic History Review* 36: 240–59.

Graaf, R. de (2011). *The Netherlands and Energy Embodied in Foreign Trade: A Decomposition Analysis of Structural and Technical Effects*. Master's thesis, University of Lund.

Grafe, R., L. Neal, and R. W. Unger (2010). "The Service Sector." In *The Cambridge Economic History of Modern Europe. Vol. 1. 1700–1870*, S. Broadberry and K. O'Rourke (eds.), pp. 187–213. Cambridge: Cambridge University Press.

Grathwohl, M. (1982). *World Energy Supply: Resources, Technologies, Perspectives*. New York: Walter de Gruyter.

Greasley, D. (1982). "The Diffusion of Machine Cutting in the British Coal Industry, 1902–1938." *Explorations in Economic History* 19, no. 3: 246–68.

Greasley, D., and L. Oxley (2000). "British Industrialization, 1815–1860: A Disaggregate Time Series Perspective." *Explorations in Economic History* 37: 98–119.

———. (2007). "Patenting, Intellectual Property Rights and Sectoral Outputs in Industrial Revolution Britain, 1780–1851." *Journal of Econometrics* 139: 340–54.

———. (2010). "Knowledge, Natural Resource Abundance and Economic Development: Lessons from New Zealand 1861–1939." *Explorations in Economic History* 47: 443–59.

Greenberg, D. (1982). "Reassessing the Power Patterns of the Industrial Revolution: An Anglo-American Comparison." *American Historical Review* 87, no. 4: 1237–61.

———. (1992). "Fuelling the Illusion of Progress: Energy and Industrialisation in the European Experience." In *Energy and Environment, The Policy Challenge*, J. Byrne and D. Rich (eds.). New Brunswick, NJ: Transaction Publishers.

Grewe, B.-S. (2007). *Der versperrte Wald: Ressourcenmangel in der bayerischen Pfalz (1814–1870)*. Köln: Böhlau.

Griffin, E. (2010). *Short History of the British Industrial Revolution*. Basingstoke: Palgrave Macmillan.

Grigg, D. (1974). *The Agricultural Systems of the World. An Evolutionary Approach*. Cambridge: Cambridge University Press.

———. (1982). *The Dynamics of Agricultural Change*. London and Melbourne: Hutchinson.

———. (1992). *The World Food Problem*. Oxford: Blackwell.

———. (1995). "The Nutritional Transition in Western Europe." *Journal of Historical Geography* 21, no. 3: 247–61.

Griliches, Z. (1971). *Price Indexes and Quality Change: Studies in New Methods of Measurement*. Cambridge, MA: Harvard University Press.

Groote, P., R. Albers, and H. De Jong (1996). *A Standardised Time Series of the Stock of Fixed Capital in the Netherlands, 1900–1995, appendix 3*. http://www.ggdc.nl/publications/memoabstract.htm?id=25.

Gross, N. T. (1973). "The Habsburg Monarchy 1750–1914." In *The Fontana Economic History of Europe. The Emergence of Industrial Societies, Vol.1*, C. M. Cipolla (ed.), pp. 228–78. London: Fontana.

Grübler, A. (1998). *Technology and Global Change*. Cambridge: Cambridge University Press.

———. (2004). "Transitions in Energy Use." In *Encyclopedia of Energy*, C. J. Cleveland (ed.), pp. 163–77. Burlington, MA: Elsevier.

Grübler, A., and N. Nakicenovic (1996). "Decarbonizing the Global Energy System." *Technological Forecasting and Social Change* 53: 97–110.

Guerra, A.-I., and F. Sancho (2010). "Rethinking Economy-Wide Rebound Measures: An Unbiased Proposal." *Energy Policy* 38, no. 2010: 6684–94.

Gunnarsson, C., and M. Andersson (2011). *Hållbarhetsmyten – Varför ekonomisk tillväxt inte är problemet*. SNS.

Gustafsson, B. (1996). "The Industrial Revolution in Sweden." In *The Industrial Revolution in National Context*, M. Teich and R. Porter (eds.), pp. 201–25. Cambridge: Cambridge University Press.

Habakkuk, H. J. (1962). *American and British Technology in the 19th Century*. Cambridge: Cambridge University Press.

Hagberg, J.-E. (1986). "Tekniken i kvinnornas händer. Hushållsarbete och hushållsteknik under tjugo- och trettiotalen." *Linköping Studies in Art and Science*. Malmö: Liber Förlag.

Haimson, L. H., and C. Tilly (ed.) (1989). *Strikes, Wars, and Revolutions in an International Perspective: Strike Waves in the Late Nineteenth and Early Twentieth Centuries*. Cambridge: Cambridge University Press.

Hanley, N., P. McGregor, J. Swaies, and K. Turner (2009). "Do Increases in Energy Efficiency Improve Environmental Quality and Sustainability?" *Ecological Economics* 68: 692–709.

Hannah, L. (1979). *Electricity before Nationalization. A Study of the Development of the Electricity Supply Industry in Britain to 1948*. London: Macmillan.

Harberger, A. C. (1998). "A Vision of the Growth Process." *American Economic Review* 88: 1–32.

Harley, C. K. (1972). "The Shift from Sailing Ships to Steam Ships, 1850–1890." In *Essays on a Mature Economy: Britain after 1840*, D. N. McCloskey (ed.), pp. 215–34. London: Methuen.

———. (1988). "Ocean Freight Rates and Productivity, 1740–1913: The Primacy of Mechanical Invention Reaffirmed." *Journal of Economic History* 48: 851–76.

Harley, K., and N. Crafts (2000). "Simulating the Two Views of the British Industrial Revolution." *Journal of Economic History* 60: 819–41.

Harris, J. (1978–79). "Recent Research on the Newcomen Engine and Historical

Studies." *Newcomen Society for the Study of the History of Engineering and Technology* 50: 208–13.

———. (1992). "Introduction." *Essays in Industry and Technology in the 18th Century: England and France*. Brookfield: Variorum.

Harris, W. (2011). "Bois et déboisement dans la Méditerranée antique." *Annales HSS* 1: 105–40.

Hartwell, R. M. (1967). "A Cycle of Economic Change in Imperial China: Coal and Iron in North-East China, 750–1350." *Journal of the Economic and Social History of the Orient* 10: 478–92.

Hasel, K., and E. Schwartz (2006). *Forstgeschichte. Ein Grundriss für Studium und Praxis*. Kessel: Norbert.

Hatcher, J. (1993). *The History of the British Coal Industry, I, Before 1700*. Oxford: Clarendon Press.

———. (2003). "The Emergence of a Mineral-Based Energy Economy in England, c. 1550–c. 1850." In *Economia e energia Secc. XIII–XVIII*, S. Cavaciocchi (ed.), pp. 483–504. Istituto Internazionale di Storia economica "F. Datini." Firenze: Le Monnier.

Haudricourt, A. G., and M. J.-B. Delamarre (1955). *L'homme et la charrue à travers le monde*. Paris: Gallimard.

Hausman, W. J. (1987). "The English Coastal Coal Trade, 1691–1910: How Rapid Was Productivity Growth?" *Economic History Review* 40, no. 4: 588–96.

Hausman, W. J., P. Hertner, and M. Wilkins (2008). *Global Electrification: Multinational Enterprise and International Finance in the History of Light and Power, 1878–2007*. Cambridge: Cambridge University Press.

Hawke, G. R. (1970). *Railways and Economic Growth in England and Wales, 1840–1870*. Oxford: Clarendon.

Hayami, A. (1990). "Introduction." In *Economic and Demographic Development in Rice Producing Societies: Some Aspects of East Asian Economic History, Tenth International Economic History Congress (Leuven, August 1990)*, A. Hayami and Y. Tsubouchi (eds.), pp. 6–20. Leuven: Leuven University Press.

Hayami, A., J. De Vries, and A. Van der Woude (eds.) (1990). *Urbanization in History. A Process of Dynamic Interactions*. Oxford: Clarendon Press.

Hayami, Y., and V. W. Ruttan (1985). *Agricultural Development: An International Perspective*. (Rev. and expanded ed.) Baltimore: Johns Hopkins University Press.

Heilbron, J. L. (1979). *Electricity in the 17th and 18th Centuries*. Berkeley, Los Angeles, London: University of California Press.

Hennessey, R.A.S. (1972). *The Electric Revolution*. Newcastle upon Tyne: Oriel Press.

Henning, F.-W. (1996). *Deutsche Wirtschafts- und Sozialgeschichte im 19. Jahrhundert*. Paderborn: Schöningh.

Henriques, S. (2009). *Energy Consumption in Portugal 1856–2006*. Napoli: ISSM–CNR.

———. (2011). *Energy Transitions, Economic Growth and Structural Change: Portugal in a Long-run Comparative Perspective*. Lund: Lund University Press.

Henriques, S., and A. Kander (2010). "The Modest Environmental Relief Resulting from the Transition to the Service Economy." *Ecological Economics* 70: 271–82.

Herman, I. P. (2007). *Physics of the Human Body*. Berlin: Springer.

Herman, R., S. A. Ardekani, and J. H. Ausubel (1990). "Dematerialization." *Technological Forecasting and Social Change* 38: 333–47.

Hermele, K. (2002). *Vad kostar framtiden? Globaliseringen, miljön och Sverige.* Stockholm: Ordfront förlag.

Herranz-Loncán, A. (2006). "Railroad Impact in Backward Economies: Spain, 1850–1913." *Journal of Economic History* 66: 853–81.

Herrigel, G. (1996). *Industrial Constructions: The Sources of German Industrial Power.* Cambridge: Cambridge University Press.

Hertwich, E. G. (2005). "Consumption and the Rebound Effect." *Journal of Industrial Ecology* 9: 85–98.

Hertwich, E., K. Erlandsen, K. Sorenson, J. Aasness, and K. Hubacek (2002). *Pollution Embodied in Norway's Import and Export and its Relevance for the Environmental Profile of Households. Life-cycle Approaches to Sustainable Consumption.* IIASA Interim Report IR-02-073.

Heywood, J. B. (1988). *Internal Combustion Engine Fundamentals.* New York: McGraw-Hill.

Higounet, Ch. (1966). "Les forêts de l'Europe occidentale du Ve siècle à l'an mil." *XIII settimana di studi del Centro italiano di studi sull'alto Medioevo (Spoleto 1965),* Spoleto: CISAM: 343–99.

Hills, R. L. (1989). *Power from Steam: A History of the Stationary Steam Engine.* Cambridge: Cambridge University Press.

Historical Crude Oil Prices, 1861 to Present, ChartsBin.com; viewed February 29, 2012 at http://chartsbin.com/view/oau.

Hoffmann, W. G. (1965). *Das Wachstum der deutschen Wirtschaft seit der Mitte des 19. Jahrhunderts.* Berlin: Springer.

Holtfrerich, C. L. (1973). *Quantitative Wirtschaftsgeschichte des Ruhrkohlenbergbaus im 19. Jahrhundert. Eine Fuehrungssektoranalyse.* Dortmund: Ardey.

Hornborg, A. (2011). *The Power of the Machine: Global Inequalities of Economy, Technology and Environment.* New York: Altamira Press.

Horrell, S., J. Humphreys, and M. Weale (1994). "An Input-Output Table for 1841." *Economic History Review* 47: 545–66.

Houpt, S., P. Lains, and L. Schön (2010). "Sectoral Developments 1945–2000." In *The Cambridge Economic History of Modern Europe, volume 2: 1870 to the Present.* S. Broadberry and K. O'Rourke (eds.). Cambridge: Cambridge University Press.

Howarth, R. (1997). "Energy Efficiency and Economic Growth." *Contemporary Economic Policy* 15: 1–9.

Huebner, J. (2005). "A Possible Declining Trend for Worldwide Innovation." *Technological Forecasting & Social Change* 72: 980–86.

Hughes, T. P. (1983). *Networks of Power: Electrification in Western Society, 1880–1930.* Baltimore: Johns Hopkins University Press.

———. (1987). "The Evolution of Large Technological Systems." In *The Social Construction of Technological Systems: New Directions in the Sociology and History of Technology,* W. E. Bijker, P. T. Hughes, and J. T. Pinch (eds.). Cambridge, MA: MIT Press.

Hulme, M., and E. M. Barrow (eds.) (1997). *Climates of The British Isles: Present, Past and Future.* London: Routledge.

Humphries, J. (2011). "The Lure of Aggregates and the Pitfalls of the Patriarchal

Perspective: A Critique of the High Wage Economy Interpretation of the British Industrial Revolution." *University of Oxford Discussion Papers in Social and Economic History*, 91.

Huntington, H. G. (2005). "US Carbon Emissions, Technological Progress and Economic Growth since 1870." *International Journal of Global Energy Issues* 23, no. 4: 292–306.

Hyde, C. K. (1977). *Technological Change and the British Iron Industry, 1700–1870.* Princeton: Princeton University Press.

IEA (2006). World Energy Assessment 2006.

———. (2009). World Energy Outlook 2009. http://www.iea.org/speech/2009/Tanaka/WEO2009_Press_Conference.pdf.

———. (2010). World Energy Outlook 2010, http://www.iea.org/weo/docs/weo2010/weo2010_london_nov9.pdf;

IEA Statistics. Electricity Information 2008, Part III.

Ingelstam, L. (1997). *Ekonomi för en ny tid.* Stockholm: Carlssons.

International Energy Agency (2008). *World Wide Trends in Energy Use and Efficiency. Key Insights from IEA Indicator Analysis.*

IPCC (1997). *Intergovernmental Panel on Climate Change, Greenhouse Gas Inventory Reference Manual: Revised 1996 IPCC Guidelines for National Greenhouse Gas Inventories.* Paris.

Iriarte-Goñi, I. And M. I. Ayuda (2012). "Not only Subterranean Forests: Wood Consumption and Economic Development in Britain (1850–1938)." *Ecological Economics* 77: 176–84.

ISTAT (Istituto Nazionale di Statistica). (1958) *Sommario di statistische storiche italiane (1861–1955).* Rome: ISTAT.

Jacobs, A., and H. Richter (1935). *Die Großhandelspreise in Deutschland von 1792 bis 1934.* Hamburg: Hanseatische Verlagsanstalt.

Jakobsson, E. (1996). *Industrialiseringen av älvar. Studier kring svensk vattenkraftsutbyggnad 1900–1918.* Göteborg.

Jevons, W. S. (1866). *The Coal Question: An Enquiry Concerning the Progress of the Nation and the Probable Exhaustion of Our Coal-Mines.* (2nd ed.) London: Macmillan.

Johansson, T. B., and J. Goldemberg (2002). *Energy for Sustainable Development, United Nations Development Programme, New York.* Sweden: Rahms i Lund.

Jones, C. F. (2010). "A Landscape of Energy Abundance: Anthracite Coal Canals and the Roots of American Fossil Fuel Dependence, 1820–1860." *Environmental History* 15: 449–84.

Jones, C. I. (2002). *Introduction to Economic Growth*, 2nd ed. New York: Norton.

Jones, C. I., and P. M. Romer (2010). "The New Kaldor Facts: Ideas, Institutions, Population and Human Capital." *American Economic Journal: Macroeconomics* 2, no. 1: 224–45.

Jongman, W. M. (2007). "The Early Roman Empire: Consumption." In *Cambridge Economic History of the Greco-Roman World*, W. Scheidel, I. Morris, and R. Saller (eds.), pp. 592–618. Cambridge: Cambridge University Press.

Jörberg, L. (1973). "The Industrial Revolution in the Nordic Countries." In *The Fontana Economic History of Europe. The Emergence of Industrial Societies. Vol.2*, C. M. Cipolla, pp. 375–485. London: Fontana.

Juda, L. (1996). *International Law and Ocean Use Management.* London: Routledge.

Kahn, H. (1979). *World Economic Development: 1979 and Beyond* (paperback ed.). New York: Morrow Quill.

Kaijser, A. (1986). *Stadens ljus—Etableringen av de forsta svenska gasverken.* Linköping.

———. (1994). *I fädrens spår. Den svenska infrastrukturens historiska utveckling och framtida utmaningar.* Carlssons förlag.

Kaldor, N. (1960). *Essays on Economic Stability and Growth.* London and Southhampton: Camelot Press.

———. (1961). "Capital Accumulation and Economic Growth." In *The Theory of Capital*, F. A. Lutz and D. C. Hague (eds.), pp. 177–222. New York: St. Martins Press.

Kander, A. (2002). "Economic Growth, Energy Consumption and CO2 Emissions in Sweden 1800–2000." *Lund Studies in Economic History* 19, Lund: Almqvist & Wicksell International.

———. (2003). "Pre-Industrial Energy Use and CO2 Emissions in Sweden." In *Economia e energia Secc. XIII–XVIII*, S. Cavaciocchi (ed.), pp. 799–822. Istituto Internazionale di Storia economica "F. Datini." Firenze: Le Monnier.

———. (2005). "Baumol's Disease and Dematerialization of the Economy." *Ecological Economics*, 55: 119–30.

———. (2012). Article XVIII. "The NEGA-Emissions—A Necessary Complement to the Multiregional Input-Output Method for Assessing Environmental Debts." Paper for the World Economic History Conference in Stellenbosch, July.

Kander, A., and M. Lindmark (2006). "Foreign Trade and Declining Pollution in Sweden: A Decomposition Analysis of Long-term Structural and Technological Effects." *Energy Policy* 34, no. 13: 1590–99.

Kander, A., and L. Schön (2007). "The Energy-Capital Relation, Sweden 1870–2000." *Structural Change and Economic Dynamics* 18, no. 2007: 291–305.

Kander, A., and P. Warde (2009). "Number, Size and Energy Consumption of Draught Animals in European Agriculture." *Centre for History and Economics Working Paper.* http://www.histecon.magd.cam.ac.uk/history-sust/animals.htm.

———. (2011). "Energy Availability from Livestock and Agricultural Productivity in Europe, 1815–1913: A New Comparison." *Economic History Review* 64, no. 1: 1–29.

Kanefsky, J. W. (1978). *The Diffusion of Power Technology in British Industry 1760–1870.* PhD thesis, University of Exeter.

———. (1979). "Motive Power in British Industry and the Accuracy of the 1870 Factory Returns." *Economic History Review* 32: 360–75.

Kaplan, J. O., K. M. Krumhardt, and N. Zimmermann (2009). "The Prehistoric and Preindustrial Deforestation of Europe." *Quaternary Science Reviews* 28: 3016–34.

Kellenbenz, H. (1974). *Schwerpunkte der Eisengewinnung und Eisenverarbeitung in Europa 1500–1650.* Köln, Böhlau.

Kelly, M., and C. O'Grada (2010). "The Economic Impact of the Little Ice Age." *UCD Center for Economic Research*, WP 10/14, Working Paper Series.

Kenwood, G., and A. Lougheed (1992). *The Growth of the International Economy 1820–1990.* London: Routledge.

Kerpely, A. (1873) *A vaskohászat gyakorlati s elméleti kézikönyve.* Budapest: Légrády Ny.

Khazzoom, J. D. (1980). "Economic Implications of Mandated Efficiency in Standards for Household Appliances." *Energy Journal* 1: 21–40.

King, P. (2005). "The Production and Consumption of Bar Iron in Early Modern England and Wales." *Economic History Review* 58, no. 1: 1–33.

———. (2011). "The Choice of Fuel in the Eighteenth-Century Iron Industry: The Coalbrookdale Accounts Reconsidered." *Economic History Review* 64, no. 1: 132–56.

Kjaergaard, T. (1994). *The Danish Revolution, 1500–1800. An Ecohistorical Interpretation*. Cambridge: Cambridge University Press.

Kleinschmidt, C. (2007). *Technik und Wirtschaft im 19. und 20. Jahrhundert*. Munich: Oldenbourg.

Koch, M. J. (1954). *Die Bergarbeiterbewegung im Ruhrgebiet zur Zeit Wilhelms II.: (1889–1914). Herausg. von der Kommission für Geschichte des Parlamentarismus und der politischen Parteien in Bonn*. Düsseldorf.

Koetse, M. J., H.L.F. de Groot, and R.J.G.M. Florax (2008). "Capital-Energy Substitution and Shifts in Factor Demand: A Meta-Analysis." *Energy Economics* 30: 2236–51.

Komlos, J. (1998). "Shrinking in a Growing Economy? The Mystery of Physical Stature during the Industrial Revolution." *Journal of Economic History* 58: 779–802.

Koning, N. (1994). *The Failure of Agrarian Capitalism: Agrarian Politics in the UK, Germany, the Netherlands and the USA, 1846–1919*. London: Routledge.

Kopsidis, M. (1996). *Marktintegration und Entwicklung der westfälischen Landwirtschaft 1780–1880: marktorientierte ökonomische Entwicklung eines bäuerlich strukturierten Agrarsektors*. Münster: Lit.

Koslofsky, C. (2011). *Evening's Empire: A History of the Night in Early Modern Europe*. Cambridge: Cambridge University Press.

Kostrowicki, J. (1980). *Geografia dell'agricoltura. Ambienti, società, sistemi, politiche dell'agricoltura*. Milano: F. Angeli.

Krantz, O. and L. Schön (2007). *Swedish Historical National Accounts 1800–2000*. Lund: Almqvist & Wicksell International.

Krausmann, F., and H. Haberl (2002). "The Process of Industrialization from the Perspective of Energetic Metabolism. Socioeconomic Energy Flows in Austria, 1830–1995." *Ecological Economics* 41: 177–201.

Krausmann, F., M. Fischer-Kowalski, H. Schandl, and N. Eisenmenger (2009). "The Global Socio-Metabolic Transition: Past and Present Metabolic Profiles and Their Future Trajectories." *Journal of Industrial Ecology* 12: 637–56.

Krengel, J. (1983). *Die deutsche Roheisenindustrie 1871–1913: eine quantitativ-historische Untersuchung*. Berlin: Duncker & Humblot.

Kuhndt, M. J., V. Geibler, S. Moll Türk, K. Schallaböck, and S. Steger (2003). "Virtual Dematerialization and Factor X." *Digital Europe, WP3*, Wuppertal, Germany: Wuppertal Institute.

Kunnas, J., and T. Myllyntaus (2009). "Postponed Leap in Carbon Dioxide Emissions: The Impact of Energy Efficiency, Fuel Choices and Industrial Structure on the Finnish Economy, 1800–2005." *Global Environment* 3: 154–89.

Kuznets, S. (1930). *Secular Movements in Production and Prices: Their Nature and Their Bearing upon Cyclical Fluctuations*. Boston: Houghton Mifflin.

————. (1955). "Economic Growth and Income Inequality." *American Economic Review* 65: 1–28.

Laffaut, M. (1983). "Belgium." In *Railways and the Economic Development of Western Europe, 1830–1914*, P. O'Brien (ed.). London: Macmillan.

Lagendijk, V. (2008). *Electrifying Europe*. Amsterdam: Aksant.

Laitner, J.A.S. (2010). "Semiconductors and Information Technology." *Journal of Industrial Ecology* 14: 692–95.

Laitner, J.A.S., C. H. Knight, V. L. McKinney, and K. Ehrhardt-Martinez (2009). *Semiconductor Technologies: The Potential to Revolutionize U.S. Energy Productivity, Report number E094*; http://aceee.org.

Lamb, H. H. (1984). "Climate and History in Northern Europe and Elsewhere." In *Climatic Changes on a Yearly to Millennial Basis*, N. A. Mörner and W. Karlén (eds.), pp. 225–40. Dordrecht-Boston-Lancaster: Kluwer.

Landau, E. (2006). *The History of Energy*. Minneapolis: Twenty-First Century Books.

Landes, D. (2003). *The Unbound Prometheus: Technological Change and Industrial Development in Western Europe from 1750 to the Present*. Cambridge: Cambridge University Press.

Langdon, J. (1986). *Horses, Oxen and Technological Innovation. The Use of Draught Animals in English Farming from 1066–1500*. Cambridge: Cambridge University Press.

————. (2003). "The Use of Animal Power from 1200 to 1800." In *Economia e energia Secc. XIII–XVIII*, S. Cavaciocchi (ed.), pp. 213–21. Firenze: Le Monnier.

Langton, J. (1979). *Geographical Change and Industrial Revolution Coalmining in South West Lancashire, 1590–1799*. Cambridge: Cambridge University Press.

Lattimore, O. (1962). *Studies in the Frontier History*. Paris: Mouton.

Lawn, P. A. (2001). "Goods and Services and the Dematerialisation Fallacy: Implications for Sustainable Development Indicators and Policy." *International Journal of Services Technology and Management* 2: 363–76.

Layton, C., D. De Hoghton, and C. Harlow (1972). *Ten Innovations: An International Study on Technological Development and the Use of Qualified Scientists and Engineers in Ten Industries*. London: Allen & Unwin.

Le, T., J. Gibson, and L. Oxley (2003). "Cost- and Income-based Measures of Human Capital." *Journal of Economics Surveys* 17, no. 3: 271–307.

Le Roy Ladurie, E. (1967). *Histoire du climat depuis l'an mil*. Paris: Flammarion.

Lee, A. J. (1976). *The Origins of the Popular Press in England, 1855–1914*. London: Croom Helm.

Lefebvre des Noëttes, R. (1931). *L'attelage. Le cheval de selle à travers les âges. Contribution à l'histoire de l'esclavage*. Paris: Picard.

Lenzen, M. (1998). "Primary Energy and Greenhouse Gases Embodied in Australian Final Consumption: An Input–output Analysis." *Energy Policy* 26, no. 6: 495–506.

Leunig, T. (2006). "Time Is Money: A Re-Assessment of the Passenger Social Savings from Victorian British Railways." *Journal of Economic History* 66, no. 3: 635–73.

Levander, T. (1991). *Koldioxid –Utsläpp och beräkningsmetodik*. Stockholm: Nutek, Rapport 1991/12.

Levi, G. (1991). "L'energia disponibile." In *Storia dell'economia italiana*, R. Romano, (ed.), pp. 141–68. Torino: Einaudi: II.

Li, Bozhong (1998a). "Changes in Climate, Land, and Human Efforts. The Production of Wet-field Rice in Jiangnan During the Ming and Qing Dynasties." In *Sediments of Time. Environment and Society in Chinese History*, M. Elvin and L. Ts'ui-jung (eds.) Cambridge: Cambridge University Press.

———. (1998b). "The Production of Wet-Field Rice in Jiangnan During the Ming and Qing Dynasties." In *Sediments of Time. Environment and Society in Chinese History*, M. Elvin, and L. Ts'ui-jung (eds.), pp. 447–84. Cambridge: Cambridge University Press.

Lindmark, M. (2002). "An EKC Pattern in Historical Perspective: Carbon Dioxide Emissions, Technology, Fuel Prices and Growth in Sweden 1870–1997." *Ecological Economics* 42: 333–47.

———. (2006). "Estimates of Norwegian Energy Consumption." Working Paper, obtained from author.

Lipsey, R. G., K. Carlaw, and C. Bekar (2005). *Economic Transformations: General Purpose Technologies and Long Term Economic Growth*. New York: Oxford University Press.

Lis, C., and U. Soly (1979). *Poverty and Capitalism in Pre-industrial Europe*. Bristol: Harvester.

Livi-Bacci, M. (2000). *The Population of Europe: A History*. Oxford: Blackwell.

Ljungberg, J. (1990). *Priser och marknadskrafter i Sverige 1885–1969*. Lund: Studentlitteratur.

Ljungberg, J., and H. Lobell (2010). "Innovation and Aggregate Economic Performance." Paper presented at the 12th Annual SNEE European Integration Conference.

Lo Cascio, E. (ed.) (2000). *Mercati Permanenti e Mercati Periodici nel Mondo Romano* Bari: Edipulgia.

Lohele, C. (2007). "A 2000-Year Global Temperature Reconstruction Based on Non-Treering Proxies." *Energy and Environment* 1049–58.

Lohele, C. and J. H. McCulloch (2008). "Correction to: A 2000-years Global Temperature Reconstruction Based on Non-Tree Ring Proxies." *Energy and Environment* 19: 93–100.

Lovins, A. B. (1985). "Saving Gigabucks with Negawatts." *Public Utilities Fortnightly* 115: 19–26.

———. (1991). "Energy, People and Industrialization." In *Resources, Environment and Population. Present Knowledge, Future Options*, K. Davis and M. S. Bernstam (eds.), pp. 114–25. Oxford: Oxford University Press.

Lucassen, J., and R. W. Unger (2000). "Labour Productivity in Ocean Shipping, 1500–1850." *International Journal of Maritime History* 12, no. 2: 127–41.

Ludwig, K.-H. (1994). "Die Innovation der Nockenwelle im Übergang vom Früh- zum Hochmittelalter. Eine Skizze Quellenprobleme unter besonderer Berücksichtigung der Walkmülen." *Technikgeschichte* 61: 227–38.

Lunardoni, A. (1904). *Vini, uve e legnami nei trattati di commercio*. Italia Moderna, Maggio.

Lupo, M. (forthcoming). *The Port of Genoa and the Modern Growth in Italy: An Analysis Based on the Imports of Coal (1820–1913)*.

MacLeod, C. (1988). *Inventing the Industrial Revolution: The English Patent System, 1660–1800*. Cambridge: Cambridge University Press.

——. (2004). "The European Origins of British Technological Predominance." In *Exceptionalism and Industrialisation: Britain and its European Rivals, 1688–1815*, L. Prados de la Escosura (ed.), pp. 111–26. Cambridge: Cambridge University Press.

Maddalena, A. de (1974a). *Prezzi e mercedi a Milano dal 1701 al 1860*. Milano: Università Bocconi.

——. (1974b). "Rural Europe (1500–1750)." In *The Fontana Economic History of Europe*, C. M. Cipolla (ed.), pp. 273–353. Glasgow-London: Collins, II.

Maddison, A. (2001). *The World Economy. A Millennial Perspective*. Paris: OECD.

——. (2003). *The World Economy: Historical Statistics*. Paris: Development Centre of the Organisation for Economic Co-operation and Development.

——. (2006a). *Chinese Economic Performance in the Long Run*. Paris: OECD (1st ed. 1998).

——. (2006b). *The World Economy. Volume 1: A Millennial Perspective*. Paris: OECD.

——. (2006c). *The World Economy. Volume 2: Historical Statistics*. Paris: OECD.

Madison, M. G. (1997). "'Potatoes Made of Oil': Eugene and Howard Odum and the Origins and Limits of American Agroecology." *Environment and History* 3: 209–38.

Mäenpää, I., and H. Siikavirta (2007). "Greenhouse Gases Embodied in the International Trade and Final Consumption of Finland: An Input–Output Analysis." *Energy Policy* 35, no. 1: 128–43.

Maizels, A. (1963). *Industrial Growth and World Trade: An Empirical Study of Trends in Production, Consumption and Trade in Manufactures from 1899–1959, With a Discussion of Probable Future Trends*. Cambridge: Cambridge University Press.

Makkai, L. (1981). "Productivité et exploitation des sources d'énergie (XIIe–XVIIe siècle)." In *Produttività e tecnologie nei secoli XII–XVII*, S. Mariotti (ed.), pp. 165–81. Istituto Internazionale di Storia Economica "Datini." Firenze: Le Monnier.

Malanima, P. (1986). "The First European Textile Machine." *Textile History* 17: 115–27.

——. (1988). *I piedi di legno. Una macchina alle origini dell'industria mediewale*. Milano: Franco Angeli.

——. (1996). *Energia e crescita nell'Europa preindustrialne*. Roma: NIS.

——. (2001). "The Energy Basis for Early Modern Growth, 1650–1820." In *Early Modern Capitalism. Economic and Social Change in Europe 1400–1800*, M. Prak (ed.), pp. 51–68. London: Routledge.

——. (2002). *L'economia italiana. Dalla crescita medievale alla crescita contemporanea*. Bologna: Il Mulino.

——. (2006a). *Energy Consumption in Italy in the 19th and 20th Centuries*. Napoli: ISSM-CNR.

——. (2006b). "Energy Crisis and Growth 1650–1850. The European Deviation in a Comparative Perspective." *Journal of Global History* I: 101–21.

——. (2009). *Pre-modern European Economy. One Thousand Years (10th–19th centuries)*. Leiden-Boston: Brill.

——. (2010a). "Urbanisation 1700–1870." In *The Cambridge Economic History of Modern Europe, vol 1: 1700–1870*, S. Broadberry and K. O'Rourke (eds.), pp. 236–64. Cambridge: Cambridge University Press.

————. (2010b). "Energy in History." *Encyclopaedia of Life Support Systems (UNESCO-EOLSS)*.

————. (2011). "The Long Decline of a Leading Economy. GDP in Central and Northern Italy 1300–1913." *European Review of Economic History* 15/2/2011: 169–219.

————. (2013). *Energy Consumption in the Roman World*, in *The Ancient Mediterranean Environment between Science and History*, ed. by W. Harris, Leiden. Brill: 13–36.

————. (forthcoming). "Energy." In *Oxford Handbook of Economies in the Classical World*, A. Bresson, E. Lo Cascio, and F. Velde (eds.). Oxford: Oxford University Press.

Malthus, T. R. (1798). *An Essay on the Principle of Population, as it Affects the Future Improvement of Society*. London.

Mangini, A., C. Spötl, and P. Verdes (2005). "Reconstruction of Temperature in the Central Alps during the Past 2000 yr from a δ18O Stalagmite Record." *Earth and Planetary Science Letters* 235, nos. 3–4: 741–51.

Mann, M., and P. D. Jones (2003). "Global Surface Temperatures over the Past Two Millennia." *Geophysical Research Letters* 30, no. 15, August.

Mann, M. E., E. Gille, R. S. Bradley, M. K. Hughes, J. Overpeck, F. T. Keimig, and W. Gross (2000). "Global Temperature Patterns in Past Centuries: An Interactive Presentation." *Earth Interactions* 4, no. 4.

Markandya, A., S. Pedroso-Galinato, and D. Streimikiene (2006). "Energy Intensity in Transition Economies: Is there Convergence towards the EU-Average?" *Energy Economics* 28: 121–45.

Marks, R. (1998). *Tigers, Rice, Silk and Silt. Environment and History in Late Imperial South China*. Cambridge: Cambridge University Press.

Martin, J.-M. (1988). "L'íntensité Energetique de l'activite economique dans les pays industrialises. Les evolutions de tres longue periode livrent-elles des enseignements utiles?" *Economies et Sociétés* 4: 9–27.

Masefield, G. B. (1967). "Crops and Livestock." In *Cambridge Economic History of Europe*, E. E. Rich and C. Wilson (eds.), pp. 276–307. Cambridge: Cambridge University Press.

Mathias, P. (1984). *The First Industrial Nation. The Economic History of Britain 1700–1914*. London: Routledge.

Mathias, P. (2003). "Economic Expansion, Energy Resources and Technical Change in the Eighteenth Century: A New Dynamic in Britain." In *Economia e energia Secc. XIII–XVIII*, S. Cavaciocchi (ed.), pp. 23–40. Istituto Internazionale di Storia economica "F. Datini." Firenze: Le Monnier.

Matthews, R.C.O., C. H. Feinstein, and J. C. Odling-Smee (1982). *British Economic Growth, 1856–1973*. Oxford: Clarendon Press.

McCloskey, D. (2006). *The Bourgeois Virtues. Ethics for an Age of Commerce*. Chicago: Chicago University Press.

McNeill, J. R. (2000). *Something New under the Sun. An Environmental History of the Twentieth Century*. London: Penguin.

McNeill, W. H. (1982). *The Pursuit of Power. Technology, Armed Forces and Society since A.D. 1000*. Chicago: University of Chicago Press.

Meissner, C. M., D .S. Jacks, and D. Novy (2010). "Trade Costs in the First Wave of Globalization." *Explorations in Economic History* 47: 127–41.

Michaelowa, A. (2001). "The Impact of Short-term Climate Change on British and French Agriculture and Population in the First Half of the 18th Century." In *History and Climate. Memories of the Future?* Ph. Jones, A. Ogilvie, and T. Davis (eds.), pp. 201–18. New York: Kluwer.

Millward, R. (2005). *Private and Public Enterprise in Europe*. Cambridge: Cambridge University Press.

Milward, A. S., and S. B. Saul (1973). *The Economic Development of Continental Europe, 1780–1870*. London: Allen and Unwin.

Milward, A. S., and S. B. Saul (1977). *The Development of the Economies of Continental Europe, 1850–1914*. London: Allen and Unwin.

MingSheng, L., Z. HuiMin, L. Zhi, and T. LianJun (2010). "Economy-Wide Material Input/Output and Dematerialization Analysis of Jilin Province (China)." *Environmental Monitoring & Assessment* 165: 263–74.

Mitchell, B. R. (1975). *European Historical Statistics 1750–1970*. New York: Columbia University Press.

———. (1984). *Economic Development of the British Coal Industry 1800–1914*. Cambridge: Cambridge University Press.

———. (1988). *British Historical Statistics*. Cambridge: Cambridge University Press.

———. (2007a). *International Historical Statistics, Europe 1750–2005* (6th ed.). New York: Palgrave Macmillan.

———. (2007b). *International Historical Statistics, Africa, Asia and Oceania 1750–2005* (5th ed.). New York: Palgrave Macmillan.

———. (2007c). *International Historical Statistics, The Americas 1750–2005* (6th ed.). New York: Palgrave Macmillan.

Mitchell, T. (2009). "Carbon Democracy." *Economy and Society* 38: 399–432.

———. (2011). *Carbon Democracy, Political Power in the Age of Oil*. London: Verso.

Mokyr, J. (1990). *The Lever of Riches. Technological Creativity and Economic Progress*. New York–Oxford: Oxford University Press.

———. (1999). "The Second Industrial Revolution, 1870–1914." In *Storia dell'Economia Mondiale*, V. Castronovo (ed.). Rome: Laterza. Available online at http://www.faculty.ecn.northwestern.edu/faculty/mokyr/castronovo.pdf.

———. (2002). *The Gifts of Athena, Historical Origins of the Knowledge Economy*. Princeton: Princeton University Press.

———. (2009). *The Enlightened Economy. An Economic History of Britain 1700–1850*. New Haven and London: Yale University Press.

Molina, A. H. (1989). *The Social Basis of the Microelectronics Revolution*. Edinburgh: Edinburgh University Press.

Montesquieu, Ch. L. de Secondat (1979). *De l'esprit des lois*. Paris: Garnier-Flammarion.

Morell, M. (2001). *Jordbruket i industrisamhället, 1870–1945, volume 1*. Stockholm: Natur och Kultur/LT.

Morell, M., and J. Myrdal (2011). *The Agrarian History of Sweden: from 4000 BC to AD 2000*. Lund: Nordic Academic Press.

Morris, I. (2010a). "Social Development." Available online at www.ianmorris.org.

———. (2010b). *Why the West Rules—for Now. The Patterns of History, and What They Reveal About the Future*. New York: Farrar, Straus and Giroux.

Mosley, S. (2001). *The Chimney of the World: A History of Smoke Pollution in Victorian and Edwardian Manchester*. Cambridge: White Horse.

———. (2003). "Fresh Air and Foul: The Role of the Open Fireplace in Ventilating the British Home, 1837–1910." *Planning Perspectives* 18, no. 1: 1–21.

Mowery, D. C. (1983). "Innovation, Market Structure and Government Policy in the American Semiconductor Industry: A Survey." *Research Policy* 12, no. 4: 183–97.

Mowery, D. C., and T. Simcoe (2002). "Is the Internet a US Invention?—An Economic and Technological History of Computer Networking." *Research Policy* 31, nos. 8–9: 1369–87.

Mukerji, C. (2009). *Impossible Engineering. Technology and Territoriality on the Canal du Midi.* Princeton: Princeton University Press.

Muldrew, C. (2010). *Food, Energy and the Creation of Industriousness.* Cambridge: Cambridge University Press.

———. (2011). *Food, Energy and the Creation of Industriousness: Work and Material Culture in Agrarian England, 1550–1780.* Cambridge: Cambridge University Press.

Mumford, L. ([1934] 1963). *Technics and Civilization.* New York: Harcourt, Brace & World.

Mundaca, L., M. Mansoz, L. Neij, and G. Timilsina (2013). "Transaction Cost Analysis of Low-carbon Technology." Climate Policy, DOI: 10.1080/14693062.2013 .781452.

Munksgaard, J., J. C. Minx, L. B. Christoffersen, and L.-L. Pade (2009). "Models for National CO2 Accounting." *Handbook of Input-Output Economics in Industrial Ecology: Ecoefficiency in Industry and Science.* Dordrecht: Springer.

Munksgaard, J., L.-L. Pade, J. Minx, and M. Lenzen (2005). "Influence of Trade on National CO2 Emissions." *International Journal of Global Energy Issues* 23, no. 4: 324–36.

Munro, J. H. (2003). "Industrial Energy from Water-Mills in the European Economy, 5th to 18th Centuries: the Limitations of Power." In *Economia e energia Secc. XIII–XVIII*, S. Cavaciocchi (ed.), pp. 223–69. Istituto Internazionale di Storia economica "F. Datini." Firenze: Le Monnier.

Munting, R. (1996). "Industrial Revolution in Russia." In *The Industrial Revolution in National Context*, M. Teich and R. Porter (eds.), pp. 329–49. Cambridge: Cambridge University Press.

Murphy, D. J., and C.A.S. Hall (2011). "Adjusting the Economy to the New Energy Realities of the Second Half of the Age of Oil." *Ecological Modelling* 223, no. 1: 67–71.

Murtishaw, S., and L. Schipper (2001). "Disaggregated Analysis of US Energy Consumption in the 1990s: Evidence of the Effects of the Internet and Rapid Economic Growth." *Energy Policy* 29: 1335–56.

Musson, A. E. (1976). "Industrial Motive Power in the United Kingdom, 1800–70." *Economic History Review*, 29, no. 3: 415–39.

——— (1978). *The Growth of British Industry.* London: Batsford.

Nash, G. D. (1968). *United States Oil Policy 1890–1964.* Pittsburgh: University of Pittsburgh Press.

National Research Council of the National Academies (2006). *Surface Temperature Reconstruction for the Last 2,000 Years.* Washington, DC: National Academies Press.

National Statistics UK, Office for National Statistics, Quarterly Energy Prices.

Needham, J. (1956–2004). *Science and Civilization in China.* Cambridge: Cambridge University Press.

Nef, J. (1932). *The Rise of the British Coal Industry.* London: Routledge & Sons.

———. (1936). "A Comparison of Industrial Growth in France and England from 1540 to 1640." In *The Conquest of the Material World.* Chicago and London: University of Chicago Press, 1964.

———. (1952). "Mining and Metallurgy in Medieval Civilization." In *Cambridge Economic History of Europe, II*, M. M. Postan and P. Mathias (eds.), pp. 691–761. Cambridge: Cambridge University Press, 1989.

Nemetz, P. N. (1981). *Energy Crisis—Policy Response.* Montreal: Institute for Public Policy.

Nerén, J. (1937). *Automobilens historia.* Stockholm.

Neumayer, E. (2004). "Does the 'Resource Curse' Hold for Growth in Genuine Income as Well?" *World Development* 32, no. 10: 1627–40.

Nilsson, L. J. (1993). "Energy Intensity Trends in 31 Industrial and Developing Countries 1950–1988." *Energy* 18: 309–22.

North, D. C., and R. P. Thomas (1970). "An Economic Theory of the Growth of the Western World." *Economic History Review* II s., 23: 1–17.

———. (1973). *The Rise of the Western World.* Cambridge: Cambridge University Press.Nuvolari, A., B. Verspagen, and N. von Tunzelmann (2006). "The Diffusion of the Steam Engine in Eighteenth Century Britain." In *Applied Evolutionary Economics and the Knowledge-Based Economy*, A. Pyka and H. Hanusch (eds.), pp. 166–200. Cheltenham: Edward Elgar.

———. (2011). "The Early Diffusion of the Steam Engine in Britain, 1700–1800: A Reappraisal." *Cliometrica* 5, no. 3: 291–321.

Nye, D. E. (1998). *Consuming Power: A Social History of American Energies.* Cambridge, MA: MIT Press.

O'Brien, P. (1983). "Transport and Economic Development in Europe, 1789–1914." In *Railways and the Economic Development of Western Europe, 1830–1914*, P. O'Brien (ed.), pp. 1–28. London: Macmillan.

O'Brien, P., and L. Prados de la Escosura (1992). "Agricultural Productivity and European Indsutrialization, 1890–1980." *Economic History Review* 45, no. 3: 514–36.

Officer, L. (2008). English wages series in http://www.measuringworth.com/aboutus.php.

Ó Grada. C. (1995). *The Great Irish Famine.* Cambridge: Cambridge University Press.

Olsson, S-O (1992). "Energiorganisation i Norden." Varberg: Br Carlssons Boktryckeri.

O'Mahony, M., and M. P. Timmer (2009). "Output, Input and Productivity Measures at the Industry Level: The EU KLEMS Database." *Economic Journal* 119, no. 538: F374–F403.

Ordway Jr., S. H. (1956). "Possible Limits of Raw-Material Consumption." In *Man's Role in Changing the Face of the Earth*, W. L. Thomas (ed.), pp. 987–1019. Chicago: University of Chicago Press.

O'Rourke, K. H. (1997). "The European Grain Invasion, 1870–1913." *Journal of Economic History* 57, no. 4: 775–801.

O'Rourke, K. H., and J. G. Williamson (1999). *Globalization and History: The Evolution of a Nineteenth-century Atlantic Economy.* Cambridge, MA: MIT Press.

O'Rourke, K. H., A. M. Taylor, and J. G. Williamson (1996). "Factor Price Convergence in the Late Nineteenth Century." *International Economic Review* 37, no. 3: 499–530.

Overton, M. (1996). *Agricultural Revolution in England: The Transformation of the Rural Economy 1500–1850*. Cambridge: Cambridge University Press.

Overton M., and B.M.S. Campbell (1999). "Statistics of Production and Productivity in English Agriculture 1086–1871." In *Land Productivity and Agro-systems in the North Sea Area (Middle Ages-20th century)*, B.J.P. Van Bavel and E. Thoen (eds.), pp. 189–208. Turnhout: Brepols.

Owen, E. W. (1975). *Trek of the Oil Finders: A History of Exploration for Petroleum*. Tulsa, OK: American Association of Petroleum Geologists.

Pamuk, S. (2000). "Prices in the Ottoman Empire." *International Journal of Middle East Studies* 36: 451–68.

Pamuk, S., and J. L. van Zanden (2010). "Standards of Living." In *The Cambridge Economic History of Modern Europe. Vol. 1. 1700–1870*, S. Broadberry, and K. O'Rourke (eds.), pp. 217–34. Cambridge: Cambridge University Press.

Panayotou, T. (1993). "Empirical Tests and Policy Analysis of Environmental Degradation at Different Stages of Economic Development. Working paper WP238." *Technology and Employment Programme*. Geneva: International Labour Office.

Panciera, W. (1988). "Ancien Régime e chimica di base: la produzione del salnitro nella repubblica veneziana." *Studi Veneziani* n.s., 16: 45–92.

Parra, F. (2004). *Oil Politics: A Modern History of Petroleum*. London: I. B. Tauris.

Parthasarathi, P. (2011). *Why Europe Grew Rich and Asia Did Not: Global Economic Divergence, 1600–1850*. Cambridge: Cambridge University Press.

Paulinyi, A. (2005). "Good Ore but No Coal, or Coal but Bad Ore. Responses to the British Challenge in the Habsburg Monarchy." In *The Industrial Revolution in Iron*, C. Evans and G. Rydén (eds.), pp. 95–110. Aldershot: Ashgate.

Perkins, D. H. (1969). *Agricultural Development in China 1368–1968*. Edinburgh: Edinburgh University Press.

Perlowski, A. A. (1980). "Application of the New Technology, The Smart Machine Revolution." In *The Microelectronics Revolution*, T. Forester (ed.). Cambridge, MA: MIT Press, pp. 105–24.

Persson, K. G. (2010). *An Economic History of Europe: Knowledge, Institutions and Growth, 600 to the Present*. Cambridge: Cambridge University Press.

Peters, G. P., J. C. Minx, C. L. Weber, and O. Edenhofer (2011). "Growth in Emission Transfer via International Trade from 1990 to 2008." *Proceedings of National Academy of Science* 108: 8903–8908.

Pfister, Ch. (1988). *Klimageschichte der Schweiz von 1525–1860. Das Klima der Schweiz und seine Bedeutung in der Geschichte von Bevölkerung und Landwirtschaft*. Bern: Haupt.

———. (1992). "Monthly Temperature and Precipitation Patterns in Central Europe from 1525 to the Present." In *Climate since 1500 A.D.*, R. S. Bradley and P. D. Jones (eds.). London: Routledge.

Piasecki, P. (1987). *Das deutsche Salinenwesen: Invention, Innovation, Diffusion*. Idstein: Schulz-Kirchner.

Pielke, R. A. (2009). "Decarbonization Figures for India and China Unconvincing." *Nature* 462: 158–59.

Pierenkemper, T. (1992). "Grundzüge der Wirtschaftsgeschichte Oberschlesiens in der Neuzeit." In *Industriegeschichte Oberschlesiens im 19. Jahrhundert*, T. Pierenkemper (ed.). Wiesbaden: Harrassowitz.

Pierenkenper, T. and R. Tilly (2004). *The German Economy during the Nineteenth Century.* Oxford: Berghahn.

Pigou, A. C. (1920). *The Economics of Welfare.* London: Macmillan.

Political and Economic Planning (1955). *World Population and Resources. A Report by P E P.* London.

Pollard, S. (1981). *Peaceful Conquest: The Industrialization of Europe 1760–1970.* Oxford: Oxford University Press.

Pomeranz, K. (2000). *The Great Divergence. Europe, China, and the Making of the Modern World Economy.* Princeton: Princeton University Press.

———. (2002). "Political Economy and Ecology on the Eve of Industrialization: Europe, China, and the Global Conjuncture." *American Historical Review* 107: 425–46.

Porter, M., and C. Van Der Linde (1995). "Toward a New Conception of the Environment-Competitiveness Relationship." *Journal of Economic Perspectives* 9, no. 4: 97–118.

Porter, R. (1995). *Disease, Medicine and Society in England, 1550–1860.* (2nd ed.). Cambridge: Cambridge University Press.

Post, J. D. (1977). *The Last Great Subsistence Crisis in the Western World.* Baltimore: Johns Hopkins University Press.

Postel-Vinay, G., and D. E. Sahn (2010). "Explaining Stunting in Nineteenth Century France." *Economic History Review* 63, no. 2: 315–34.

Pounds, N.J.G. (1979). *A Historical Geography of Europe, 1500–1840.* Cambridge: Cambridge University Press.

Pounds, N.J.G., and W. N. Parker (1957). *Coal and Steel in Western Europe: The Influence of Resources and Techniques on Production.* London: Faber and Faber.

Prados de la Escosura, L. (2003). *El progreso económico de España, 1850–2000.* Bilbao: Fundación BBVA.

Prados de la Escosura, L. and J. R. Rosés (2010a). "Capital Accumulation in the Long-Run: The Case of Spain, 1850–2000." *Research in Economic History* 27: 93–152.

———. (2010b). "Human Capital and Economic Growth in Spain, 1850–2000." *Explorations in Economic History* 47: 520–32.

Pustufa, Z. (1992). "Deutsche Kapitalanlagen in der Schwerindustrie des Königreichs Polen. Die oberschlesischen Direktinvestionen 1856–1914." In *Industriegeschichte Oberschlesiens im 19. Jahrhundert,* T. Pierenkemper (ed.), pp. 263–303. Wiesbaden: Harrassowitz.

Putnam, P. C. (1953). *Energy in the Future.* New York: van Nostrand.

Radetzki, M. (1990). *Tillväxt och miljö.* Stockholm.

Ramelli, A. (1588). *Le diverse e artificiose macchine.* Paris.

Reddy, A.K.N., and J. Goldemberg (1990). "Energy for the Developing World." *Scientific American* 263: 111–18.

Reichard, R.W. (1991). *From the Petition to the Strike: A History of Strikes in Germany, 1869–1914.* New York: P. Lang.

Reynolds, D. B. (1996). "Energy Grades and Economic Growth." *Journal of Energy and Development* 19, no. 2: 245–64.

Reynolds, T. S. (1983). *Stronger than a Hundred Men. A History of the Vertical Water Wheel.* Baltimore-London: Johns Hopkins University Press.

Ricardo, D. (1821). *On the Principles of Political Economy and Taxation.* London: Murray.

Richards, J. (1990). "Land Transformation." In *The Earth Transformed by Human Action*, B. L. Turner (ed.), pp. 163–78. Cambridge, MA: Cambridge University Press.

Riello, G., and P. Parthasarathi (2009). *The Spinning World. A Global History of Cotton Textiles 1200–1250.* Oxford: Oxford University Press.

Rockström, J., W. Steffen, K. Noone, and A. Persson (2009). "A Safe Operating Space for Humanity." *Nature (London)* 461: 472–75.

Rodrik, D. (2006). "What's so Special about China's Export?" *China & World Economy* 14: 1–19.

Rolt, L.T.C., and J. S. Allen (1977). *The Steam Engine of Thomas Newcomen.* Hartington: Moorland.

Romano, R. (1962). "Per una valutazione della flotta mercantile europea alla fine del secolo XVIII." *Studi in onore di A. Fanfani*, Milano, Giuffré, 5: 573–91.

Rossi, G. (1915). *Manuale del costruttore navale.* Milano: Hoepli.

Rossignoli, D. de (1922). *Guida allo studio delle macchine a vapore marine e loro accessori.* Trieste: La Editoriale libraria.

Rostow, W.W. (1960). *Stages of Economic Growth: A Non-communist Manifesto.* Cambridge: Cambridge University Press.

Rubio, M.d.M. (2005). Economía, Energía y CO2: España 1850–2000. Cuadernos Económicos de ICE 70, vol. 2: 55–71.

Rubio, M.d.M., M. Folchi and A. Carreras (2010). "Energy as an Indicator of Modernization in Latin America 1890–1925." *Economic History Review* 63: 769–804.

Rubner, H. (1967). *Forstgeschichte im Zeitalter der industriellen Revolution.* Berlin: Duncker & Humbolt.

Ruttan, V. (2001). *Technology, Growth, and Development. An Induced Innovation Perspective.* New York–Oxford: Oxford University Press.

Rydén, G. (2005). "Responses to Coal Technology without Coal. Swedish Iron Making in the Nineteenth Century." In *The Industrial Revolution in Iron*, C. Evans and G. Rydén (eds.), pp. 111–27. Aldershot: Ashgate.

Saito, O. (2009). "Forest History and the Great Divergence: China, Japan, and the West Compared." *Journal of Global History* 4: 379–404.

Salter, W.E.G. (1966). *Productivity and Technical Change.* Cambridge: Cambridge University Press.

Sánchez-Chóliz, J., and R. Duarte (2004). "CO2 Emissions Embodied in International Trade: Evidence for Spain." *Energy Policy* 32, no. 18: 1999–2005.

Sarti, R. (1999). *Vita di casa. Abitare, mangiare, vestire nell'Europa moderna.* Roma-Bari: Laterza.

Saunders, H. D. (1992). "The Khazzoom-Brookes Postulate and Neoclassical Growth." *Energy Journal* 13: 131–48.

Schäfer, I. (1992). "*Ein Gespenst geht um." Politik mit der Holznot in Lippe 1750–1850. Eine regionale Studie zur Wald- und Technikgeschichte.* Detmold: Naturwissenschaftlicher und Historischer Verein für das Land Lippe.

Schipper, F. (2008). *Driving Europe, Building Europe on Roads in the Twentieth Century.* Amsterdam: Aksant.

Schön, L. (1988). *Development Blocks and Transformation Pressure in a Macro-Economic Perspective—A Model of Long-Term Cyclical Change.* Skandinaviska Enskilda Banken Quarterly.

———. (1990). *Elektricitetens betydelse för svensk industriell utveckling.* Vattenfall.

———. (1995). "Growth and Energy in Sweden—on Innovation, Efficiency and Structural Change." In *Expanding Environmental Perspectives. Lessons of the*

Past—Prospects for the Future, L. Lundgren, L. J. Nilsson, and P. Schlyter (eds.). Lund: Lund University Press.

———. (2000). *En modern svensk ekonomisk historia. Tillväxt och omvandling under två sekel.* Stockholm: SNS förlag.

———. (2006). "Swedish Industrialization 1870–1930 and the Heckscher-Ohlin Theory." In *Eli Heckscher, International Trade and Economic History*, R. Findlay, R.G.H. Henriksson, H. Lindgren, and M. Lundahl (eds.). Cambridge, MA: MIT Press.

———. (2010). *Vår världs ekonomiska historia. Den industriella tiden.* Stockholm: SNS förlag.

Schott, D., B. Luckin, and G. Massard-Guilbard (2005). *Resources of the City. Contributions to an Environmental History of Modern Europe.* Aldershot: Ashgate.

Schremmer, E. (1988). "Faktoren, die den Fortschritt in der deutschen Landwirtschaft im 19. Jahrhundert bestimmten." *Zeitschrift für Agrargeschichte und Agrarsoziologie* 36: 33–77.

Schulze, M. S. (2007). "Origins of Catch-up Failure: Comparative Productivity Growth in the Habsburg Empire, 1870–1910." *European Review of Economic History* 11, no. 2: 189–218.

Schurr, S. H., and B. C. Netschert (1978). *Energy in the American Economy, 1850–1975. An Economic Study of its History and Prospects.* Baltimore: Johns Hopkins University Press.

Scientific American 2009, March issue.

Scott, W. (2010). *Powering the Alaska Pipeline.* Available online at http://www .brighthubengineering.com/fluid-mechanics-hydraulics/84796-powering-the -alaska-pipeline/.

Segers, Y. (2004). "Nutrition and Living Standards in Industrializing Belgium (1846–1913)." *Food and History* 2: 153–78.

Serre-Bachet F., N. Martinelli, O. Pignatelli, J. Guiot, and L. Tessier (1991). "Evolution des temperatures du Nord-Est de l'Italie depuis 1500 A.D. Reconstruction d'après les cernes des arbres." *Dendrocronologia* 9: 213–29.

Sharp, P., and J. Weisdorf (2012). "French Revolution or Industrial Revolution? A Note on the Contrasting Experiences of England and France up to 1800." *Cliometrica* 6, no. 1: 79–88.

Shorter, E., and C. Tilly (1974). *Strikes in France, 1830–1968.* Cambridge: Cambridge University Press.

Siddayao, C. M. (1986). *Energy Demand and Economic Growth. Measurement and Conceptual Issues in Policy Analysis.* Boulder and London: Westview Press.

Sieferle, R. P. (1982). *Das Ende der Fläche: zum gesellschaftlichen Stoffwechsel der Industrialisierung.* Köln: Böhlau.

———. ([1982] 2001). *The Subterranean Forest. Energy Systems and the Industrial Revolution.* Cambridge: White Horse Press.

Singer, P. (2010). "Increasing Energy Efficiency." *Solid State Technology* 53: 5–6.

Smil, V. (1988). *Energy in China's Modernization.* New York: M.E. Sharpe.

———. (1994). *Energy in World History.* Boulder-San Francisco-Oxford: Westview Press.

———. (2004). *China's Past, China's Future: Energy, Food, Environment.* New York and London: Routledge Curzon.

———. (2005). *Creating the Twentieth Century*. Oxford: Oxford University Press.

———. (2008a). *Energy in Nature and Society*. Cambridge, MA: MIT Press.

———. (2008b). *Oil—A Beginner's Guide*. Oxford: Oneworld Publishers.

———. (2010). *Prime Movers of Globalization*. Cambridge, MA: MIT Press.

Smith, A. (1776). "An Inquiry into the Nature and Causes of the Wealth of Nations." E. Cannan (ed.). Chicago: Encyclopedia Britannica, 1952.

Smith, A.H.V. (1997). "Provenance of Coals from Roman Sites in England and Wales." *Britannia* 28: 297–324.

Smulders, S., and M. de Nooij (2003). "The Impact of Energy Conservation on Technology and Economic Growth." *Resource and Energy Economics* 25: 59–79.

Solar, P. (2003). "The Linen Industry in the Nineteenth Century." In *The Cambridge History of Western Textiles* II, D. T. Jenkins (ed.), pp. 809–24. Cambridge: Cambridge University Press.

Solow, R. M. (1956). "A Contribution to the Theory of Economic Growth." *Quarterly Journal of Economics* 70: 65–94.

———. (1957). "Technical Change and the Aggregate Production Function." *Review of Economics and Statistics* 39, no. 3: 312–20.

———. (1974). "Intergenerational Equity and Exhaustible Resources." *Review of Economic Studies* 29–45.

Sörlin, S., and P. Warde (eds.) (2009). *Nature's End. History and the Environment*. New York: Palgrave Macmillan.

Sorrell, S. (2010). "Energy, Economic Growth and Environmental Sustainability: Five Propositions." *Sustainability* 2: 1784–1809.

Sprandel, R. (1981). "Zur Produktivität in der Eisenproduktion des Spätmittelalter." In *Produttività e tecnologie nei secoli XII–XVII*, S. Mariotti (ed.), pp. 417–21. Firenze: Le Monnier.

Standish, A. (1611). *The Commons Complaint*. London: Printed by William Stansby. Statistik des deutschen Reichs.

Steffen, W., P. J. Crutzen, and J. R. McNeill (2007). "The Anthropocene: Are Humans Now Overwhelming the Great Forces of Nature?" *Ambio* 36, no. 8: 614–21.

Stern, D. I. (1997). "Limits to Substitution and Irreversibility in Production and Consumption: A Neoclassical Interpretation of Ecological Economics." *Ecological Economics* 21: 197–215.

———. (2004). "The Rise and Fall of the Environmental Kuznets Curve." *World Development* 32, no. 8: 1419–39.

———. (2006). "Reversal in the Trend of Global Anthropogenic Sulfur Emissions." *Global Environmental Change* 16, no. 2: 207–20.

———. (2010a). "Energy Quality." *Ecological Economics* 69: 1471–78.

———. (2010b). "The Role of Energy in Economic Growth." *USAEE–IAEE WP* 10–055.

Stern, D. I., M. S. Common, and E. B. Barbier (1996). "Economic Growth and Environmental Degradation: A Critique of the Environmental Kuznets Curve." *World Development* 24: 1151–60.

Stern, D. I., and A. Kander (2011). "The Role of Energy in the Industrial Revolution and Modern Economic Growth." *CAMA Working Paper Series*, WP 1/2011, available online at http://cama.anu.edu.au.

Stopford, M. (2009). *Maritime Economics*. (3ʳᵈ ed.). London: Routledge.

Stork, J. (1975). *Middle East Oil and the Energy Crisis*. New York: Monthly Review Press.

Sun, J. W. (2000). "Dematerialization and Sustainable Development." *Sustainable Development* 8: 142–45.

Sung, Ying-Hsing (1966). *Chinese Technology in the Seventeenth Century*. E. Tu Zen, Shiou-Chuan Sun (eds.). Mineola-New-York: Dover.

Szreter, S., and G. Mooney (1998). "Urbanization, Mortality, and the Standard of Living Debate: New Estimates of the Expectation of Life at Birth in Nineteenth-Century British Cities." *Economic History Review* 51, no. 1: 84–112.

Tann, J. (2004). "James Watt." In *Oxford Dictionary of National Biograph*. Oxford: Oxford University Press.

Tapio, P., D. Banister, J. Luukkanen, J. Vehmas, and R. Willamo (2007). "Energy and Transport in Comparison: Immaterialisation, Dematerialisation and Decarbonisation in the EU15 between 1970 and 2000." *Energy Policy* 35: 433–51.

Tavoni, M., and R.S.J. Tol (2010). "Counting only the Hits? The Risk of Underestimating the Costs of Stringent Climate Policy." *Climate Change* 100: 769–78.

Tawney, R. H. [1932] (1979). *Land and Labour in China*. New York: Progress.

Tello E., and G. Jover (forthcoming). "Economic History and the Environment: New Questions, Approaches and Methodologies for the Environmental and Economic History of Pre-industrial and Industrial Societies." *Encyclopaedia of Life Support Systems*.

Temin, P. (1997) "Two Views of the British Industrial Revolution." *Journal of Economic History* 57: 63–82.

Thomas, M. (2004). "The Service Sector." In *The Cambridge Economic History of Modern Britain*, R. Floud and P. Johnson (eds.), pp. 99–132. Cambridge: Cambridge University Press.

Thompson, F.M.L. (1983). *Horses in European Economic History. A Preliminary Canter*. Reading: British Agricultural History Society.

Thorsheim, P. (2006). *Inventing Pollution. Coal, Smoke and Culture in Britain since 1800*. Athens: Ohio University Press.

Tilly, R. (1983). "Per Capita Income and Productivity as Indices of Development and Welfare. Some Comments on Kuznetsian Economic History." In *Productivity in the Economies of Europe*, P. O'Brien, and R. Fremdling (eds.), pp. 30–56. Klett-Cotta, Stuttgart: Historisch-sozialwissenschaftliche Forschungen; Band 15.

———. (1996). "German Industrialization." In *The Industrial Revolution in National Context*, M. Teich and R. Porter (eds.), pp. 95–125. Cambridge: Cambridge University Press.

Timmer, M. P., M. O'Mahony, and B. van Ark (2007). "Growth and Productivity Accounts from EU KLEMS: An Overview." *National Institute Economic Review* 200: 64–78.

Tipton, F. B. (1976). *Regional Variations in the Economic Development of Germany during the Nineteenth Century*. Middletown, CT: Wesleyan University Press.

Tol, S.J.R., S. W. Pacala, and R. H. Socolow (2009). "Understanding Long-Term Energy Use and Carbon Dioxide Emissions in the USA." *Journal of Policy Modeling* 31: 425–45.

Toniolo, G. (1983). "Railways and Economic Growth in Mediterranean Countries: Some Methodological Remarks." In *Railways and the Economic Development of Western Europe, 1830–1914*, P. O'Brien (ed.), pp. 227–36. London: Macmillan.

Toutain, J.–C. (1961). "Le produit de l'agriculture française de 1700 à 1958, I, Estimation du produit au XVIIIe siècle." *Cahiers de l'Institut de Science économique appliquée* 115: 1–216.

Toynbee, A. (1884). *Lectures on The Industrial Revolution in England* (2nd ed.). London: Rivingtons.

Tsubouchi, Y. (1990). "Types of Rice Cultivation and Types of Society in Asia." In *Economic and Demographic Development in Rice Producing Societies: Some Aspects of East Asian Economic History*, A. Hayami and Y. Tsubouchi (eds.), pp. 6–20. Tenth International Economic History Congress (Leuven, August 1990). Leuven: Leuven University Press.

Tunzelmann, G. N. von (1978). *Steam Power and British Industrialization to 1860*. Oxford: Clarendon Press.

———. (1995). *Technology and Industrial Progress: The Foundations of Economic Growth*. Cheltenham: Elgar.

Turnbull, G. (1987). "Canals, Coal and Regional Growth during the Industrial Revolution." *Economic History Review* 40: 537–60.

Turner, M. (2004). "Agriculture, 1860–1914." In *The Cambridge Economic History of Modern Britain. Vol. II. Economic Maturity, 1860–1939*, pp. 133–60. Cambridge: Cambridge University Press.

Tylecote, R. F. (1962). *Metallurgy in Archaeology: A Prehistory of Metallurgy in the British Isles*. London: Arnold.

Unger, R. W. (1978). *Dutch Shipbuilding before 1800: Ships and Guilds*. Assen: Van Gorcum.

———. (1980). *The Ship in the Medieval Economy*. London-Montreal: Croom Helm: McGill-Queen's University Press.

———. (1984). "Energy Sources for the Dutch Golden Age: Peat, Wind and Coal." In *Research in Economic History 9*, P. Uselding (ed.), pp. 221–53.

———. (2004). *Shipping, Energy and Early Modern Economic Growth*. University of British Columbia, available online at http://mauricio.econ.ubc.ca/pdfs/unger.pdf.

———. (ed.) (2011). *Shipping and Economic Growth 1350–1850*. Leiden: Brill.

Utterback, J., and A. Murray (1977). *Influence of Defense Procurement and Sponsorship of Research and Development on the Development of the Civilian Electronics Industry*. Cambridge, MA: MIT Press.

Uytven, R. van (1971). "The Fulling Mill: the Dynamic of the Revolution in Industrial Attitudes." *Acta Histoire Neerlandica* 5: 1–14.

Valentinitsch, H. (1983). "Idria und Fragen der Umweltgestaltung." In *Wirtschaftsentwicklung und Umweltbeeinflussung (14.–20. Jahrhundert)*, H. Kellenbenz (ed.), pp. 57–72. Wiesbaden: Steiner.

Valturio, R. (1462–70). *De re militari*. Verona, 1472 [first printed edition].

Van Zanden, J.-L. (1985). *De economische ontwikkeling van de Nederlandse landbouw in de negentiende eeuw. 1800–1914*. Utrecht: HES.

———. (1991). "The First Green Revolution: The Growth of Production and Productivity in European Agriculture, 1870–1914." *Economic History Review* II s., 44: 215–39.

———. (1999a). "The Development of Agricultural Productivity in Europe, 1500–1800." In *Land Productivity and Agro-systems in the North Sea Area (Middle Ages-20th Century)*, B.J.P. Van Bavel and E. Thoen (eds.), pp. 357–75. Turnhout: Brepols.

———. (1999b). "Wages and the Standard of Living in Europe, 1500–1800." *European Review of Economic History* 3: 175–97.

———. (2001). "Early Modern Economic Growth: A Survey of the European Economy, 1500–1800." In *Early Modern Capitalism*, M. Prak (ed.), pp. 69–87. London: Routledge.

Vecchi, G., and M. Coppola (2006). "Nutrition and Growth in Italy, 1861–1911: What Macroeconomic Data Hide." *Explorations in Economic History* 43, no. 3: 438–64.

Vergani, R. (2003). "Gli usi civili della polvere da sparo (secoli XV–XVIII)." In *Economia e energia Secc. XIII–XVIII*, S. Cavaciocchi (ed.), pp. 864–78. Istituto Internazionale di Storia economica "F. Datini." Firenze: Le Monnier.

Vietor, R. H. (1984). *Energy Policy in America since 1945: A Study of Business-Government Relations*. Cambridge: Cambridge University Press.

Vigneron, P. (1968). *Le cheval dans l'antiquitè gréco-romaine*. Nancy: Annales de l'Est.

Ville, S. P. (1987). *English Shipowning during the Industrial Revolution: Michael Henley and Son, London Shipowners, 1770–1830*. Manchester: Manchester University Press.

Voigtlander, N., and H. J. Voth (2006). "Why England? Demographic Factors, Structural Change and Physical Capital Accumulation during the Industrial Revolution." *Journal of Economic Growth* 11, no. 4: 319–61.

Vries, P. (2003). *Via Peking Back to Manchester: Britain, the Industrial Revolution, and China*. Leiden: Leiden University.

Vringer, K., and K. Blok (2000). "Long-Term Trends in Direct and Indirect Household Energy Intensities: A Factor in Dematerialisation?" *Energy Policy* 28: 713–27.

Warde, P. (2003). "Forests, Energy and Politics in the Early Modern German States." In *Economia e energia Secc. XIII–XVIII*, S. Cavaciocchi (ed.), pp. 585–97. Istituto Internazionale di Storia economica "F. Datini." Firenze: Le Monnier.

———. (2006). "Fear of Wood Shortage and the Reality of the Woodland in Europe, c. 1450–1850." *History Workshop Journal* 62: 28–57.

———. (2007). *Energy Consumption in England and Wales 1560–2000*. Napoli: ISSM-CNR.

———. (2009). *Energy and Natural Resources Dependency in Europe, 1600–1900*. Brooks World Poverty Institute.

Warr, B., and R. U. Ayres (2012). "Useful Work and Information as Drivers of Economic Growth." *Ecological Economics* 73: 93–102.

Warr, B., R. Ayres, N. Eisenmenger, F. Krausmann, and H. Schandl (2010). "Energy Use and Economic Development: A Comparative Analysis of Useful Work Supply in Austria, Japan, the United Kingdom and the US during 100 Years of Economic Growth." *Ecological Economics* 69, no. 10: 1904–17.

Warr, B., H. Schandl, and R. U. Ayres (2008). "Long Term Trends in Resource Energy Consumption and Useful Work Supplies in the UK, 1900 to 2000." *Ecological Economics* 68: 126–40.

Weber, C. L., J. G. Koomey, and H. S. Matthews (2010). "The Energy and Climate Change Implications of Different Music Delivery Methods." *Journal of Industrial Ecology* 14: 754–69.

Weber, M. (1898). *Agrarverhältnisse in Altertum*. Tübingen: Mohr.

Wheeler, D. A. (2009). *The Most Important Software Innovations*. Revised version. Available online at http://www.dwheeler.com/innovation/innovation.html.

Whittaker, R. H. (1975). *Communities and Ecosystems*. New York: McMillan.

Whittaker, R. H. and G. E. Likens (1973a). "Primary Production: The Biosphere and Man." *Human Ecology* 1: 357–69.

———. (1973b). "The Biosphere and Man." In *Primary Productivity of the Biosphere*, H. Lieth and R. H. Whittaker (eds.), pp. 305–28. Berlin, Heidelberg, New York: Springer.

Wilhelmy, H. (1981). *Welt und Umwelt der Maya*. München: R. Piper Verlag.

Willan, T. S. ([1938] 1967). *The English Coasting Trade 1600–1750*. Manchester: Manchester University Press.

Williams, E. (2002). "The 1.7 kg Microchip: Energy and Chemical Use in the Production of Semiconductors." *Environmental Science & Technology* 36, no. 24: 5504–10.

Williams, E., R. U. Ayres, and B. Warr (2008). "Efficiency Dilutions: Long-Term Energy Conversion Trends in Japan." *Environmental Science and Technology* 42: 4964–70.

Williams, M. (1990). "Forests." In *The Earth Transformed by Human Action*, B. L. Turner. Cambridge: Cambridge University Press, pp. 179–201.

Williamson, J. (2011). *Industrial Catching Up in the Poor Periphery 1870–1975*. *Working Paper 16809*. National Bureau of Economic Research.

Wilson, R., P. Ashton, and T. Eagan (1980). *Innovation, Competition and Government Policy in the Semiconductor Industry*. Lexington: Lexington Books.

Wollstonecraft, M. (1796). *Letters Written during a Short Residence in Sweden, Norway and Denmark*. London: Penguin (1987).

World Bank (1992). *World Development Report 1992*. Development and the Environment. Washington, DC: World Bank.

———. (2001). *World Development Indicators 2001*.

———. (2009). *World Development Indicators 2009*.

Wright, T. P. (1936). "Factors Affecting the Cost of Airplanes." *Journal of the Aeronautical Sciences* (February).

Wrigley, E. A. (1962). "The Supply of Raw Materials in the Industrial Revolution." *Economic History Review* 15: 1–16.

———. (1985). "'Urban Growth and Agricultural Change: England and the Continent in the Early Modern Period." *Journal of Interdisciplinary History* 15: 683–728.

———. (1988a). *Continuity, Chance and Change. The Character of the Industrial Revolution in England*. Cambridge: Cambridge University Press.

———. (1988b). "The Limits to Growth. Malthus and the Classical Economists." In *Population and Resources in Western Intellectual Traditions*, M. S. Teitelbaum and J. M. Winter (eds.), pp. 30–48. Cambridge: Cambridge University Press.

———. (2004). *Poverty, Progress, and Population*. Cambridge: Cambridge University Press.

———. (2006). "The Transition to an Advanced Organic Economy: Half a Millennium of English Agriculture." *Economic History Review* II s., 59, no. 3: 435–80.

———. (2007). "English County Populations in the Later Eighteenth Century." *Economic History Review* 60, no. 1: 35–69.

———. (2010). *Energy and the English Industrial Revolution*. Cambridge: Cambridge University Press.

———. (2013). "Energy and the English Industrial Revolution." *Philosophical Transactions of the Royal Society A*.371:20110568. https://dx.doi.org/10.1098/rsta.2011.0568.

Yarranton, A. (1681). *England's Improvement by Sea and Land*. London: Everingham.

Young, H. P. (2009). "Innovation Diffusion in Heterogeneous Populations: Contagion, Social Influence, and Social Learning." *American Economic Review* 99, no. 5: 1899–1924.

Zahedieh, N. (2013). "Colonies, Copper and the Market for Inventive Activity, 1680–1730." *Economic History Review* 66, No. 3: 805–25.

Zamagni, V. (1989). "An International Comparison of Real Industrial Wages, 1890–1913: Methodological Issues and Results." In *Real Wages in 19th and 20th Century Europe. Historical and Comparative Perspective*, P. Scholliers (ed.). New York-Oxford-Munich: Berg.

———. (1993). *The Economic History of Italy, 1860–1990*. Oxford: Clarendon.

Zannetos, Z. S. (1987). "Oil Tanker Markets: Continuity amidst Change." In *Energy: Markets and Regulation*, Gordon, R. L., H. D. Jacoby and M. B. Zimmerman (eds). Cambridge, Mass.: MIT Press.

Zapico, J. L., N. Brandt, and M. Turpeinen (2010). "Environmental Metrics: The Main Opportunity for Industrial Ecology." *Journal of Industrial Ecology* 14: 703–39.

Zeeuw, J. W. de (1978). "Peat and the Dutch Golden Age. The Historical Meaning of Energy-Attainability." *A. A. G. Bijdragen* 21: 3–32.

Zittel, W., and J. Schindler (2007). *Crude Oil: The Supply Outlook. Report to the Energy Watch Group*. EWG-Series No 3/2007.

Index

THE PRINCETON ECONOMIC HISTORY OF THE WESTERN WORLD

SERIES EDITOR

Joel Mokyr